PORTFOLIO AND PERFORMANCE ASSESSMENT

Helping Students Evaluate Their Progress
as Readers and Writers

Second Edition

PORTFOLIO AND PERFORMANCE ASSESSMENT

Helping Students Evaluate Their Progress
as Readers and Writers

Second Edition

Roger Farr
Indiana University

Bruce Tone

Harcourt Brace College Publishers

Fort Worth Philadelphia San Diego New York Orlando Austin San Antonio
Toronto Montreal London Sydney Tokyo

Publisher	Earl McPeek
Acquisitions Editor	Jo-Anne Weaver
Product Manager	Don Grainger
Developmental Editor	Tracy Napper
Project Editor	Elaine Richards
Art Director	Lora Gray
Production Manager	Andrea A. Johnson

Cover photo: Chris Blay

ISBN: 0-15-505402-3
Library of Congress Catalog Card Number: 97-73098

Address for orders:
Harcourt Brace College Publishers
6277 Sea Harbor Drive
Orlando, FL 32887-6777
1-800-782-4479

Address for editorial correspondence:
Harcourt Brace College Publishers
301 Commerce Street, Suite 3700
Fort Worth, TX 76102

Web site address:
http://www.hbcollege.com

Printed in the United States of America

7 8 9 0 1 2 3 4 5 6 066 9 8 7 6 5 4 3 2 1

To Lonnie Sullivan

Some readers may have heard me tell the story of how my mother taught my brother-in-law Lonnie to read when he was an adult. Lonnie passed on unexpectedly in the summer of 1993. He was a wonderful person and an inspiration to me because he made the very best of what he had. I will miss him very much.

Roger Farr

To Sylvia E. Bowman

Hundreds of former students will not forget that this outstanding scholar, editor, university administrator, author, and professor was also once a magnificent junior high and high school teacher and publications adviser. She taught us to be aware of audiences that were eager to hear our untrained but unique voices, which she recognized, respected, encouraged, and trained.

Bruce Tone

ABOUT THE AUTHORS

Roger Farr

Dr. Roger Farr is the Chancellor's Professor of Education and director of the Center for Reading and Language Studies at Indiana University. He also serves as the associate director of the ERIC Clearinghouse on Reading, English, and Communication and as associate dean for research and the university graduate school. A former elementary school teacher and junior and senior high school English teacher, as well as a school district reading specialist in New York state, Farr has been employed at Indiana University since 1967. During his years at Indiana University he has served as director of the Henry Lester Smith Center for Research in Education, director of the Reading Clinic, associate director of the Division of Teacher Education, associate dean for research in the School of Education, and dean of research and graduate development for the university.

Farr has been a leader in the International Reading Association for a number of years. He served as IRA president in 1979–1980, and he was a member of the board of directors from 1974–1977. He served as co-editor of the Reading Research Quarterly for 12 years, and he also chaired a number of IRA national committees including the Evaluation of Tests Committee and the Committee to Advise the National Assessment of Education Progress.

Farr is regarded as an authority in the field of reading assessment and instruction. He is the author of the *Metropolitan Achievement Test: Reading* and the *Iowa Silent Reading Tests*. He recently co-authored the *Language Arts Performance Assessments,* a series of integrated language arts performance assessments for grades 1 to 8 published by Harcourt Brace Educational Measurement. He has developed performance assessment batteries for numerous other publishers and school systems, to report on student language development and thinking as well as a range of other subject matters. He has written hundreds of articles and monographs on reading, including co-authoring of *Reading: What Can Be Measured?* published by IRA and *Teaching a Child to Read* published by Harcourt Brace and Company. Farr is a senior author in the area of measurement and evaluation for the language arts programs published by Harcourt Brace and is the senior author of *Treasuries of Literature* published by Harcourt Brace and Company.

In 1970, Farr's research monograph, *Reading: What Can Be Measured?* was selected by Pi Lambda Theta as one of the twenty outstanding books in education. In 1984, the International Reading Association awarded Farr the William S. Gray award for outstanding lifetime contributions to the teaching of reading. In 1986 he was elected to the Reading Hall of Fame of the International Reading Association. And in 1988 IRA selected him as the Outstanding Teacher Educator in Reading. In 1993, he was honored with the outstanding alumnus award by the State University of New York at Buffalo.

Bruce Tone

Bruce Tone has been a writer of educational and research-related materials for 35 years and has served as director of publications at ERIC Clearinghouses, where he initiated several monograph series for teachers, parents, and researchers. He is an experienced writer of reading and reading-writing assessments, of articles on language education and student achievement, of book chapters on educational research, of materials for developing the strategies of young readers and thinkers, and of reports on projects evaluating major educational programs. He was editorial associate for the Reading Research Quarterly and other academic journals and has edited several books on student language development. He has taught students at levels spanning grades 7 through 12 and college undergraduates, and he has advised numerous award-winning student newspapers, annuals, and creative writing magazines that they published.

PREFACE

Over recent decades, research and theory have helped us understand language use and development as meaning-making processes that link reading, writing, speaking, and listening. That emphasis on language use as a process has, in turn, focused educators and assessment professionals on a primary goal: to devise methodologies for assessing reading and writing that examine it in process. Long-registered criticism of an overemphasis on standardized testing with multiple choice items has gained more credibility as the results of that traditional form of testing have been argued to be product—not process—oriented.

Assessment of students' abilities has long been a matter of high public priority. This happened as declines in scores on various standardized tests and increased costs for education created intensifying criticism and scrutiny. That concern for more accountability complicated the challenge of devising process-oriented, theory-based language assessment, since the approaches that goal recommends are less easily made reliable. It could be argued that they were more valid, but evaluating writing and reading comprehension in application was far more subjective than scoring assessments designed for a tally of correct answers to multiple-choice items.

It is in this state of tension that both portfolio assessment and performance assessment have gained increasing popularity. As more information and testimonies on portfolio use have accrued, it has been easy to explain how the methodology reflects the theory that has emerged, and equally easy to demonstrate how it can effectively guide good instruction—this is, in effect, effective instruction itself. That addresses a long-held educational goal, obviously, to make assessment more closely match or reflect teaching.

New to this edition: Intensive observation and contact with teachers since the book was first published has given us an ever-keener understanding of how portfolio assessment succeeds. This is reflected in a cleaner, clearer design and description of the book's content. As in the first edition of *Portfolio and Performance Assessment,* we are humbly grateful for the privilege of talking to, observing, and learning from many excellent teachers and their students.

The first five chapters of this edition are still dedicated to presenting a rationale for portfolio assessment (Chapter 1), considerations for getting started with portfolio collecting (Chapter 2), detailed discussion of what to collect (Chapter 3), what to look for in the collections when analyzing their contents (Chapter 4), and the all-important student/teacher conferencing that we consider vital to the success of portfolio assessment (Chapter 5).

The message of Chapter 6 has become even more important—assessment is a practice that serves a variety of needs and audiences, and an eclectic approach to assessment is the only obvious way to meet them all. Understanding that this is an issue-oriented perspective, we have attempted to ground that discussion in more sources, hoping that the referencing will lead to expanded considerations of the argument there. Also emphasized in the revision of this chapter is the discussion of exactly what role portfolios can play as a backup, clarifying source in the complex mix of assessment needs.

The placement of Chapter 6 was always intended to explain the importance of performance assessment and its role in the whole assessment picture. It is an appropriate way to introduce the final two chapters on performance tests, how they are constructed, and how they are used and interpreted. While Chapters 7 and 8 can still be used as a blueprint for constructing performance assessments, they have been redirected to also serve those who might be selecting performance assessments from the growing number available on the market. We have never tried to imply that building performance assessments is anything less than a highly-demanding task, yet we recommend it as a way of clarifying what one believes about language development and instruction. We have also added a discussion of a new type of performance assessment which reflects more traditional ways of evaluating reading and writing. At the end of each chapter, we have added a dozen bulleted points summarizing the high points of the content.

Despite these changes, this book is still packed with highly practical ideas and suggestions related to these assessment methodologies that teachers can take and apply immediately in their classrooms. A final appendix of blackline guide and record sheets can be modified or copied for any use that serves the reader's need. Our intent has been to guide educators and to promote the development of self-assessors among their students.

ACKNOWLEDGMENTS

We are grateful to the readers who provided feedback for this edition: Brenda Betts, California State University, Stanislaus; and Craig Cleland, Mansfield University.

CONTENTS

Chapter 3
DECIDING WHAT GOES INTO THE PORTFOLIO   64

Chapter 4
ASSESSING PORTFOLIO CONTENTS   98

Chapter 8
DEVELOPING RUBRICS AND ANCHOR PAPERS   252

PORTFOLIO AND PERFORMANCE ASSESSMENT

*Helping Students Evaluate Their Progress
as Readers and Writers*

Second Edition

PROLOGUE:

THE KING AND THE

CARPENTERS

Once upon a time, long ago and far away, there lived a wonderful kingdom full of happy people. They had plenty to eat and were not harassed by fire-breathing dragons. However, as in all fairy tales, there was one problem: There was a shortage of houses in the kingdom. Their carpenters and plumbers were old and not many were building houses any longer. No one was teaching children to build houses anymore. (Everyone seemed to think the kingdom would be better off with more bankers and lawyers, and teaching house-building just didn't seem interesting and important.)

"This cannot continue," lamented the people. "If some of the children do not learn to build houses, many of us will soon be without roofs over our heads."

They went to their King for help. He was a wise old fellow, and he knew exactly what to do. He charged off to the schools and said to the administrators and teachers, "You must start teaching the children to build houses!"

"But," said the teachers, "we have been teaching accounting and jurisprudence. We know little about house building ourselves. How are we to teach the children to do it?"

The King pondered the problem. "There are still some old carpenters and plumbers," he said, "and others in our land who know how to build houses. We will hire them to teach the children."

"Oh, no," argued the teachers, "those carpenters and plumbers may know how to build, but they do not know how to teach."

"They are not Kingdom Certified Teachers," said one venerable school administrator. "They must be certified to teach."

"Well," said the King, "then you educators can teach them how to teach. We will have special workshops called ITT (I'll Teach Trades)." (Later the ITT workshops came to be known as *Intensive Teacher Training*, but that is another story.)

THE PROGRAM GETS UNDER WAY

After the carpenters and plumbers had completed their special training, they were certified as specialized teachers, and off they went to the schools to teach children how to build houses. Many of the children were very happy to learn how to build things since their previous classes in accounting and litigation had only taught them to count and argue. It seemed great fun to get a chance to make something.

Each morning the carpenter and plumber teachers would gather the children about them to discuss their plans for building for that day. (Those were called "Cooperative

Learning Groups.") The children would plan the houses and discuss how to get the job done. They seemed to learn the most, however, from actually building houses. At times things did not go well, and the teachers and students would sit together and discuss what they thought had gone wrong. Then they would set about making changes (revisions) in order to produce the kinds of houses they could all be proud of.

Everyone in the kingdom seemed very happy. The children who were learning about building houses had lots of work to do. Houses were being built that were the envy of the surrounding kingdoms. The King was pleased. Once again he had solved a great problem for his people.

The King himself was in need of a new house, and he had the new house-building graduates build a strong and beautiful palace for him and his Queen. Near bliss settled over the land.

THE KING ENCOUNTERS SKEPTICISM ON THE ROAD

One day the King announced to his wife that he had heard about a great education conference that was to be held in a nearby kingdom. "They will have meetings," he told his wife, "so we Kings can learn all about education. I think I will go to the Great Education Conference to see if I can learn more to help our teachers."

When the King returned from the conference, he told his wife about the special bragging meeting that was held during the Great Education Conference. "All of the Kings from all the lands were there," he told her excitedly. "They all told about how much the children in their Kingdoms were learning. I told them about the wonderful houses our children have learned to build," he said.

"But, they laughed at me," he moaned. "They said that just *telling* about houses was not admissible in the bragging meeting. They said that I needed test scores to really show what the children are learning. They said that test scores were the only reliable and valid way to show what students are learning.

"Just telling doesn't count," he lamented to his wife. "I even told them that I would bring pictures of the great houses, and they said that pictures didn't tell what the children were learning. They said that only test scores would count," he said sadly. "They even told me that if we do not have test scores, people from other lands will not know how good our schools are and they will not bring their new businesses to our kingdom. I must go to the schools to ask the teachers about the children's test scores."

The next week the King met with all of the teachers and asked if the children were really learning anything. "Of course," said the carpenter and plumber teachers. "Just look at the wonderful houses in our land. Indeed, you live in one of those houses."

"I know, I know," replied the King, "but I went to the Great Education Conference of the great kingdoms, and other kings showed their test scores. They had splendid graphs and charts in many colors and with lots of numbers showing how much their children have learned." (Some may think that the moral of this tale is that you should not send your Kings to conferences, but there is more to this story.)

"Can we have test scores?" asked the King. "Can I have graphs and charts to take to the next Great Education Conference? There is a bragging meeting where all of the kings show their test scores. If we show our test scores, people in other lands will see how much our children have learned and how good our schools are. They will want to move to our kingdom and bring their businesses here. We will prosper even more. I must have test scores!"

The carpenter and plumber teachers shyly responded that they did not know how to make tests. They said that they knew only how to make houses and other kinds of buildings, and to teach children to build houses.

"Then I will bring a test builder to our kingdom," the King shouted. "I met many test builders at the bragging meeting. They helped the other Kings with their graphs and charts. I will find one to help us. I must have test scores so my country can flourish."

The teachers did not know what to make of all of this. However, they agreed that if the wise old King thought it was important, they certainly should try to help.

THE TEST BUILDER ARRIVES IN THE KINGDOM

Several months later, the test builder arrived in the country and came to the schools to talk with the teachers. The test builder always seemed to carry a clipboard with him. (Later the carpenter and plumber teachers developed a motto that read, *Beware of people carrying clipboards.*)

"If I am to build a test," said the test builder, "I must know what you are teaching the children. Tell me, what is it the children are learning?"

The carpenter and plumber teachers looked at each other quizzically and wondered at such a strange question. Didn't the test builder see the houses? "Why," they responded, "we are teaching the children to build houses. Surely you can see that."

"Of course, of course," said the test builder with a pained expression on his face. "I know they are building houses, but there is more to teaching than that. What is it they learn each step of the way? We must understand each skill and subskill and assess it carefully."

The teachers didn't know what to say. "They build nice houses," blurted one of the teachers, hoping that was what the test builder wanted to hear.

"No, no, no!" he responded. "What do they do first? What would someone do as the very first thing in starting to build a house?"

One of the carpenters thought the test builder's questions were all a big joke of some sort, so he yelled out, "Why, the first thing is to pick up a hammer and hammer a nail in a board to start making a wall."

"Good," responded the test builder, "now we are getting someplace."

"They have to know the names of nails," called out another teacher.

"And the different kinds of wood," another joined in.

"Excellent! You really do know what you are teaching," said the test builder.

The teachers were happy that they were able to please him.

The test builder announced that all of the teachers must attend an after-school meeting the next Friday, so they could work together to make long lists of these things the students must learn. He called it "Teacher-Guided Item Formation" or TGIF, for short.

The teachers were tired after a long week at school, but they agreed to attend since they knew the King was so excited about securing some scores. They worked very hard and produced long lists of the things the test builder seemed to want on the lists. Indeed, the longer the lists became, the happier the test builder seemed to be.

After the meeting, the test builder announced that he would take all of the wonderful lists the teachers had produced and would build a test to measure all of those things. The house-builder teachers were relieved to see the test builder leave, but some of them worried about what the test builder was going to do with all of those lists.

They had lost most of the weekend, but they were, nonetheless, eager to get back to teaching children about house building. Besides, they realized that they didn't know anything about test building. "Some people build houses," they said, "and some build tests. And after all, our wise King knows what *he* is doing. If he believes these tests are important for our country, then surely there can be nothing wrong with them."

THE SCORE GATHERING BEGINS

A year later, the test builder returned and announced that it was now time to test the children. The teachers were not shown the tests beforehand although they were very curious about what was on the tests. "Security is very important with tests," said the test builder. "We do not want anyone to know what we are testing before we test it."

That seemed strange to the teachers, since knowing what one was doing always seemed important to them when they built houses. Nevertheless, the teachers were taught how to administer the tests, an activity which did not seem to them anything at all like building houses. However, they did what the test builder asked. They told their students not to ask questions, not to work together, and not to look at each other's work. All of this also seemed strange to the teachers, since these were the very things they had always encouraged the children to do when they were learning how to build houses.

Unknown to the teachers, to the test maker, and even to the King, a storyteller was observing silently in one of the house-building classes when the tests were given. The first question on the test was the very first thing the teachers had told the test builder when he had asked them exactly what they taught their children. The test item read:

Given a wall and some nails, which of the following should you pick up?
a. a sledge hammer

b. a claw hammer

c. a ball peen hammer

d. none of the above

e. all of the above

The storyteller noticed one of the children poking the student next to him (when the teacher was not looking) and he heard the child whisper, "Hey Billy, did you know our hammers had names? I'm gonna call mine 'George.' George is not one of the choices, so I guess none of the above is what I should mark."

Many of the students were as confused as this student, and the test results were not good at all. Indeed, when the test builder returned with a huge pile of test score reports, he told the King that the students had scored very poorly. He advised that the King should not tell anyone about the test scores. "Be especially careful," he said, "to see that the scores are not published in the newspaper. And," said the test builder, "you surely cannot go to the bragging meeting with those low test scores because everyone will know what a poor education the students in your kingdom are receiving."

The King was devastated. "What am I to do?" he wailed. "I thought our children were learning, but these test scores show they know nothing. I will never be able to go the Great Education Conference again, and I will never get to brag at the bragging meeting! People will not want to move to our kingdom. We will not be able to attract new businesses to our land. Our test scores are too low."

The test builder said that he knew of other countries that had faced the same problem, and they had been able to solve the problem. "What did they do? You must tell me!" pleaded the King.

"They hired an educational consultant," said the test builder. "The educational consultant was able to help the teachers teach better. When the teachers taught better," said the test builder, "the test scores went up."

The King hurried off to tell the teachers the bad news about how poorly the children were learning. But he also told them the good news. He had a solution once again. An educational consultant would be hired to help them teach better, the children would learn more, and the test scores would go up.

Will the educational consultant carry a clipboard? the teachers wondered.

THE GREAT CONSULTATION BEGINS

Several weeks later the great educational consultant came to the land. He had no clipboard, but he had a book he had written with a picture of himself on the cover. He was very pleasant and always seemed to smile. He also carried a great bag full of all kinds of colored paper, paints, and other such things. One of the teachers said to his friend that he thought the educational consultant looked like a traveling art store.

The educational consultant met with some of the teachers to begin planning how they would improve education in the land. "What is it you teach?" he asked.

"Oh, dear," thought the teachers, "this is the same way the test builder started out. This time we must attempt to tell more exactly what we teach."

"Well," said one of the teachers, "I used to teach the children how to build houses, but the King seems to think the children are not learning anything because they have done so poorly on the test. So I guess I should teach what is on the test."

"Good," said the consultant. "You know where you are going. You have your objectives clearly in mind. Now let's look at those tests to see what it is the children must learn. Then we can conduct workshops on how to teach those things."

The educational consultant and the planning teachers scoured the tests and made lists of all the things that were asked. One of the teachers said that it seemed that they were now doing what they had done with the test builder, only now it was happening in reverse. "This education business seems very complicated," many thought, not sure that they could fully understand it. Some of the most thoughtful teachers looked bewildered. Everyone looked forward to getting straightened out at the workshops.

"Don't worry," said the educational consultant, "we are going to see just what we have to teach and then we will teach it well. The children will learn more. And," he said beaming, "the test scores will go up. Everyone will be happy once again. You'll see."

The educational consultant planned a number of after-school workshops to help the teachers learn how to teach the lists of stuff included on the tests. Some of the workshops were called "Make-and-Take Workshops." At these sessions, all of the teachers would make things to help the children learn. At one of the Make-and-Take Workshops, some of the teachers drew wonderful pictures of the different hammers on big pieces of cardboard. On the backs of the cardboard pictures of hammers, they would write the names of the hammers. These big cards were then used in classes to flash the pictures to the children so they would learn to immediately recognize the names of the hammers. These came to be known as hammer flashcards.

Another group of teachers drew pictures of the hammers in a column down one side of a sheet of paper. In a second column, they wrote the names of the hammers. However, they did not put the correct name of each hammer beside its picture. "We will have the children draw lines from the pictures of the hammers to the correct names of the hammers. This will be good practice in learning the names of hammers."

"And when they finish, they can color the pictures of the hammers," shouted one of the teachers. "That will make it fun and interesting for the children. The educational consultant has reminded us that learning is supposed to be fun."

The educational consultant was delighted and would visit the schools to see how the teachers were putting all of the new ideas to work with the children. As the educational consultant walked up and down the hallways of the schools, shouts of "Ball peen! Ball peen! Ball peen!" could be heard coming out of the rooms. The children were obviously learning from the flashcards. Later the shouts would become, "Ball peen! Claw! Sledge!" as the teachers taught more and more complex distinctions. Some of the teachers were sure they were now teaching higher order thinking skills. They all felt good because the children were learning so many things.

"I am naming the hammers, so I can tell them apart," one self-conscious student bragged, blushing nonetheless. His teacher's chest swelled with pride. The student was practicing metacognition.

However, some of the teachers worried about the class time all this was taking. Would the children be able to use this new knowledge to once again build houses? "Of course," the educational consultant explained, "but first they must know all of the skills. Once they know the skills, the rest will be easy."

THE PLAN BEGINS TO PAY OFF

The King was so pleased that he issued a proclamation that all school administrators should select the new curriculum. For several years the new education program was implemented in the schools throughout the Kingdom. It was called the School-Licensed Improvement Program (SLIP) and was dedicated to developing Effective Schools.

"This is a grass-roots movement," said the educational consultant. "The teachers defined what they taught and they helped plan the workshops." Some teachers had taught other teachers. Some talked of how they had "adopted management practices to restructure their schools." It was heady and heavy stuff.

Some teachers did notice that there wasn't much house building going on. However, no one seemed very concerned, since the children were telling their parents about all that they were learning and carrying home many practice sheets with pumpkin faces and other honorific stamps on them. Some parents even bought their own sets of the hammer flashcards so they could help their children at home.

Each year the test scores showed more improvement. The King was happy and knew that before long he would be able to once again go to the Great Education Conference and for the first time show off his test scores at the bragging meeting. However, he wanted to wait until the test scores throughout his country were sure to be the highest of all the kingdoms.

THE SCORES GET HIGHER DESPITE ONE DROP

As he waited, he and his wife decided to have an addition built onto the summer mansion they had built years before—long before there was a shortage, before the test score program, and before the new education system. "A new addition built by children with such high test scores will surely be wonderful," the King told his wife.

As the addition began to take shape, the Queen looked at the work with growing concern. "It doesn't look very solid," she said, "especially the new balcony on the back. I think it is drooping to one side."

"Don't worry," said the King, "that addition is being built by children who have the highest test scores in the history of our kingdom. Those are the best-educated house builders we have ever had in our land."

Before the new addition was completed, the latest test scores were released and they had once again gone up. "These new test scores are marvelous!" the King cried, puffing up. "I can now go to the Great Education Conference and attend the bragging meeting. I will show my test scores and be the envy of all the kings. People will want to come to our kingdom because of our great education system. We will have new businesses. Our kingdom will be the envy of all."

Off the King went to the Great Education Conference. He took his educational consultant, his test builder, and even several teachers to tell all about education in their land. However, when it came time for the bragging meeting, the King didn't want anyone to speak for him. "I alone," he announced, "will tell the other kings about our test scores."

The King had charts and tables with bar graphs. They covered an entire wall and were of many colors. They included percentiles, stanines, squizziles, and staybecks with many lines, bars, and connected dots. (Squizziles and staybecks were new ways of presenting scores developed by the King's test builder just for this meeting.)

Everyone at the bragging meeting was astounded! Such high test scores! Such sophisticated charts! Such wondrous analyses! This is the best bragging they had ever heard. This is a king who is truly a great education leader.

The King returned to his country and a special parade was given in his honor. "Long live the Education King," the people shouted. The King had never been more popular nor more certain that he knew how to help his people. "You just have to set targets," he thought to himself, "and then find out where you are and where you have to go. The test builder and the educational consultant really knew what to do."

The King and his wife returned home at the end of the celebration to find that the addition to their house was now finished. It looked kind of shaky, but the King was sure that was just a benchmark of modern architecture. His wife said it looked not only shaky, but also dangerous! She announced that she wasn't going out on the balcony until it was proven to be safe.

The King scoffed at her concern and reminded her that the balcony had been built by students who had achieved the highest test scores in the history of their kingdom. "These are the highest test scores of all the kingdoms," he proclaimed. He seemed always to be giving speeches now.

The King took his test score reports and marched out on the balcony. There was a terrible noise, like thousands of nails being ripped from their places. The balcony swayed . . . and then buckled . . . and *then crashed to the ground!*

Somewhere in some kingdom, there is joy in the land. Somewhere in some kingdom, laughter can be heard. But not in this kingdom, where the newer houses had all begun to fall apart.

The moral of this story became obvious to even the most faithful subjects of the king. It was written and read as a kind of qualification or caveat at his memorial service. Can you put it in words yourself? You are encouraged to try if you like. There will be no test on it, however. (Your answer is sure to be as valid as mine, but you can find out what I believe the moral is by going to the first question in Appendix A on page **[[279]]**.)

—Roger Farr

CHAPTER

ONE

WHY PORTFOLIOS AND PERFORMANCE ASSESSMENT?

The use of portfolios in instruction is not new. Nor is their use in assessment a new practice. Portfolio assessment has been of considerable interest to teachers for nearly two decades now (Arter, 1990; Tierney, 1991; Valencia, et al., 1994; Horowitz, 1995). Before that portfolios were an approach used primarily in teaching the arts, in supporting career education, and in assessing and crediting experiential learning in higher education.

Performance assessment of language use—*reading to write* and *writing about what you have read*—has been developing for a shorter period (Stiggins, 1987; Henk, 1993). Good teachers have always used reading as a motivation for writing, of course; and *language experience* approaches have used writing to promote reading. But integrated reading and writing activities designed intentionally to *assess* those abilities are relatively new.

Enthusiasm for both language arts portfolios and performance assessment has led to attempts to make them major alternatives for producing educational information (Wolf, et al., 1992). Often the intent has been to recommend them as replacements for more traditional assessments of language development (Grady, 1992), but experience has begun

Appendix B at the back of this book is a reading list of key sources about portfolio and performance assessment.

Chapter 6 of this book discusses how these alternative assessments fit into the whole of educational assessment and information needs.

to suggest that while they can play an important role, they will not soon supplant standardized testing (Cizek, 1991; Hamp-Lyons and Condon, 1993).

The issues regarding these alternative assessments—like those that surround educational assessment in general—continue to be hotly debated (Smith, 1990; Goldberg and Kapinus, 1993). In discussing the ongoing concerns about the role of assessment in general, the Resnicks (1989) discussed the problems related to alternative assessments but compared them favorably to standardized and criterion-referenced tests. They argued that traditional forms of testing:

> . . . embody a view of education that defines knowledge and skill as a collection of bits of information and they demand fast non-reflective replies. Alternative performance assessments . . . including open-ended writing examinations (essays) and portfolio assessments, help release educators from the pressure toward fractionated low-level forms of learning that are rewarded by most current tests, and they also set positive standards for an educational system that strives to cultivate thinking. Tied to curriculum and designed to be taught to, performance assessments can be essential tools for raising authentic educational achievement.

This kind of endorsement suggests that the role of performance assessment may be broader than that of portfolio assessment and be a vital link to both portfolios and more traditional assessments that serve other informational needs. While portfolios, in particular, can be basic in directing classroom decisions, they seem destined to play a subordinate, if important, role in educational accountability (Arter, et al., 1995).

WHAT ARE THESE METHODOLOGIES?

Even though they have been around for some time now, it cannot be assumed that all teachers know what these methodologies are.

WHAT IS PORTFOLIO ASSESSMENT?

Portfolio assessment is not merely the collection of work samples. A portfolio is a concept that has been a part of all good teaching. The portfolio assessment concept has a student gather the materials he or she has been working on under one cover. Then the student talks with his or her teacher about how to do the work better. The teacher takes the role of a coach who helps the learner focus by asking why a particular project didn't turn out the way the student wanted it to turn out—and how it might be done better the next time. Thus the teacher as coach gets the student to self-assess what he or she is attempting to do.

This book will describe how a teacher can implement that concept of portfolio assessment in a classroom, using the materials that are collected. Language arts portfolios are—in the very simplest terms—collections of things students write, materials they have used in writing, and information and ideas they intend to use when writing and expressing themselves. Ideally much of this "stuff," as some students come to call it, will consist of responses to things the student has read. While some may incorporate expressions reliant on computer technologies and audio and visual media, overall, the portfolio will consist primarily of lots of different kinds of student writing (Farr, 1991).

The varied materials that go into the portfolio can be placed there by both the student and the teacher. The container or holder of these items can be an expandable folder, a box, a shopping bag, or just space on a shelf. But the portfolio is far more than just a holder or just a bunch of papers. It becomes a developing repository of a student's thought and expression. Above all, it becomes a powerful tool for managing the student's development as a language user and a thinker.

This happens on a daily basis as the students in a classroom take out their portfolios and add materials to the collections. These might include notes about stories, books, or articles they have read. They pull unfinished work out of the portfolios to complete, or batches of papers to organize. They are seen conferring with classmates about what they are doing with the collection, and the portfolios become the focal point of student/teacher interaction and discussion. On occasion, the teacher recommends the inclusion of a paper, explaining to the student why it would be a good thing to have in the portfolio.

Most simply put then, *portfolio assessment* is the practice of saving lots of things that a student writes so that the student and his or her teacher can look at the collection and see how they are doing. In slightly more complex terms, portfolios are those collections organized in such a way as to reflect, promote, and report a considerable amount of thinking that students have applied to the contents in them.

Language arts portfolios should be paper trails of idea and language processing. Among the many examples of student writing, the collections should include some done on instructional tools (sheets and forms) designed to promote more substantive writing and to assist the students in analyzing and organizing it. Hopefully, students will value and include sources or indications of where their ideas were derived or of what provoked them. Ideally they will include drafts of the same idea or piece of writing as it became more incisive, audience-focused, and polished.

Thus each portfolio will contain the evidence of language and thought *processing*. This display can be the basis for an emerging sense of who its owner is becoming as a reader, writer, and thinker—a metacognitive laboratory directed by a developing *self-assessor*.

At the same time, the portfolio can inform the teacher about the student's progress as a thinker and language user, while indicating how effective instruction has been and what additional instructional emphases are needed.

WHAT ARE PERFORMANCE ASSESSMENTS?

Unlike the portfolio, performance assessments are not a student-selected collection of writing. They are a one-time response to reading presented by the teacher or the assessment instrument. They are similar to portfolio assessment in that they integrate reading and writing behavior. Yet the topics that such assessments focus on are not fully controlled or selected by the students—except as the people who design these assessments try to select topics, purposes for writing, and texts that they assume students will find meaningful, and thus reasonably authentic.

If teachers create their own performance assessments, they can help assure some authenticity, since they probably know their students as well as any adult. If they have a say in selecting which published performance instruments will be used and some options in how they are administered, they will also have some opportunity to assure that the tests are a more authentic match with their students' backgrounds, interests, and needs.

Very basically described, a performance instrument that assesses a student's language use will require the student to write in response to a text—often referred to as the *passage* or *prompt*. These may often include charts, graphs, pictures, diagrams, and maps. The student's written response employs the prompt in some way directed by the assigned task for reading and writing. It may react to it and/or incorporate syntheses or citations to the content of the prompt. Thus writing and reading are occurring in conjunction as thinking vehicles.

A reliable performance test should supply the teacher or other rater with a carefully thought-out rubric describing each score possible in each category being rated.

The test package should also include examples of at least two papers that raters have given each possible score in each category. If there were two behaviors being rated (say, *reading* and *writing*), there would be six cells in the rating rubric and twelve examples or *anchor papers*. With these samples, teachers can compare how each student has done in comparison to responses that have been collected in tryouts and selected as models for each of the cells in the rating rubric.

WHAT IS THE ATTRACTION?

The use of language arts portfolios and performance assessment has gained widespread popularity in recent decades because they both promote and assess the *application* of language. Both methodologies reveal student writing, reading, and thinking in action while providing practice as well as assessment of these integrated behaviors. The primary evidence is writing that reveals comprehension of reading and is tied to authentic purposes for communicating and the thinking involved in fulfilling them.

The portfolio collection can reveal numerous authentic purposes for reading and thinking about it in writing. The performance assessment assigns such a purpose as a

PORTFOLIO ASSESSMENT AS AN APPEALING CONCEPT

The concept of the portfolio as a collection of one's personal work has grown from the meaning initially attached to the holder or carrying case. But it is not difficult to see how the term has come to stand for a collection of some sort that is representative of an individual's abilities and interests. In the business investment world, *portfolio* means the collection of stocks, bonds, and other investments that a person owns or controls at a particular time—very much a picture of that individual in the eyes of other investors. In England, the term came to mean the documents carried by a particular officer of state. Politically, it added the meaning of the experience and qualifications that might recommend a person to conduct the business of an important post.

Thus the use of the term *portfolio* to designate a collection used to evaluate or assess something related to an individual has standing in our culture. In education, the term has for several decades described an evaluation technique which allows a student—often an adult returning to education—to present responses to a set of requirements or assignments to get credit toward graduation. In some systems, teachers prepare extensive portfolios for professional evaluation. These are prepared from a careful analysis of one's whole professional contribution and are the results of the kind of thinking that is developed by language arts portfolio assessment. The selection process in preparing these portfolios is, however, closer to the *show* as opposed to the *working* portfolio.

The distinction between what is shown and the collection it is selected from becomes clearer when considering the types of portfolios in certain professions. To artists and photographers, the portfolio is a key concept. In a very real sense, the artist's *working* portfolio spreads across a studio or production area, to the racks or space holding finished works and works in progress, and to places where the work is displayed by the artist or by his or her patrons. Artists select from their working portfolios to create what might be called their *show* portfolios. The pieces selected are what the artist has decided are representative of the range and best examples of his or her work.

The portfolio of a photographer is quite similar. Negatives and prints are all part of the working portfolio, which will include a range of "shots" similar to, but in the final analysis not as good as, the ones put into the show portfolio or displayed at a gallery. The photographer, like graphic artists, often has an actual portfolio full of prints of his or her best work to show to possible clients. Models have similar show portfolios created for them, made up of photos of themselves chosen from a much wider collection to demonstrate a range of presentations of themselves. Fashion designers, decorators, architects, and other creators of various sorts also have variations of *working* and *show* portfolios.

The distinction between the two kinds of portfolios is important in understanding portfolio assessment in the language arts. While there may be occasions for your students to select show portfolios for particular audiences, it is working with and thinking about their working portfolios that will develop them as self-assessors. The same can be said about artists' or models' analyses of the contents of their working portfolios. A painting, for example, may not be a success; but the artist can learn much by considering why it was not.

Over the years, some teachers have used the portfolio methodology with success. Only in recent years, however, has the language arts portfolio become a more widely used methodology.

task that is deemed reasonable and authentic for the students tested. Often the performance assessment rates the student's response to the task as well as his or her reading and writing.

Proposals to use portfolios in language arts instruction and assessment have, as Elaine Parker has noted (1995), always been rationalized metaphorically, comparing the methodology to aspects of humanistic development and to many careers and life situations in which portfolios are used. The intent has been to emphasize the methodology's potential to reveal both process and product—not just to the teacher but also and *primarily to the student as a developing self-assessor.*

Portfolios do this with a broad range of reading and writing activities that integrate the two behaviors as a single thinking process. Across most proponents of using portfolios in assessment, one primary appeal of portfolios has been that they display student progress and instructional effectiveness *authentically*—by providing a look at language as it is actually used (Coleman, 1978; Wiggins, 1989). Finally, the portfolio is an approach to assessment that can effectively incorporate performance assessment and inform the teacher about the student's progress while keeping the ownership of the process in the student's hands.

PORTFOLIOS ENCOURAGE AND DEVELOP SELF-ASSESSMENT

Portfolio assessment is founded on the realization that effective assessment begins with the learner. If any student is to improve, he or she must be able to see the need for that improvement. The student must be able to self-assess and to consider how to improve—by identifying both strengths to be practiced and perfected and areas that need strengthening through focused practice on them. Hopefully, what is self-assessed leads to that kind of application outside the classroom. The goal of education ought to be to develop students as persons who can continue to learn when the teacher is not around to direct that learning and development.

In an effective portfolio program, then, students take control of their own learning. They think about their goals and review their work with a focus on what they think they must do to improve. Keeping the portfolio enables a student to become an active learner and to become his own teacher.

Just looking at the material collected and deciding what order to put it into requires evaluating it in some significant way related to categories the student has decided apply to it. Conferring with the teacher or a classmate about these decisions invites verbalizing/explaining what was done and why. This is just one way that portfolios promote self-analysis and allow students to take responsibility for their own development as readers and writers.

When a student reviews a written piece and decides to revise and improve it, the student engages in self-assessment. This effort, which is not well-served by any score on a multiple-choice test, is focused on the student-produced language. The process is motivated by ideas that are of interest to the student, who has processed them to produce the materials reviewed. And the process extends with the high potential of the material for future meaning making. Analysis of the same material may tell the teacher a lot about the student and indicate instructional needs and emphases, but the key objective is to involve the student in the assessment—to train the student as a self-assessor. It is the student, after all, who will effect changes in language processing and thinking that the assessment may recommend; and it is the student who can continue to assess his or her thinking and expression in an ongoing way.

Portfolio assessment can help the student learn to look at his or her work in an evaluative and analytic way. The portfolio is kept primarily for this purpose, not just so the teacher can look at it and evaluate the student's progress. If you are using portfolio assessment that succeeds in developing students as self-assessors, it has become one of the most important instructional components in your classroom because it is teaching your

So central is this objective and its potential that much of Chapter 4 is dedicated to detailing how portfolios can encourage students to become self-assessors.

T I P   A NATURAL WAY OF LEARNING

To get a sense of how introspection is related to self-assessment, you might think about something you have taught yourself to do or make at some time or other. How did the thing you were learning to do or make turn out the first time you did it? Did it turn out just as you hoped it would? Or did your first attempt produce less than completely desirable results?

Regardless of the outcome, think of whether you had a model in your mind as to what you thought the outcome would be. As you taught yourself to do this, were you comparing the outcome to what you envisioned as the ideal outcome of your effort?

---

students to think about the ways that *they* can improve their language strategies, skills, and behavior.

PORTFOLIOS PROVIDE VARIED AND BROAD PERSPECTIVES ON LANGUAGE USE

Chapter 3 is dedicated to discussing the variety of materials that can go into a portfolio. Chapter 4 explains how logs and other self-detailed records serve the student's and the teacher's assessment of the student's progress as a language user and thinker. Models of these records, which can be reproduced and used in the classroom, are in Appendix C of this book.

Portfolios should contain all kinds of writing and materials related to texts that a student has read or might be inclined to read. The balance of the materials in the portfolio will depend on that individual student's interests, habits of thinking, sources of ideas, etc. Individual interests should also dictate materials a student includes in the portfolio as ideas that can be developed in the future. This "open-ended" or relatively "unprescribed" nature of the portfolio is vital to ensuring that the student will have a genuine sense of ownership if the collection is to promote self-assessment.

The portfolio can contain many different work samples in the form of finished products, first and unfinished drafts, written products such as original stories, journals meant to be read by others, lists of ideas, pictures drawn by the student or clipped from old publications, and other materials. In addition, portfolios can contain organizational, evaluative, and analytical records supplied by the teacher and filled out as activities that promote and guide self-analysis of single pieces or groups of papers in the portfolio. Some of these inform both the student and the teacher. These sheets include logs, tables of contents, summary and evaluative tools, and notes about the portfolio content and language use of the student made by the student, classmates, and the teacher.

A key characteristic of portfolios that serves assessment effectively is that they are *inclusive,* not *exclusive.* Students should be encouraged to include almost anything they want, and teachers should add what they think will inform their assessment of the student and that will promote self-assessment by the student. The portfolio should not, however, become a repository for *everything* done in class. The portfolio includes those things the students want to keep, the things they want to share with their teacher, the ideas they have about their reading and writing, and their ideas about what they may want to read and write next.

Although teachers may want to discourage students from packing their portfolios with lots of workbook sheets, they should not set up inclusion/exclusion criteria that limit what students may and may not include.

Also, teachers should watch for students whose analysis of the portfolio contents leads to continual culling of materials, and discourage this. Earlier drafts of a rewritten paper, for example, should remain in the portfolio with the latest draft. So should any material in the portfolio that may have prompted a particular piece of writing. The student—particularly one who is worried about the portfolio appearing tidy—may feel that he or she is finished with papers related to preceding steps and be eager to throw away first drafts that include errors. But those are vital papers that reveal the process you hope the student will learn to analyze.

DEALING WITH BULK

TIP

When your students' portfolios get awkwardly bulky, pass out some large rubber bands and advise the students to put them around the content and start over. You might want to do this as often as three or four times a year.

You may want to give your students an opportunity to keep some of the portfolio contents—especially early drafts of unfinished work.

Make sure that the banded materials are available to students who want to look back over them and that the students can get to the materials they have "weeded out" without asking where they are.

Students who are perfectionists, and who may be overconscious of audiences who might view their portfolios, are apt to want only the things they think are their best work to be in the collection. What they are attempting to do, in effect, is to limit the collection as a show portfolio. The teacher can coach these students as they prepare show portfolios for particular audiences, but if the working portfolio collection is culled in this way, its potential to support analysis of process will be severely limited.

Opportunities to see many classrooms using portfolios across the United States has led to this observation: We have never seen a fat, untidy portfolio that was deemed ineffective. Extremely neat ones and thin ones, on the other hand, have become a kind of warning sign that those portfolios are seldom used and provide little insight when they are. When most of the portfolios in a class look like that, it seems fairly clear that they are deemed by everyone to be the property of the teacher, who may be more interested in developing neatness than language abilities.

This primary point bears repeating: Portfolios should be collections of reading and writing activities that students can use to learn how to self-assess. That means that a portfolio is not filled with just one's best work. Things that don't turn out well, first drafts, notes and thoughts about what one wants to accomplish are all part of a comprehensive working portfolio.

Will the sheer bulk of portfolios make it too difficult for students to manage them—to analyze and sort their contents? The tendency is rather that inclusive portfolios tend to generate the need for *more* ongoing student analysis, sorting, and assessment of the contents.

PORTFOLIO CONTENT INTEGRATES
READING AND WRITING WITH THINKING

The underlying processes that a writer uses are similar to those a reader uses in constructing meaning while reading (Tway, 1985). This understanding may not be new, but the emphasis on it is. For too long, schools focused on reading and writing as if they were separate components of literacy development. Today many teachers are encouraging their students to read like authors; and instructional attention to visualizing one's audiences encourages writers to write like readers.

Moreover, the teaching and use of reading and writing are integrated throughout the school day—as students read stories and write their reactions, gather sources of information to develop a report, read letters and respond, and write stories to extend an unfinished plot or to mimic the style of an author. And this integration crosses most subject matter.

Just as this understanding has affected instruction, it has had a serious impact on the assessment of language behavior. This is effectively accommodated by the portfolio, but it will be necessary to ensure in some way that a considerable amount of the writing collected relates to texts the student has read. That is, a number of pieces in the collection should react or respond to written text, expand it or modify its meaning in some way, report on the text, apply it to an extended context, or rely on the content of the text in some other primary way. Reading, we have come to know, is as much a process of constructing meaning as is writing. Common bases of these processes are *thinking* and the influence of the *affective* realm, which link all language use—including speaking and listening—as one basic process that extends to all meaning-making behaviors (Maiorana, 1992; Manzo, 1995).

Integrated reading/writing assessments can be constructed, administered, and analyzed without the use of portfolios, but the nature of the two is so interactively supporting that they make ideal instructional component partners. They are not identical twins, but like the portfolio, the more formalized performance assessment activity can indicate how well students comprehend what they read and how well they can write about those ideas. It also gives an indication of how the student has fit what was read into his or her understanding of, and attitudes about, the world.

Such assessments are now available from major publishers, including those who publish reading and literature basals and other series and include performance assessment at the unit level. Teachers in some schools and in school districts have been constructing their own. The differences between these instruments as a group and the portfolio include these: The portfolio does what the test does but on a much broader, more expansive scale, employing many more kinds of materials; and the student is apt to have far more control over the selection of the text read and over the written response to it. The integrated performance assessment does so with a single activity that frames a purpose for reading.

The controlled assessment begins with the student reading the supplied text and culminates with the student writing a somewhat directed response designed to promote use of details and concepts in the text. The portfolio can contain writing samples of similar activities, and it may also contain writing not directly based on a text. Such samples, however, reveal interests and background that inform on the student's reading behavior and suggest potential texts that the student may enjoy reading and reacting to.

Although it is advisable to place the results of such an integrated test in the portfolio, once there, the test becomes but a single sample, which may or may not include preliminary drafts. On most integrated performance assessments, redrafting is optional and drafts and notes are not analyzed as a part of the student response. Yet this processing material should go into the portfolio.

Perhaps the most important difference between the portfolio and the integrated language arts performance test is that the student is not usually the evaluator of the test; with the portfolio, however, the student's analysis is the key objective and outcome. Once in the portfolio, where it should be placed, however, what the student has done on the test is as open to student analysis as any other writing.

PORTFOLIO CONTENTS SHOULD BE AUTHENTIC

The goal of developing students' language abilities has long been to develop them so that they are applied in ways that are meaningful and real to the learner (Valencia, 1990). This is currently described by the term *authentic*. Given enough control to select a majority of the content in the portfolio and to determine how it is organized, students should find portfolio content more authentic than many other materials they are encouraged or required to work with while they learn. The thoughtful selection of a good performance assessment instrument can strive to achieve the same thing.

If teaching with authentic motivations is a difficult thing to do, assessing the language development that results from the learning in an authentic way is doubly challenging. The prescriptions for using portfolio and performance assessment that are in this book try to respond directly to that goal. As this text will attempt to demonstrate, both methodologies can integrate assessment as instruction, making both challenges easier to meet by compounding their impact. Performance assessment and portfolio assessment

PORTFOLIO ASSESSMENT PUTS THEORY INTO PRACTICE

The trend toward portfolio and performance assessment of reading, writing, and thinking abilities indicates that important theory about language development (Farr and Tone, 1994) is having widespread impact on the teaching of language behaviors. Ideally we assess what we believe we should be teaching, and theory that has been gaining prominence for the past twenty-five years or so describes language behaviors as meaning making.

Generally, the emphasis in classrooms where instruction responds to reading and language development theory is on having students read and write as much as possible. The belief is that the best way to determine whether an individual can construct meaning with and from language is to look at meaning that the language user has constructed. From this same analysis, we can also infer things about the process that created it. If we have access to various stages of meaning construction—as in the form of notes or drafts—we get a better view of the process. And another way to observe process, of course, is to watch for opportunities to observe while it is actually taking place.

There are other important methods, instructional materials, and approaches that have grown out of what we have decided about language behaviors. But the effectively used language arts portfolio and increasing interest in performance assessment are among the most evident indications of the understanding of language use as an integrated, interactive process for thinking, communicating, and enlarging one's understanding and appreciation of the world (Courtney, 1965; Valencia, et al., 1989; Farr and Tone, 1994).

The fact that these methodologies are better than multiple-choice test items in displaying how well a student reads and writes should be obvious. Making a mark beside one of several options that complete a statement or answer a question about a text passage is approving or endorsing a supplied meaning, not making it; and it applies the comprehension of the text in only the most minimal way. The annotated reading list at the end of this book contains a section of good sources that explain language and language development theory and its impact on instruction and assessment.

are by definition student language in use, so the student practices and learns during the assessment.

Our understanding of language use as the construction of meaning has led to an increased instructional emphasis on having students write for "real" audiences. In many classes, that means that the audience for a writing activity is identified as someone other than the teacher, for whom legions of students wrote book reports and essays about what they did last summer. Developing as genuine a purpose as possible has become as relevant for reading as the student's reason for writing. The connection between a reader's background and how well he or she comprehends now helps dictate the selection of reading material the student is asked to read as surely as a student's life experiences have always been tapped to promote and support writing.

All this demands that language instruction be a real experience—that what we ask students to do in the classroom be a worthwhile life experience if possible, or that it at least emulate something that might happen outside the classroom. The term *valid* has too specific and technical a meaning in testing to apply to this easily. It is better to think of the need for instruction and for the assessment that reflects it to be *authentic*.

Assessment is an essential, guiding aspect of good instruction; so the assessment of language behaviors like reading and writing needs to be authentic, as well. This has been the major complaint about assessing reading with multiple-choice questions or writing ability with multiple-choice items about language usage. It has become increasingly clear to effective teachers that while multiple-choice items can determine how well a reader comprehends details, a much surer way to find out if the student has comprehended a text's message and intent is to have the student write something that explains or applies what the reading text contains.

Performance assessment and *authentic assessment* are often discussed as if they are synonymous terms. While the two have much in common, the proponents of performance assessment are most often concerned with a student's performance in constructing or developing some product rather than choosing a correct answer. Both traditional tests and performance assessment may be designed to deal with a topic of interest to the age of the student to be tested. But performance assessments tend to appear more authentic

WHO HAS THE CONTROL?

T
A
B
L
E

1
•
1

Assessment Feature	Multiple-Choice Test	Performance Assessment	Portfolio Assessment
Identification of the topic/issue to be studied	Test-developer	Test-developer	Student/teacher
Form of the response	Test-developer	Test-developer	Student/teacher
Specific questions/ issues to be answered	Test-developer	Test-developer (with modifications)	Student/teacher
Criteria for success	Test-developer	Test-developer (with modifications)	Student/teacher
Length of time for the assessment	Test-developer	Teacher/student	Teacher/student
Resources to be used	Test-developer (usually none allowed)	Test-developer (usually allowed)	Teacher/student
Collaboration	Test-developer (usually none allowed)	Test-developer (sometimes allowed)	Teacher/student
Selection of best response	Test-developer	Test-developer (with modifications)	Student/teacher

because the student creates a response in writing—often to complete a realistic task. Given this emphasis, a multiple-choice test would not be considered a performance assessment, while a written essay would be.

Authentic assessment, on the other hand, looks more like a real-life task rather than like an activity that was constructed as a test that does not resemble much that happens beyond the test—let alone beyond the classroom.

Most of the alternative assessments that are being proposed in education today attempt to be both authentic and performance-based. Yet, it should be noted that in addition to the definitions posed above, many educators believe that for assessment to be both authentic and performance-based, the student must be the primary evaluator. Portfolio assessment responds most directly to that specification.

One can decide how authentic and performance-based an assessment is by considering the degree to which the student is in control of the assessment. For example, a multiple-choice test is under the control of the test giver and not the learner; a performance-based assessment seems to share control between the test giver and the learner; and authentic assessments are primarily under the control of the learner. Portfolios come quite close then to being clearly authentic, but they are also performance-based.

Table 1.1 indicates how these assessments differ from each other and from standardized testing (usually multiple-choice) in terms of who controls a number of important factors.

Portfolios that are successfully used for assessment of language abilities contain ample examples of writing that integrate reading and writing that is authentic for the

GETTING A SENSE OF
WHAT IS AUTHENTIC

Ask your students to bring to class something they have read and something they have written that they feel is "important to them." Have volunteers explain reasons for their selections and press for details with questions that show respect for their choices.

Next make a list of tasks and topics that this session has suggested as being of "authentic interest" to your students. After this activity, do you have any better sense of what kinds of topics, language, and purposes for using it are most important to your students?

students. To be authentic, the texts the students read need to relate to things that are interesting and real—that are meaningful for the student; the purposes for reading need to be convincing. The writing activities ought to represent the kinds of writing and thinking that the student is doing at school and at home.

This concern relates again to ownership, for if the portfolio is to contain authentic writing as reactions to reading, the student is most apt to know what that is and must have some authority in deciding what goes into the collection.

A considerable amount of the writing and reading that students do at school may yet be typical of the kinds that have traditionally been required of students as "learner/ scholar literacies" within traditional disciplines. Yet if the student doesn't buy into a text or a writing activity, any authenticity the activity has will be forced at best. If papers related to such assignments get into the portfolio, the student is probably going to look at them as requirements that are clearly owned by those who impose them. This may be the case even if the student, for some reason (probably because the student assumed that the teacher expected to see them included), decided to put them in.

Some activities that result in student writing are done with the clear purpose of getting a passing grade. Getting promoted is a valid concern for a student, but the activities may have no other convincing authenticity for the student and are unlikely to establish the sense of ownership of the portfolio or promote the regular thoughtful engagement with the collection that will develop self-assessment.

Many students, of course, will enjoy and get involved in texts and writing assignments related to good instruction. Ideally the portfolio will contain ideas that both the student and the teacher feel have *real* importance and interest and complement purposes for using language—inside and outside of school. Striving for this kind of authenticity in portfolio content will help ensure it in your instructional activities as well.

THESE METHODOLOGIES INFORM
THE TEACHER AS A COACHING PARTNER

Over the years, the portfolio methodology has been used successfully by some teachers. Only in recent years, however, has the language-arts portfolio become a more widely used methodology. Developing student self-assessors remains the primary aim of the method, but the teacher plays a vital role in that development, using the portfolio for assessment that can effectively guide individualized instruction. As the teacher and student work together, *the student's working portfolio can become a highly effective tool for managing the student's language development.*

The student self-assesses, often with the teacher's guidance. The rich mixture of content that accrues in portfolios is a powerful source of information that helps the teacher learn a great deal about the students. The questions that can guide the teacher's analysis of the portfolio are innumerable! Here are just a few samples:

- What kind of texts and what topics have authentic appeal to each of the students? What kinds of writing do different students appear to like and create most effectively? What are the major strengths of each student's use of language? What recurring themes, topics, images, and details used in writing and selected in reading suggest individual students' interests and information needs? Which texts that the student has read have seemed to contribute to these? Are any texts read clearly models for the writing?

- What kind of affective responses does this boy and that girl have to different kinds of texts? What does their writing or their choices of reading materials reveal about their backgrounds and their individual strengths and potentials? Which stories and reading materials are which students' favorites and why? Which are most meaningful to them? What does all that tell the teacher about generating authentic purposes for motivating students to read and write and think?

- How do different students use the material they read? How is the meaning constructed applied and how effectively? Does the use suggest a high level of comprehension? What does the student's handling—organizing, analyzing—of the collection suggest about his or her development as a reader, writer, thinker, and self-evaluator? What kind of thinking is going on in the materials gathered and massaged in each portfolio?

Obviously, the student and the teacher can also look at writing samples in the portfolio and identify language strategies and skills the student can target for improvement. Even a very limited and skill-focused analysis, for example, can reveal that the number of misspellings or grammatical errors makes it difficult to grasp some ideas the student is trying to express. Ideally, students will begin to recognize these aspects of their writing in their own self-assessment so that the teacher does not need to focus on them too repeatedly.

Paragraphing and idea organization, use of detail, diction selection, and almost any other aspect of writing that has been a particular focus of the teacher or the curriculum as a stated instructional objective can be examined in the light of the student's writing included in a portfolio. Hopefully this will not be overemphasized at the expense of the ideas revealed; and the analysis of skill-focused teachers need not emphasize negative examples. The teacher can, for example, point out effective word choices, expressions, and descriptions and comment on why they enhance the written communication. The reactions to books and other texts can be noted in terms of their clarity, originality, etc. Better yet, the teacher can lead the student to make such observations!

Portfolios can be used to compare pieces of writing written recently to those written earlier in order to note the development of ideas, arguments, and language use. Is there evidence that a strategy that teacher and student have agreed should be developed has been used? Is there evidence of changes in the student's positions or feelings about certain things? And the reactions that integrate reading and writing can be used to analyze texts more traditionally as well—again hopefully not at the expense of the power of the portfolio to focus on ideas and on how effectively they are transmitted.

Does the student display the ability to grasp the main themes and ideas of texts and to gather textual detail around them? Is there understanding of character motivation in stories? Is there evidence of appreciation of writing styles? Records such as reading logs can be coupled to writing in determining such things.

The portfolio is a warehouse of the ideas important to an individual student and should indicate purposes the student has for using language to clarify, convey, and use those ideas. The teacher can learn a lot about the student; more importantly, the student's analysis of the content becomes a kind of blueprint for future reading and writing. The portfolio, for example, can ensure that even the writing in the collection that the student considers the most completed becomes a fuse for future expression.

Reading experience, too, can grow on the basis of portfolio assessment. In the portfolio's contents, the student discusses and reacts to texts he or she has read; that writing/thinking has helped synthesize what the student knows and feels about the topic of a text. Almost invariably the student's attention to the text has directly or indirectly helped frame questions generated by the increased understanding. So thinking about the contents of the portfolio should act as a springboard to promote additional reading.

STUDENT/TEACHER DISCUSSION IS THE KEY TO ASSESSMENT SUCCESS

The portfolio becomes a focal point for student/teacher discussions about ideas that have been encountered in reading and writing. The ideas themselves are primarily important, but at the same time, the conversation is also about language and how it can be used most effectively. Portfolio assessment provides regular opportunities for the teacher to talk with students about their developing prowess as language users. It affords the chance to reveal their attitudes toward, and interests related to, reading, writing, and thinking. Sometimes those kinds of things that can be learned from portfolios must be inferred from discussions that focus on the specific content of the writing—trying to clarify it and increase its impact on a reader.

This kind of exchange between teacher and student may be ongoing in the classroom, but of prime importance to the success of portfolio assessment are conferences that the teacher schedules with each student, ideally four times a year. The one-on-one meeting uses the collection as a demonstration of the student's developing strengths and interests and as an indicator of possible instructional focuses for the future. At these sessions, the teacher and student pull together all their notes and ideas gained from examining the portfolio frequently between the conference sessions and in preparation for the conference.

So essential and important are the student/teacher conferences that center on the portfolio that all of Chapter 5 is dedicated to discussing ways to make them a success. In that chapter, too, twenty-five strategies for facilitating the scheduling of the four one-on-one conferences with each student are offered.

Working together, the student and the teacher can make the portfolio the focal point for managing the student's language development.

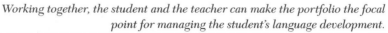

As they do this, the collection lies open and accessible between them as the focal point of their analysis of the student's work and interests. Both participants keep notes during the conference and share them. A special two-sided sheet is recommended for this to ensure the open nature of the meeting and the sharing of assessments.

Not all the portfolio assessment done by the teacher occurs while talking with the student. Just as the student often works alone with his or her collection, the teacher may approach the portfolio independently to review the progress of, and to learn more about, individual students.

In a classroom with portfolios, one can see the teacher viewing the collections after school or while the students are doing other work. This analysis is very helpful as the teacher plans future instruction—for the individual student, for small groups, and for the class as a whole. Such teacher analysis may also contribute to the student's preparation to inform reports to parents, administrators, and educator specialists.

SOME INDICATIONS ABOUT THE STATE OF THESE ALTERNATIVES

While this book will explain formal uses of portfolios, a majority of the advice on using them is for classroom instruction and is, therefore, a form of informal assessment. Unfortunately, the term *informal* is often connoted as "unplanned" or "casual," which in turn may mean "less valid" or "less informative" to some readers. Yet many highly useful types of informal assessment are used by effective teachers in an ongoing way, and portfolio assessment is a very powerful assessment *and* instructional tool.

For all the potential advantages of these two methodologies, it seems realistic and advisable to acknowledge that while these methodologies are now favored and popular, they have not "swept" the educational scene to become the primary ways of producing information for assessment. An attempt to fit portfolio and performance assessment into the whole educational assessment picture has led to several temporizing realizations in recent years:

- While portfolio assessment is a highly attractive methodology that is initially appealing to many teachers, it requires commitments that some teachers have found difficult to make. Yet it remains a highly viable and useful methodology because it (1) integrates assessment as very effective instruction and (2) extends the impact of instruction indefinitely by developing the student as a self-assessor.

- Attempts to use portfolios in "high-stakes" assessments—those in which student, teacher, and school accountability are involved—have not been highly successful. It appears that there is too much subjectivity involved in evaluating portfolio contents to generate substantial "public" trust.

- When this concern results in attempts to standardize portfolio contents so that ratings of them can be more reliable, the nature of the portfolios is controlled. This tends to disenfranchise students and to forfeit the sense of ownership that is essential to developing self-assessors. Thus using portfolios in large-scale assessments is not highly compatible with the methodology's potential in the classroom.

- A clear role for portfolios as mediation in "high-stakes" assessment is emerging. It suggests that portfolios can be vital as a "backup" to other assessment information that informs educational decision makers and others interested in educational accountability. In this role, portfolios of a percentage of students for which classroom and test performance differ can be used to qualify indications of the test data and to modify and better inform educational decisions.

Thus portfolios can be used to avoid potential mistakes that might be made due to overreliance on standardized and criterion-referenced test data. When such test data do not seem to reflect a student's actual ability, the decisions dictated can be unfortunate. Portfolios are now recommended to mediate such situations.

- This use of portfolios distinguishes between *working* and *show* portfolios. The *working* portfolio is an essential prerequisite to developing the student as self-assessor, but the use of portfolios to mediate in high-stakes decisions leads to selecting samples from the working portfolio to make a *show* portfolio.

- Performance assessments have been somewhat more successful than portfolios in winning the trust of administrators and the public. These tests, which can assess a combination of different thinking and language skills, have been in development for about a decade now. A variety of published batteries are available, and different types of performance assessments now accompany all reading and language arts textbook series. In winning this acceptance, however, the degree of integration of the language abilities rated has been compromised on some fronts; and some performance assessments have been modified to reflect more traditional assessments.

- These two general developments—(1) the use of portfolios in developing the self-assessor and in a backup role for educational decision making and (2) the increasing reliance on performance assessments—now recommend that performance assessments results become an essential inclusion in portfolio collections. They can initially model the kind of document sets the student will want to collect and can be used to demonstrate improvement.

HOW ACCEPTED IS
PORTFOLIO ASSESSMENT?

It is becoming increasingly clear that teachers who use portfolios as *successful* assessment tools invest a considerable amount of time in the methodology. This commitment is not just in teacher time spent analyzing the content of portfolios. It is primarily in class time dedicated to giving the students the opportunity to build and assess their own collections.

This kind of commitment must also be tied to instructional time committed to showing students how to examine, analyze, and assess their own work. Successfully putting together a portfolio requires the interlocking of assessment and instruction—long an objective of viable and defensible assessment (Wilson, 1981).

The teaching that successful portfolio assessment requires may be practiced as different combinations of whole-class activities, small-group assistance, and one-on-one tutoring. Individualized attention, however, is basic to many teachers who have come to rely on portfolios. Working one-on-one with a student allows the teacher to customize the assistance given so that it matches the individual student's interests and identifies the particular instruction that can help that student develop as a language user. Furthermore, one-on-one assistance can be offered during the class time that needs to be committed to allow students to work with their collections.

Regardless of *how* the teacher shows students ways to build, analyze, organize, and draw directions from their portfolios—that kind of commitment is essential if portfolio assessment is to work. It is the only way that portfolio assessment can lead the student to set personal goals and objectives as a language user and to assume metacognitive habits that monitor language use and development.

Many teachers who have started out with enthusiastic intentions to develop and use portfolio assessment have abandoned that ambition in the face of essential time commitments that may appear, at least initially, to be unreasonable. Or they have continued having their students keep portfolios in such a way that the collections have limited value as assessment or instructional tools.

Portfolios that grow fatter and fatter with materials have great *potential* for revealing their students' language processing—to both the students themselves and to their teacher—but that doesn't happen with the collections just billowing in some corner of the classroom. Nor will portfolios that are slimly selected little showcases of a student's favorite or "best" work have much long-lasting value in developing the self-assessor and goal setter: the primary promise of portfolio assessment.

So portfolio assessment is not some panacea to teachers hard-pressed for time, but more of a challenge to create classroom opportunities for students to work with the collections. This may be less of a problem than that observation suggests, however, because what these teachers also find is that portfolio assessment becomes a rather intricate part of their instruction. Even so, the reluctance of many teachers who begin portfolio assessment to commit to the time required for success leads to many collections becoming little more than an attractive filing system for lots of student products.

HOW WELL DO PORTFOLIOS WORK IN ACCOUNTABILITY ASSESSMENT?

The enthusiasm for portfolio assessment as an authentic measurement of a student's language use and development has led understandably to an interest in using it for large-scale accountability assessment. While the ultimate results of this movement are not in, it seems clear that using portfolios in this way is a considerable challenge (Guskey, 1994).

It seems sensible to want to show language *in use* in an age when demands for accountability led to the use of standardized or criterion-referenced tests in a majority of states (Afflerbach, 1990). Multiple-choice, short-answer tests could not, it has been argued, simulate real-world uses of language. As the primary way to express thinking, language needed broader and more authentic contexts to fairly hold students accountable for minimum competencies, it has been argued (Valencia, 1990). What could seem fairer than to have students keep portfolios demonstrating with writing that they can comprehend reading, can think, can create, and can solve problems?

Among the large-scale use of portfolios for accountability testing are programs in states like Vermont, New Mexico, and Kentucky (Fontana, 1995; Wesson, 1993). The problems with this kind of testing should have been easily predicted (Herman and Winters, 1994). Just collecting the portfolios from all the students in a school district, let alone a state, presents a logistic problem necessitating some plan for sampling or for evaluation within each school.

Even with just a sampling of students, reviewing and reacting to the bulk that this initiative creates is another extremely demanding challenge. Practical considerations in one state led to teachers rating portfolios in their own school and having to avoid doing so for students they knew (Callahan, 1996). The analysis of the contents of thousands of different portfolios could end up being an understandably subjective task. The problem of how the many raters who are necessarily involved could rate or rank the collections fairly and without bias and with any consistency or reliability across the whole assessment is a reasonable concern (Bond, 1995; Black, 1993).

The role that portfolios can play in more formal, high-stakes accountability assessment will be discussed realistically in this book without recommending it as a replacement of standardized, criterion-referenced, or performance tests. That would not be a good idea for several reasons. Perhaps the most important is that if portfolios attempt to fulfill the information needs met by standardized tests, for example, structured and narrow specifications would be enforced on them. They would be overpowered by certain inclusions that would allow their evaluation using relatively specific criteria. They would not promote the sense of ownership that is an essential of student self-assessment.

One way to help assure fairness and reliability in ranking or rating portfolio collections is to make sure that the contents of the collections are alike to some degree. This means requiring a certain number of particular kinds of writing that must be included (Case, 1994). A requirement for a state assessment might be, for example, that a portfolio include a piece of descriptive writing, a persuasive essay or editorial, two responses to reading that fulfill assigned tasks, a letter, and other specific types of writing. More specific purposes for writing might also be required.

Such portfolios would have to be show portfolios selected from students' working portfolios. But to be sure that the kinds of papers required would be available for selection from the working portfolio would mean requiring that they be there. So such attempts to make sure that portfolios in large-scale evaluations have comparable and somewhat standard content severely limits student ownership of them and has negative effects on the use of portfolios as classroom assessments that can develop self-assessors (Benoit, 1996). It might be good that portfolios have these kinds of writing, but ownership has clearly shifted beyond the student keeping the collection.

There are other understandable concerns about large-scale portfolio assessment. It is argued that since the portfolio-keeping process promotes close collaboration between student and teacher, among students, and sometimes between students and parents, it is not possible to be assured that the work being rated has integrity (Gearhart and Herman, 1995). Is it truly an indication of what the student can do as opposed to what the student can do with considerable consultation and assistance?

This possibility, along with the problem of some degree of subjectivity across raters, leaves some members of audiences who are interested in educational accountability less than confident in the results of portfolio assessment. In addition, the ratings given portfolios are far less sensitive than scores on standardized tests: It may be a matter of

---

T I P

THINK ABOUT IT.
WHAT WOULD YOU USE?

Although the recommendation is to assure a bit of reliability by selecting portfolios for this purpose randomly, it would be a good idea early in your portfolio program to start thinking about what portfolio contents can be most informative to you. Here is an interesting exercise you may want to try:

Look through your roster of students and pick several whose language development has, in your estimation, shown significant improvement and several whose development is not clear to you. Think about how you would explain your assessment of their status as language users to their parents or to the teacher they will have next year.

- What papers in the portfolio do you think are most revealing? Why?

- What else would you base your analysis on? What would show that to the parent?

- Would you be inclined to use the standardized test scores for these students? Would they help explain why the student has improved and how? Would they reveal why there is little apparent improvement and suggest why?

- What conclusions could you draw about these students and how could you detail them?

- Would their developing portfolios help report to such audiences?

comparing scores that range from *1* to *3* or *4* to scales that range across double digits. Audiences interested in high-stakes assessment appear far less than willing to give up the kinds of assessments that are familiar to them in order to accept portfolio assessment as a replacement. It may be accepted in conjunction with the standardized and/or criterion-referenced test scores, but it is not viewed as a dependable substitute.

It seems clear that portfolios are not some silver bullet that can target and eliminate all the problems and criticisms of more traditional assessment methodologies. Rather, they are an important missing link in a comprehensive evaluation and assessment program. Nonetheless, school board members, school administrators, and parents seeking a more comprehensive understanding of what is being accomplished in language arts classrooms can randomly sample and review portfolios. With a bit of training as to how to look for and appreciate process, these could even be working portfolios, not some show collections selected specifically for the review.

A collection of ten portfolios selected randomly, for example, from all classrooms at one grade level could provide a valid perspective of what is going on in language arts instruction. Coupled with more traditional assessment reports, this kind of analysis adds depth to the view such audiences get of a school. Creating show portfolios from randomly selected working portfolios would be an excellent exercise for the teacher, however, and is another approach.

WHAT VALUE IS THERE, THEN, IN HIGH-STAKES PORTFOLIO ASSESSMENT?

With all these qualifications, it may seem surprising that large-scale portfolio assessment has survived at all. There is one persuasive argument for not giving up the effort. In at least two states portfolio assessment is reported to be driving educational reform (Callahan, 1996; O'Neil, 1992). This is a clear indication of accountability assessment driving instruction. It is interesting that no one appears to be arguing the case often made against high-stakes standardized testing—that teachers tend to drop the kind of instruction that they believe is best fitted to their students to teach to such tests.

In the case of large-scale portfolio assessment, the fact that it has led teachers to more integrated instruction of reading and writing and to valuing thinking ability and clear, effective expression is acknowledged as a positive result. In Kentucky, for example, portfolio assessment was mandated as a part of legislated school reform. Not all teachers were pleased with the emphases; yet everyone seemed to acknowledge that evaluating portfolios as part of the accountability process had resulted in changes in instructional emphases that the reform seemed designed to bring about (Kannapel, et al., 1996).

In addition, another important role related to accountability assessment now seems clear for portfolios. Anyone who has taught for a number of years is sure to have had students who did not score well on standardized or criterion-referenced instruments used in large-scale accountability testing. How does the teacher, who has the most direct indication of a student's ability, prevail against decisions that do not appear to be in the student's best interests but are apt to be made in response to low test scores? How does the teacher avoid a negative evaluation of methods or emphases that the teacher knows—by looking at what a student writes and reads—are effective in teaching a student and in promoting his or her thoughtful expression?

It is recommended here that teachers in this situation pull a show portfolio from the student's working collection to demonstrate what the teacher believes the test scores do not show. The student can have a hand in selecting the pieces, but the ultimate purpose of this portfolio is to show educational decision makers who do not have access to the student's daily and authentic language performance that the student is more capable than the test scores indicate.

The selection should be made as well with consideration for the amount of time available to the audience intended for the "backup" portfolio. The mediating portfolio needs to make its point directly and efficiently. It may take some accompanying analysis from the teacher to effectively explain this relevance to the situation, but the collection needs to demonstrate adequate and effective application of skills on which the student did not score well on the test. Once this kind of mediating with portfolios becomes an accepted practice in a school or system where teachers have been using it, the procedure becomes easier and more efficient.

Beyond just waiting for the need to produce this *backup* portfolio for a particular student, it is recommended here that a teacher make an informal but systematic analysis of which students may need portfolio backup mediation. This can be done easily by taking the portfolios for a class and sorting them into four piles. One pile can be of portfolios for students whose work appears to be exemplary—students whose writing, use of texts, and thinking patterns are either quite strong for the age/grade level or are improving dramatically. Another pile can be for students who are clearly in need of individual and other instructional attention in order to develop into effective readers, thinkers, and writers.

The teacher should create two piles of portfolios between these: one for students whose work appears to be strong yet does not quite fit the teacher's estimation of exemplary and one for students whose work is weak but shows enough promise to keep it out of the pile of those in need of the most help. Starting from the pile of the strongest portfolios, each student should be rated with a *4, 3, 2,* or *1*.

Using student test scores from some recently administered standardized test or a criterion-referenced measure that is of high significance in the accountability system that reports on the students and school, the teacher should use some system to rank the scores from *4* (top) to *1* (lowest). Quartiles or some such simple system can be used to do this.

Next, the teacher compares the two rankings for each student: portfolio strength versus test score rank. If there is a discrepancy of *2* or *3* ranking points for any students, the teacher has identified those who need "backup" portfolios. There will not be many. This simple system should, therefore, not overburden the busy teacher.

A student who scores in the lowest quartile on the test, for example, but has a portfolio in the pile rated as *3*s, has a discrepancy of *2*. That student's working portfolio should be used to prepare the show portfolio. It should be shown to whoever may rely on the test scores in making decisions about that student. The point that the "backup" portfolio will make is that the scores are not compatible with what it demonstrates.

Almost invariably, when there are discrepancies between portfolio and test score ratings, the lower of the two is the test score. This is, no doubt, explained by a student's fear of tests and test environments; or perhaps a student just had a bad day on the day the test was administered. The authentic nature of the tasks and purposes that lead to portfolio contents and the fact that they are collected over many days makes them the perfect instrument to suggest that that is what has happened.

What, one may wonder, should a teacher do if the portfolio is the weaker of two ratings with a discrepancy of *2*? The possible explanation for this unusual occurrence might be that the student has an unusual skill for tackling tests, known as *test-wiseness*. This situation may recommend using the show portfolio to argue for any special attention that the teacher feels such a student needs. The portfolio could also point out that opportunities promoted by high test scores require the very kind of language application that the portfolio displays is not well developed for the student. A "backup" portfolio might protect such a student from being placed in a position where too much is automatically expected of him or her, and failure is a possible result.

It is important to note that this use of portfolios for backups to other large-scale assessment avoids most of the problems inherent in using the methodology for accountability: The number of portfolios involved is dramatically limited, and the attention that needs to be paid to their contents is very limited. Since the teacher's judgment is being valued in considering the backup collection in the first place, questions about the integrity of the student's work can be answered on the spot. There are no concerns about the

The development of backup and other show portfolios is discussed in Chapter 6.

subjectivity of raters or about consistency of value judgments across raters. The "backup" portfolio is there to examine. The contents can speak for themselves as there is no "rating" of the portfolio using some standardized scale. Nor are there concerns about the contents of the "backup" portfolio. It has been selected to respond to particular performance and test score discrepancies for a particular student. Its contents are not expected to be comparable to the contents of the portfolios of other students. The intention is to customize the contents to the situation, not to make sure that they are a match for the contents of other students' portfolios.

With these concerns alleviated, the use of the portfolio as a backup to large-scale assessments seems highly recommended.

CAN PERFORMANCE ASSESSMENT SERVE LARGE-SCALE ASSESSMENT?

In many important regards, performance assessment is more like traditional tests than like portfolio assessment. Compared to assessing portfolio collections, far less time is required to rate the performance of numerous students. Because of this, it is not surprising that it is being considered and employed by an increasing number of schools and states (Khattri, et al., 1995).

With performance assessment, the assessment does not have to subjectively synthesize student performance across a variety of tasks or written expressions in order to draw conclusions as is the case in portfolio assessment. A performance assessment can clearly target tasks and purposes for using language, so it is clearer to the high-stakes audience what schools, teachers, and students are being held accountable for. The task or purpose for reading and writing that is assigned can require the comprehension of particular texts, can target particular audiences, and can assess any other aspects of reading, writing, and thinking that the high-stakes assessment audience may value.

Chapters 7 and 8 of this book present logical and descriptive steps for developing an integrated language arts performance test and present an example of the non-integrated approach. These chapters are not necessarily meant to promote the development of such tests but are intended to inform those who may be selecting them of what to look for.

The ratings of student responses on performance assessment can be rather explicitly defined within categories and subcategories. This is done using scales that are also carefully defined in rating rubrics so that there is less concern about subjectivity in evaluating the student product. On most such assessments, the fitting of particular student responses to these scales is sensibly guided by ample examples of actual student papers that have received particular scores in particular categories.

For example, most language-use performance assessments will rate at a minimum the two categories *reading* and *writing*—and minimally, the rating scale will run from *1* to *3*. The matrix for this simplest of performance assessment designs would result in a rubric with six cells for ratings *1* through *3* in each major category. It would describe what constitutes each possible score in each category. More importantly, the assessment package would include at least two samples of responses from actual students taking the assessment for each of the six cells to guide the rating procedure and make it more reliable.

But if performance assessment is more like traditional assessments in matters such as these, it is far more like portfolio assessment than like standardized or criterion-referenced tests. Performance assessment requires the *application* of language skills in responses that are considerably more substantive than any test made up of multiple-choice items. As the tasks, audiences, and texts assigned and involved are picked with the intent to serve authentic language use for the age assessed, these tests can be considerably more authentic than traditional assessments.

In addition, the performance assessment can provide documentation of steps or phases in responding to the task. Sometimes administration of the performance assessment makes creating these optional, but more often than not, they are followed to some degree and the notes and drafts involved are made available to the rater. Whether they are actually rated or not, these notes and drafts can help create a performance assessment paper set that can serve both the student and teacher as a source of examining and analyzing language/thinking processes. In this regard, performance assessment can reveal process at least as effectively as the portfolio does.

There is, as well, in performance assessment, considerable assurance that the language skills assessed are integrated. Answering multiple-choice questions to demonstrate comprehension of a passage covers reading, but writing is not involved and thinking is reduced to selecting the correct answer that results from the test maker's thinking. Integrated language skills are far more apt in performance assessment to require the thinking necessary to write something that responds to the assigned task. In many performance assessment packages, that thinking is assessed as a major category. More likely, however, a third category related to how well the assigned task is performed is added to performance assessments as an indication of the thinking and application of the reading and writing done to respond to the task.

The case for the integration of the behaviors or skills involved, however, can be stated more strongly for one of two general types of performance assessment than for the other. There are two prevailing approaches to performance assessment. One approach *integrates* the assessment of behaviors such as reading, writing, and the completion of a task assigned as the purpose for reading and writing. In fulfilling it, the student writes a single response based on the passage or passages supplied and read. This single response is analyzed and rated on each of the behaviors being assessed.

An example of this kind of performance assessment might provide the student with three texts: one outlining a social problem, one presenting some tabular or charted information helping delineate the problem, and one suggesting several solutions and offering critical summaries of what is best and worst about each. Sometimes these texts are not congruent. The student can be directed to read the texts, decide on the most promising solution, and write an argument to some specified audience about why it is the best. The resulting writing would then be evaluated on all aspects of language that the test professes to assess. For example, how well and accurately were the texts comprehended and used in the writing, how directly and effectively did the student tend to the task assigned, and how clearly and persuasively did the student write?

This design for performance assessment has been received by educators with less enthusiasm than another, more traditionally based approach. That type of test rates student responses as short written answers to several questions about the supplied passage or passages (to reveal reading comprehension). Then it rates the student's writing ability using another sample of writing that has been motivated in a very general way by what was read. The sample for writing analysis is often a creative response sparked by the topic of the texts, but need not demonstrate any other use of them. The responses to the reading are not rated for writing ability, and the writing does not reflect comprehension of the passage supplied. The reading part of this assessment is basically akin to the short-essay answer test, and the writing part is rated similarly to the way that writing test samples have always been rated.

Which of these types of performance assessment should the educator choose? The answer to that appears to depend on the audience. Those used to more traditional assessment tend to lean toward the format in which the responses are less integrated. Even teachers who are more comfortable with what is familiar to them have tended not to select performance assessment where several categories of language behaviors have to be assessed from a single response.

Proponents of performance assessment have tended to encourage teachers to get involved in creating their own performance assessments. The argument has been that when done in collaboration with a group of fellow teachers, this is an excellent curriculum development activity. It will force teachers to articulate their philosophies about language instruction and to carefully consider the needs and interests of their particular students. But it is also a very time-consuming and even grueling task.

The steps to constructing a successful performance assessment instrument include these: The reading prompt and an authentic task must be selected together. The rubric (evaluation matrix) that will guide the rating of student responses (and which articulates what the teacher values in language behavior) must be devised. A close-to-final draft must be tried out and revised according to analysis of initial student responses. The revised test must be field-tested in order to select anchor samples from responses that will match the different scores in the rubric and serve as a guide to raters.

A group of teachers can learn a great deal about their priorities and objectives in teaching by developing such a test as a team. Yet few teachers have the time to get that involved in test development. Thus it becomes more significant, perhaps, for educators to understand the process followed in developing a performance test in order to select one from the published language/thinking performance instruments on the market.

While performance assessments have many of the qualities of both traditional assessments and portfolio assessment, the high-stakes audiences will need some help in understanding what can be learned from them. For this reason alone, most use of performance assessment has been coupled to standardized and criterion-referenced measures rather than being used as a replacement for them.

WHAT DO THESE DEVELOPMENTS SUGGEST FOR INSTRUCTION?

As the remainder of this book will attempt to demonstrate, portfolio and performance assessment have tremendous potential as instructional tools. Both can inform the teacher about how effective instruction is in developing a student's language use; and both can show the student how well he or she is doing. Each can contribute to developing the student as a self-assessor. While the portfolio may be the most powerful of the two tools for accomplishing this, it is far more effective when used in conjunction with the performance assessment.

This book will describe practices that can help make the portfolio the centerpiece of effective performance assessment *and* of reading and writing instruction. While some pages in the book will describe options for incorporating other language behaviors and symbol-based products in a portfolio—particularly at the lower grade levels—the emphasis throughout is on using portfolios as assessment tools to teach reading and writing as an *integrated process*.

As Chapter 2 will argue, a performance assessment instrument can jump-start the analytical self-analysis that the portfolio is meant to promote. It demonstrates what a look at process can do by providing a set of notes and drafts leading to the fulfillment of a reasonable task. It sets the pattern for tying reading, writing, and thinking into one activity to be analyzed. And it serves as a kind of pre-performance against which subsequent performance tests and sets of notes and drafts can be compared.

SUMMARY: A DOZEN COMPELLING ARGUMENTS FOR PORTFOLIO ASSESSMENT

- Students learn so much from it that it serves as instruction itself, expanding the effective use of language.
- The approach it embraces reflects the best accruing knowledge and theory about language use as meaning-constructing behavior. It emphasizes both content and performance.
- It promotes the integration of reading and writing. It guides and invites the synthesis of reading and writing experiences to formulate understanding, beliefs, and evolving interests.
- It is compatible with reliance on thinking as the common language behavior, promoting the use and development of more incisive and powerful thinking strategies.

- It supports student ownership of, and responsibility for, language development. It's primary goal is to develop habitual self-assessors!

- It helps keep the focus of instruction on genuine purposes for reading and writing; thus it is as *authentic* as the instructional experience it complements should be. It reveals student interests and genuine needs that language can serve.

- It promotes writing with audience awareness and a sense of how one's language use is a presentation of one's self.

- It supports an emphasis on reading and writing activities that reflect and build on individual student backgrounds and interests. It not only promotes, but helps ensure, highly individualized instruction.

- It is ongoing, serving good instructional planning and outcome evaluation.

- It helps develop positive attitudes about language and its uses, including appreciation of literature, clarity, ideas, and other traditional educational goals.

- It promotes student/teacher interaction and serves collaborative learning.

- It models a more formalized, integrated test that can help provide the assessment demanded for educational accountability.

CHAPTER TWO

CONFIRMING BELIEFS AND MAKING DECISIONS

The idea of starting portfolio assessment from scratch may seem very demanding to teachers who have not used any similar system. Some may feel uneasy about relying on an assessment methodology that depends on relatively subjective judgment; yet these same teachers make subjective judgments daily in their instruction—decisions that are informed by observation and other informal assessment techniques.

Other teachers may consider portfolio assessment cautiously, wondering how much time it will take. How much class time will have to go to building the collections? Some teachers worry about how they will attend to the ongoing, daily teacher/student exchange that is required to develop the habit of self-assessment in students. And those one-on-one conferences with each student each semester—won't working those in create a scheduling crunch in the classroom? Interestingly, it is the rare teacher who has already made time for the all-important conferences who worries about this, suggesting that the benefits gained from conducting them have made the effort to find the time worthwhile.

THINK ABOUT IT!   **TIP**

How many decisions did you make in your classroom today or yesterday? Pick two or three of them. What were your options in each? Why did you pick the one that you did? Was your decision based on very concrete, countable data, or were several factors or reasons mixed in such a way that the decision had to be made subjectively?

Portfolios won't do their job just sitting on a shelf gathering papers. Your students will need guidance—your interest and feedback—in learning to assess their own language behaviors. Building and using portfolios will require some class time, but since the payoff turns assessment into instruction so effectively, that ought not to be a problem. In effect, portfolios help accomplish what good teachers have been doing for a long time: They bring instruction and assessment together.

You may find your students wanting to work with their portfolios more than you had expected, but that doesn't mean you will feel pressured because of it. Successful portfolio assessment can be so involving for *both* teacher and student that it becomes a kind of habitual activity that sustains itself rather automatically as natural, useful, and even essential learning. And as students develop as self-assessors, working with their portfolios on a daily basis, much of the management of the portfolios is accomplished by the students themselves!

Teachers with concerns like those mentioned above are already asking about some of the aspects of portfolio assessment that make it successful. Perhaps they have heard talks or read articles by teachers who have used portfolio assessment attesting to its effectiveness and manageability, and that has stoked professional interest in the methodology. They are attracted by the indication that any sincere effort to use portfolios pays dividends by developing students' awareness of themselves as readers, writers, and thinkers.

Testimonials aren't the only reason to consider portfolio assessment. Chapter 1 has reviewed numerous reasons for you to follow whatever interest led you to this book. Portfolio assessment is a hands-on approach to developing language abilities in students, so the best way to find out if it's worth the effort is to give it a try. With a rationale for your interest, the next step is to think about how you would get started. That, of course, raises a lot more questions.

GETTING STARTED WITH A DEMONSTRATION OF PROCESS

Fortunately for the teacher who is just beginning portfolio assessment, the educational environment is now more supportive and attuned to assessment methodologies that actually look at the way students use language to make meaning. This is not to argue that portfolios are now strongly proposed as replacements for all standardized and criterion-referenced tests that factor those behaviors into skills. But it is a happy recognition that educators and the public are paying respectful attention to attempts to measure language development more authentically.

One reason for this broader acceptance is the increased use of portfolios. Another is the rather rapid and intensive development of what we now call performance assessments. There are many types of performance assessments used across the curriculum. In the language arts, two formats for performance assessments have emerged:

1. Assessment of a student's reading, writing, and thinking (task-fulfilling) performance using a single response that integrates these activities.
2. Assessment that produces shorter written responses intended to assess the comprehension of a particular text and a writing product that is only thematically linked used to evaluate writing ability.

HOW DO PERFORMANCE ASSESSMENTS DIFFER?

In the fully integrated performance assessment, a task is assigned that requires reading a text (the *prompt*) and applying comprehension of it in some authentic form of writing. The student, for example, may read a story about a character with a problem and is asked to write the character a letter offering advice that might solve the problem. An effective response requires comprehending the story and is thus assessed for reading ability; it is also assessed for writing ability. In addition, the integrated performance instrument may assess how well the student has fulfilled the assigned task.

The second format claims to be integrated but is called analytical here to distinguish it from the fully integrated type. The analytical format is more akin to traditional assessment methodologies; the student is asked to write short essay answers to several questions intended to reveal how well the passage has been comprehended. These are rated for reading ability only. Then the text is used thematically to motivate a piece of writing that is used to assess writing ability.

Both of these types of performance assessment rate the student using some kind of scale, often ranging from *1* to *4* or *1* to *3*. With the different factors being rated, this usually creates from 6 to 12 possible scores that can be assigned to the student. Other features that help describe the two general types are summarized in Table 2.1.

Performance assessment appeals to many educators because it can be standardized to some degree. An accountability audience, for example, has *ratings* that will help

Chapters 7 and 8 give a relatively extensive description of the different types of performance assessment while describing how to construct and/or select one that can serve your needs.

TABLE 2.1 FULLY INTEGRATED AND ANALYTICAL PERFORMANCE ASSESSMENTS

Type of Performance Assessment	How Reading Ability Is Assessed	How Writing Ability Is Assessed	How Raters Are Guided in Assessing	Other Distinction
Fully Integrated	By looking at a single written product that responds to text(s)	By looking at the same written product used to assess reading	Usually with rubrics describing each score for each factor rated and sample papers of each possible score	Frequently the response to the assigned task (task fulfillment) is also assessed.
Analytical	By looking at short essay responses to several questions	By looking at a separate written product that is usually related thematically	Usually with rubrics describing each score for each factor rated and sample papers of each possible score	

describe improvement over time and support other comparisons. The analytical type has appeal to many because it can be used as two separate tests. The writing part can be administered without administering the reading section.

Teachers tend to like either the fact that the reading and writing are considered in separate responses in the analytical format or that the fully integrated assessment evaluates the reading and writing in the single response.

Both types of performance assessment create a credibility bridge to the kind of product/process analysis done in portfolio assessment. Performance assessment links portfolios to more traditional forms of assessment and suggests an important role for them in a complete assessment program.

This role is so important that it is mentioned numerous places in this text and is described in some detail in Chapter 6. The relationships and distinctions between product and process are also explained in that chapter.

WHEN SHOULD I USE PERFORMANCE ASSESSMENT?

So reinforcing, as a matter of fact, are portfolio and performance assessment that a key feature of this book is an almost adamant recommendation that teachers begin student portfolios with their responses to some performance assessment! To do that, you will need to understand more fully what a performance assessment is, where you have access to some that are already constructed, how to select one that reflects your instructional goals, and how to administer it and evaluate the results.

Some might argue that you should develop this assessment yourself, and as we will examine in later chapters, doing that is a very rewarding experience. But it is very demanding and time-consuming, and that would defeat the purpose here of administering this instrument to give your students a jump-start in compiling their portfolios. Wait until you have a couple of performance assessments administered and scored and your portfolios under way before taking on the task of building your own.

Beginning student portfolio contents with a performance assessment accomplishes more than merely demonstrating your faith in authentic assessments and your belief that they are closely related. It gives you a wonderful opportunity to learn about how your students process thought and language. It allows you to teach your students a lot about those processes and about how their written products can reveal them.

It can also provide the student with a model of the *kind* of content that will be most useful in the portfolio because it usually includes the notetaking, outlining, and drafting that reveal language processing. It can also serve as a kind of pretest against which performance on a similar instrument administered later can be compared to note progress and development.

While your students complete the performance assessment, you will have a wonderful opportunity to observe them as readers, writers, and thinkers. Do not hesitate to discuss what they are doing with them—that is another advantage of performance assessment: It is not subject to the concerns for absolute adherence to directions and procedures that are necessary for norm-referenced assessments. Take some notes as you do this. From this experience, you can learn a great deal about strategies and techniques that individual students use and also about problems they are having.

Scoring the results of the assessment can be very instructive! Using the rubrics and anchor papers supplied by the instrument, you will get an excellent idea of what the test makers (including all the teachers and other persons who participated in developing its rubrics and selecting its anchor papers) think make good, average, and weak responses. You could, if you want, try to involve the students in this process: Let them discuss the rubrics and read anchor papers aloud and respond to and critique them. If you can manage this kind of class activity successfully, you will create an effective learning experience and develop a genuine sense of ownership among your beginning portfolio keepers.

It is at least equally effective to use individual conferences and small groups in discussing the results of the initial performance assessment and comparing them to anchor papers and rubrics. And, if you have fellow teachers who have or are using the same assessment, it is very instructive to discuss these guides with them.

HOW DO I TIE PERFORMANCE ASSESSMENT AND PORTFOLIO ASSESSMENT TOGETHER?

Most performance assessments will lead the student through some preliminary writing activities that involve reacting to the provided text through notetaking, categorizing, outlining, and drafting. These are sometimes optional, but you are advised to encourage students to follow them. Doing that creates a set of papers that clearly demonstrates language process as the first entry in their portfolio collections because all the evidence of thinking and language processing that led up to the written product is there. The set of papers should include the test itself with its reading prompt if that is possible.

It is a good idea to take some time to discuss the results of this assessment with your students. Point out how all aspects of the performance assessment experience demonstrate that reading and writing are linked and that making meaning out of something one reads by writing about it is indeed a *process* demonstrated by that first performance assessment test. Explain that sets of papers that show the process of thinking, reading, and writing in this way are *exactly* the kind of materials that will be useful in their portfolios.

Later in the semester, you should make a point to administer at least one other performance assessment, and the results should be added (again as a complete set demonstrating process) to the portfolios. You should take some time working individually with the students to help them compare this later performance with the earlier one. Get them to articulate how they think the two sets of papers demonstrate their development as thinkers and language users.

Beginning with their performance on the first assessment, your students will add numerous other papers to their collections and will analyze, evaluate, sort, and organize the contents over time. This activity will be the heart of the portfolio experience, and a majority of this chapter and book are dedicated to explaining it.

After you and your students gain some competence in analyzing their written product in order to reveal process, you may want to tackle the development of a performance assessment of your own. You may wish to do this with other teachers, but it is a wonderful experience for your students if they can be involved. Begin by discussing the kind of reading and writing that are most authentic for your students. This will entail discussing purposes for reading and writing.

It is a considerably demanding task. Not many teachers or students do it, or complete it if they start it. Those who do learn a great deal about what they believe language development is.

Meanwhile, your students will be ready to start putting together show portfolios to use in a variety of ways to inform audiences like their parents, your school's administrators, and others.

With all that you have learned, you will be ready to take a hard look at your plan for authentic assessment using portfolios and performance assessments to see how you can improve it for the next time you implement it. Thus, administering an initial performance assessment becomes the first step of a long-range portfolio assessment program that could be outlined like this:

1. Select a performance assessment to administer.

   • Observe the students and take notes as they complete the assessment. Note their strategies, techniques, problems.

   • Score the assessments and discuss the criteria, rubrics, and anchor papers.

   • Discuss the performance assessment results with the students, emphasizing how product can reveal process.

   • Direct the students to put the entire performance assessment set into their portfolios, explaining the value of showing their writing and thinking processes with notes and drafts.

2. Assist and advise as students add other papers to their working portfolios, which can ultimately include other performance assessments.

3. Assist and advise the students as they analyze, evaluate, sort, and organize their portfolio contents on a regular basis.

4. Review the portfolios with students regularly in conferences.

5. From the working portfolios, have your students pull show portfolios to present to particular audiences: parents, administrators, next year's teacher, the press.

6. Review your portfolio/performance assessment plan to determine how the process can work better.

7. Begin the development of your own classroom or local performance assessment, involving the students if possible, and fellow teachers if appropriate.

8. Try out the local performance assessment to revise it if necessary, to develop a rubric for it, and to select anchor papers to exemplify the rubric. Again, involve students and fellow teachers.

Step 7 of this plan might not begin until the second year of your program, and Step 8 could extend into the third year.

THINKING ABOUT YOUR PLAN

This chapter will offer advice you need to get off to an effective start with portfolios. There are some operational decisions that you can make right away based on some guidelines about portfolios.

Some of the seemingly obvious and practical decisions that you must make relate to key aspects of portfolio assessment. You will decide, for example, what to advise the students to put into their portfolios as they begin to collect their work; but you may want to know more about that and other aspects of portfolios as your program proceeds. Generally, the answers to these questions are a catalog of possibilities for you to choose from; you can even try most of them as the use of portfolios becomes a learning experience for you and your students.

If you agree with the practice that language arts portfolios should be as open, unrestricted, and student-controlled as possible and that once your students are collecting papers for them, you and your students should use them vigorously, your subsequent decision-making tasks should be something like taking a shopping trip.

Before you begin to make these decisions about how your program will begin operating, however, take a little time to give some thought to three rather major considerations that relate directly to developing self-assessors. Your answers to these questions can help you in initial and ongoing decision making about portfolio assessment:

- What benefits do I expect from using portfolios?
- Should I try to get other teachers in my school involved in portfolio assessment?
- How will my beliefs about language learning affect my use of portfolios?

The first of these will reveal your expectations and perhaps trim them down to what is realistic and possible; the second relates to how broad a portfolio assessment experience your students will have. If you decide to promote a school- or even districtwide program, you will want to answer the third question in terms of what most of the teachers you work with believe. You may want to review the philosophies and theories of language

Key aspects of portfolio assessment, such as what can go in them, how they can be used to promote self-assessment, and what can be learned from them are treated in much more detail in following chapters.

development that you buy into as a group. Your school's curriculum should figure in the third consideration, no matter what scope you pursue for your program initially.

WHAT BENEFITS DO I EXPECT FROM USING PORTFOLIOS?

Begin with sensible expectations. No one can answer these questions for you—especially the first. So to get off to a realistic start, it seems wise to be honest with yourself. This project will require some degree of enthusiasm if it is to yield successful results; yet we all know that skepticism is a function of careful thinking. Do you really believe that portfolios might help you develop self-assessors? If you can answer "Yes" to that, you have reason enough to proceed; if not, you may want to hold off, at least until you have read more of this book and can articulate a rationale that reflects claims made for the methodology.

On the other hand, you shouldn't initiate portfolio assessment as some kind of panacea or silver bullet to cure, resolve, or even target all of the assessment problems in your classroom. It cannot answer all the concerns and criticisms of four or more decades that have focused in large part on the way we have taught reading and writing and on the not highly authentic ways we have assessed those efforts. Nor will using portfolio assessment assure that you will teach with a particular approach, such as whole language.

It can, nonetheless, change the emphasis of language arts instruction in some classrooms. It could also lead some teachers to reexamine their theories relevant to language development and how it can best occur. If it doesn't modify or otherwise change the way you view language development, it should reaffirm your understanding of reading and writing as integrated processes of meaning construction.

This is not to argue that portfolio assessment is some revolutionary approach that is sure to shake the professional convictions of many teachers. If anything, it is apt to gain force in a classroom because it serves the goals and objectives of most of the language arts instruction already in place there. It should endorse an authentic experience for many students because it can put increased emphasis on natural, commonsense practices that have more meaning for your students.

Portfolio assessment claims to look at the way your students actually *use* language— that is, to examine how they are developing as language users by taking a look at the way they are actually using it. But it need not commit you to opposing other forms of assessment that you may have used and value or that may seem particularly important to audiences other than students and teachers. Portfolio assessment clearly complements other assessment methodologies, such as performance assessment and observation; and it can also provide a valid perspective to accompany information provided by dramatically different assessments, such as standardized multiple-choice tests.

Thus the results of portfolio assessment can be reported in conjunction with the scores on standardized and criterion-referenced tests. Whether it tends to endorse or contradict those assessments, it should be of keen interest to all assessment audiences. The public may be more ready for evaluation of instruction based on portfolios than you think. The press and other audiences, which have been far from reluctant to criticize our schools on the basis of standardized test scores, may think that looking at students' actual work to see how they're doing makes a lot of common sense.

There are, then, some important broad benefits that you can expect from a successful portfolio assessment program. Its major strengths are that it:

- Informs your instruction by identifying individual students' strengths and needs as well as authentic purposes for them to read and write.
- Helps you communicate with your students.
- Gets students to accept the major responsibility for becoming better readers and writers.
- Provides a focus for managing the development that assures that improvement.

SHOULD I TRY TO GET OTHER TEACHERS INVOLVED IN PORTFOLIO ASSESSMENT?

Your students will not become self-assessors overnight, but the habit may be developing nicely for many of your students after a semester or two. Such good habits, however, are not sustained without practice over time. That is, after all, the essential part of the definition of a habit: a repeated and ingrained behavior. So what happens to your self-assessors when they leave your classroom? Suppose no one else in your school is using portfolios: Will the habit of self-assessing their language processes and products be so ingrained in your students that they will continue to do that for long?

A portfolio assessment system adopted school- or systemwide will help assure that your students get the opportunity to truly develop the *habit* of self-assessing. So you might consider doing a bit of stumping before or as you use portfolio assessment in your classroom in order to persuade other faculty members in your school that portfolio assessment is worth a try.

It is not necessarily recommended here that complete portfolio collections be passed along from grade to grade. Yet the practice of collecting papers anew and using them from grade to grade gives students the opportunity to develop self-assessment as an invaluable life habit that can prevail long after they have stopped keeping portfolios. Developing a portfolio each year enables students to become more incisive self-evaluators—to see more and more precisely as they use language what they can do to improve their reading comprehension, written expression, and thinking abilities.

Some students may keep portfolios on their own if they move on to a different classroom where doing so is not part of the instruction; however, if there is no opportunity to discuss their observations with their teachers, the self-evaluating habit will surely fade as it is practiced less and less frequently and teacher/student conferences that focus on it are no longer a part of the instructional system.

You may decide to begin promoting language arts portfolios among your colleagues as soon as you feel you can do so with a degree of genuine enthusiasm. This could be done informally in the teachers' lounge and over lunch or coffee, or with department heads or in faculty or departmental meetings. At the very least, you may want to earmark the teacher or teachers that your students are apt to have after they leave your classroom and explain what you intend to do and why you think it is important that it be a long-range experience for students.

Having fellow professionals who can share experiences in using portfolio assessment can only benefit you, them, and your students. For one thing, discussing portfolio assessment, the rationales for using it, and the experiences you have while using it is sure to lead to sharing thoughts about the instructional objectives and goals that are valued across classrooms. The philosophies and theories that endorse these aims are apt to be cited and articulated, and the instructional techniques for achieving them described. A school with that kind of interaction among teachers is invariably an excellent learning environment for students.

SPREAD THE WORD   T I P

Use any of the rationales or arguments in Chapter 1 or other places in this book if you think they are persuasive. You may decide to get copies of articles cited in Chapters 1 and 6 or recommended in Appendix B of this book in order to help explain portfolio assessment to other teachers. As your program develops in your classroom, you can report regularly and informally on how it is working. With enough experience using the methodology, you may seek opportunities to share what you have learned with other teachers through reports at professional meetings and professional publications.

T I P   TRY A NEWSLETTER!

If your enthusiasm for portfolio assessment grows with experience, you may find other ways to promote it. You might, for example, use the duplicating facility at your school to put out a portfolio newsletter that explains what is happening using portfolios in your classroom. You could involve your students in writing and producing it, and the intended audience might expand past the language arts teachers at your school to parents, supervisors, administrators, and any of the public who get a chance to read a copy. If portfolio assessment is under way in several or all classes at your school, you and your associates could produce the newsletter together and circulate it in your school system or district in hopes that the methodology might be used with that scope and become a system. A model page from such a newsletter is in Appendix C. Feel free to use ideas and expressions from its stories to create your own.

This is one of several types of show portfolios that are explained in Chapter 6.

Even when the exchange that a widely implemented portfolio assessment system promotes leads to the delineation of differences among teachers, the clarification and focus that results from such discussion should be invaluable for individual teachers. In team-teaching efforts, this kind of professional openness and exchange is essential. In short, your promotion of portfolio assessment can spark a keener sense of professionalism and a genuine concern for the welfare of students in your working environment.

Because self-assessors are developed over time, the payoff for keeping portfolios is potentially the greatest when they become a schoolwide—even systemwide—way of assessing student language development. In such programs, it is an excellent practice for students to cull from their portfolios at the end of a year or semester samples of their work as a kind of *show portfolio* with which to introduce themselves to their next teacher.

How and when you suggest portfolio assessment to other teachers in your school may depend on how comfortable you feel about explaining it. This book is an attempt to help you with that, but you may decide to wait several months until you have some experience with using portfolios. Having a successful program in place—even for a semester or more, if necessary—may give a lot of persuasive power to your suggestion that portfolio assessment be used by a fellow teacher or department or school district. By that time, the enthusiasm of your students should be initiating the promotion for you, if the portfolios are being used in a successful way. Meanwhile, you may have some close associates in the school whose input and insight would be invaluable if you all were initiating the new system together. You should make it clear to all fellow faculty members what you are doing and that you will be willing to share what you know and are learning with any who want to try the system.

Suppose, however, that you are unable to generate any interest in portfolio assessment among your fellow teachers. It is not the intent here to encourage delay among teachers who face the prospect of being the only person to initiate portfolios in their schools; their experience and example might be the best way of promoting continuing opportunities for their students to develop as self-assessors using portfolios.

So if you're less inclined to be a reformer than an explorer, begin your trip; and may this book make the journey more satisfying. On the other hand, don't hide what's happening in your classroom or the reasons you are doing it under a bushel basket—even if that is what some student has decided to use as a receptacle for his or her collection.

HOW WILL MY BELIEFS ABOUT LANGUAGE LEARNING AFFECT MY USE OF PORTFOLIOS?

One of the best aspects of having students keep portfolios as self-assessors is that it should lead you to think about and articulate your beliefs about language use and development.

One way to promote portfolio assessment in your school is to let your students produce a portfolio newsletter reporting what they are doing and explaining how the system works.

Adopting portfolio assessment is a perfect opportunity to reexamine what you believe about language development and the way to promote it. One of the major reasons for a growing dissatisfaction with the way we have assessed language abilities has been our increasing understanding of those behaviors as thinking behaviors.

Emerging theory about reading and writing that describes them as interrelated *meaning-constructing* processes has gained wide acceptance (Farr and Tone, 1994). Whether you look on that as newly emerging theory or a better, more broadly accepted articulation of what many educators have always contended, it has had genuine impact on the way many teachers teach and has intensified their need for performance assessments.

Some teachers have always based their analysis of student improvement on a broad and accruing sample of student work; some have always placed a high priority on getting their students to do that kind of assessment themselves. In effect, some excellent teachers have always used portfolio assessment, with or without holders for the material or the term *portfolio*.

For all of the new appreciation of language as process, we are still looking at examining and evaluating *products* when we use the contents of a portfolio to assess someone's ability to comprehend, write, and think—to apply ideas and understanding acquired, for example. To examine process more directly, we need to look over students' shoulders as they read and write—to ask them questions about what they are doing, to get them to talk about the way they are processing ideas when reading and writing.

Some researchers are waiting until students have finished reading and writing in order to ask them what they can recall about what was going on as they processed and used language. While that approach remains much more immediate than portfolio assessment, it is not unlike what happens during the conferencing that is so essential to

A technique of examining reading processing is known as using *think-alongs*. The process has proven particularly successful in research attempting to understand and describe reading-related concepts, such as *comprehension*, the role of background in reading comprehension, how students deal with problems with understanding and comprehension.

successful portfolio assessment, and it argues effectively for the frequency of student/teacher conferences.

Another argument that is critical of almost any kind of assessment being used by any teachers is that we cannot really understand how well a student processes language without following him or her around to see how language is used in real-life situations. To get a more exact picture, we would need to observe when the reading and writing take place, how language is used and for what purposes, and how well it achieves those purposes—how what is learned from reading is applied in real-life situations, for example. Even then, however, we would have to draw inferences and conclusions about what we are seeing.

So no matter how we assess students' *processing* of language, we are invariably looking at *products* or outcomes. Accepting that, it seems reasonable to endorse the use of portfolios that contain a broad assortment of student writing, much of which applies and reacts to reading in some way and is done to fulfill numerous purposes. The fact that most of the things selected to put in these collections are chosen by the student tends to help ensure that the language use is authentic in these products, which must then represent the processes used to create them.

One thing is generally accepted: The products examined in portfolio collections pull together several steps between process and product when compared to traditional test results. Student writing in a portfolio is most certainly a more direct result of the process of using language than are the results of selecting answers from among the options on a multiple-choice test preconstructed by someone else.

Another thing seems apparent. Performance assessments, including portfolios, must depend on someone's analysis of the product. You and your students will be the analysts in your classroom. So before you make decisions about the portfolio program you will initiate—particularly what will go into the portfolios—it is important to begin with some consideration of what your *theory, understanding,* or *philosophy* of language development is and of what you believe about how it can best be taught and developed.

What purposes for reading and writing and types of writing and reading are most typical of what your students will do with language all their lives? What products are most related to developing effective thinkers? How related is creative freedom to effective thinking and language use?

What you do with portfolios and what you can expect to get out of them depends a lot on what you believe about language development. If, for example, you believe primarily in the power of skill-drill, mind-to-the-grindstone instruction, and lots of exercises to teach the recognition and avoidance of offending usage, then portfolio assessment—at least the kind described here—may not be the most useful (or honest) kind of assessment system for you to use.

It is possible that having a collection of writing samples will enable you to judge how acceptable the usage of students is and whether it is improving. But if that is all—or even

THE BEST APPROACH JUST ISN'T VERY PRACTICAL

We might, in this age of technology, follow each student around with a video camera, recording everything that he or she says and writes. If possible, we would use the camera to note everything that the student reads. It wouldn't be easy—particularly getting a perspective that shows what meaning an individual is constructing in his head when reading.

With our eavesdropping camera, we would get some kind of record of how language is being used, but any assessment of that would depend on subjective analysis of what we got on tape. Actions would tell us some things, but we would have to rely on what the student says, writes, and does to determine very completely how he is using what has been read and to find out what the student is thinking. The whole procedure would probably make the student self-conscious and ensure that the situation we were recording was far from normal or real.

Can you imagine doing this at one time for each member of a whole class? What a mess, and how cumbersome and expensive! It's not feasible.

On the other hand, portfolio collections can approximate the ways that students are actually using (processing) language. In many ways they're not unlike the video record would be, and they're far less intrusive on daily use of language in the classroom.

primarily—what you are assessing with the portfolio, it cannot be argued to be the most efficient way to do that. And the portfolio's potential to train the student as self-assessor may also be lost.

It is difficult to visualize a student spending considerable time analyzing his or her development as a writer, reader, and thinker by looking at a collection of worksheets like those that are predominant in some classrooms. What conclusions might a student draw about himself or herself as a user of language doing that? (They would be very tactical indeed: "I have misspelled fewer words this quarter. I do not make as many number errors. I had only six pronouns that did not have clear antecedents.") Packed into a portfolio, what might a bunch of worksheets tell us about any actual student writing or thinking that managed to get in there as well?

Table 2.2, "How a Teacher's Goals Help Structure the Portfolio," gives just a few examples of what some teachers might identify as things they want to achieve, and it shows how those objectives can help a teacher make decisions about the portfolios his or

HOW A TEACHER'S GOALS HELP STRUCTURE THE PORTFOLIO

TABLE 2.2

Instructional Goal/Objective/Emphasis	How to Use Portfolios to Achieve This
The teacher wants her students to react more personally and more freely to texts. She notes that her students invariably wait to hear "official" interpretations before responding to what they read.	The teacher uses texts early on in the semester as models for student writing, and she encourages students to write and keep new beginnings, endings, and episodes for stories they read. She creates many opportunities for students to express their opinions, especially in writing, and is careful to respect them and to recommend that they go in the portfolios. She recommends a journal-like format in the portfolio called "What I Think."
The teacher believes that reading and writing develop when students are given genuine reasons to read and write. He wants to learn more about what interests individual students while showing them that reading is a good way to learn about things that are interesting.	Students are allowed to shop from a large and varied group of books borrowed from the library and are asked to write a paragraph or more telling about the book they selected and why they liked it or were disappointed with it. The review goes into the portfolio and may first be posted on a bulletin board or be published in a class magazine or newsletter for fellow students to read. Students are encouraged to use what they have read in creative ways. Projects that use texts are encouraged and plans for and reviews of them are kept in the portfolio. The student is encouraged to frame related questions and to seek additional texts to answer them.
A major objective for the year is to get students to identify audiences and purposes for reading and writing particular things.	The students are given guide sheets to help them to interpret texts in terms of the intent of their authors. Other sheets help them to write for particular audiences with particular intentions. They are asked to select details from one text that they have read to present to two distinctly different audiences, and they are asked to include the two in the portfolio with a note explaining the audiences they are written for. The teacher spends some time discussing this assignment during portfolio conferences.

continued

T A B L E 2 • 2	continued		
	Instructional Goal/Objective/Emphasis	**How to Use Portfolios to Achieve This**	
	The teacher wants the students to understand reading and writing as a *process* and to examine their own processes for using language.	On several occasions the teacher prepares several texts for students to choose from, presenting each on just the left side of the pages they are printed on. Students are encouraged to make notes in the other column indicating their thoughts about what they are reading—after the teacher models the process as a *think-along,* by reading something else aloud and pausing to tell what s/he is thinking while reading. In conference, the teacher and student discuss what the student thought was going on in the reading process. The teacher then takes a piece of the student's writing and tries to get the student to recall what language processing was going on when he or she wrote particular parts of it. The teacher encourages (and even requires) the collection of several sets of papers that show several of the following steps in creating a particular product: the notetaking, information gathering, outlining, drafting, revising.	
	An important objective for the year is to get students to recognize the importance of details in descriptions.	Several assignments ask the students to pick a setting or event from a story read and to draw a picture of what they liked about it. They next write about the picture, under it or on a sheet to go with it. The picture goes into the portfolio, and the teacher asks questions during the conference about the details; and with students who have used few, the teacher presses to identify additional details that could have been used. The student can draw a second sketch if he or she wants. The student is encouraged to add to the details of the setting creatively and to write a new story to match it. Then the student is encouraged to identify and examine details that were added and to discuss how they changed the story in any significant way.	
	The teacher feels that his students revise what they write only minimally, and he is eager that they learn the value of revision.	The teacher stresses the importance of including all the drafts of things that go into the portfolios, demonstrating ways of keeping the different drafts of a single piece of writing together and in order as a unit. During conferences the teacher asks questions that promote the closer examination and comparison of drafts and discusses changes that the student has made with the student, admiring them and trying to get the student to remember and explain why they were made. Students pair off in teams as readers or editors of each other's work. The writer revises on the basis of the editing/reaction. All drafts and revisions go into the portfolio.	

Instructional Goal/Objective/Emphasis	How to Use Portfolios to Achieve This
A major objective of the teacher is to get her students to draw conclusions *inductively,* as a primary method of thinking that involves classification.	Students are asked to keep fact sheets on a topic of their choice as a set of *jot notes.* On occasion, the students sort the notes into categories by marking letters in front of the jot notes. Periodically, the student is asked to write summaries for each category and then a major summary for what has been learned to that time about the topic. The results go into the portfolio as a set.
The teacher wants her students to learn to challenge generalizations and other deductive reasoning.	The students are encouraged to listen for generalizations in ads and conversations and to identify them in reading (categorical: All redheads have bad tempers; hypothetical/causal: If you buy a certain product, you will be popular; dilemma: Either you like a certain kind of music or you have bad taste/are a nerd). Then the student makes a list of exceptions and writes a challenge to the generalization. The set of papers goes into the portfolio for discussion later.
A major classroom objective for the year is to get the students to consciously synthesize and compare different texts that they read.	The teacher requires that each portfolio have a collection of things that the student has written about one favorite topic (animals, baseball, doll collecting, country music, for example). Two of the things added to the portfolio between teacher/student conferences must be about the topic. Each month or so, the student writes a summary of what she or he now knows about the topic, and ends with questions that have arisen about what can be learned. All this is kept as a set in the portfolio.
The teacher wants her students to explore the complexity of causal relationships without becoming fearful of how complicated such exploration can become.	A portfolio project begins with the students writing about something that has happened that they find fascinating. Next they make lists of all the possible causes of that event/phenomenon. By interacting in small groups and with the teacher they are encouraged to expand the causal possibilities. The teacher explains that the cause of each event or phenomenon need not be singular—that perhaps two or more of the causes considered worked together in some way to produce the result. Some students are encouraged to chart the cause/effect relationships. Finally, the students are encouraged to anticipate what effects might result from the event itself as a cause. The teacher explains to the class, using some of their causal chains, how those chains develop with effects becoming causes. Some students present chains explained by the paper sets in their portfolios to the class.

her students will keep. Remember: The purpose of this chart is not to offer particular objectives for teaching language use to students. Rather it is an attempt to *illustrate* how understanding your objectives can help you design portfolios that will help you assess and achieve your goals.

A wide adoption of portfolio assessment across a school, district, or even state may lead to tying portfolios to curriculum objectives, but that need not prohibit you from promoting the kind of portfolio that will serve your instruction best. You may need to decide how to modify portfolio content or to balance emphases that will reflect any objectives you have that are not covered in the existing curriculum without denying those that are emphasized in such a prescription. When you have an open policy toward portfolio content and are not setting limits on content, this balancing is easier to accomplish. Your students will create emphases to match their interests, and you will need to add work to the portfolio that reflects goals and objectives that you think are important, while tending to the objectives in the curriculum.

"How," some teachers may reasonably ask, "am I to use portfolios to cover a host of goals articulated in the curriculum guide for usage, such as punctuation rules, without pulling the focus away from the ideas expressed and killing the students' interest in conducting the analysis of their work?" That concern is one worth raising, and that teacher has several options:

- She can devise some activity that causes students to focus on the mechanics in selected pieces of writing in the portfolio while also focusing on the importance of their ideas and audiences. She can, for example, develop classroom publications and have students submit from their collections pieces that are then edited by peer groups that include the writers, instructing the editors to help their fellow writers weed out mechanical errors.

- She can cover the objectives that focus on very specific mechanics or are worded as "avoidance goals" with instruction that is unrelated to the portfolios and then ask students to find examples in their writing where they have used the language correctly in those regards. For example, after some board work on plural possessives, she can ask students to find two examples in their writing in the portfolio where they have used *s'* to indicate ownership by more than one person or thing.

- If the usage emphasis warns, "Do not use singular verbs with plural nouns," students can find and highlight examples of how they have used plural verbs with plural subjects and singular verbs with singular subjects. Or the teacher could invite students to select examples from stories and other texts that they have read and xerox a copy of a page with a model of the correct usage in question. They are highlighted and the page is stapled to a piece of the student's writing in the portfolio that also has an example of the usage.

Besides providing material that will reflect goals and objectives you and the curriculum have set, the portfolios your students keep should be potentially revealing about instructional objectives that emerge as you teach particular students and groups using a variety of materials. Portfolio assessment, in fact, is apt to give notice of the need for new, emerging objectives. Even a skill as tactical as using quotations correctly can be included in portfolio analyses without destroying it as a meaning-focused place. Having noted that the class as a group was having trouble using quotation marks, a teacher might promote the writing of stories that include lots of dialogue and then encourage students to collaborate in reviewing how well they punctuated what they wrote.

MAKING SOME OPERATIONAL DECISIONS

Having set your thought processes in motion about the broader considerations just discussed, you are ready to proceed to some practical decisions about portfolio assessment.

A host of initial questions about using portfolios in your classroom must have popped up by now:

- What will we use to hold our portfolio collections?
- Where will we keep the portfolios?
- When will my students work on them?
- Who will be allowed to see them?
- Who will pick what goes into the portfolios?
- What criteria will be used to pick?
- How will I get the students involved in self-assessment?
- How should the portfolios be evaluated?
- Who will do it?
- What criteria will be used?
- Will they be graded?
- What should I tell others about my new assessment plan?
- What else should I be doing to get ready for portfolio assessment?

The questions presented here may not include all that have crossed your mind, but they are typical of those asked by many teachers. They relate to each other so closely that it's difficult to discuss one without discussing one or more of the others. Consequently, some of the questions are answered as groups.

WHAT WILL WE USE TO HOLD OUR PORTFOLIO COLLECTIONS?

This is an easy one to answer! Let your students decide. By letting each student pick his or her own portfolio holder, you take an important step in establishing the ownership you want your students to feel. You can set some limitations, of course. You probably won't have room for 20 to 35 orange crates in the classroom, and while a manila mailing envelope will serve a student for up to a week, perhaps, the collection will certainly outgrow it quite quickly.

What goes into the portfolio is paramount, of course, as is what is done with a portfolio. But the physical portfolio holder is important, too. Basically it is a place where each student can collect samples of his or her work. It could be as simple as designated space on a shelf where each student can collect and stack samples of what he or she writes, draws, and finds interesting. A container of some sort is better, however, because it keeps what will become an assortment of different-sized materials together, provides a degree of privacy, and invites personalizing that will help establish a sense of ownership.

Physically, student portfolios can look like many things, but for them to contribute to a successful assessment system, there are a few basic things to consider in selecting or helping students select them:

1. The portfolio should be large enough to hold most student writing and art without folding the contents and to hold a substantial variety and amount of materials, including papers, audiotapes, videotapes, etc.
2. The portfolio holder should be sturdy enough to withstand frequent handling by both the student and the teacher.
3. Students should be allowed and encouraged to personalize their portfolio holders by painting them, marking them with crayons, gluing colored paper onto them, etc. Student names can be part of the design but need not be required. This personalizing of the holders is even more important when the

structure of the holders is uniform for the class. Being allowed to create a holder uniquely one's own contributes substantially to developing a sense of student ownership.

4. Ideally, students will be given the freedom to select their own holders, resulting in a variety of structures that are difficult to keep together in one place but that have a surprising amount of whimsy and charm.

Some teachers may use specially printed folders that come with particular reading programs or sets of materials. If a holder is basically a file folder, however, it is important that it have a fan fold at the closed edge to allow for adequate expansion. The kind of portfolio recommended in this book can soon outgrow even those.

Paper briefcases or file holders are available in office supply stores, but be careful about recommending them. Those that have flaps and attached strings or bands for closing are especially appealing, but they are surprisingly expensive! You probably should have some potential holders on hand for those children who may be unable to find anything at home. Some teachers provide each student with a half-open cardboard file box, like those made to hold magazines in libraries; but they are relatively expensive, too. Some teachers have collected the nicely lidded boxes that envelopes come in from large office complexes.

Other teachers acquire the corrugated boxes that fanned computer printer paper comes in and cut the flaps off the top. We have seen teachers who have supplied each child with two paper grocery bags—one inside the other for strength. The upper edges are carefully folded down to give them more structure and so they will not be too deep. Twenty-some portfolios made in this way will sit on the floor in one corner of the classroom, each uniquely colored and decorated and bearing the name of its owner, who can easily spot it among the others.

Some teachers encourage ownership by allowing students to select their own holders. In doing this, of course, it is necessary to help those students who do not have access to interesting boxes or bags by providing some to choose from.

Not long after the students have put several items into their folders, you should give them some class time to design and decorate the outside if they wish. Besides assuring a

HOW TO MAKE PILLOWCASE PORTFOLIOS

An active portfolio program in Palm Springs, Florida, led to one teacher designing pillowcase holders that hang on the back of the students' chairs. The simple directions have helped teachers in many schools create them:

1. Fold the open end of a pillowcase back eight inches to form a cuff. (This cuff will eventually slide over the back of the student's chair.)

2. Sew the cuff down to the pillowcase *on only one side.* Leave the other side free to slide over the back of the chair. (Be careful not to sew the pillowcase shut!)

3. Sew facing pieces of Velcro on the inside of the pillowcase just below where it opens so the portfolio can be held shut.

4. Have the student write his or her name across the front of the pillowcase. Fabric paints are also available for this purpose and are very effective.

5. Let the student individualize the holder by decorating it with markers, paints, glitter, ribbons, photographs, or whatever appeals to the student's fancy. Teachers or parents can sew buttons or patches on the portfolios. Anything goes!

Allowing students to express their individuality when they make portfolio holders can lead to quite an interesting portfolio collection.

sense of ownership, this can lead to a classroom collection that is bright and whimsical with original art and ideas—not a collective eyesore, but something delightful to look at! You may or may not decide to suggest that students do this decorating right away; you may want to wait a week or so—until they have some sense of what the contents of the portfolio may come to mean to them. You may wish to keep the focus on what goes into the portfolios until you have established the concept with your students.

WHERE WILL WE KEEP THE PORTFOLIOS?
WHEN WILL MY STUDENTS WORK ON THEM?
WHO WILL BE ALLOWED TO SEE THEM?

Again, these are easy questions to answer: Keep the portfolios where your students can get at them—easily! Then allow them as much free access to them as possible. It is absolutely essential that your students can get at their portfolios as quickly and easily as possible. This allows students to elect to work on their portfolios during short periods of time when you allow students to set their own priorities. You should structure a half an hour or more at least once a week when all your students are required to examine, think about, and reorganize their portfolios.

They should be encouraged to write notes about their thoughts on their collections and to update their records, adding stories and other texts they have read to their reading log, for example. You should be circulating among them and be available for informal

AN INGENIOUS CLASSROOM COLLECTION

With almost unlimited possibilities, classroom portfolio collections are often very ingenious. Allowed to create what they wanted, one elementary class came up with a variety of holders:

- Two brought tinted plastic boxes made for storing clothes. One was decorated with designs applied with colored Magic Markers; the other had a combination of such markings and cutouts from construction paper glued on it. Each bore the first name of its creator.
- One girl used a box that had contained four dinner plates. Its dimensions were slightly bigger than $8\frac{1}{2} \times 11$ inches and it was about 6 inches deep. It opened at the narrow end and had an attached lid with a flap. The box was completely covered with red construction paper glued to it securely. On all four sides, cutouts of yellow, blue, green, and orange construction paper made different scenes—one of buildings in a city, one of a starry night with a cradle moon, one of an abstract drawn around big lettering of the student's name. All the designs were tied together with lines drawn with crayons of different colors.
- Two children used paper grocery bags—one with hand-drawn pictures pasted on it, the other plain on the outside but lined with vivid pink contact paper applied carefully to the inside.
- Several students had used flat-bottomed shopping bags from department stores. One girl fringed the upper edges and stapled colored construction paper over the handles; two were heavy plastic, one relying on the store's distinguished logo to set that student's collection apart, and the other with the student's name carefully pasted over the store's name.
- One student decorated a corrugated box from an office. It had held a ream of stationery and had a nice lid. Another student had a similar but deeper box from his father's office. Its only decoration was a border neatly glued over the upper edge.
- Several students used expandable file holders of various types. One was plain manila open at the top; it was decorated very carefully with designs drawn with crayons. Another, which opened wider, had a flap and an attached elastic band to hold it closed.
- The teacher supplied big mailing envelopes to one student while he looked for a replacement for a shoe box that required him to fold everything and to another student whose big cardboard tube curled its contents and kept rolling off the shelf.

one-on-one exchanges about portfolio content. If the portfolios are close to where the students often work and are very easy to get to, that allows your students to make use of almost all of the time you block out specifically for working with portfolios; little time goes into distributing or putting them away.

Do not keep students' portfolios put away so that they must be handed out and are accessible only when there is time to do that. Do not establish a "hands-off-unless-I-say-otherwise" policy. Ideally the portfolios will be within reach or a few steps from where

NO SELF-ASSESSMENT GOING ON HERE!

The very worst collection of portfolios one of the authors has seen was totally inaccessible to the students in the class. The teacher was proud of the fact that a drawer in a metal file cabinet near the teacher's desk had been cleared so that it could be dedicated to student portfolios. These were in neat folders with each student's name marked by the teacher's hand and kept in alphabetical order. Each folder appeared to be about the same thickness, and, the observer was assured, contained responses to the same set of assignments.

The file drawer was kept shut and was opened only by the teacher; its contents were too important to her

ongoing assessment, she explained, to allow free student access. She passed out the "portfolios" periodically, she said, and the students followed careful directions on how to handle them—on what to add, how to organize them, etc.

Whatever teacher assessment those folders supported could be interesting indeed and might, on analysis, demonstrate student progress and needs. But they certainly did not belong to the students and were contributing little or nothing to developing self-assessment. They were about as appealing to the students, it is safe to guess, as the teacher's grade book.

students do a great deal of their work. The idea is to assure the students that the portfolios are truly theirs and to eliminate class time used to get them out and put them away.

Your students should be allowed to work with their portfolios almost any time they wish. You don't want a student getting up to get his portfolio in the middle of a lesson while you have everyone else's attention, of course, so there are limits. But generally, anytime you allow your students to work on their writing, to read, or to do their homework, they should feel free to get their portfolios and study them.

WHO WILL PICK WHAT GOES INTO THE PORTFOLIOS? WHAT CRITERIA WILL BE USED TO PICK?

Directions for using portfolio assessment almost always mention giving students some say as to what goes into their portfolios. Students are to be allowed to add things on their own but are required to have so many pieces of nonfiction, so many stories, so many poems, as well as other inclusions that will hopefully promote some self-assessment.

Whatever prescriptions the teacher or school or district enforce on portfolio content, the student should be allowed to add almost anything else that seems appropriate to him or her. Somehow the intention of encouraging that freedom sounds quite cosmetic in the descriptions of some portfolio programs. If that is the case—if the students get very limited opportunities to control what goes into their collections—their sense of responsibility for analyzing what is collected will be not more sincere than the stated intent of the program.

There are many ideas about the kinds of materials that can go into portfolios in Chapter 3.

To assure that portfolios will promote a genuine sense of ownership, it is essential that both the student and teacher be allowed to put things into it. The student should have the primary control and can, after some experience with organizing and analyzing portfolio contents, articulate criteria for both the inclusion and organization that have emerged in the process. But the student should know from the beginning that you, too, may be adding some things to the collection.

Meanwhile the teacher needs to observe each student's selection process—not to evaluate it or criticize it but to make sure that the portfolio contains examples of the student's work that the teacher feels will reveal whether the student is reaching the objectives and goals the teacher—and perhaps the school, district, or state—have set for that grade. The teacher should feel free to ask the students to add material that can be analyzed to determine particular instruction that the teacher feels the student needs, including any that will help the student meet standards set outside the classroom.

Suppose that you have several students who are not selecting material that you feel will inform adequately on how well your instruction has met certain goals. Suppose some are not picking the pieces of writing that you think are their best or that under self-analysis would suggest ways to improve their writing or that would recommend future reading. Suppose you have students who are not picking many materials that relate the reading and writing processes. Or perhaps some are not including notes and drafts that reveal process. What do you do?

You should not chastise or criticize such students. You should not order them to select certain things for their portfolios. What you might do is confer with them, focusing on things they *have* selected and asking questions that reveal why certain pieces of writing were included. What you are doing is asking the student to articulate his or her criteria for selection so you can compare them with the criteria that answer to your needs for information and what you value in language behavior. You may even ask a student why a piece you feel is strong, interesting, or revealing has not been included.

You should not criticize the student's selections or selection criteria, although you may ask the student to consider certain aspects of his or her use of language that you feel should qualify products for the portfolio—explaining carefully why you think the additional criteria should be considered. In the final analysis, you are negotiating a settlement of selection values. If that doesn't work, you can explain that you understand the student's different opinion but request the inclusion of a paper anyway because it tells *you* something you need to know.

You can offer to attach a note to a paper you want added explaining that you asked for it and why, but more meaningful to both the student and the teacher are notes that the student adds to the portfolio *evaluating* particular papers. Students should feel free to make notes about their thoughts on a piece of paper and attach it to any appropriate piece of writing. A student might note, for example, that a piece is his favorite and why; that her mother and teacher like a story she wrote better than she does and what it is that they say they like about it; that this story is a different ending for a particular story he read and that he now plans to write a new beginning for his ending.

Appendix C includes a very simple form for such notes, but plain paper will work as well.

One good time to encourage the student to write a note is when you sense that with a bit more thought about it, the student may come to an important realization. Examining what makes a rewritten story stronger, for example, or what could have been done to make a response to a text read stronger can be a strong learning experience for the portfolio keeper. Or you might ask a student to write such a note rationalizing a particular selection because you believe some potentially revealing pieces are being overlooked by the student and you want to create the opportunity to nominate them, possibly using the student's criteria, not your own. Still another time is when you feel the student is packing his portfolio with an overbalance of materials that are not clearly enough related to his reading or writing or have little potential to reveal much about him or those behaviors. You ask for the note hoping that writing it may reveal that to the student.

Finally, the teacher has some influence over what goes into portfolios because she creates or selects many of the classroom activities that result in the writing and other student products that may be selected for inclusion. The teacher may even require on occasion that all students include a particular piece of writing done in class. This is most likely to occur when the activity that led to the writing is a response to something read. It can give the teacher a sense of how the student performs on a particular task compared to his or her classmates.

The way that these forms encourage students to think about the content of their portfolios is discussed in Chapter 4.

Even with this amount of teacher influence over the portfolio's contents, it must yet remain the students' domain. If students are allowed to add whatever they see as appropriate, they can easily ensure that a very significant balance of the content is student-selected. This is particularly true when the student does a reasonable amount of reading and writing outside of class and is encouraged to include that kind of product.

Clearly, however, we are recommending here that the teacher have some say about what goes into the portfolio and about what is, therefore, eligible for analysis. Virtually all sources advise teachers to require some types of portfolio content, such as the simple records that students are asked to keep and that promote thought about the reading and writing recorded on them.

Requiring these is a kind of preemptory exercising of your option to include what you think is important and promotes self-analysis. These records are not difficult to initiate or maintain, but you are advised to introduce them in a session dedicated to the portfolios when you can move among the students and assist one-on-one. This would be done after the semester is under way and you are certain that the students have something in or ready to put in their portfolios—and information about these inclusions to put on the records. You will need to introduce them with first-graders during an early conference, when you can help each student as extensively as possible.

It must be recognized in responding to these most basic questions about portfolio assessment that the individual teacher and student do not always have *complete* control about what goes into the portfolios. In schools, systems, and/or states where the methodology is most fully exploited, the department, school, or district set clearly articulated purposes for portfolio assessment that tend to dictate what will be collected.

Among several prevalent rationales for limiting and/or specifying portfolio content is the intention that the portfolio be more "manageable." Others include making it easier for the teacher to compare the students' work to objectives and to use the results in reporting that particular kind of information to other audiences. But while portfolio assessment programs that extend across grades are very desirable, such goals are sometimes accomplished at the expense of dulling the edge of the portfolio's major potential: to promote the kind of thinking that will develop students as self-assessors!

With the categories of the contents so clearly lined out and the range of quality limited, a good share of the thinking we would have students do when using portfolios is accomplished *for* them—even when the student is involved in setting the criteria for inclusion. In that sense, such portfolios are not very *manageable* at all; they have already been managed!

Limiting portfolio content is almost invariably coupled to some articulation of criteria for what will be included. What standards must a piece of writing or other item meet to be selected for the portfolio? Who will decide if they have been met? Most advocates of portfolio assessment insist that both the student and teacher be involved in deciding which student efforts will go into the collection to fulfill the quotas, so it would be natural to get the student involved in helping to articulate the criteria used to select them. That is certainly an excellent idea, if limiting portfolio content is to be acknowledged as necessary.

When the criteria are very limiting, they systemize the development of collections in such a way that a *show* portfolio tends to be the result. The criteria usually help the students pick the pieces of writing that they consider "their best" representations of certain types of writing. Doing that is a thoughtful activity for the student to be involved in, for in accomplishing this screening, the student is indeed exercising evaluative judgment. But how much analysis and self-assessment is left for the student to do using a selection once it is in the portfolio? It is limited to deciding what it is that makes the selection good.

In summary, the contents of portfolios should, quite simply, be relevant to developing better readers and writers. Besides samples of writing and responses to reading and records that track both reading and writing, the contents should include things like plans for language-related projects, notes about what has been read and written, pictures, and other materials that represent ideas and individual interests that can figure in future use of language.

One other generalization is also worth noting: A portfolio should reveal ideas that can be shared. It should contain material that the student is willing to have others read and consider. Thoughts and preferences that the student would harbor from the teacher, his or her parents, other adults, and even fellow students should not be included in portfolios, which will be studied and examined by others, including fellow students. Since portfolios must be kept in a highly accessible place, it is very likely that classmates will browse the portfolios of others without any special permission.

HOW WILL I GET THE STUDENTS INVOLVED IN SELF-ASSESSMENT?

A student who is asked to select his or her "best stuff" to go into a portfolio that meets school, district, or state requirements will need to do that from most of what he or she has written. Papers that are less than "the best" can be studied in terms of how they could be improved. There are earlier drafts of the "best efforts" that show how the desired outcome emerged and what was done to make it strong.

If a look at a portfolio collection is limited to just one's "best" efforts, the analysis is basically limited to some self-praise. The papers that were rejected for inclusion in the "prescribed" portfolio will never be compared to those that passed the test of the criteria—whoever sets them. And that's an important opportunity lost! Portfolios are ideal places to mull over all kinds of relationships and connections between ideas.

So in schools where even semirigid prescriptions are set for portfolio content, teachers should have their students select from working portfolios to create the requirements as show portfolios. In this way, the tendency to overstructure portfolios with specification for contents—the attempt to control that content for quality, and the articulation

> **T I P**　　　　　　　　　　　　　　　　　　　　HAVE A LOOK
>
> See if you can collect two or more drafts of several pieces of student writing or of your own. Lay them out in sequence and study them, noting differences. What kind of revision was going on? Was it substantial or minimal? What does it tell you about the process involved?

of criteria for doing that—need not be a mistake. In preparing for such standards, students can develop as self-assessors as they struggle to manage the contents of their working portfolios. It is the need to deal with a reasonable bulk and variety of material that sets the student to looking at the contents to make some sense and order of them.

This kind of activity tends to link the origin of an idea to its expression—a picture to a story it inspired or a reaction in a reader's log to an essay or editorial about the same topic. It links one version of an expression to the next draft, demonstrating the process of language use. The analysis that recognizes those links develops a sense of language as a thought-driven process.

If everything in the portfolio is already determined to be "best" and much of it is included to fill prescribed slots set for genres or instructional objectives, things are pretty much already taken care of. Whatever analysis takes place within the limited collection deductively follows the selection criteria. Meanwhile, the student with a *working* portfolio is inductively trying to make sense out of its many materials.

The student with the *show* portfolio can think about the content of the specific pieces, looking for relationships among them and for directions for future reading, thinking, and writing. That's all good metacognitive activity, what there is of it within a folder containing a limited number of pieces of writing and reactions to reading that all passed a single set of criteria. But the students have been excused from the really tough and initial evaluative challenge: They don't have to make some manageable sense out of an accruing collection of material with a much wider range. They have been spared the realistic and ongoing experience of inductively developing order out of the many things that they think are of some interest and of identifying *emerging* criteria for ranking all the stuff they and the teacher have collected.

Chances are that the student is pleased to escape this responsibility. As experience reveals, the need to think and seek order amid the eclectic mess created when their uninhibited interests collect an unlimited portfolio is a demanding, if not frustrating, chore for many students. They begin the necessary step of enforcing some meaning on their collections with rather crude major sorting categories:

- Stuff I like, stuff I'm not sure about, stuff I'd just as soon take out of here.
- Pieces that I consider finished, pieces that I intend to work on some more, unfinished pieces that I've decided not to finish.
- Records of my work, stories and poems, essays and reports, daily writing, ideas and miscellaneous favorite stuff.
- Pictures of my favorite things, names and words from stories I liked, drawings for stories I like to tell.

These are just a few of the general categories that students often come up with when forced by the bulk of their own creations to establish some initial order. Some never progress beyond these, although a successful student/teacher conference could promote more refined analysis. Even so, the thinking and evaluation that such sorting requires is more varied, and perhaps more complex, than deciding if each piece of work is good enough to go into the portfolio according to a set of criteria thought out sometime before and probably by someone else. And what's to keep that "best . . . acceptable . . . not so good" evaluation from being laid on the materials in the fuller portfolio to create a sub-layer of categories *within* one of the schemes just mentioned?

The more selective portfolio also tends to limit two other vital potentials of the methodology. When only "best" efforts are included in portfolios, any evidence of process that led to the paper selected tends to be eliminated by definition. It is the final draft that goes into the portfolio; earlier drafts are almost certain to be considered inferior or they wouldn't have been revised. Thanks in significant part to portfolio assessment, we now know that students do precious little, and usually only perfunctory, revision.

What little revision is done does not get into portfolios with content that has been overly screened, so there is practically no chance that the student will be looking at two or more drafts of a piece of writing and considering how it evolved. If evidence of revision is not collected, the kind of metacognition that self-assessment develops using portfolios will not include an understanding of how polished expression evolves. And in many portfolios, that trail will not be laid out for the teacher to consider.

The same selection process is even more apt to separate student expression from the source that promoted it. It takes a fairly extensive collection to reveal, for example, that a story read (and reported in the reader's log) provoked a critical reaction, then something more personal like a poem or journal entry, which in turn prompted the student to read other texts related to the same topic. The only thing the selective portfolio might include is a final narrative that pulls together selected ideas from texts and reader reactions into a story whose source is in the reader's log but not identified there.

That is another limitation of the overly selective portfolio. Without the freedom to pack it with pictures drawn and cut out, with notes about things viewed and read, with unfinished and unpolished drafts of pieces written, a portfolio may reveal little about the student to the teacher. The full, messy portfolio, on the other hand, tells the teacher a lot about what interests the student, where he or she gets ideas, and how some of them are developed and used. It is a rich source of good information that the teacher and student can review to provoke ideas about future reading and writing activities. The overly screened show portfolio is far less revealing.

The reading and writing logs evolve across time, and you or the student may decide to switch from one type to another. You may decide, for example, that the logs that leave less room for reactions and allow more entries per page are likely to promote as much student analysis as those which leave more room for the students.

Another form that many teachers require students to keep in their portfolios is the "Contents" or "Table of Contents," which should match and explain the order the student is keeping the material in at the particular time. The table of contents should be re-done occasionally as the student adds materials and shifts the organization of them.

Other types of records can be included in portfolios. One of these is the survey of student interests. The rationale for including it in the portfolio is to have it convenient when you and the student are looking at and analyzing the portfolio's contents.

These and other forms are discussed more thoroughly in Chapters 3 and 4. Usable models are offered in Appendix C, as are other forms that promote student self-assessment. You are encouraged to modify and use any of them you wish, or to copy and use them as they are.

How Should the Portfolios Be Evaluated?
Who Will Do It?
What Criteria Will Be Used?
Will They Be Graded?

You don't need the answers to these questions to get started with portfolio assessment, but they are apt to arise not long after the portfolios in your classroom are started. What you should understand as you begin is that the portfolio program will effectively help your students develop their reading and writing abilities so directly that you will think of it not as assessment but as the effective instruction that it really is.

If you have ever longed to teach to individual student interests and needs more ef-fectively, you will have an assessment/instructional methodology that serves that goal

Chapter 4 will detail how a teacher can assess students' language development.

Some teachers will feel that they are under considerable pressure to grade their students' portfolios as projects that have taken a considerable amount of class time. They may even be required to do so by their departments, school systems, or states. This possibility is discussed in more detail in Chapter 6, which has some suggestions for guiding the teacher who feels it necessary to grade portfolios.

directly. The portfolio can provide as complete and informative access as you have ever had to student backgrounds and interests, and your analysis using it should point up individual student needs in regard to reading and writing instruction. At the same time, your analysis will allow you to focus on student strengths and the ideas and content that express those interests and experiences.

If the time that individualized instruction requires has been one of the reasons you have done less of it than you would like, the same concern may apply to portfolio assessment. Yet as your students learn to assess their own strengths and what they can do to improve as language users, they are actually helping you manage their instruction as well as their portfolios. In this sense, portfolios can make your job easier.

What the rather rosy and idealistic tone of that promise suggests is that the best way to evaluate your students' portfolios is to determine whether they are indeed guiding your instruction in an effective way. If you have decided that getting students to think about their reading and writing experiences, abilities, and progress is a primary instructional goal, and your students are using their portfolios to do that, then the portfolios are a success.

It would be a serious mistake, we believe, for the teacher to grade portfolios. Portfolios are for assessment—both teacher assessment of progress and a student's self-assessment, but they are not meant to be graded. Too often in education we have confused assessment (finding out what is needed to plan and improve instruction) with grading (the labeling of an outcome). Grading portfolios could easily destroy all the genuine sense of responsibility for their own language development that you have instilled in your students with the portfolios; some students—probably those who have given the most thought to their collections—would feel betrayed, even if you had indicated all along that the portfolios would be graded.

At the same time, however, your analysis of the collections and your one-on-one conferences and regular contacts with the students as they work with their portfolios will give you a distinct sense of the effort that went into each one. You should have as well some sense of whether it has had some effect on the student's ability to construct meaning from reading and writing and on his or her awareness of that growth. Of course, what the portfolio demonstrates may have some substantial effect on your grading—usually to create more appreciation of the student's ability or attempt to improve. Interestingly, should you need to support whatever grade that judgment might help dictate, the portfolio is apt to be one of the first things you would get out to show to a parent, for example.

The portfolio, in fact, can play a major role in providing assessment data to parents as well as to teachers and students. In addition, portfolio assessment can act as a backup methodology in informing educational decision makers, a rather encompassing term that tends to include school administrators, lawmakers, the media, and education-conscious taxpayers. While many of those groups' information needs are best served by standardized and performance tests, they can, by looking at a sample of student portfolios collected randomly, gain perspective on student achievement that may not be revealed by the other assessments.

Suppose, for example, that the decision makers were proposing to act on information from standardized tests that indicated that the students in their schools were not meeting many objectives related to language usage. The teachers in their schools are surprised by those results, which they feel fail to depict the way their students use and think with language. They persuade the decision makers to examine a set of portfolios selected at random from several different grades.

After doing this, the decision makers come away surprised that their students are so creative, are so involved with ideas, react in such substantive ways to what they read, are relatively prolific readers, and have such diversified and specialized interests. Many from this audience are unable to come into the classroom and observe what is happening there. What the portfolios can do is give them a sense of the range of reading and writing that students do and of the rich language environment of their classrooms and of their lives in general.

WHAT SHOULD I TELL OTHERS
ABOUT MY NEW ASSESSMENT PLAN?

How you can inform your fellow teachers and your administrators about the portfolio assessment plan has already been discussed. But there are others who should know about the program you are initiating. Most parents, of course, will be interested. Explaining portfolio assessment to them should be a lot easier than explaining standardized testing in a way that will tell them what it means and cue them to misuses of the information it produces. Once parents learn that they are going to have an opportunity to look at their child's actual work—and at actual things the child has written and at indications of how effectively the child has read—you may almost hear them breathe a sigh of relief. When they find, as well, the degree of reflection and understanding that many student portfolios reveal, parents often express genuine surprise and gratitude for a chance to see them.

Watch for opportunities to present information about the portfolio plan to groups of parents. Perhaps back-to-school night is early in the year or falls relatively soon after you have begun portfolio assessment. If not, check with your administrators to see if you can invite your students' parents and guardians to a special session some evening to explain. Actually, it might work best the first time you present such a session to do so after your students have their portfolio collections under way and you have had more experience with the methodology. That would allow you to give the parents a general introduction to portfolios and how they are being used and then let them take the portfolios their children are constructing and examine them while you move about answering any questions they have.

If it works best to wait a bit for what might be called a parent workshop on portfolios, use some other method to inform them that the procedure is under way. You could write an announcement to send home with the children or mail to their homes.

Some teachers prepare their announcements like a newsletter; they let their students help prepare it, and they actually send home several issues each year. Not only will this be a way to inform parents, but it will also intensify your students' interests in their portfolios.

However you inform parents, emphasize that they can help by encouraging the child to bring any writing done at home and any reactions to stories and books read at home to school to put into the portfolio. Explain, too, however, that it is the child who is to make the decisions about whether most of the things done go in or not. The parent's role can be to react to language-related experiences at home and to encourage the child.

Once your students find out that the portfolio is important enough to merit all this attention, it may intensify their interest in their collections. "Gee," a student may think, realizing his parents are going to actually look at his portfolio when they come to the school, "putting this stuff in here must really be important. I better give some extra thought to the way I am arranging it. I hope they understand what this is really all about. I better write them a note about it and put it right in front of the table of contents. I wonder what Dad will think when he reads this story about us cleaning the garage. Maybe I can take that out if he comes to look at it, or I could put a note on it and tell him I'm kidding. Or just one that says, 'Hi, Dad!'"

Teachers appear to disagree when telling us about their experiences with allowing students to take their portfolios home to show their parents. Some who report the possibility of never seeing some of the collections again sound convincing. With limits, the portfolio probably should reside in the classroom, and ownership would not extend to taking it wherever the student pleases.

What you might consider is sending home the part of the collection that the student closes off when the collection has become too cumbersome and the student has evaluated its contents enough to select some items to transfer to the beginning of a new collection. Put a rubber band around the papers to go home. Both the papers culled and those kept

Models of such announcements can be found in Appendix C. Modify the announcement in any way that seems appropriate, but be sure to include the part about inviting the parents to school to discuss the portfolio. A sample of a page from a newsletter about portfolios is also in Appendix C. Once again, use anything from that model that is useful. Perhaps you can use the masthead or make up your own.

T I P   A MEMORABLE IDEA!

Do you remember saving your report cards and special papers from school? Have they tended to disappear over the years? What would you give to see them one more time?

Acquire some corrugated or cardboard boxes about $8\frac{1}{2} \times 11$ inches and 8 to 12 inches deep. They should have lids. When class time allows over the course of the semester or year, let your students decorate them. Then send them home with a note to parents that they can be put on a shelf to hold samples of their child's work, which will be coming later. As you are sure that you and the students are basically through with papers culled from their portfolios every few months, have the students gift wrap them and take them home as presents to be examined by parents and to be put into the storage boxes they have made.

These boxes can be large enough to hold what has been culled from the collections for the entire school year—everything except pieces that are going into special show portfolios that might be created at that time for special audiences, such as next year's teacher. One teacher who used this approach had her third-graders write to themselves as if they were writing to a person who is 21 years old. What a thrill it would be for the student to look at the portfolio collection and the letter as an adult and to be reminded of one's own thoughts as a third-grader. And, what a challenge for a third-grader to think about what to write to explain to this adult what has been read and written in the third grade and why.

for the new portfolio should contain a copy of a summary the student writes of what he has learned about his reading and writing from his portfolio to that date.

If the bulk of the earlier part of the collection were to be lost outside the classroom, it would not be a severe setback. If you do this, be sure that you have had a last look at what is going out of the classroom and at the pieces and summaries the student is using to begin collecting again. You may want to write a summary yourself and to put a copy of it in both sections of the student's portfolio.

You can also recommend that each student write a memo addressed to his or her parents or guardian. And enclose another explanation of portfolio assessment and/or an issue of your newsletter in the package with two copies of a form that invites parents to react to what they are seeing. Keep the form simple so that it is easy to respond to. At the end of the school year—after the student selects some materials for a show portfolio to introduce himself to his new teacher—the student can take the complete year's collection home.

It may seem that an unusual amount of contact with parents over the portfolio is being recommended, but it actually involves only several attempts at contact each year, and in terms of the potential benefits, this is actually minimal. If parents buy into the assessment program, they can have a remarkable impact on the attitudes of their children toward language, and they can encourage writing and reading at home.

WHAT ELSE SHOULD I BE DOING TO GET READY FOR PORTFOLIO ASSESSMENT?

There remains the most important group of all who need to understand the portfolio assessment program: your students! They need to know what is coming and why you think it is a good idea to do it. Be as open and informative as you can with them; that will encourage them to approach portfolio building and evaluation with a positive and even enthusiastic attitude.

THINGS YOU NEED TO EXPLAIN TO
YOUR STUDENTS IN INTRODUCING PORTFOLIOS

- **What a portfolio consists of:** Writing that they think can tell something about the way they use language—the way they express ideas; writing that tells what ideas are interesting and important to them. Particularly writing related to things they have read—that shows what they remember about certain books, stories, and articles. Writing that tells what they think about things they have read. Materials like pictures that interest them, clippings, and notes about authors they like. Records that show what they have written, what they have read, and what they have put into the portfolio. Records that show the order it is in. Notes that explain what they think about the materials in their portfolios after looking at them and studying them. Notes that show what other people who have looked at the portfolio think. Notes from conferences where you and they sit down and talk about what is in the portfolio. Notes that they and you attach to certain things that have been put into the portfolio, explaining why it is there and what you think of it. Other "stuff."

  Emphasize the importance of keeping different drafts of things written and other materials that show how the student's ideas have developed. Explain that the portfolios may contain audiotapes, videotapes, computer discs, and any other records if students use them. Encourage them to bring things they have written outside of school to put into their portfolios.

- **Who will pick things to put in the portfolio and why:** Usually the student, but also you on occasion, because the selections are of special interest, are good examples of how the student thinks with language, are something the student is proud of or that you think is really good work,

  are something that the student is working on and intends to finish.

- **What the student will do with the portfolio:** Look at the things in it and think about them; use special sheets to analyze them; put them in order and reorder them later after thinking about them again; use special sheets to keep a record of the order they are in; rewrite them if they like; write about them; select them to put in show portfolios or to show to someone in particular or to use for some special project or purpose.

- **Who else will look at it:** Parents on some occasions, the principal and perhaps other adults at the school—but never without the student knowing ahead of time that they are going to do that. Explain that you may be looking at the portfolios at times when the students are out of the classroom so that you too can think about them.

- **What you will look for in the portfolio:** Signs of how they think with language; information about things that interest them and why; examples of the kinds of reading and writing that they do really well; indications of things the student can work on to become an even better reader or writer and things you can do to help.

- **What all the papers will be kept in:** Explain your plans for letting the students pick their own holders and what they need to be like or describe what you plan to supply; you may wish to hold off on explaining that they can be decorated or mention it at the beginning.

- **What the conferences you have with them will be like:** How many, about when, the kinds of things you will discuss with them; the notes you and they will take; what they need to do to get ready for the conferences.

Prepare an introduction using the ideas in the box "Things You Need to Explain to Your Students in Introducing Portfolios" and decide how much of it to introduce at one time. Don't overwhelm the students with information, however. Keep your introduction relatively simple, and keep in mind that the portfolio assessment process will become real for them as they actually make and collect their papers.

Conference time will be the key experience that makes the process meaningful and clearer. But introduce portfolios, nonetheless, and allow plenty of time for questions. Be patient and respectful as you go over some aspect of the portfolios for what may seem to you the nth time. Adopt the tone that keeping portfolios will be important because it will be fun and helpful, but it is really no big thing. Explain to your students that they are just going to keep a collection of their stuff so you and they can talk about it—especially so they can tell you about it.

There are interest surveys in Appendix C that can be copied and used as is or modified to serve your particular needs. Note that there is one for kindergartners and first-graders and one for students in grades two and above.

BE SURE YOU KNOW YOUR STUDENTS' INTERESTS   When you are reviewing the kinds of things that can be put into portfolios, you have an opportunity to stress one of the portfolio's strengths: to tell you a lot about its owner. Explain why knowing their interests is of importance to you as a teacher. If you haven't done so already, you may want to pass out an interest survey for them to fill out. Explain that it is one of the things you want to go into the portfolio because it helps you understand the other things that will be in there. Doing this, of course, cues the students that (1) whether they are interested in something is a key criterion for selecting things for the portfolio and (2) although they are to be the prime selector, you, as teacher, will be interested in what goes into their collections.

USE A MODEL OR MODELS   Have an example of the kind of portfolio you hope each of them will collect so that you can show things in it as you talk about them and as you answer questions the students are sure to have. Perhaps you know a teacher who is using portfolios with students who will be willing to let you borrow a few of them for a day. Perhaps you have a portfolio you have been keeping. Perhaps you know some other adult who keeps a portfolio that can be borrowed for the purpose. After you display and discuss the contents of the model or models you use, give the students time to look through the portfolio themselves.

BRING IN PEOPLE WHO USE PORTFOLIOS   Arrange for one or more professionals who use portfolios to bring them to class to show your students. Perhaps you know an artist, a graphic designer, an architect, a clothes designer, or someone else who would be willing to show your students the portfolio he or she uses and to explain its importance. Explain to your volunteer ahead of time that it is vital that students' collections be working portfolios and see if you can prevail on the guest to be sure some drafts, sketches, and other unfinished ideas are in the portfolio brought to your class. Be sure to allow time for the students to ask questions of the visitor.

You might be able to arrange for the class to visit an artist's studio, explaining that the whole place is his or her *working* portfolio.

HAVE EXAMPLES OF THE HOLDER OR HOLDERS   If you are supplying uniform holders, have some ready for inspection. If you are allowing the students to pick their own, have a range of samples—the kinds of things students might find at home that will do the job. In a final introduction section, you might have students show what they have selected to each other, or pass out the ones you have selected for them to use.

HAVE THE RECORD FORMS READY   Look through Appendix C and select the forms you expect to use with or without adaptation. Adapt as you wish and have copies of the logs and other forms that the students will be asked to use ready. Hand out copies for them to look at. They are sure to have some questions about them, but be sure to point out that you will be close by to help them get started using these aids when it is time for them to use each of them. You may want them to begin right away filling in the reading

---

TIP   BE THEIR MODEL!

If you don't have a portfolio of your own, start keeping one now! Give this priority attention so that your collection will be ready to show your students as you introduce the plan. Make it convincing—not something that appears to have been concocted for your purpose. If your students believe that you and/or other adults are keeping a portfolio yourselves, their attitudes will open positively to the new project.

and writing logs, and if so, allow adequate time for them to do it calmly as you move about the room to answer questions and assist.

STRESS THE CONFERENCE   Be sure to explain the conferences that you will be scheduling with the students and describe the kinds of things you and the student will talk about during them. Hand out a copy of the note sheet you intend to use for these conferences. You might want to arrange with one student to read a paper he or she has written and to discuss it with you.

Have some questions ready that demonstrate the kinds of things that might be discussed in a conference: Why did you write this? Who would you like to have read it? Where did you get the idea? Do you think it is one of your best papers? Why or why not? For the lowest grades, you might have a student bring a favorite picture and discuss why he or she likes it and what kind of story it suggests. Be sure, however, that the conference is a time for your students to talk and discuss rather than just a time for you to ask questions. Asking too many questions can turn the conference into a teacher interrogation rather than a time for you and the student to discuss.

If you are giving each student the responsibility of scheduling his or her conference, you might want to have a sheet with scheduled opportunities on it ready to pass around, even though this would be too early for a student to sign up with any certainty that he or she could be ready.

GET THE STUDENTS INVOLVED   Explain how the students will be allowed different times to look at, add to, and rearrange their portfolios and how it is important that the collections be somewhere where the students can get at them easily. Let them suggest arrangements for keeping their collections in the classroom and discuss their merits among themselves. If possible, let them decide as a group where to keep the portfolios initially on a trial basis.

HELP THEM GET STARTED   Have several papers from each student to hand out to them and have volunteers describe what they have so the class can discuss why those items might or might not be selected to go into a portfolio. This idea gives you a perfect opportunity to include, if any are available, more than one draft of something a student has written and to explain how ideal it would be to put all of the drafts into the portfolio in the order that they were written.

Perhaps some student has written a report on something read and has then done something original based on it. Again, you have a perfect example of a pair of papers that would be wonderful in a portfolio because they show where an idea came from. These and any other examples that show *process* should be displayed and their value described in the early days of portfolio building.

You will have many opportunities to enlarge, reinforce, and even improve your introduction of portfolio keeping as the process actually gets under way and you block out time to assist the students one-on-one while they work with their accruing collections.

Specifics about how to conference with students are included in Chapter 5. Concern with finding time for conferencing is expressed so frequently by teachers who come to workshops and other informative sessions about portfolios that more than two dozen hints for finding the time for portfolio conferences with students are also described in a special chart in that chapter.

SETTING UP A BASIC SCHEDULE
TO IMPLEMENT YOUR PLAN

Good luck with portfolioing! Chances are that you're in for one of the most interesting and rewarding projects you've ever conducted in your classroom. Before you get too far or even actually start, however, check out the more detailed discussions about the way portfolio assessment works in the chapters that follow.

Also, if you can set up a basic routine, you will find it much easier to get the portfolio process established in your classroom. Table 2.3 is a model of a basic schedule that you can follow to start the portfolio process in your classroom.

T
A
B
L
E

2
•
3

SAMPLE OF A BASIC SCHEDULE FOR STARTING A LANGUAGE ARTS PORTFOLIO PROGRAM

Activity	Schedule	Student's Responsibility	Teacher's Responsibility
Teacher administers a performance assessment and observes as students complete. Results are discussed thoroughly and form the initial entry in portfolios.	This needs to be done once as early as possible. It can be repeated several times at later dates.	Taking the assessment, saving all notes and drafts to put into the portfolio, learning about how product reveals process.	Observing the students' processes in completing the assessment, using the results instructively, helping students understand how the results model language/thinking processing.
Students keep Writing Logs that list the date and title of each piece included—along with comments.	Daily, or as often as writing is completed or revised	Completing the Log, which is kept in the portfolio	Encouraging and reminding students to maintain the Log; responding to it
Students keep Reading Logs that list the date finished, title, and author of texts read—along with comments.	Daily, or as often as something of interest has been read	Completing the Log, which is kept in the portfolio	Encouraging and reminding students to maintain the Log
Students and teachers collect writing samples including those written in response to reading. Samples should include notes, preliminary drafts, and final drafts. Unfinished materials should also be included.	Every two weeks minimally, but daily as samples are developed and selected	Selecting materials to be included	Selecting materials to be included
Portfolio materials are reviewed and analyzed. Notes are made about reading and writing interests as well as reading and writing strengths.	Minimally once a week	Organizing the materials and making notes, table of contents, and other analytic materials	Analyzing materials and making notes; discussing contents with student informally
Conferences: Portfolio materials are assessed and judgments are made about each student's developing literacy interests and abilities.	At least four times a school year or as often as student's need to review develops	Organizing materials and making notes; summarizing for conference; making conference notes and setting new objectives	Meeting with student and making notes; helping student set new objectives; summarize student's strengths/needs

SUMMARY: A DOZEN THINGS TO TEND TO IN GETTING STARTED WITH PORTFOLIO ASSESSMENT

- Start off by administering a performance assessment that can serve as a model for the kind of papers that should go into the portfolio to reveal integrated reading/writing/thinking processing.

- Approach portfolio assessment with the expectation that it can inform your instruction and help you communicate to the students that they can become self-assessors and manage their own development as language users and thinkers.

- Let your fellow teachers know what you are doing with the hope of developing a schoolwide, multiyear portfolio assessment experience for your students.

- Verify that portfolio assessments complement your philosophy and theory of how language abilities develop, are used, should be taught, and can be assessed.

- Make sure that the portfolios your students keep will answer to your instructional needs, objectives, and goals as well as to any school, district, or state standards that may apply.

- Let the students decide what they will keep their collections in and where they will be kept so that they can get to them easily and frequently.

- Give your students a sense of ownership by explaining how they will pick most of what goes into the collections while explaining the kinds of contents that let portfolios reveal the process and progress of language users.

- Promote from the start the concept of the *working portfolio* that includes idea sources, notes, outlines, drafts, and revisions of single pieces of writing.

- Give your students some idea of how they will use their materials by introducing them to some of the basic and required forms that they will use, such as the Log, the Table of Contents, and a few of the sheets that guide them in assessing individual pieces of writing.

- Understand the dangers of grading portfolios and learn to evaluate them as revelations of their owners.

- Introduce your portfolio assessment program to parents, administrators, and the public in ways that emphasize its unique window on authentic use of language; and understand the potential of using show portfolios for a variety of purposes that report to those audiences and to teachers your students will have in the future.

- Have a clear plan and a schedule for doing these things that can be explained to the students and evaluated and revised for the implementation of portfolios in the future.

CHAPTER THREE

DECIDING WHAT GOES
INTO THE PORTFOLIO

Getting started on portfolio assessment is as simple as having the students begin to collect their work. "But what papers should I have them collect?" you ask, quite reasonably. The short answer to that question is:

> The portfolio should include whatever the student and teacher feel depict that student's development as a user of language—as a thinker with numerous purposes for reading and expressing himself or herself.

SOME GENERAL OBJECTIVES
FOR PORTFOLIO CONTENTS

Ideally, the collections in your classroom will contain what the students *want* to collect, not what you *have* them put into their portfolios; but that doesn't mean you should not provide some guidance and motivation for including the kinds of materials that will support the development of self-assessors.

Given the need for a sense of student ownership that comes by having students rationalize why they have included a particular paper or set of papers, there are some important guidelines that apply to portfolio contents. The collections should, over time, include:

- Sets of papers that will reflect writing and thinking as a process.
- A quantity of papers that will allow the student to sort and categorize them in meaningful ways.
- A variety of types of writing, targeted at as many audiences as possible and reflecting numerous purposes for writing and reading.
- Whatever forms and guides are necessary to promote the analysis of the contents and organization extending from that analysis.

What Kinds of Student Papers Will Show Process?

When students and their teachers look for signs of progress and improvement, as well as for skills and behaviors that students can improve, they are almost always looking at *products*. The beauty—the real power—of portfolio assessment is that it gives us a genuine way to examine the student's writing and thinking *processes*. Assessing process is usually done through observation, but portfolios have the potential to use products in a way that can reveal process as well.

Product refers to just the evaluation of the final result, while *process* refers to how the result is achieved. For example, the score of a baseball game might be 1 to 0. That score is the product, but it tells us little about how the game was played. We might infer from the product that the game was a pitcher's duel and that there were few hits during the game. However, if we had observed the game to add to our understanding of process we might have learned that there were actually many hits during the game but the runners were left stranded on base.

We might also have learned that the infield for both teams had made many spectacular plays to cut off runners as they streaked for home. We might add to that a conversation with a third baseman. He explains that he moved in toward the batter because he knew his pitcher often got the batters to hit ground balls and he was sure he could handle the grounders and throw out the runners.

Simply put, product is the score or the result—it is how well something is accomplished. Process, on the other hand, is how we do the thing. You can learn about process by inferring it from the product, but much more is learned by watching the person as he goes about the task—and by talking with him after he completes the task and explains how he went about it.

It is important that the student reflect about his or her reading and writing since the most important person to learn about process is the student. The student should not just assess *how well* he or she did something. The goal is to get the student to understand *how* it was done.

The portfolio conference is the time when you coach your students to think about how they can do what they want to do better, but a view of process can also emerge from the examination of a spectrum of student products kept across time. That spread of materials can reveal progress and development of various abilities, interests, and attitudes over a period of weeks or across a semester. Noticing how writing becomes more incisive and expressive is a prime benefit, but the inclusion of writing assignments that are about favorite topics or are special in some other way makes a portfolio a cache of ideas that appeal to and intrigue or concern the student. So in a sense, the collection can depict a developing individual.

In a successful portfolio assessment program, the student begins to get a sense of how he or she is growing. The student does this by studying the collected products. Examining

There is a discussion of product and process—their distinctions, relationships, and relevance to assessment of student progress—in Chapter 4.

T I P

EIGHT STRATEGY ICONS CAN GUIDE YOU TO PROCESS!

One of the surest ways to assure that a student's portfolio will reveal process is to consider the eight icons of language strategies that will be detailed in Chapter 4 when discussing the development of self-assessment as metacognition. They can be copied as a checklist on the sheet "When you read and write REMEMBER" in Appendix C and pasted into the inside cover of the portfolios as a guide students can use in looking over their collections.

Encourage your students to ask themselves the questions accompanying the icons:

1. What do I want to know?
2. What do I already know?
3. Do I think about the ideas before I start to read and write?
4. Do I think about what is coming next?
5. Do I picture what is happening?
6. Do the ideas make sense to me?
7. Do I make changes if things don't make sense?
8. Do I get help when I need it?

These assessments are described more thoroughly in Chapters 7 and 8, which discuss how to construct and select them. Chapter 6 explains how they can link portfolios to fuller accountability assessment programs.

and organizing the materials in the portfolio show the process of thinking with language and how writing can grow out of, and respond to, things read. This is particularly obvious in sets of papers that show thought emerging from disorganized notes and then outlines that direct written expression across different drafts and revisions.

Consequently, the inclusion of more than just the finished written product is a primary way to demonstrate the process with which students express themselves. The sources of ideas can sometimes be kept in the portfolios, too—as clippings, notes about stories, pictures from magazines and newspapers, snapshots of friends and important events, and other artifacts. If the student uses some kind of jot note technique to explore the idea, the notes represent an important step in the process. Any attempt to organize those notes as some kind of outline is also vital evidence of the process. One of the primary products that becomes a very revealing part of a process set of papers is a draft. Sequenced before and compared to the latest draft it can be a clear indication of the writing/thinking process.

Not all of the products a student puts into his or her portfolio will consist of all these steps, but most of it can confirm how expression comes out of background, interests, and other sources. Hopefully, many papers will reveal how language is being used to frame those expressions.

An excellent way to demonstrate the value of a set of papers that show such a process is to make the student's response to a performance assessment an early part of the portfolio collection.

It is a wonderful experience to develop your own performance assessment, but there is probably not enough time to accomplish that at the beginning of your portfolio project. If you do eventually develop one or more, they can be saved and used early on in another year or semester. But in beginning portfolio assessment, you should look for a published instrument that leads the student through a thinking, note-making, and outlining activity as a prewriting process. If the instrument you select does not have such a prewriting feature, be sure to devise one yourself to go with it.

More than just an evaluation and a record of student performance, such an assessment is a full piece of writing that should inform well on the student's ability to read and write. Often the prewriting activities are presented on performance assessment instruments as optional steps, but you should require them of your students, who should be helped to construct and use them and be instructed to save them. Then, after you have scored or rated the results that grow out of that process, have your students put the final product in their portfolios, *preceded by all the prewriting papers they created.*

What you have in this set of papers is a good example of the kind of sequenced products that taken together provide some insight into writing and thinking processes.

Name *Alisha Morgan*		
A Comparison/Contrast Chart to Use in Responding to "Redistricting the Schools"		
Details to Compare/Contrast	West Side Junior High	Central Junior High
The building/facilities	*It's old! Roof leaks! Gym's too small, crowded but shouldn't be after change. No tennis courts. No pool!*	*Brand new building. Best science rooms in town! Huge home ec area. Gym holds 1500 fans! Has new tennis courts and a pool!*
The teachers	*A lot of teachers are older, more experienced (Mom and Dad had some). The teachers there always win awards.*	*New and younger teachers. Know latest ways to teach. Have lots of spirit, not a lot of experience.*
The traditions	*Eagles are best team in the city! Always great teams in girls' sports. Colors = gold + blue (Mom still has her pom-poms!!!).*	*Bobcats won 3 championships last year. Band looks really snazzy in green and white uniforms!*
The students	*Most of my best friends will go to West Side! I get better grades than most of the students there.*	*Kids at Central are "the smart ones!" They win academic contests. Special courses there. Harder to get A's!*

In one performance assessment, the students read a news story about how a school board drew new district lines. It split the students at Barthowlon Middle School almost in half. Half would go on to West Side Junior High and half to Central Junior High. Before the new lines were drawn, all Barthowlon students went to West Side Junior High.

A second story was a feature that described what people believed about each school. The student was asked to pretend that she was a student at Barthowlon Middle School who would go to Central Junior High. She was to write how she felt about that.

These are the notes she took on a worksheet provided with the test. From this, she was asked to make an outline and then write. After exchanging with a friend, she was to revise and rewrite. All four papers would go into the portfolio: these notes, the outline, the first draft, and the final draft.

(Whales have sensitive skin. They can stay under water for about an hour. Whales have very good hearing.)

Performance assessments are now commonly administered to students at all levels—even in kindergarten. Here is an example of how such a procedure reveals early language processing. This child was read a text about whales and was asked to draw a picture about the content. Then the student was asked to write beneath the picture what it showed. After that, the teacher or researcher sat down with the child and had him read what he had written. The child's transcription of his own writing was then recorded.

Explain to your students how this is so, using some of their sets of papers as an example. Then get them to discuss how they did the tasks. You can add your own observations of what you have seen them doing in class, but you should remember that the portfolio conference is to get the students to discuss and think about how they can accomplish what they want to accomplish. In doing that, you will be modeling how they can analyze any such sets added over time to their portfolios.

Be sure to explain, too, that the purpose for reading is frequently to apply what we learn from a text, noting that their sets of papers also display reading process in that sense. Make sure that they at least understand that the set of papers that are going into their portfolios in this early stage are a good model of the kind of *sets* you hope they will add to it all along.

Many teachers would correctly object to including scores from standardized reading and writing tests in student portfolios because they tend to work against the purpose of the portfolio. The results of integrated reading/writing performance tests, on the other hand, seem highly appropriate because they echo the kinds of integrated reading/writing activities that many teachers try to create in the classroom and want the portfolio to reflect. In them, the student responds in writing to a reading prompt or prompts. A purpose for responding in writing is dictated, but it allows the student some leeway in applying the details from the prompt as advised.

Whereas the teacher learns what works by using such activities in the classroom, published performance tests of this type are tried out with large numbers of students in different schools. Some integrated language arts performance tests are developed by the teacher or a group of teachers in a school or school district. These tests, too, go through trial stages to see if they successfully engage a majority of students. In a sense, this verifies their authenticity.

Student performance on these tests is rated, usually within several categories, that cover reading comprehension, writing, and the interaction between the two as it is necessary to perform a prescribed task. The rater follows a rubric that describes the rating range (*1* through *4*, for example) within each category, and the tryouts have produced samples of actual papers that got each of the scores in each category. The rater can use these as anchors in assigning ratings to students who take the test after the tryouts.

Some schools test students several times a semester in this way, using different prompts and writing activities. Inclusion of sets of papers from these tests can show progress quite clearly as well as performance tying the comprehension of different text genres to different writing purposes. Another argument for their use and for their inclusion in the portfolio is that they are so like good instruction that they can be used primarily as an instructional tool; but the primary reason remains that the inclusion of the results on one performance assessment at the beginning of portfolioing provides an excellent model of a paper set that illustrates process.

WHY SHOULD I ENCOURAGE THE STUDENT TO SAVE LOTS OF PAPERS?

The second of these general objectives is served nicely by efforts to give the student as much leeway as possible in selecting the contents. The need to organize portfolio contents that accrue from an open-ended policy about what students can select—one not rigidly controlled by criteria the student must follow—is one of the surest ways to ensure that students examine and think about portfolio contents.

As they do this and organize the materials—often one way and then another and possibly in the crudest kinds of categories—students are taking the first step to becoming self-assessors. If they are to tackle this with a sense of responsibility for their language development, they will need to believe that they really do own—or at least have a major control over—what goes into the collection.

It is probably a good idea to encourage students to begin articulating some criteria for selection *some time after they have accumulated a sizable number of papers, tapes, and whatever they and the teacher have added to the portfolio.* The point in doing so at that time is to encourage the students to think about what they have collected and why. Even then, however, it should be stressed that these criteria are descriptive of what is *in* the portfolio and that the student can develop and change them in terms of guiding what will be added; they are not a set of rules to *limit* future selection for the student's collection.

Here are some examples of the kind of criteria that students often devise:

- I enjoyed writing this.
- I think this is written really well.
- This tells about a book I liked a lot.
- This was a difficult paper to think out and write.
- I really relate to this topic/idea: I "feel for" the character; it tells how I felt when I was up/down; it cracks me up; it is the first time I have ever been able to say what I think/feel about this.

STUDENTS COME TO ESTABLISH MEANINGFUL CRITERIA FOR PORTFOLIO CONTENTS

One of Linda Rief's fifth-graders wrote a rationale that would be a good guide for any student beginning portfolio assessment: "Now I know that in order to write something well, you have to care about it. The first important thing is that you like a piece of writing, then you worry if anyone else likes it. . . . I've learned to add detail to get something across. I've learned to care about my writing and write in order to resolve things, because even when I read a piece over, I always learn something."

See Rief's article in *Educational Leadership* cited under "Sources Cited and Other Relevant Reading" in Appendix B.

- I feel strongly about this and I think my arguments might be used to persuade someone.
- This made me feel happy/sad/excited.
- I think this is funny/exciting/entertaining, and I would like to share it with people.
- I think it's important to remember what I did; how to do this; why I thought this; why I like this author; etc. I don't want to forget this stuff/these facts/this character.
- This really shows how my writing/reading/thinking has changed.
- My mother/dad/friend/teacher likes this one. I think people will feel that this is a good story/essay/piece.
- This is an idea I had that I would like to use sometime. I think that I have more to say about it.

With student control of what goes into language arts portfolios, they can vary a great deal from student to student within some classrooms. Across classrooms, where the school activities that provide many opportunities to select materials may vary, portfolios will differ as a group as well. The more ownership that students have of their portfolios, the more variance one is apt to see in terms of content—and presumably, the better the portfolios serve their owners.

WHAT TYPES OF WRITING WORK BEST IN A PORTFOLIO?

Almost any kind of writing that expresses some idea and for which there is some purpose can serve portfolio assessment. As has been noted already, that writing can range from notetaking to a draft of a story or paper that the student considers finished—at least for the time being.

Numerous materials related to writing and reading can be selected. Most are writing products—some of which are developed as class activities and some totally "free writing." Some is more clearly related to reading; some is highly creative, and the influence of life experiences and reading is not so directly obvious.

A list of the types of writing that can be saved could be quite extensive, but here are some examples:

- Stories, poems, essays, personal narratives, think-pieces, and other free writing done at home and at school.
- Notes and brainstorming—often accompanying clippings, stories, pictures, or other sources about ideas that interest the student.
- Memos and various notes analyzing and/or explaining portfolio contents, sometimes directed toward potential viewers.
- Longer reactions to things read, including extensions or revisions of stories read.
- Responses to performance assessment tasks.
- Informative writing, including directions, rules, and information the student wants to remember.
- Argumentative and persuasive writing.
- Agreements, contracts, proposals, articulated goals.
- Lists of things the student wants to do, read, or write about.
- Letters, memos, and formal and informal notes to friends and relatives or ones from them that need answering.

- Journals, diaries, or other ongoing self-reflections.
- Assigned writing that the student is proud of and considers his or her best work or wants to revise.
- Classroom and school publications that contain work by the student.
- Audio- and videotapes of student (and often friends and classmates) reading aloud or making some form of presentation.

Very broadly, it can be said that nearly everything—including experiential essay reports (often still called "themes"), letters, new story endings or beginnings, school-based reports, free writing, and so on—produces student written expression worth including in portfolios.

One cannot prescribe a particular package of examples as the ideal portfolio combination; yet it would be difficult to go wrong by encouraging students to include many of them. Written papers are best acquired by providing reading and writing experiences that will authentically involve the student and thus can produce something that the student *wants* to save. This also allows the teacher to promote certain contents for the portfolio without laying down too many requirements for it and usurping ownership.

EXAMPLES OF LANGUAGE-RELATED ACTIVITIES THAT PRODUCE PORTFOLIO CONTENT

- Have your kindergartners or first-graders draw self-portraits. Then record their voices one at a time on audiotape as they tell about their pictures. Make some notes about each student's oral use of language, and put the audiotape in his or her portfolio. Conduct a similar activity later so you can compare the student's language on the two recorded tape segments. Make notes about the comparison.
- If you give your students opportunities to work on and present projects, let them write up reports on each project finished that can go into the portfolio. You can do this with small-group projects as well; allow the members of a project team to collaborate on planning their reports and in reacting to what their teammates write, but have each student write his or her own.
- Use whatever type preparation and reproduction technologies are available to you in order to produce one or more classroom publications. Students suddenly look on their writing quite differently when they realize that it is going into a class creative writing magazine or newsletter that will be read by numerous readers. The newsletter could be themed to explain portfolios to parents. Plan the publication as a group and appoint revolving editors or small editorial groups to work with writers to edit, standardize spelling, or whatever they decide is necessary. Make sure that each student is represented in each issue of a publication and do not do the editing yourself.
- Let discussions of the themes and topics in instructional units lead to different types of expression about them: story extensions, creative writing modeled on what has been read, poems, essays, etc.
- Get students "whipped up" on some topic and let them try some poems. Indicate that the poems need not rhyme. Encourage each poet to read his or her creation aloud, changing words until the poem can be read smoothly.
- Have students write parodies of favorite poems or stories, or copy unusual stylistic features in some stories to write their own.
- Let some students start "Thought-for-the-day" journals to keep in their portfolios. Give them about 15 minutes at least every other day to work on entries in this journal.
- Let students make up new lyrics for songs they like, or rap copy.

- Help some students get started writing the script for a scene in a play.
- Let students retell and record stories appropriate for particular holidays or seasons.

It is not the purpose of this book to attempt to classify the many kinds of student writing that can be developed in the classroom and encouraged outside of class or to provide a catalog of teaching ideas. But beyond this list of examples, we will discuss here several general types that have proven to be valuable inclusions that support self-assessment. It is worth illustrating how some of the best instructional ideas serve portfolio assessment quite well.

WRITING THAT SYNTHESIZES AND SUMMARIZES LEARNING CAN BE INCLUDED   Obviously, the student will be inclined to include writing that is done in the classroom. In some classrooms that may often be a kind of reportlike synthesis or summary of something a student has learned by reading and by watching and listening: the habits of an interesting animal, the customs of an alien land, or a scientific phenomenon, for example. It is best, of course, when such writing includes the individual student's reaction to what has been learned.

This kind of writing is now understood to be an effective way to learn material, a methodology sometimes called *writing to learn*. The material is thus more established in memory and/or as part of comprehension, along with the inclination to apply it when

Writing from all subject matters is suitable for inclusion in the portfolio, and most often that takes the form of a kind of synthesis of information.

the opportunity arises. The student is apt to create the opportunity himself or herself by picking the topic of this type of writing for a subsequent reading and writing experience.

As the student progresses in school, this kind of writing and thinking will continue to be important. So it is not out of place at all for such efforts to be collected so the student can analyze them and look for ways to improve this important kind of writing and thinking.

REVEALING PORTFOLIOS INCLUDE THE STUDENTS' CREATIVE EXPRESSIONS   Writing that summarizes and synthesizes should not, however, dominate the overall contents of a portfolio. No particular genre should do that. Creative writing has as much potential to link reading and writing thinking processes as does nonfiction. Fictional text is a terrific ignition to student writing that is perhaps the best way of all for the student to demonstrate both comprehension and appreciation of the story. For decades, teachers have developed and used successful methods of getting their students to write about stories they read. The fiction in readers and other books becomes models for genres and style that the students mimic to some degree. Or stories become the cornerstone of creative efforts that add to them, using and often expanding the set of characters or the settings and events presented in a story.

You are almost certain to have numerous successful techniques that produce creative efforts by your students. Student efforts that use literature as models, that create new events for characters in stories read, that analyze the problems and behaviors of characters in stories, and that provide new endings or beginnings are obvious ways to link reading and writing. And as experience demonstrates, students love to read their own writing and that of their peers. They will also show keen interest in analyzing them to note their development as readers, writers, and thinkers.

JOURNALS MAKE REVEALING ADDITIONS TO PORTFOLIOS   One of the numerous techniques used in many contemporary classrooms that can help students develop fluency as writers is the journal, and there are several types. Students can keep their journal entries in many ways. Relatively inexpensive books of bound blank pages are available, but the journal does not need to be so booklike. Ring notebook covers work fine with lined or unlined paper as it is needed, and they allow the student to easily transport entries from home to school. Plain paper will do, for that matter, and can be punched and bound or even merely stapled together whenever the journal keeper wishes.

Teachers have devised several types of journals with different purposes, but the aim is to keep the writing and expression in them as unrestricted and fluent as possible:

- **Personal journals:** Students are encouraged to write whatever they wish in these—with the understanding that the teacher will read them, parents may

AHEAD OF HER TIME?

Fifty years ago Catherine McLaughlin set aside two hours a week for her fifth-graders to read books of their choice. No reports on the books or record-keeping was required; she could see who was reading and who wasn't.

Soon she noticed that several of her students were writing rather than reading. Calmly she asked what they were composing and learned that they were writing original stories modeled on or inspired by the stories they had read.

That was just fine with Miss McLaughlin!

Soon about half of her students were budding authors. Caught up in their own narratives, many were taking them home to work on them—every night. As the stories were completed, class time was devoted to having volunteers read their stories aloud. The students loved the tales written by their classmates, and as a couple were finished, broke into enthusiastic applause.

That was all that there was to it. Miss McLaughlin didn't press for discussions tying the original stories to any books read. It was obvious to her that time allotted for reading had generated a keen appreciation of storytelling and of what it means to be an author and to write for an audience. It was a very simple activity, and quite simply one of the most memorable experiences her fifth-graders were to have that or any other year.

A Pizzaman's Adventure

One cold night in Milwaukee there is a pizzaman
name Gary. Gary was a poor man that live with
his Parents. He love this job delivering pizzas.
That's what he does for a living. He doesn't
has a high shool deploma, becaose his perents
didn't have enough money, they only have
enough money for food and cloth. Gary
is 21 year-old. When he didn't go to school,
he learn's at home with he mom and
dad. Gary live with his parents because
his parents don't has enough money to
bye a home. They live in a small
town and a small neiberhood. Everybody in his block knows him. Many people
in his block give Gary family stall like, food,
cloth, and furnicer. Gary's family lives in
a apartment, on the third floor. It is a small
apartment with two bedrooms. Gary's parents
sleep in on bedroom. and Gary sleep in the
other room. Gary has a jar where he keep
his tips and his pay checks. Every time it
get full he pots it In the bank. So
far he has $109.57. That is alot of
money forhim. He doesn't work in a
famous pizza place. so he doesn't get
lots of money. The pizza place he works

in is called pizza palace, Not many people know the
place. One night when Gary was at work, some thing strn:
happened. Gary, his boss yelbed. You got another ordc
O.k, give me the address and the pizza and I'll
go said Gary. I'll just give you the adress, and
you can get the pizza later. What! Do I
have to go to 1306 Baff street, Gary yelled. What is wrong
with that Why don't you like 1306. No it not that, I
don't mean 1306, I ment Boff street. I hate that neit
hood! It's so creepy, and theres more. It's weird, ugly
strange. The people are weird and the houses, thier
like the house on those old monster movies, they
give the creeps! How do you know? Because I
went to that neiberhood trying to finda house.
Gary answered. SO wat. I'm not going, yes you
are, I'm not going, yes you are. I'm not going,
it you jot, O.K. I'll go. Gary smiled. When
he got there, his legs was shaking. He got
closer and knoked the door. knok, knok,
knok. Oh hello there. AHH! He almost droped th:
pizza. Oh sorry about that. The old man gave
him a calone bottal instead of tip, the old
man said it will help him on his adventure. The
next morning Gary took out the trash. The
trash can was In the ally. Garx was always
sceard to go there. He herd some gun shots!
He went in the room. The guys saw him
they chase Gary down the bbck to a ally.
he keapt look back. Then he hit a wall.
It was a dead end! The crooks came
closer. We got you now boy.

To Be Continued....

This creative effort by a sixth-grader was so involving for its author that it generated a serial.

see them, and other students might somehow get hold of them. The teacher
is sometimes advised to be especially cautious in using these for any assessment, and certainly not to rate or grade them. They are valuable in revealing
much about student interests, including reading interests, backgrounds relevant to constructing meaning with language, and other language-relevant
information.

- **Dialogue journals:** These are kept by the student with another person—the
  teacher or a classmate. The participants both make entries, responding to each
  other, exchanging written comments on a regular basis. This kind of evolving
  exchange can become an important and meaningful experience for some students, and it tends to loosen the pen, so to speak.

  Teachers who partake in dialogue journals with students often ask questions
  of the student in writing intended to encourage longer written responses.
  The teacher's entries should indicate a sensitive and careful reading of what
  the student has written but avoid provoking personal revelations that cannot
  safely be kept in the portfolio. At the same time, however, the teacher reveals
  some of his or her feelings, opinions, and experiences.

10-13-92

Dear Brenda,

Hi how are you? I'm fine., I am 10 years old. My birthday is April 5, 1982. How old are you? I have one brother no sisters. Do you have any brothers or sisters? What kind of muisc do you like? Can I have a picture of your baby? My favorite kind of music is rock and roll and rap. What is your favorite group? Mine is Def leppord. Write back.

Your friend,
Bevie

Dear Bevie,

I am 23 years old. My birthday is on March 22nd. I have one brother who is 26 and one sister who is 31. I like all kinds of music, but my favorite is country. Yes, you may have a picture of my baby. I will try to remember to bring it next week. My baby's name is Christian. He was born on May 8th.

What other kinds of things do you enjoy besides music? Do you have any pets? Do you like to go shopping? Do you have any favorite games? I like to play softball, and collect clowns of all types. I also like to cook. My favorite things to cook are anything chocolate!

What are you doing your research on? Are you working with anyone on your research? What are you going to do with the information you find while doing your research?

Have a good week! I will see you monday!

Brenda

In an actual dialogue journal, a student and the college intern working in her class get to know each other.

With reasonable care, such entries can demonstrate that writing is an appropriate means of risk-taking. As successful exchanges develop, students often begin to respond with eagerness. Teacher/student dialogue journals often lead to the student quickly establishing such an exchange with one or more classmates.

- **Literature response journals:** In this type of journal, students write informally about things that they have read. Some teachers promote reading and their use by requiring a minimal number of entries a week. Class time is often structured for students to share from these journals, and some teachers conduct occasional or regular "reading conferences" in addition to portfolio conferences. The literature response journal is the focus of these reading conferences.

- **Issue journals:** The teacher presents topics that are controversial or present problems or needs for public decision making, and students are invited to respond to the presentation in the issue journal. Or the teacher may note a topic of keen interest to a particular student and encourage him or her to start and keep a running journal of entries on that topic.

Traditionally, a journal is a kind of record into which someone writes thoughts that are frequently dated and are sometimes personal and introspective. A journal is something like a diary, often written in the first person, as a diary is; but unlike a diary, the journal is not intended necessarily as a daily record of events. A faithful diary keeper feels obligated to note that nothing worth recording has occurred on a particular day, but a journal keeper usually awaits an idea, an inspiration, or some other reason for making an entry in the journal.

Although a journal may indeed record interesting things that happen or are witnessed on particular days, it can also record *any* thoughts the journal keeper has. Some diaries are actually journals in that they contain longer, more descriptive entries that reveal many of the diarist's thoughts. In some journals, diarylike accounts may be spliced among essays that present the journal keeper's thoughts on various issues and topics. Other entries may be poems or sketches, which may be entered with the intention of using them later in stories or other pieces of writing.

Journals invite more creative entries. Those of literary or historical merit are often beautifully descriptive, philosophical, or historically informative. Many, like the *Diary* Samuel Pepys kept in code for nine years, describe events and personalities of the times. Pepys was eventually jailed for the political thoughts he revealed in his diary. Anne Frank's diary of her family's existence while hiding out in an attic in Holland from the Nazi troops gains stature as a journal both because it is hauntingly affective and because it documents historically significant experience from a unique perspective. It also reads like a kind of novel, creating great suspense and intense empathy for the people in it.

In explaining journals to your students, it is not vital for you or them to distinguish between diaries and journals in any definitive way; it is acceptable to explain that they are so alike in may ways that diaries can become journals, and journals can be quite diarylike.

Both journals and diaries reveal a great deal about their keepers. The style of a journal is sometimes *stream of consciousness*. That is, the writer tends to record thoughts as they occur and can be put down on paper. The values, interests, and concerns of your student become quite apparent in a journal that is kept for any length of time—even if the journal is stylized more as informal little essays rather than as personal revelations.

These personal aspects of journals can disqualify them as good inclusions in portfolios. Students should understand that any journal kept in their portfolios will almost certainly be read by others. You will read it, and since the portfolios will be kept out where they are accessible, it is quite possible that other students will read it as well, even if you ask the class not to do that without the owner's permission. So students who keep journals in their portfolios should write for an audience that is bigger than just

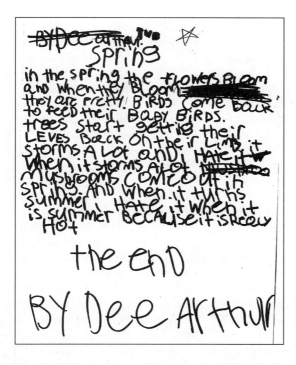

Journal entries can lead to very personal reactions as in this page from the journal of a third-grader.

themselves. That kind of audience focus is not uncommon among journals and journal keepers, who have often kept them with the intention that they be published.

On the other hand, the kind of informal, stream of consciousness that journal keeping tends to promote needs to be valued in order to promote writing. Some students cannot write that way if they are overly conscious of an audience other than themselves. For this reason, teachers may decide not to include the journal in portfolios kept in an easily accessible place in the classroom, but to collect them occasionally and at the same time as they are examining the portfolios.

Despite the problem of their being vulnerable to uninvited readers, journals can be very valuable inclusions in portfolios. They are, first and foremost, warehouses of ideas that students can develop in other writing. Journals can be full of snippets, tidbits, and capsulated stories. They can be trial space for expressing ideas that may make good essays. They can allow a writer to play with language—to test diction and phrasing, some of which may be turned into poetry later, some of which may find its way into presentations before the class or other groups. They are ideal places for sketches and descriptions that can be used in stories. For many students, they provide the connections from the ideas they have read to stimuli for stories they write. Students should be encouraged to use their journal entries in this way.

One way to do that is for the teacher to note in a student's journal the entries and ideas that are potential seeds for longer efforts and to suggest that the student develop them. It is not a good idea for the teacher to mark on the student's journal, so you will have to make a mental note to do this, or attach a temporary note in some way. It is one thing to strike an agreement that the journal will be exposed to the teacher, who will discreetly respect the student's privacy; but it is another matter for someone other than the student to actually write in the journal unless it is intended to support a dialogue.

Above all, journals are a wonderful place to reflect on oneself, what one understands, believes, and dreams. Primarily, the joy of a journal materializes as entries accrue and the student senses that by writing about feelings and ideas, he or she can clarify what he believes, prefers, disparages, and the like. Journals can teach their writers a lot about

WHAT MAKES A JOURNAL SO SPECIAL?

The household goods belonging to a stylish woman were being sold at a small country auction. There were excellent old quilts and watercolors of Paris and other places the woman had visited. There were two small illuminated manuscripts with notes that said they were hundreds of years old; there was large pot signed by Picasso. There were many unusual, interesting, and beautiful books.

Other auction-goers had been eyeing a large cardboard box of oil paints and other supplies. It also held a tiny ringed notebook that had been manufactured, perhaps to hold addresses. On its plain looseleaf pages were terse but thoughtful entries written by the woman aboard the Queen Mary during an Atlantic crossing in the late 1930s. These included detailed descriptions of leisurely activities and of fellow voyagers. In the margins there were delicate little ink sketches of stylishly clad passengers lounging in deck chairs, climbing stairways, and leaning against the rails. Each illustration accompanying the words about life aboard that luxury liner was washed with watercolors.

Crossing on such a ship had to be the appropriate place—the ideal time perfectly paced—to keep a journal. The tiny volume had been tossed into the box by someone cleaning out the woman's home. It lay amid half-squeezed tubes of oil paints, canvas stretchers, a broken easel, and other supplies. Perhaps, one bidder mused optimistically, no one else had noticed it—or valued it much if it had been examined and tossed back into the box.

But when the selling of that lot began, the bids came from all over the crowded little room, and in barely more than a minute the box was out of the financial reach of all but one. A small crowd gathered around the prevailing bidder. Was she an artist after the supplies? Had she noticed the journal? Would she sell it?

Slowly she reached far down into the box to claim the prize. The losers watched wistfully, regretting that they hadn't bid higher. They would think of that wonderfully personal and beautiful little book often, wishing they could see it again, could read, study, and enjoy it at their own paces.

themselves. So journals are an excellent place for a student to evaluate the total contents of the portfolio—to note things about his or her reading and writing experiences.

If all of this sounds a bit sophisticated for use with younger students, please keep in mind that the journal lays practically no requirements on the writer—as to form, diction, or content. The only thing required of a journal keeper is some degree of frequency in making entries. It need not be daily; on the other hand, it may include several entries in the same   day. Realize, too, that the writing in a journal is probably as close to *verbal doodling* as a writer can get. Many journals, including those kept by adults, are heavily adorned with drawings and sketches. In short, journals are uniquely what their keepers make of them, and having one or more in a portfolio helps establish a clear sense of ownership.

OTHER KINDS OF PERSONAL CORRESPONDENCE HAVE A HIGH POTENTIAL TO BE AUTHENTIC   Letter writing is a language use that continues through most persons' lives, so it follows that letters that can be shared with audiences other than the addressee should be highly authentic portfolio inclusions. It can be argued, as well, that letters are among the easiest type of writing that one can need to do—because the audience, and often the primary topic, are so clearly focused and defined.

There are, of course, concerns about correct letter form that often dominate a young writer's, and often a teacher's, attention and can smother any intention to emphasize content. But if letters kept in the portfolio are treated as drafts, the attention to form can be far less adamant, and the emphasis can be on content.

Similar to letters are notes, memos, and cards. These are particularly valuable formats to promote for the portfolio, because they can be done relatively quickly when your students have only a matter of 10 or 15 minutes or so to work on their collections.

KEEP YOUR LIMITED OPTION TO SELECT PAPERS TO GO INTO THE PORTFOLIOS   The teacher may also place pieces of student work into the portfolio. Some may be assignments that all class members are required to include. You may also select a piece that a student has overlooked or has considered and rejected. If the student

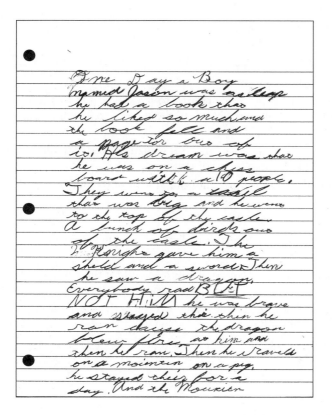
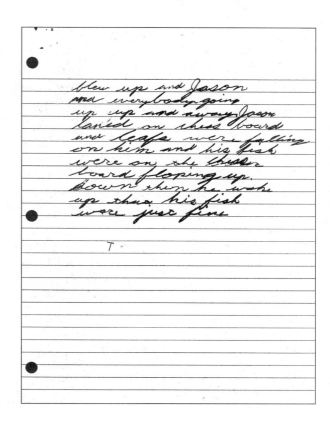

Here is a very unpolished draft that a boy had decided not to put into his portfolio until his teacher suggested that it had the seed for an interesting story and encouraged him to revise and expand it.

asks, or if you sense that you have inadvertently challenged the student's sense of controlling the collection, it is important that you explain why such a piece is being selected. You may even staple a note to it if you wish, explaining why it has been included. One way to try to avoid this feeling in the student is to be sure that you give the student adequate opportunity to select the piece you want in the collection.

Even though it is not recommended that the teacher set out criteria for including materials in the portfolio, the teacher will need to indicate to the students the different kinds of things they can consider for inclusion. In beginning portfolio collections, students cannot be expected to understand all their options and why they might want certain things in their collections. They will have to rely on their teacher to point out what they might collect and why.

Here are some criteria that teachers often use in selecting pieces for inclusion in the portfolio:

- Will having this in the portfolio help show the breadth of a student's reading and writing and give a more complete picture of how the student's language ability is developing?
- Will this show growth and development as a reader, writer, and thinker?
- Is this evidence of how the student is using language outside of school?
- Will this promote—or is it evidence of—self-assessing and changes in language use based on self-evaluation?
- Does this show the student organizing thought and using thinking strategies; solving problems by using comparison, categorizing, induction or deduction, synthesis, summarizing?

- Does this demonstrate a clear purpose for writing and reading, such as persuasion or informing a particular audience?
- Does this inform on and relate to the student's interest and background?
- Does this represent an authentic experience?
- Does this fulfill a personal goal or objective related to language use? Is it a statement of a new objective or goal, or could it lead the student to formulate a new objective or goal?
- Is the structure of this piece of writing revealing? Is it well organized? Should the student consider its organization in terms of revision?
- Does this reveal the student's sense of the author of a text or of the audience for a piece of writing?
- Is there an appealing voice to this piece?
- Does this demonstrate the student's command of diction or the need to command a more powerful vocabulary?
- Is there clarity and focus in this expression, or is there a need for the student to identify the lack of those qualities?
- Does this show new evidence of how well the student controls the mechanics of language when expressing himself or herself?
- Is there an indication of how well the student uses details to develop and modify ideas?

HOW CAN I GET STUDENTS TO START ANALYZING WHAT THEY COLLECT?

Much of the analysis that your students do can be promoted by good questions you ask about the pieces in their collections. This will be happening informally as they work with their portfolios during class time and during the all-important student/teacher conferences that you should schedule regularly.

In addition, you can encourage your students to use numerous guide sheets that promote the sorting (categorizing), organization, analysis, and evaluation that constitute the self-analysis that you hope will become habitual. Some of these direct the student to organize and catalog; others focus on the analysis and/or evaluation of individual pieces in a student's collection; others promote analysis across numerous pieces of writing. Some of these are designed to reveal progress and development in language and thinking skills and behaviors and to direct and articulate subsequent activities and goals. They also can help your students understand their own interests, needs, and feelings, as reflected by the things they read, write, and think.

SOME GOOD ADVICE FROM TEXAS

In a guide for teachers on how to use portfolio assessment, the state of Texas suggests that teachers may want to be sure that portfolios do not overlook outstanding student work that shows:

- Unusual presentations of ideas.
- Advanced work beyond age or grade level.
- Complex or intricate presentations of ideas.
- Evidence of in-depth understanding of ideas or skills.

- Resourceful and/or clever use of materials.
- Evidence of support of research for an idea.
- Organization that communicates effectively.
- Evidence of high interest and perseverance.

The source of this list is cited in Appendix B under a citation to Evelyn L. Hiatt in "Other Sources About Portfolio Assessment."

Here are some of these specific records and guides:

- The Reading Log.
- The Writing Log.
- Table of Contents.
- Notes kept during student/teacher conference.
- Checklists that guide student self-assessment.
- Notes about self- and teacher observations, rationale for inclusion of particular pieces, metacognitive analyses of particular materials.
- Reading and writing response sheets.
- Periodic synopses/analyses/progress notes.
- Notes/explanations written by the student for portfolio viewers.
- Artifacts, and notes related to ideas, issues, and topics of interest that become the grist for future language use.
- Anecdotal records of phenomena the teacher notes that are relevant to the student's development as a language user.

The student should keep these sheets to initiate the kind of evaluative thinking important to self-assessment. They lead the student to thinking that involves comparison, classification, sequential considerations, and cause-and-effect relationships. They promote the brainstorming and notetaking and jot listing that stimulate and guide other writing.

There are numerous forms that generate analysis in Appendix C and a discussion of how to use them in Chapter 4. Some are designed particularly for younger students. There are also small notes for the reactions of parents, teachers, and fellow students. As your students are using them for the first time, be available to assist them if necessary.

READING AND WRITING LOGS ARE THE FIRST STEP IN ORGANIZING THE PORTFOLIO   The reading log and the writing log—or a combined reading/writing log—are, quite simply, a list of what the student writes and reads with room to indicate when it was done and to make notes about the language experience. Most descriptions of portfolios recommend keeping a separate log for what is read and one for what is written. The current emphasis on the integration of the two language activities, however, has led some teachers to have students keep one combined log with a column indicating whether the entry is for reading or writing.

To begin their logs, students write their names on the top of each page and number it. As they finish reading or listening to stories and other texts, they enter the title in the left-hand column and the author's name in the column to the right of that. If it is a combined log, an *R* is entered to indicate it is a reading experience and a *W* if it is a piece of writing.

The forms are kept as simple as possible for very young readers, who may need some assistance in getting started nonetheless. A column for the date is optional, but can help clarify the sequence indicated by the order of the entries. Finally, reactions or annotations are circled or written on the right. The far right-hand column is a place for the student to rate the piece of writing or the text read or heard.

Some teachers create logs with columns on "What the writing or text is about" and that tell why the student likes or does not like the text or piece of writing. It should be

LET THEM LEARN
FROM EACH OTHER

TIP

Permit your students to work in pairs or small groups at different times, to look at each other's work, and to make collaborative recommendations for additions to the portfolios.

kept in mind, however, that it is relatively easy to overload the student with procedural requirements and thus press all of the joy out of the portfolio experience! It is recommended that adaptations of suggestions made in this book simplify rather than complicate procedures.

One very useful activity that you might have students who keep a combined log engage in before they conference with you is to draw lines and arrows from things they have written to those stories they have read that their writing reminds them of. Beginning to write like a favorite author, borrowing ideas and language structures, and being able to note these are the mark of growing sophistication of readers and writers.

Brod Bagert penned a short poem "Good Models," that emphasizes this connection. It is reprinted here from *The Gooch Machine: Poems for Children to Perform*, Honesdale, PA: Boyds Mills Press, 1997, p. 30.

I read my first poem
And I felt like frowning,
It sounded too much
Like Elizabeth Browning.

Then in my next poem
I noticed a change,
I was Emily Dickinson—
Quiet and strange.

Now it's happened again,
Please don't think I'm weird,
But today I'm Walt Whitman,
Without the long beard.

When I read all my writing
I discover a rule:
I write like the poets
We're reading at school.

Brod Bagert

The last two lines of Brod Bagert's poem capture the essence of the connection between reading and writing and the combined reading/writing log and the student's effort to note the comparisons between their writing. It explains how what they have read will pay rich benefits in producing more thoughtful and insightful writers—and readers.

As the log is introduced, time should be allowed for the students to make their first entries to see if they need one-on-one assistance. It will be difficult—especially at first—for some students to remember the names of the stories they have heard or read, so it would be helpful for you to write the titles and authors' names on the chalkboard.

Allow some time at least every few days for students to go to their portfolios and fill in the log. The updating of reading/writing logs could become a regular Friday activity. Making the activity a routine practice will emphasize the importance of the log and will cause the students to remind themselves to remember what they have been reading and writing.

If the pieces of writing or pictures do not have titles, have the students print tag names for them on the top of each piece added to the portfolio. Be sure to invite students to enter stories read to them at home on their logs and to bring things written or drawn there to enter and add to the portfolios. Stress that it is all right if they do not remember the exact title or know the author's name. With the title in the author column, help the student print "home."

Since all research in reading and writing indicates that those students who read and write more become better readers and writers, it is very important that you applaud and encourage the growing logs. Students need to see for themselves that the more they do of it, the better they will be—and the better they become at reading and writing the more enjoyable and useful it will be for them. The logs are your (and their) insights into their developing reading and writing habits.

THE TABLE OF CONTENTS SHOWS THE STUDENT'S ORGANIZATION SCHEME   An important step in the self-assessment process calls for the student to organize the material in the portfolio after a number of pieces have been collected. A good time for students to do this is just prior to teacher/student conferences. When the student is organizing or reorganizing the portfolio he or she is reviewing and reflecting about what has been read and written. This requires the examination of the portfolio contents in order to categorize it. It may also include discarding things the student feels are unimportant.

The organizing is accomplished by putting the papers into different piles according to some categorization scheme that is meaningful to the student. The scheme, for example, could be as simple as things the student is most proud of, those he is not sure about, or those he feels are not his best. It could be based on topics or types of writing or some other sorting distinction. The piles are put in some order meaningful to the student, and some order (often based on when the papers were created) may be created within the piles before the papers are returned to the portfolio.

Then the student should create a table of contents showing the order in which things are included in the portfolio, a written explanation of the organization scheme, or both. The table of contents lists the title of each item included in the order in which it appears. Some students may decide to number their pages so they can put the page numbers on the table of contents.

> # The Story of my Portfolio
>
> On the front is a picture of me. I have blue eyes. I have blonde hair, but there's not a blonde crayon so I used purple instead because I like purple. I have fingers and toes because I need them. When I wrote my name, I had to put it backwards because there's not room to put it the other way.
>
> On the back is a picture of a turtle. I am getting a turtle. I want to name it Mikie so I hope it is a boy. He is a happy turtle because he likes me.

Along with their table of contents, students can attach a written explanation of their organization scheme, as this third-grade girl has done.

Like the log, the table of contents can have a place for comments about the inclusions as a kind of annotation. The table serves as a guide to finding things in the portfolio, of course; but more importantly, creating it leads the student to the first genuine analysis of the work collected by requiring attention to the nature of each piece.

Some students keeping a combined reading and writing log may become confused by the fact that the reading entries will not show up on the table of contents. Explain patiently that the table is for listing things actually in the portfolio. The combined log also includes all the things a student reads.

Wait until most of your students have enough in their portfolios to organize and then introduce the table of contents and explain how to use it, moving about the room to assist as needed. Depending on the length of your portfolio sessions, you may need to devote more than one to filling out the table of contents for the first time.

A problem with the table develops if it inhibits the student from rethinking and reorganizing materials later in a different way that has new meaning for the student after subsequent analysis of portfolio contents. The objective should be to challenge them to reanalyze in ways that can reveal more about their progress as language users, thinkers, and individuals.

There is a blackline master of the "Student/ Teacher Conference Notes" sheet in the teacher section of Appendix C. It is not vital that you introduce the form to the entire class since you will be with each student during his or her conference to explain how it works. Effective approaches to conferencing and keeping notes are in Chapter 5.

THE STUDENT/TEACHER CONFERENCE NOTES ARE ESSENTIAL

During each formal student/teacher conference that you will be scheduling, the student and teacher write notes about their joint evaluation. This can be done on separate pieces of paper or on a shared, two-sided record like the one provided in Appendix C. Passing the sheet back and forth in order to record observations and decisions and to react to each other's comments is a bit awkward, but the combined sheet assures that both the student and teacher get to read what the other has written. If separate sheets are used, they should be divided by a vertical line so the student can add comments to the left of the teacher's on the teacher note sheet and the teacher can do the same on the student sheet. They need to be passed back and forth at times during the conference so this can happen.

Conference notes should tend to cite improvements and development that you and the student agree upon and discuss. It is a good idea to encourage the student during the conference to set one or more goals for language development and to make notes on the sheet to that effect. There are, as well, other sheets that summarize student progress that can be used during the conference, as well as at other times during informal exchanges with the student. But there should be note sheets for at least four formal conferences in the portfolio by the end of the year.

OTHER NOTES AND MEMOS CAN PROMOTE SELF-ASSESSMENT

Other types of notes can promote self-assessment. Periodically, as the collection is analyzed, the student may choose to write a kind of synopsis of what has been learned about his or her language development over a period of several weeks. This may be fairly inclusive or can focus on one or more major observations. A good time for the students to do this is right before each student/teacher conference or as a front-piece for a show portfolio that will be on display during back-to-school night or is pulled from the working portfolio for some other purpose.

Other notes that student and teacher may include in the portfolio are optional and should not be required. If you are requiring that the student keep a log, keep updating a table of contents, and perhaps write periodic synopses of his or her analysis of the collection, you are using the portfolios as an effective teaching tool. However, you can add other activities to make the portfolio even more analytical and meaningful by asking the students to add their own anecdotes or rationale notes when there is time to do so. Such additions to the collection are valuable. If a student seems eager to say something about one of the things he or she has written, to write a reaction or takeoff on something read, or to contribute a special self-observation, be sure to encourage that it be done.

Special response sheets can be made available to your students as options so they can use them to write about particular texts or to react to their own writing. Small notes rationalizing particular inclusions can be filled out by either the student or the teacher and stapled to the papers they refer to.

Anecdotal observations that you wish to share with a student about his or her language behavior can be added when the occasion arises. You may wish to use checklists of approaches or steps to self-analysis to assist the students when they are working with their portfolios.

Examples of this kind of tool are found in Appendix C and can be duplicated for use.

SOME GENERAL ADVICE ABOUT INCLUSIONS

While there is no absolute prescription of what a portfolio should contain, and students and/or teachers can select from numerous types of materials, some general guidelines are worth noting.

YOUR STUDENTS' COLLECTIONS SHOULD BE WORKING, NOT SHOW, PORTFOLIOS

One factor clearly distinguishes the successful student language arts portfolio from the show portfolios that have been used for many years to evaluate the performance of various kinds of professional workers and students in some subject areas. The successful language arts collection is not a *show* portfolio made up primarily of final drafts and/or just the student's best work; it should be a *working* portfolio!

If a language arts portfolio is to serve assessment and instruction and the development of the student as a self-assessor, it needs to be a continually growing collection both of work in progress and of finished work. It can be, in addition, a packet of ideas waiting like seeds to be planted and cultivated as new writing, thinking, and directed reading. It is also a place where the student keeps his or her personal records that are relevant to the collection—such as logs of things read and written. All these kinds of materials are found in a *working portfolio.*

Chapter 1 noted how artists, photographers, models, and other professionals rely on the show portfolio when setting out to interview for a commission or job. The collection is normally selected as the kind of work the artist thinks will be preferred by whoever will look at it. Without an exact handle on what the audience may be looking for, the artist attempts to display some range of his or her best work. This portfolio is selected from many sketches or photographs that have led to the more finished work in it.

It is back amid all the work unfinished, in progress, rejected, and so on that the artist feels most at home, contemplates his or her progress, and plans what will be drawn, painted, sculpted, or photographed next. *The artist is apt to spend considerable time examining it, critiquing it, and rearranging it.* The collection, which may fill the entire studio and other areas, is the equivalent of the artist's *working portfolio.*

Like the artist who might breathe a sigh of relief and of relaxed ownership and control when returning to the familiar studio after interviewing for work, the student should feel a distinct territorial comfort when opening and working with his or her portfolio in the classroom. It is then that the student enters his or her "space," so to speak. Portfolio assessment depends on being able to use working portfolios in an ongoing, evolving process that allows students to grow and learn about themselves as thinkers and language users. The portfolios also allow the teacher to learn this, as well as to get an indication of how effective instruction has been. Too often, prescriptions for student classroom language arts portfolios visualize the kind of portfolios used to assess the work of artists, designers, and the like. But the *self-assessment* that the classroom portfolio should promote, encourage, and support depends on a range of work that covers much more than just examples of the student's best finished work.

Some teachers may prefer to have the student select and build a show portfolio from the working portfolio for a particular audience and/or a particular occasion—to be on display during back-to-school night, for example, or to be submitted to a supervisor or principal as a demonstration of the student's progress. Yet even in those instances, the classroom-based portfolio is different from the professional show portfolio.

One of the key interests of others who examine a student's portfolio should be to look for the processes the student uses, how well she or he commands language behaviors, and what development of language ability is obvious over time. Thus, any show portfolio a student selects and arranges ought to include drafts and stages of some of the finished work included.

Selecting and arranging an occasional show portfolio is a possible way to involve the student in analyzing the contents of the working portfolio. On the other hand, this activity can be exercised on the whole working portfolio as well to ready it for analysis and assessment by others. In short, when the bulk of the material and other factors allow, the working portfolio can serve the assessment needs met by show portfolios and may well serve them better—while serving additional assessment concerns as well.

APPEARANCE SHOULD NOT BE OVEREMPHASIZED

The working portfolio will never look as "presentable" as a show portfolio. It is important for others who look into portfolios in order to assess a student's reading, writing, and thinking to understand that they are not intended as tools to develop good housekeeping skills. If, like the authors of this book, you had the opportunity to view the more successful language arts portfolios in use in many classrooms, you, too, would come to the following generalization: A messy portfolio—one that is packed with a variety of materials of different sizes, colors, stock, and so forth that tend to stick out of the sides of whatever holder is used—is, more often than not, a good and useful portfolio.

Such a portfolio is probably being used regularly by a student who is developing a habit of self-assessing. It looks as it does because the student is adding to it and is including pictures and clippings of things that interest him or her. Once in the holder, the materials, which are apt to vary in shape and size, are shuffled around periodically; and as they are put and/or fall into place in some order meaningful to the student, they may well become a bit "dog-eared."

There almost always tends to be a genuine sense of student ownership of such collections. An extremely tidy portfolio is probably *not* a working portfolio and thus does not provide the student and teacher the opportunity to observe process and note progress or to review, confirm, and relate interests. Generally, one observes that very tidy portfolios are not used very often and may not even be readily available to the students, who sense that they are actually the property of the teacher.

PORTFOLIOS SHOULD REPORT ON INSTRUCTIONAL GOALS AND OBJECTIVES

Your philosophy of language development and your instructional objectives and goals should set the criteria of what you add to the portfolios students keep in your classroom. Indirectly, your instructional goals and objectives should have considerable influence on what the student selects as well. It just makes sense. The portfolio will contain writing from things your students are doing in school and out. And you will be hoping to get your students involved in activities that you feel will develop their abilities to read and write and think.

What you believe about language development should set your instructional objectives and goals, and they, in turn, should help structure the learning experiences you want your students to have. If the materials in their portfolios include the products that result from those experiences, you will be able to assess your students' progress in achieving those objectives and goals. If it sounds simple and logical, that's because it is!

The table "How Your Beliefs Affect Your Portfolio Assessment Program" gives examples that are not uncommon among the many that teachers hold and that help structure curricula. With them are suggestions of the kind of reading/writing activities

HOW YOUR BELIEFS AFFECT YOUR PORTFOLIO ASSESSMENT PROGRAM

TABLE 3 • 1

What Teacher Believes	Activities the Belief Recommends	What Goes Into the Portfolio	Assessment the Portfolio Supports
Language development occurs mainly from using language; thus promoting fluency is a primary objective.	Students write and/or draw several times a day to create pictures with captions, papers, letters, journals, notes, etc. The teacher reads to students and/or has them read frequently.	The portfolios contain many samples of writing as papers, on pictures, etc. The quantity of writing beyond lower elementary grades is of many types, and both pictures and writing frequently respond to reading.	The sheer quantity of portfolio contents demands sorting and other attention, engaging the students in self-assessment. Reading and writing logs grow with interesting reactions.
Readers comprehend more effectively when they understand their purposes for reading particular texts.	Before reading to kindergarten and first-grade children, the teacher talks about the story so they can identify favorite things to listen for. Many assignments grow out of student expression of things students want to accomplish. The teacher relates these to texts recommended and made available and translates the student objective into opportunities to write.	The captions with pictures in lower elementary grades reveal reactions to stories read and read aloud to them. Many pieces of writing included in the portfolio translate what has been read into syntheses that demonstrate understanding and into arguments that persuade, etc.	Teacher questioning is able to guide student to analysis/evaluation of his/her captioned drawings and/or reading/writing to decide how well objectives have been met, how they have changed, etc.
Effective writers almost always have an audience in mind and write to meet its needs.	Many writing activities are geared to types that promote audience awareness—letters, news stories, reports, editorials, etc. Captioned reactions to reading at lowest grades are addressed to parents.	Teacher requires students to select a minimum of several pieces a week to put in their portfolios, assuring materials for audience analysis. Original captioned drawings are sent home to parents and copies go into portfolio.	Students are required to sort materials (temporarily) by audience and to consider what they did in writing to write especially for different audiences. In conference, children are asked to remember how parents reacted to drawings taken home.

continued

	continued		
T A B L E 3 • 1	**What Teacher Believes**	**Activities the Belief Recommends**	**What Goes Into the Portfolio**	**Assessment the Portfolio Supports**
	An acceptance of the importance of mechanical correctness comes with the awareness that being clear depends on it.	Students work in teams as writers/editors of each other's stories to produce newsletters and other products. While respecting and valuing inventive spelling, teacher notes words spelled traditionally and praises students.	Copies of things each student writes for the publication go in the portfolio as they were edited by classmates along with the finished product and samples of editing done on classmates' writing. Students highlight traditionally spelled words in collection.	Teacher questioning guides student to analyze and note mechanical aspects of language that have been considered important for clarity. Teacher praises both traditional and inventive spelling.
	Good fictional style is subconsciously enjoyed by readers who show their appreciation by adopting it as a model.	Activities provide opportunities to tell or write new beginnings, endings, other story events, parodies, etc. Teacher picks at least one patterned story that students can imitate.	The portfolio should contain an ample amount of this kind of creative writing or, in the case of youngest students, tapes of tellings that match drawings.	The portfolio supports discussion of fiction features in terms of writing style and reading appreciation.
	One basis of most comprehension and written expression is some treatment of detail.	Activities relate to texts and writing assignments that are or should be detail-rich. Youngest students are given chance to retell, and are encouraged with good questioning to use details.	The samples in the portfolio collection are probably rich in details.	The way students organize their collections can reveal much about their grasp of/interest in particular details. Teacher questioning can focus on how details have been related— comparison, sequence, classification, etc. Based on drawings and taped retellings, teacher presses younger students for some details during conference.

that could facilitate reaching them, the kind of emphasis the portfolio collection might have, and just one or two assessments that the collection should support. There are separate suggestions in the chart for kindergarten and first-grade children and for the grades above these.

The intent of presenting these is not to suggest what you should believe about language development or that the activities suggested here for the objectives have priority over those you may think of yourself. The point is to demonstrate how teacher beliefs/ philosophies and instructional objectives can relate to what goes into portfolios.

AS MUCH WRITING AS POSSIBLE
SHOULD RESPOND TO READING

Tying writing activities to reading and vice versa is a vital general instructional approach that should be reflected in assessment, so it is important that portfolios contain as many examples of student responses to reading as possible. Doing this is not just a matter of being theoretically correct or in tune with our increasing understanding of how language develops; methodologies based on the theory have gained broad endorsement because they have proven effective.

Theory about language development tells us that to be most effective, reading and writing instruction should be authentic. When students write about what they read, comprehending the material gains some authenticity for them—particularly if they are reacting freely to what has been read. When reading is prompted and/or directed by what has been written, it is far more certain that it has a genuine purpose and will be an authentic experience. When the two language activities are truly interactive, the possibilities of the experience really meaning something to the student are greatly increased.

Students can be encouraged to extend nonfiction explanations or descriptions as a genuine reaction, to take or add personal perspectives to issues depicted in texts, to support or contest argumentative essays, or to build on or react to texts in other ways. The characters in stories read to or by beginning readers can be personalized so that student reactions tend to be expressing concern for new friends and/or are addressed directly to the characters.

Of course, a teacher can require reading that may serve little purpose for the students other than fulfilling the teacher's demand and then require the student to write something about it—and then based on what is written, require additional reading or rereading. But to fulfill their potential to involve the student, the reading and writing need to serve a purpose that students value; that is, be minimally related to a topic of interest to them.

Meanwhile, writing about or in response to what has been read promotes comprehension and leads students to seek new texts to read about what has been learned, hoping to learn more. The authenticity and appeal of that reading is assured by the student-set purpose.

Experienced teachers and professional journals are replete with original ideas that will generate writing about reading. Here are just a few examples:

- For kindergarten and first-grade students, read a story aloud and have them draw their favorite part, writing what they can and wish to note on the picture. Print key words from the story title on the chalkboard for students to copy onto the paper. If necessary, reread the story and invite them to write reactions as you read. Their writing will probably contain some inventive spelling and it may range from single words to whole ideas, so if necessary, help students attach a sheet of paper to the drawing. When they are finished, suggest that they may want to put the effort into their portfolios.

USE PREDICTION!   **TIP**

As your students are finishing reading or listening to a story, pause to have them predict how it will end. Then finish the story and see how well they predicted. Finally, have your students predict what might happen next in the story.

You could let volunteers take turns looking into a crystal ball or tea leaves, and have them draw and caption their predictions. Remind them that they can add these things to their portfolios.

A First-Grader Gets It Exactly Right!

A brief example from one first-grade classroom highlights the value of tying reading and writing together. Patti Felton, a first-grade teacher we know, had been integrating reading and writing for her students for several years. One activity she used to help students learn about writing from reading was to keep a box of books for each of the students' favorite authors. When the students wanted to read a book by Shel Silverstein, Eric Carll, Dr. Seuss, or others they could go to the appropriate box and get the book. This teacher thought boxes worked better than shelves, which are often too high for the students, and the boxes could be moved around the room to be in close proximity to comfortable reading corners she had set up around the room.

She emphasized the reading/writing connection by having the students write their own stories in the style of Eric Carll, Shel Silverstein, or other authors and add each of them to the appropriate box. The students learned to read the books carefully so they could write like their favorite author. Often the students' stories were only drawings that mimicked the favorite author, and sometimes they were about the same topic as the book by the favorite author. However, the students were all sure they wrote like their favorite author and they were always ready to argue that their stories were just about as good as those created by their favorite authors.

One of the authors of this book thought it would be a useful teaching tool if he could videotape these first-graders. The teacher agreed and a small group of the first-graders was asked to sit around a table and discuss with their teacher how they wrote like their favorite authors.

"I want to go first, Mrs. Felton."

"OK, Alice, you can go first." Alice always wanted to be first at everything. Some of the first-graders thought Alice was very smart and others just thought that Alice thought she was very smart.

"I'll read my story about the clouds," said Alice. She read her story, and Patti commented that it was a very nice story. Alice quickly responded that it was her Eric Carll story. Patti asked why it was her Eric Carll story.

"Because," said Alice, "Eric Carll uses a lot of color words in his story, and I used a lot of color words in my story." Neither Patti nor any of the first-graders at the table seemed surprised by this comment since they were always talking about how they wrote like their favorite authors.

"Do others of you write like a favorite author?" Patti prompted.

"Nope, not me!" Josh seemed to almost shout out. Josh was a first-grader who never seemed to want to do what anyone else was doing. "I don't write like my favorite author at all," he said with a proud smirk on his face.

"No, not you," said Patti in a very accepting and gentle response.

"Nope, not me!" Josh repeated.

Patti went on talking with the first-graders about their writing, and a few minutes later, Josh was heard to state almost too quietly to be picked up by the microphone, "I do sorta get my ideas from some of them."

Clea raised her hand and asked if she could read her story.

"Certainly," Patti replied.

"Good," Clea clapped. "I write like my favorite author just like Alice does."

"Ugh, who wants to be like Alice," Josh said as he looked at Patti to see if he was going to once again be told to respect others.

"Who is your favorite author?" Patti asked.

"Oh, I can't remember," answered Clea, "but he writes that silly stuff."

"Shel Silverstein," shouted out Alice.

"No, not him, the other one," said Clea with a furrowed brow. "I just can't remember his name."

"Oh, now I remember," smiled Clea. "I write like Dr. Seuss!"

"Well," said Clea, "Dr. Seuss taught me that when you write, it doesn't have to make any sense."

Patti smiled and the first-graders giggled just a bit. Even the cameraman smiled at Clea's comment.

Then Clea stated, with a big wonderful smile on her face, "IT JUST MATTERS IF YOU LIKE IT."

There it was: the most important statement about the connection between reading and writing. It just matters if you like it. A first-grader who summed it up in seven words. When you write, you are your first reader—and when you read what you have written, you must think about it because it is your words and ideas. The thinking connection that ties reading and writing together was knotted and adorned with a big ribbon by a first-grader in Patti Felton's first-grade classroom. A moment to be cherished and remembered: It just matters if you like it.

- Read a story aloud, modeling your reactions to it out loud (as a think-along). You may wish to pick a story with a theme you believe will catch the interest of most students, such as kindness to animals, keeping friends, or being a good winner. Then reread the story, pausing to encourage students to insert their

---

PLAY "PICK-A-PAL"!

Write the names of characters from several stories read in class recently. Ask students to write a description (or for youngest students, draw a picture) of the character they would like to have as a best friend. They should be careful not to use the character's name.

Then let volunteers read their descriptions or hold up their pictures so the rest of the class can guess who it is. When the character has been identified, have the student explain why he or she picked this pal.

Have students write their character pal's name on the back of the sheet and have them write why that character would make a good friend. Have younger students caption their drawings with these reasons as best they can on the front of the sheet.

Have the pictures added to the students' portfolios, and repeat the activity later in the year so you can compare the effort to note whether and how some students develop descriptive and persuasive powers.

---

reactions aloud. Next have students write (or draw and write) their reactions to the story. Suggest that the work can go into their portfolios if they wish.

- Have volunteers describe an interesting setting from a story read. Ask: Have you ever seen a place like this? Ask students to write and describe a place they have seen that reminds them of the story setting.

- Ask students to write a letter to someone in stories read recently, telling them about something that has happened to the students that is like or different from something that happened to the character.

- Have students read some directions for making something. Then ask them whether they could actually use the directions to make what is described. Ask them to write why or why not.

- Have students write to the author of a story or other text to tell him or her what they liked best or least in the text or to ask about something that is not clear to them. Let beginning readers draw what they have in mind and caption it. Suggest that students at higher levels tell the author what could have been done to improve the story. (Try to have an address for the author if some students want to mail their letters, or find the publisher's address. Ask whether anyone who is mailing the letter wants to have it copied for his or her portfolio.)

- Have students write and/or draw personal anecdotes that relate to a story read.

- Ask students to retell, in writing or on audiotape, something that happened in a story *but from a different point of view,* the way someone mentioned in the story might see it.

- Tell or write a story using characters in a story read but putting them in some other place/context.

- Write a letter to a friend telling what you think of a book you have read recently.

- Write something that could have happened to the characters in a story read before it begins.

Fiction can generate writing as effectively as nonfiction. Student writing that uses literature as models for creative writing, that creates new events for characters in stories read, that analyzes the problems and behaviors of characters in stories, or that provides new endings or beginnings or internal episodes makes an ideal addition to the portfolio.

The NAEP study as reported by Claudia Gentile is packed with examples from student portfolios and makes very interesting reading for teachers setting out with portfolio assessment. It is listed in Appendix B under "Sources Cited and Other Relevant Reading."

PORTFOLIO INCLUSIONS THAT REVEAL THINKING STRATEGIES ARE VERY VALUABLE

When the National Assessment for Educational Progress studied the use of portfolios by having a large sample of teachers and students send samples for analysis, it found that only 5 percent of the portfolios from eighth-graders, the oldest students in the study, contained any attempts to persuade. This traditionally accepted purpose for writing may be neglected, the study indicates; and the thinking strategies that serve it may not be practiced as much as one would wish either.

It is not the purpose of this book to stump for the teaching of higher-level critical-thinking behavior, but it can be appropriately noted that if such goals or objectives are being pursued in a classroom, one should certainly be able to appraise the results with portfolio collections. Minimally, it seems reasonable to encourage the teacher to use portfolios to develop students' abilities to summarize and synthesize, for this can be done with relatively uncomplicated activities.

Among the inclusions in your students' portfolios there should be some single pieces of writing that respond to more than one piece of reading. You can assure this by structuring an activity in which the student responds to multiple writing prompts: the same event described from two different perspectives; a descriptive piece accompanied by charts, graphs, or tables with information that is not in the text; two letters taking different sides of an issue.

At the lowest levels, you can read aloud or have students read two stories with distinctively different characters and then have the students make up stories that include at least one character from each of the stories. You may need to model this activity by having an original story of your own based on the stories to read aloud or tell.

This is a good way to promote synthesis, classification, comparison/contrast, and other analyses that tie thinking to reading comprehension and to effective written expression. This kind of activity can take texts from distinctively different genres that deal with the same general topic and let the student respond in one or more of them.

George Henry (1969) proposed the layering of such textual stimuli one at a time to build more intricately latticed concepts. His classic example began with a poem that extols the beauty of nature, moved to a journalistic report of a natural disaster, then to a piece about the prospects of humans harnessing nature for power, and finally to a persuasive piece on environmental concerns about the need to respect and protect nature from human misuse. Each stimulus is added as students are encouraged to synthesize and respond to the enlarging concept of *nature*.

George Henry's fascinating book is listed among the sources in Appendix B.

For elementary children, Betsy Byar's story, The Midnight Fox, which depicts the conflict between a boy's concern for the animal and his uncle's determination to protect his poultry from the fox, could be coupled to texts that describe the animal and its habits, and to parables that stress the trickiness of the animal. To encourage synthesis, students could be asked to tell what they had learned about the animal and then to tell a story about one.

The same type of thing can be done with even younger children. For example: Stories or other texts presenting very simple but different perspectives on one of the following concepts can be read to and/or with them: the sun, water, brothers and sisters, friends. Then students could be encouraged to tell stories in small groups with the sun, water, or a brother, sister, or friend as the main character as they are recorded. Later the

---

T I P   WRITING "AHA'S"!

Ask the students to write or to draw with captions something exciting that they have learned by reading or being read to in recent days.

INVOLVING BEGINNERS!

Get your kindergarten and first-grade students started by having them bring photos of themselves and favorite family members, paper that is their favorite color, favorite pictures they have drawn, and other items that reveal their interests. Give volunteers a chance to explain to classmates what is special about one or more of the things they have brought; encourage them to caption what they are putting into the portfolio.

results can be played back or read from transcription and the students can try to recall and identify where details used came from. The teacher can read from the sources to verify that the story about the beach talks about the sun being hot, for example.

Like teaching ideas that tie reading to writing, there are a great many that promote thinking. Here are a few examples of ideas that can be used effectively with portfolio assessment:

- Acquire numerous copies of articles (editorials, news reports, letters, etc.) that relate to a community problem; have students read them and discuss the problem. Then ask them to write a solution to the problem that they think might work. Allow students to read or show early drafts to fellow students for their reactions and encourage them to revise. Be sure to suggest that this piece can be selected to put into the portfolio and encourage students who do this to include drafts (and attach one or more of the texts read if they wish).

- Cooperate with your science lab teacher to have students write a report on some experiment. Suggest that they should predict what they expect to happen, compare their results to their expectation, and discuss them. Point out that writing from different subjects can be selected to go into the portfolio.

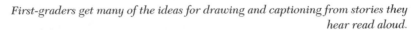

First-graders get many of the ideas for drawing and captioning from stories they hear read aloud.

- Have very young students draw two characters from different stories on separate halves of a large piece of paper. Then ask them to "make notes" on the drawings about things that are alike or different in the two characters.

- Gather sufficient copies of brochures from agencies that promote travel and vacationing in your state and in one or more neighboring states. Ask your students to select a place in one of the states for a vacation and to describe what they expect while explaining why they picked the vacation they did over one in the other state(s).

- Present one or more texts about a famous place or an animal. Find or create a chart, graph, or table with some information that is not in the texts. Or combine printed sales copy (ad, brochure) with a table of figures and/or a review of some product of high interest to your students: a skateboard, surfboard, jeans, musical album, and the like. Ask the students to write a letter to a friend telling about the item.

PORTFOLIOS SHOULD CONTAIN WRITING FROM OUTSIDE OF CLASS

It does not appear to be a mistake when students elect to include nearly everything they write in class, and as the preceding section suggests, the teacher can assure that there are numerous such opportunities. A weakness in many portfolios, however, is the failure to include examples of what a student writes outside of class. It is somewhat easier to get students in the habit of adding classroom writing efforts to their portfolios than it is to get them to bring writing that they do outside of class. But having that kind of writing in a portfolio is very important for the success of the collection. The lack of written musings, letters, unassigned stories, or accounts of personal and family experiences in a portfolio is an almost certain sign that the student who is keeping it does not feel involved in it, does not look on it as a genuine reflection of his or her real thinking or language use, and does not feel any sense of ownership. Equally important, the indication the portfolio gives of the student's language use is skewered to writing as an assignment in school.

There is, of course, the possibility that the student does little or no writing outside of class. If it is determined that this is the case through an informal conversation with the student or a parent, the teacher can encourage such kinds of writing. Students who write little because they have poor control of the language may begin writing once they realize that they can add their thoughts from outside of class to the collection without fear of them being criticized, graded, or marked by the teacher.

The teacher can encourage the student to compare pieces from home to ones done in school that are on a similar topic; the assumption here, by the way, is not that the writing produced in school will be better. It is quite possible that what the student wrote at home will be more expressive and interesting in many ways; the object of encouraging the comparison might be to get the student to realize that he or she should be more open about feelings and opinions in what is written in class. Students who do write outside of class and are interested in reading their efforts to the class should be encouraged to share them in this way.

Sometimes writing outside of class can be generated by taking class time to initiate it. Original stories or poems begun in class—individually or in groups—for example, may be finished outside of class even though doing so is an option, not an assignment. This is most apt to happen when class time is used to generate a mood or sentiment that students can relate to easily. The teacher may find a particularly effective description of some setting and read it, inviting the students to decide what happens there. Kindergarten and first-grade students can be invited to draw a picture or pictures depicting *fog, rainy days, first day of summer vacation, secrets,* or whatever the concept or mood the teacher has tried to set and has invited the students to discuss before drawing.

During conferences on the portfolio, teachers can tactfully press to see if the student does any kind of writing outside of class at all. If convinced that the answer is no, the teacher may need to encourage it by having the student write notes to a friend or some other such device. The teacher/student journal discussed below is another good way. Letters written in class may initiate an ongoing exchange or at least serve as models that will generate outside writing for the portfolios.

Many students are very involved in writing at home. More likely than not, they carry home formats that have been introduced at school—journals, stories, and letters in particular. You should make it clear to your students that they can bring things from home to put in their portfolios.

PORTFOLIOS SHOULD NOT BE PACKED WITH "SEATWORK"

Sometimes portfolios become stuffed with things like workbook and assignment sheets that have required some writing—such as a paragraph that is an open-ended response to a page's details and/or content or theme, if it has one. Or perhaps the page has generated an idea that appeals to the student and may be the starting point for future writing or reading. There is no reason that pages like these should not go into the portfolio.

On the other hand, some students are so hitched to this kind of activity that they will, with or without the teacher's encouragement, want to include a great deal of it in their portfolios. This kind of seatwork prevails in some instruction, but it doesn't promote much authentic writing. Heavy reliance on it should be tolerated only until the teacher can replace it with other types of materials.

Inclusions of workbook material in portfolios can easily suffocate examples of more meaningful language use and of good thinking—ideas connected to each other and to something of authentic concern to the student. It is not advised that you put stringent limitations on workbook/exercise material that can go into portfolios, but mention to students doing that that it is not of much interest to you. If possible, get them to think about and explain why they have included it.

When several student portfolios are overbalanced toward classroom writing and include workbook pages, the teacher has an opprtunity to use the student portfolios as an assessment of the emphases in his or her instruction. Obviously, student thinking and language development might be well served by providing students more opportunities to react to and extend the content of the instruction. And the opportunities provided should hook students on reading and writing by promoting their creative, original expression, a key kind of writing that is an important inclusion in the portfolio.

If only one or two students appear to be relying on workbook pages to flesh out their portfolios, that is an indication that they may be unwilling to risk expressing themselves in writing. The teacher can make special efforts to get them to take the risk and to assure that putting their thoughts down in writing is not at all traumatic, as they might have anticipated.

SEVERAL TYPES OF WRITING
INCLUDED SHOULD PROMOTE FLUENCY

Breaking down any stigmas about writing is an important overall aim of the use of portfolios. As the student becomes more involved in his or her collection, any negative attitudes about writing—and reading as well—may begin to fall away. This happens as the student comes to realize that the teacher is not going to be critical of the things in the collection, even though they may analyze the contents together.

Another sure way to overcome negative attitudes about writing is to encourage your students to write as much as they are inclined to write. This should eventually help create a kind of fluency for students so that they often can write quickly and extensively, if they like. Some types of writing encourage this more than others. Teachers can devise techniques that promote fluency, such as having individual or groups of students write episodic stories using characters from stories read or written earlier. Journals are also a way to develop fluency. *A key aim of the portfolio should be to make writing seem as natural and comfortable for the student as talking is.*

Once again the literature is full of wonderful and original ideas for developing fluent writers. Here are just a few examples:

- Let young students discuss settings, situations, and characters for plays that they can ad-lib and record for their portfolios. If possible, get the script transcribed for revisions when they can read it effectively and revise.
- Let students try writing their own jokes and riddles—after giving them a model.
- Some students may be able to draw their own comic strips.
- Some students may wish to try a short stand-up comic routine.
- Let students take jokes, comics, or other ideas they have clipped and put them into their portfolios and expand into stories.
- Have students who work well together form pairs to react in writing to samples of each other's writing. You may wish to supply copies of the form in Appendix C.
- Have each student record one or more of the following on an audiotape: a reading of a favorite passage, a retelling of a favorite story. Do this at the beginning of the semester and at approximately each quarter so you can compare the control of language at different points in time.
- Encourage students who wish to do so to include art projects with attached notes about them.
- You may wish to adapt journal writing as entries in a student-kept book entitled something like "reflections on life." If so, you might prompt some entries with a one-page list of experiences and questions typical to students the age of those in your class.
- Form book groups based on common student interests and allow the members of a group to share reactions to books that most have read. Ask them also to share and react to things each shares from his or her portfolio.
- Conduct a writing workshop. Explain ahead of time how many people go to workshops to learn new things and to become better at doing things. Modify one of the pages in the back of the book or copy one directly to structure the half-day affair and to supply each student with a program. Follow up by allowing time several days later for the students to react collaboratively to things they began in the workshop.

Over the course of the semester, use whatever classroom publications you have been producing to enlarge publishing ventures that promote revision. Let the students alternate as writers/reporters, editors, illustrators, and production specialists.

SUMMARY: A DOZEN WAYS TO ENSURE USEFUL PORTFOLIO CONTENT!

- Get the collection off to a good start by including all the papers resulting from the administration of a performance assessment.
- Make sure that the growing collection contains sets of papers that show writing and thinking process across sources, notes of ideas, organization, drafts, and latest versions of things written.
- Encourage your students to include many types of writing: summary analyses and syntheses from any subject area, creative efforts, letters, memos, journals, etc.

- Keep your eye on the growing collections and if necessary recommend the inclusion of papers you feel students have overlooked.
- Be sure that the students get off to a good start with an understanding of how to keep logs and sort their papers to structure a table of contents.
- Use guide sheets to get the students analyzing and assessing their work.
- Make sure that the results of teacher/student conferences go into the portfolio and help formulate each student's objective and goals for the next time period.
- Make sure that the portfolios are working portfolios that demand organization.
- Examine the growing collections to be sure that they reflect what you believe about the teaching and development of language abilities.
- Make sure that much that goes into the portfolios can be understood as response to texts that students have read or heard.
- Make certain that the portfolio contents reveal the student as a developing thinker.
- Encourage portfolio development that promotes fluency in expression.

CHAPTER
FOUR

ASSESSING

PORTFOLIO CONTENTS

As the portfolio collections grow, they should become the focus of student self-assessment. They will also be very useful to you and can inform other audiences. Students will not become self-assessors merely by picking things for their portfolios. This may happen somewhat automatically, but there are many things you can do to promote the desired result. Some of them have been mentioned in Chapter 3 as a few relatively simple records that you should require the students to keep in their portfolios.

Hopefully, your students will be involved in examining the contents of their portfolios in a variety of ways: the content and ideas in their papers, their purposes for writing, and the audiences they have written for. With your guidance, they should begin to develop the perspective of self-assessors, considering how effective their writing, reading, and thinking have been. At the same time, you can learn a great deal about the students' progress and about the students themselves from the portfolio contents. The teacher looks at portfolio contents to understand the student as a learner and a unique person and thinker; and the student is reviewing ideas of interest and how effectively he or she has communicated.

SHOW PORTFOLIOS HAVE SPECIAL PURPOSES

In teaching students to self-assess with their portfolios, be sure to understand the difference between the *working* portfolios they should be building and analyzing and *show* portfolios. Often portfolios that are shown to viewers other than teachers and fellow students are *show portfolios* selected by students from their *working portfolios* and with the particular audience, such as parents or the principal, in mind.

This activity is an excellent way of getting the student to give additional reflective attention to his or her collection. The show portfolio should be understood as a demonstration of what a student believes to be his or her best work. It is not meant to be representative. In much the same way that an artist or model would not want to show a potential employer all the work that has been done, a student can develop a show portfolio to demonstrate the best that has been accomplished.

Of course, the show portfolio should not focus merely on one type of activity, but should represent a variety of types of work that have been completed. Several factors that weigh in this problem can be solved at least partially by convincing the student that the show portfolio must be an honest representation and should show as much of the reading and writing process that he or she used to create the pieces selected as possible.

Another solution is to let the student present the working portfolio after pulling a *few* pieces that seem to have served some purpose that is no longer obvious to the student. However a show portfolio is prepared, the student can write the viewer a letter or long memo about the collection, the way it is organized, and particular pieces in it that the student is eager that a viewer examine.

These are all excellent activities for promoting student self-analysis!

These things are revealed by the diversity of the collection detailed in the previous chapter:

- Samples of many kinds of writing done at and outside of school.
- The accruing written reactions to reading, original stories, and other writing—revealing interests, attitudes, and ideas as well as grasp of genre and ability to construct meaning.
- The student's Reading and Writing Log with reactions to reading and written products—revealing amounts and some reflection.
- Table of Contents—listing contents of the portfolio as the student's analysis has organized them—often with reflective comments.
- Self-reflection notes—summarizing the student's assessment of his or her language uses to date; setting goals for development as a language user; discussing personal development in terms of an idea, concept, topic, and so forth; explaining aspects of the portfolio to potential viewers; providing introspection about language and its use; tagging, identifying, and rationalizing specific pieces/inclusions.
- Journals, letters, notes to friends, and other personal writing that reveal much about the individual and his or her attitudes about many things, including those toward reading and writing.
- Conference notes—recording student's comments based on conferences with his or her teacher and entered beside the teacher's comments, and notes from the teacher in regard to particular pieces, from anecdotal and other observations, meetings with parents, and so forth.

The evaluative purposes of the student and the teacher are treated separately here, but they are very similar and are interwoven. While the student becomes, hopefully, interested in his or her development as an effective user of language, the more immediate focus is on learning about, clarifying, and articulating particular topics and ideas. The teacher may be looking to find how effective instruction has been and what can be done in future instruction, but the emphasis is both on noting progress and student needs and on learning what ideas and purposes involve the student.

10-8-92

Jeremy

If I could turn into any animal I would like. to be a buck deer. So I could defend myself and run fast.

In his journal, a young boy's wish tells a lot about him.

9 - 3 -92

My favorite color is black and white because I just like it

9-4-92

The best thing that could happen to me would be... When my sister moves out of house.

9-8-92

I wish parents knew that that my sister punches me.

9-14-92

I was really sorry I hate my sister.

9-15-92

If I were a teacher, I would be nice to the students.

9-16-92

I wish grown ups would give you fifty dollars.

9-17-92

A funny thing that happened to me once was... When I was swinging and I fell out the back of it and hit my head on a big rock.

This elementary school girl's journal displays some typical-sounding sibling rivalry and then her guilt about expressing it.

ENCOURAGE SELF-ASSESSMENT OF LANGUAGE PROCESSES

- Provide opportunities for your students to talk about what they read and write. When they have such exchanges, they think about the ideas that have been most interesting to them, why they liked certain selections, and how they can become more successful as readers and writers. Such discussions are based on reflection, and reflection tends to focus on process.

- When allowing time for the students to look over their portfolios, structure a final portion for writing down what they think of their reading and writing. You may want to have them finish by answering: What one thing can I do now to become a better reader? Or a better writer?

- Modify or use the blackline masters in the back of this book in Appendix C to promote student self-reflection. Let students who want to use them fill out "Thinking about My Reading" and "Thinking about My Writing."

- Structure interaction among your students over their portfolios or set aside time for such informal interaction. This will tend to create real audiences for student expression, peer reaction, and even editing of written expression.

- Promote free reading—on class time and outside of class—that responds to student needs and interests, that builds on individual student backgrounds, and that provides real audiences for student expression.

- Give your students a chance to write and revise using computers. This requires, *without exception,* the opportunity for students to print out and to read to revise.

- Use school reproduction facilities to prepare classroom publications that are edited by rotating groups: class newsletters, creative writing publications, original stories and books for a classroom library.

Much of what the student learns about constructing meaning from reading and writing comes from experiences structured and encouraged by the teacher's instruction. Much of the experience the student gains as a self-assessor comes from teacher-guided activities that model what both the student and teacher hope will become habitual behavior.

So the teacher is interested in exactly the same goals the student is interested in, and primarily in how good a self-assessor the student becomes. The object is to enable the student to guide his or her own life-long development. The teacher's training, maturity, and expertise, of course, enlighten and direct that perspective, but it is not easy to distinguish what is appropriate for the teacher's evaluation from the criteria and objectives that should dictate the student's. That is why informal portfolio conferences should take place as often as possible as students work on various projects that involve reading and writing. This goes on informally, of course, all the time; but these conferences are planned to help both the student and the teacher evaluate the student's performance more in depth. That is why the conference can be said to be the heart of the portfolio assessment approach. As you conference with your students about their portfolios, you will come to understand this concept better.

Equally important is allowing the students class time to look through their portfolios, checking their reading and writing logs to see if they are up to date and thinking about the accruing materials. It is recommended that you designate *at least* a half an hour every week or so as "portfolio time." At first, tell the students that they can do whatever they want with their portfolios during this class time. After a session or two, you can encourage the students to engage in some of the activities discussed in this chapter; some of them you may require. Move about the room during these sessions for working with portfolios and ask questions of individuals:

- When did you add that story?
- Is that a drawing of the boy in the story we all read together?
- That's a very interesting collar on that dog; tell me about it.
- I'm glad you put in that story about moving to an apartment. What was *your* reason?
- You really seem to be interested in the kinds of animals that live on farms, but you live in a big city. Have you ever lived on a farm? Would you like to?
- Show me where you entered this paper about the rainy day in your log. Did you notice that you can make a note on the log about the paper—that you can say that I like it more than you do? You can say anything you want about it— why you like it, why you put it in the portfolio, what you may plan to do with it, anything.

One teacher we know uses a Friday afternoon class period to have her students get their reading and writing logs up to date. They spend some talking about what they have read and written. The teacher keeps her own log and shares with the students some of her own reading and writing. When necessary, she prompts them about some things that may have been written the previous week as class assignments.

This teacher also has the students draw lines and arrows on their logs from the things they have written to stories, books, and poems that "are like" what they have written. The likeness may be in the content, the writing style, or any other feature the student notices as being similar.

This little activity takes no more than a few minutes, but it reinforces for the students the connection between what they have read and the pieces they are writing. During portfolio conference time, the teacher notes these connections and tries to prompt the student to explain them. The students begin to take pride in how they write like their favorite authors, and the reading/writing connection is strengthened.

The simple objective is to get the students thinking about the things they have read and written so that they understand themselves better as language users. As they do this, they can be encouraged to use questions that promote the metacognitive activity even more.

In the final analysis, that is the job of the portfolio: *To help students understand themselves as language users and to enlarge the teacher's understanding of students—what they are interested in, what they think and why, and how they are using language and developing as language users!* That should be your objective as the person who plans the instruction and who promotes experiences designed to help the student become a more effective language user.

That is also the purpose of the portfolio when it is shown to parents. It is what makes the portfolio a superb backup system to help administrators and others interested in educational effectiveness *understand* the role that language is playing in the development of student thinking ability, interests, values, knowledge, and learning strategies.

In this chapter we will review how students use portfolios to assess their progress and then ways that the teacher can examine portfolio contents and assess the student's progress and the effectiveness of the instruction.

The first part of the discussion of student use of the portfolio for assessment deals with different emphases that students can have in collecting papers. Then after discussing general considerations related to the student's use of the portfolio, the kinds of reflecting will be discussed as eight steps designated by icons that help make them memorable.

The second part of the general section on student self-assessment discusses particular steps that lead to successful self-assessment. The use of the log is described in some detail as is the table of contents that is created by analyzing and organizing the

David

"I can read bider."
"I look at the pichrs."
"I look at the ferstarrd
"Indding" "I Gis". "I read on?"
"I can sowd out the
reads." "That is it."

Dear, Ms. Anderson,

    Do you really think I have a talent for writing. I have thought about getting some of my stuff published. But I didn't know if they were good enough or not. So do you really think I should really try to get them published.

    This is all I've been thinking about. Every since I read your part of this journal. I really would like to see about getting some of my things published. I talked about this to my mom and even she said I have a talent for writing. She told me if I really wanted to try to get some of my storys and poems published I should go for it.

              Sincerely
              Tracy

Even first-graders can begin to think about their language use as a process, as David's self-analysis (top) demonstrates. Below that, a fourth-grade girl's note to her teacher attests to how involved with the sense of being a writer students can become.

contents listed on the log. Finally the use of guides to analyzing individual inclusions in the collection and to assess progress across papers is described, using models in Appendix C, which are available for duplication.

The discussion of the teacher's use of the portfolio in assessing the student begins with a theoretical and then practical understanding and application of distinctions between product and process. Then the teacher's use of three considerations that guide the assessment are reviewed in practical detail: the volume of the portfolio contents, the way they reveal the student's interests and attitudes, and various aspects of growth and development that can be identified. Finally, the discussion of teacher assessment focuses on the inevitable consideration of whether or not to grade the portfolio.

STUDENT USE OF THE PORTFOLIO FOR SELF-ASSESSMENT

Getting the student to use his or her portfolio to develop self-analysis, assessment, and evaluation is the prime reason for its existence. If it accomplishes that, it is surely worth whatever time and trouble its development takes! Just creating the opportunity for the student to collect pieces of his or her writing and to react to reading will have some impact on the student's self-concept as a reader and writer—provided that the portfolio does more than act as a personal file cabinet collecting a few papers and some dust.

PORTFOLIOS CAN HAVE DIFFERENT EMPHASES

Not all portfolio collections are alike, and portfolios can differ from classroom to classroom and/or from student to student according to what might be called "emphasis." Different emphases can be noted both in the type and balance of content and in the way that material is arranged. In a classroom where the portfolios differ in emphasis from student to student, there is apt to be a high degree of student control or ownership of them. In classrooms where a particular emphasis tends to appear in all or most of the portfolios, it is clear that the emphasis reflects either teacher values or particular classroom emphases.

There is nothing inherently wrong with the latter. In a classroom where the teacher is working hard through conferences and instruction to develop a sense of process, some or even many of the student portfolios can be expected to reflect the different steps involved in producing a writing product—particularly different drafts of many things the students write. In a classroom where some outlining has been required, one of the preliminary steps included in the portfolio may be the outline.

A teacher who is developing in students a strong and clear sense of audience may have students who tend to group what they write in a way that reflects that approach. Some may separate things written for themselves as a private audience from those written to particular readers; the materials might be arranged by general types of readers. In classrooms where the teacher stresses understanding one's purpose for writing and reading, the papers may be arranged according to different purposes.

This is not to say or advise that teachers should dictate such arrangements or emphases in portfolios; but students are led, in a sense, to mimic the values stressed by their teachers, whether evidence of them is required or not. Students with a strong sense of their individual writing and thinking processes, however, may want to organize their portfolios in a way that looks entirely different from the schemes used by other students more influenced by particular instruction. These individualistic writers should be encouraged to do their own thing—in effect, to develop their own methods of, and approaches to, self-analysis. In fact, if a majority of students are organizing their portfolios in the same way and it is one that the teacher admires, that teacher may need to consider whether he is not limiting the sense of ownership that students must have if portfolios are to succeed.

While particular emphases may not necessarily dictate the main organization of a portfolio, here are several that tend to be obvious from content:

- Many portfolios across all grade levels are revelations of student interests. Often there is a heavy emphasis in such portfolios on "ideas" that may be used for writing. Often these are not articulated but may be evident in pictures that caught the student's attention and were clipped and saved. In such portfolios, logs, reports on and reactions to reading, and stories and nonfiction the student has written will tend to cluster around several general topics. The grouping may reflect, for example, such interests as a preference for adventure, sports, or mysteries; a keen interest in animals or history; and/or an

Letters and personal notes are a good way to learn about emphases and interests in students' lives. These two tell a story about problems Anna is having in planning an important poster.

emphasis on interpersonal relationships. Such portfolios are often organized by such general topics or by the genre of the writing. A few may be organized according to uses of the content.

- Some portfolios become a strong articulation of student beliefs and values. Such an emphasis tends to lead to persuasive writing, sometimes in response to articles or letters read; letters to particular family members or friends or for publication are often included. Such portfolios may be organized around topics, and frequently stories are kept separate from the nonfiction. Journals and ideas for writing topics may appear with drafted or even finished material.

- Some student portfolios emphasize self-evaluation—often of a more strenuously negative nature than is conducive to fullest development of the young writer. This can be set off when such portfolios include comments from parents, the teacher, or friends about particular pieces of writing. Notes on how a piece is to be reworked are sometimes attached. Often such a student is process-conscious and the portfolio contains two or more drafts of pieces of writing, carefully arranged in the order they were written. Often the arrangement of the material is by groups rated from "Best" through "Poorest."

But sometimes students who stress the quality of their work will focus on the mechanical problems in their writing almost exclusively. It is not uncommon, for example, for younger writers in particular to rank and sort their writing strictly on the number of misspelled words the pieces contain or on the basis of how neat the handwriting is. It is possible that this emphasis reflects the primary values of parents who have been critical of the writing or of the teacher, whose job it is to try and shift a considerable degree of the student's focus to the content of the writing. Without negating the desire to spell

> Dear Ms. Redner,
>   I like to spell the words correctly and make scence and write neatly so people can read what I write. I like writing storys and Poems This is called   The Forest
>
>   The forest is nice and cold with all of the mold. The cool breeze makes me freeze. I fly my kite with alot of fright. The trees make me sneeze.
>
>   So that is my poem about the forest!! I like reading and language. Do you like reading? I do. Do you like to read mystry storys?
>
>   Sincerely,
>
>   Danielle

A fifth-grader wrote a letter to her teacher's aide about how she uses language and later included it in her portfolio collection.

correctly or to write legibly, for example, the teacher should avoid responding to the student's plaint about these mechanical flaws, but seek, instead, to involve the student in clarifying the ideas in the writing. The teacher can promote expression of opinions, feelings, and conclusions drawn from reading.

SOME GENERAL CONSIDERATIONS CAN PROVIDE THE FOUNDATION FOR SUCCESS

It is essential to the success of the portfolio system that your students be allowed adequate and regular time to get their portfolios out, to handle them, to read what is in them, and to think about how they are growing as readers and writers. It seems clear that there is some direct correlation between the amount of time students spend working with their portfolios and the benefits they derive as self-assessing language users. Even so, many attempts to develop portfolio assessment dissolve in neglect, like those intended for a piece of exercise equipment purchased and used initially with good intentions but eventually abandoned and used only rarely.

Portfolios that get only occasional attention from students may do some minimal good, but it seems a pity to limit the impact of such a promising approach. If the system is to succeed, working with portfolios must become a regular classroom activity that relates to the reading and writing that your students are doing. Time needs to be set aside *regularly,* if not daily, for your students to take out and work with their portfolios. They should not stand apart from classroom instruction. From the classroom context must come products that the students *elect* to include in their portfolios.

Just saying this—and doing it—does not assure that your students will become actively involved with building their portfolios. You are going to have to prime the pump. One way to do this, of course, is to circulate while the students are looking at what they have in their collections. Make observations and ask questions about the contents that will promote more intense focus on the contents:

- I love that picture! I'm so glad you decided to put it into your portfolio. What made *you* decide that it should go there?
- I'm interested in what you have written on your picture. I wonder if I know exactly what you mean.
- I didn't know that you like growing things. Are you going to put other things in your portfolio about your garden? I always wonder what makes a garden so much fun.
- Which of those three papers do you think is the best? Why?

There are other things you can do to promote both process and product analysis. Fortunately, you have laid some ground rules for building the portfolio that allow you to add things or to require that the student keep them in the portfolio. Remember that you are not going to overwork this option to the point that you threaten the student's sense of ownership, but you do want to be sure that certain things that will promote and support both the student's and your analysis are in the collection.

Chapter 3 has already discussed the reading/writing log, other records like conference notes, other memos and notes, letters to potential portfolio viewers, and a table of contents. How they promote and support self-assessment will be discussed further here. Among other activities that the teacher can use to encourage self-assessment are those that get the student to write self-reflective pieces. Give extra credit or encourage students in some way to write pieces on topics such as these:

- The things that make a good writer.
- Different kinds of writing I have done this year.
- Why I like certain types of writing most.

- Why these two pieces of writing I've done in the past few weeks are the best.
- The piece of my writing I would most like to do over and what I could do to it.
- The kinds of writing I'd like to do in the future.
- How my writing has changed this year.
- The easiest and the hardest things for me about writing.
- What I need to work on most as a writer.
- What I like to write about most. What I like to read about most, and why.
- The two best things I have read this semester and why I like them.
- My favorite author and why would I like to read more by him or her.
- Where I get my ideas for writing.

These kinds of considerations are often grouped on one sheet and are given to students as a guide for them to use as they look at their portfolios, but any of them is worth a student's focused attention. You might decide to pick three to five for the students to write about briefly, but ask them to choose one topic from the list and to write a page (or a paragraph) on it. The sheet can be put into the portfolio with the longer self-analysis.

Or you might decide to hold topics like those above in mind so that you can use them with students when you discover during conferencing or informal discussion that one is particularly applicable for a particular student. For example, you admire the originality of one writer and ask him where he gets his ideas. He finds the question challenging and interesting but can't answer it succinctly. So you request that he think about it and write out the answer.

Emily, Would you please write one or two comments about the books you have read? Thank you.

1) Bobbsey Twins of Lakeport
   — I have read other Bobbsey Twins and this one wasn't as good.

2) Great Advice From Lila Fenwick
   — I like that Lila is in the 5th grade.

3) Scary Stories to Tell in the Dark
   — I really liked the "jump stories".

4) Scary Stories 3
   This was really good becaus they are more modern day.

5) More Scary Stories to Tell in the Dark
   This book got boring after a while.

6) Kilroy and the Gull
   — I liked this book becaus we were studying ocean-ography and it helped us learn about whales.

❷ WRITING LOG —Emily MacMorran

Emily, Below are some titles of things you have written so far this year. Would you please write one or two comments on these pieces?

1) Going to Colorado!
   I didn't tell my mom or dad's names. It's a true story.

2) My Family — I like it. If someone else read this they would know all about my family.

3) angelfish
   I might have listed to many names. The last sentence is the best.

4) If I Were President
   It makes me sad to read now because Clinton won. Yuck!

5) The Cheetah and the Snail
   This took me a long time to write and I think I did a good job on it.

Although one sheet of these questions is labeled "log," it is a special questionnaire that the teacher has prepared specifically for Emily to promote more thinking and expression.

Still another idea is to put 8 to 10 of the topics as questions on a kind of questionnaire that calls for shorter answers. If you hand this out shortly before conferencing time, you can look over the reaction and see which questions prompt interesting answers from particular students and ask for longer explanations of their answers during their conferences.

One problem with any of these approaches to encouraging student self-analysis is that the topics can all promote such worthwhile analysis that you may be tempted to use them too often. Thus you could create a metacognitive focus that might exhaust the student's sincere interest in himself or herself as a language user. This is likely to happen when this kind of activity seriously crunches the overall time the student has to read and write, so that there may be less to analyze at the same time that there is more encouragement to self-assess.

Some teachers like to prepare short-answer questionnaires for their students after looking over the collections. In this way, the teacher is able to customize the attempt to provoke self-analysis. The example on page 108 shows what one teacher did with a fourth-grader. The teacher got the idea after noticing on Emily's log that she was reading a great deal but was not commenting on the table of contents or log about many of the titles. Just the first page of the reading questionnaire is shown, beside the one on Emily's writing.

EIGHT ICONS PROVIDE A CHECKLIST FOR THE METACOGNITIVE READER

You do not want to overload the portfolio with too many guidelines or aids directed at getting the student to follow metacognitive processes in self-assessing, but you may decide to use minimally one of the eight icons and/or one or more that you devise to reinforce your teaching. You can couple aids like these to particular instructional activities, but be very cautious not to turn guidelines intended to promote a *process* orientation into a static, workbooklike exercise that presses any joy out of real language processing by pacing it at workbook speed.

By asking themselves eight very simple questions, students can help assure that they are reading or writing effectively. While there are many more sophisticated metacognitive considerations, these have been devised to be understood even by young students. So with practice, they can develop self-assessing habits without extensive coaching. It is not a mistake to incorporate these into instructions and to invite the student to include them in his or her portfolio as a kind of behavioral checklist to guide self-assessment based on the portfolio collection.

The eight "heads" can guide the student to ongoing self-evaluation of products that is truly focused on reading and writing process. Yet it is worth noting that the strategies in the eight icons are not linear but rather overlap and should be reiterated during reading and writing processing as needed.

The icons, as they can guide reading and writing, are phrased as questions that the student asks himself or herself:

 Do I have a specific purpose as I read this story/book/text? (What do I want to know after reading this?) What is my specific purpose for writing this? (What do I want my audience to know after reading what I am writing?)

 Have I thought about what I already know about this topic before I begin to read or write (or as I am reading and writing)?

 Before I start reading and writing, have I thought about the ideas I will probably find when I read this or that I intend to write? (What do the title, the artwork, and other clues tell me?)

As I am reading or writing, do I think about what is coming next? (What do I think will happen next? What would my reader expect me to tell about next?)

 Do I picture in my mind what I am reading or writing?

 Do I ask myself as I read and write, "Is this making good sense?"

 Do I change my mind and revise the meaning I am making if necessary? (Do I make changes if things don't make sense?)

 Do I get help if I need it?

Numerous activities that promote the student's consideration of the products he or she has collected in the portfolio can be encouraged, including many that are responses to reading. Actually, many have already been suggested because they also can reveal

YOU HAVE TO STAND STILL TO FIND MUSHROOMS
By Michael Riggs

If you are going mushroom hunting this year, go to the dampest place you can get. If you stand real still and look at the ground for a couple of minutes, you will be able to see a mushroom. But, if you don't stand still, you won't see any. If you want to find a whole bunch of mushrooms, after it rains, go into the woods and look real good at the ground, and you will be able to find them. I find the grayish kind mostly. Actually they are kind of gray and brown. After you find them, you stick them in a pan of water to get the bugs out of them. If you can't get all the bugs out, you can throw them away. If you do get the bugs out, you cook them and eat them. You can only find mushrooms at certain times in the year, like around this time of the year.

THE SCARY CREATURE
By Dustin Richardson

Once upon a time my mom was driving down the road. She was just driving along, and this creature jumped out. He had brown eyes, and it was a four-eyed creature. He splatted on the window. All of a sudden, he tried to grab my sister! The creature was wearing clothes. He had a black shirt and some blue jeans with a stripe down his face. He had gum in his pocket. I just thought he was going to grab my sister, but he was trying to give her a piece of gum. He gave me a piece, too, and my mom gave him a ride home. He was a friendly creature, after all!

The mod shop 47 E. main
879-4345
Shampoo Cuts
Style Perms
Spike
Owner: Pat Woodall   2

WRESTLEMANIA EIGHT WAS GREAT
By Rodney Terrell

Wrestlemania Eight was in the Hoosier Dome in Indianapolis on April 5. The double main event had Hulk Hogan going against Sid Justice, and Rick Flair going against Randy Savage in a world title match. Macho Man won the gold by cheating, but everybody was glad that he did. At the other match Poppa Shongo ran down to the ring and was beating up Hulk Hogan. Then somebody returned as the Ultimate Warrior, and then Poppa Shongo got thrown over the top rope. Sid Justice hit the Ultimate Warrior with a steel chair, but it had no effect on the Ultimate Warrior. He tried to hit him again, but Hulkster got the chair.
Brett, the Hitman, Hart, won the intercontinental title. The Natural Disasters, a tag team, won against the Money, Inc.—the Million Dollar Man and IRS. Shawn Michaels went against El Matador, Tito Santana. There was an eight-man tag team where Sergeant Slaughter, Hacksaw, Jim Duggan, Virgil, the Repo Man, and three others tagged each other. The Undertaker won against Jake the Snake by tombstoning him outside the ring.
Hulk Hogan was hugging the Ultimate Warrior at the end. There were over 7,000 people there. I'm going to rent the video that shows the whole Wrestlemania Eight.

Gosport Nursing home
879-4242

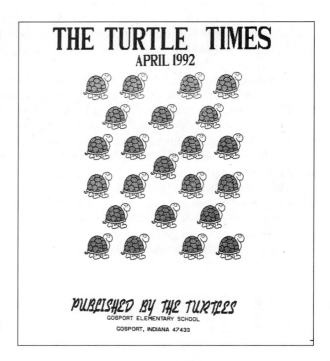

THE TURTLE TIMES
APRIL 1992

PUBLISHED BY THE TURTLES
GOSPORT ELEMENTARY SCHOOL
GOSPORT, INDIANA 47433

Although ready-made computer templates may produce dressier looking classroom newspapers, producing them the old-fashioned way can be charming, indeed—if a lot of work. An elementary class in Gosport, Indiana, published The Turtle Times using a reproduction system familiar to teacher Pam Todd. This classroom paper was published several times a semester and was often eight pages long.

SOME IDEAS FOR
CLASSROOM PUBLICATIONS

TIP

- A creative writing magazine: Let panels of editors select from pieces of writing submitted by your students—usually out of their portfolios. Stay involved in the process long enough to make sure that all students will get something in the magazine. Let those who like to draw do some simple, black and white illustrations if your reproduction system can duplicate it. Point out that the magazine should have different kinds of writing, including book reviews.

  Let some students act as editors, but point out that in creative writing, the author often has the last say as to what is changed or not changed in a poem, story, review, or whatever. Make sure that the magazine is circulated as widely as possible beyond the classroom. It is difficult to overestimate the impact of such a publication in demonstrating to parents, other teachers, and the community what a significant role language plays in student thinking and feelings.

- A newsletter: Plan a newsletter to go to parents and other readers, describing what is going on in your classroom. Let students get involved suggesting news stories, features, opinion columns, illustrations, etc. Let them make the writing assignments and appoint their own editors, who will react to the stories as the writers look on. Make sure to get everyone involved and alternate staff responsibilities for the next issue.

- Storybooks: Let students turn their own stories into language-experience books, binding them to put into a library that their fellow students can borrow from. Let them do the illustrations or get a friend to do them.

- A yearbook: Let students bring photos of themselves or draw self-portraits for a class yearbook that highlight the semester or school year to date; each student's activities, interests, and ambitions; etc. Bring some yearbooks to class for models and let the students decide how theirs will be organized and presented. If it is too difficult to reproduce the yearbook, make a single copy available in the school library and on back-to-school night.

process, but several more can indicate the possibilities. One of the most successful approaches that teachers have begun using more and more is to develop student writing—creative, reporting, reacting to reading, expressing opinions—for classroom publications.

Some teachers call the process "publishing" even when no product is distributed to an audience, and the value of that rather metaphorical application of the approach is debatable. One of the very clear benefits of having students write and edit classroom publications is that the activity provides real audiences and cements the metacognitive concept of *being aware of one's audience!* Because the students are responsible in various ways for the production of the products, the emphasis again can easily shift to the way the stories and articles are processed.

To get full benefit from this kind of activity, plan the publication with the class. Appoint groups of writers and help them decide what they will report on and write—what their assignments will be. Name editors to react to the written work, making changes to it as the writers look on. Alternate writing and editorial responsibilities after a couple of weeks or between issues so that all the students get all experiences.

One of the biggest challenges in using classroom publications to motivate language development is in printing or otherwise reproducing the copy. You may have some good ideas of your own, based on school equipment and other sources you are aware of. Do

The portfolio has powerful potential to promote both collaborative and individual analysis of the products it includes, and it leads to natural consideration of the processes involved in using language. It is essential, however, that the teacher allow the time necessary for that to happen.

not overlook the potential of some computer software available today. Many programs provide a choice of templates for newsletters, for example. Don't overlook the professional look of ever-more-available laser printers. You can easily print on both sides of a sheet if such a printer is available to you.

But if no such opportunities exist for you, you can use Xerox or other methods to duplicate; and even if the students must write and print the final copy by hand, that will give the publication a very special appeal to your audiences.

ENCOURAGE THE STUDENT TO TAG ANALYSES TO SOME PAPERS

There are other techniques that you can use to promote self-analysis using the portfolio. Make a point of explaining to students that they can react to something *they* have written or to something a friend has written. If you can get volunteers to share these kinds of inclusions in the portfolio, it will encourage other students to do this.

SELF-REFLECTION NOTES INCLUDE REACTIONS TO READING   The rather limited space on the log discussed below tends to invite the students to write or draw other reactions to things that they read, and if they feel the need to do this, it is almost certain that they will put the longer reaction into the portfolio. These kinds of notes are, as already noted, a form of self-evaluation. Often they are directly related to perspectives that are of key interest to the teacher: discussing volume and revealing attitudes and interests. You can initiate classroom activities that do the same thing. These are important additions to the portfolio because they integrate reading and writing and they tend to ensure more careful thinking and to invite more thoughtful use of detail, in order for the student to tell why he or she did or didn't like something or to explain a reaction.

You can also encourage students to write notes about their development as language users. Such an activity might even be assigned *but only once every few weeks*. Extra credit and other motivations can be created for activities like these that can generate self-analysis:

- Ask students to take up the stance of an informed critic or biographer, noticing what is characteristic about their writing or the things they like to read, how their use of language has changed over time, or what remains to be done to make a good writer.

- After a matter of weeks, have students pick what they think best shows development in their work and explain why they think so in a note.

- Let students expand on their log by creating a special notebook or pad reserved for their observations about things read in subject areas.

- Let students keep a "Speaking Up" log of experiences they have outside the classroom using language: recording memorable things they said or heard, discussing letters they wrote or received, or structuring things they thought of saying to authors they have read.

- Let students select "Portfolio Partners" to examine and respond to each other's collections. Encourage them to write some of their reactions and to respond in writing to what the partner thinks of the portfolio.

- Let students form small groups as "fellow editors" to swap work in progress for reactions. Encourage editors to write notes to attach to the drafts they

THINK ALOUD ABOUT YOUR WRITING

Dennie Palmer Wolf describes an experience of a teacher named Kathy Howard, who "faced an ordinary class of eighth-graders who had not written more than the answers to chapter questions and who had certainly never been asked to reflect on their progress as writers. In the ensuing months she began to insist that they write essays, journals, and poems.

At intervals of several months, she asked her students to select two pieces: one that didn't satisfy them and another that they liked. Her students studied these pieces and wrote down what they noticed about themselves as writers. Sometimes she left students on their own; at other times she discussed the various dimensions of their writing that they might consider. As students continued to write, they revisited their earlier choices, seeing whether old favorites held up in the light of their own evolving standards. After eight months, the climate around writing had changed dramatically: part of writing was now the responsibility to know where you were and what you thought. By early June, the classroom dialogue had acquired a sound that was tough yet meditative:

"I want you to look at what you chose last time as your most satisfying piece and your least satisfying piece. You don't have to change them, but I want to give you the chance to reevaluate them. Something that once looked good to you may look different now, or you might see something new in a piece you once thought wasn't much.

"Feel free to conference with each other. Go ahead and ask someone else's opinion. But be sure you really give them a chance to read what you have written. Don't just wave a paper in front of their face and ask them."

A student calls: "If we have two satisfying pieces, is that okay?"

"Yes, just be sure you know what you see in each of them."

Kathy pauses beside another student who is shuffling papers. "Rocky, show me what you are using."

"Is this the right one?"

"I don't care which one you choose. I'm just here to listen to your ideas."

Rocky looks quizzical.

"I want to know why you chose what you did. See, if I chose, I would probably choose different things for *my* reasons."

Source: Wolf, Dennie Palmer. (April 1989) "Portfolio assessment: Sampling student work." *Educational Leadership* 46 (7): 35–39.

read. Ask students to put the draft with notes attached into the portfolio with revisions on it or with a revised draft.

- Let pairs of students hold conferences like the one you hold with the student, and encourage them to record notes on what is said. Have them take turns playing teacher, so that the focus is on the work of one of them at a time.
- Provide the student with his or her own copy of the eight icons as a checklist to use in thinking about reading and writing. Make other checklists that guide the student to a quick written reaction of his or her own performance.

The regular student/ teacher conference is discussed in detail in Chapter 5 and is the centerpiece of portfolio assessment.

NOTES FROM THE STUDENT/TEACHER CONFERENCE ARE VERY HELPFUL   One key set of notes that relates to and that should promote additional student assessment is the set taken by the student and the teacher during the portfolio conference. Ask the student to look at any goals recorded in portfolio conference notes and to write how close he or she is to achieving them.

The aim of the conferences that you have with each student will be to create a focus on his or her writing. So the notes that you and the student make about what you each decide at this conference and record side by side should help set the student to self-assessing. These jointly kept notes may also contain goals and objectives that you and the student have decided are reasonable and important for him or her to follow in developing as a language user.

Nothing else that you do in relation to the portfolio is apt to have more impact than the conference. If it is successful in promoting student self-analysis and in confirming that you and the student are a like-minded team supporting the student's best interests, it is almost certain to have an impact on the portfolio keeper. Take special note after your first round of conferences of any attitude changes in your students both toward the portfolio itself and toward development as a language user in general. The student is almost bound to consider the collection more seriously and to be more involved in analyzing it after the conference.

Name ___*Harrison*_____

Teacher ___*Stegall*_____

About My Portfolio

Write or draw about…

What I most like to read and write about.

> *I like checking out chapter books from the school library. I like action.*

The things I write and read about the most.

> *I read chapter books the most. But I do write jokes.*

The things I want to read and write about more.

> *I want to read more action books. I've almost read every action book in the library.*

Harrison's response to the prompted review of his reading and writing is very simplistic, but it still reveals directions for the teacher: Harrison should have access to chapter books about action as well as joke books.

About This Piece of Writing

Name _Pamala Missar_ _____ Date _2–14_ _____

Name of piece I wrote: _"A Valentine for Carole"_ _____

_____

Why I wrote it: _because she needed one and she deserves one_ _____

_____

I wrote it for these people to read: _for Carole, but I wanted the other kids to see it._

_____

I got the idea for this piece from/by _watching her face._ _____
                  She needed a long valentine.

This is the __ first X second __ third   draft of this piece.

The hardest thing about writing this was _finding room to say all the stuff why she is such a good friend._

Things I could do to make this a better piece of writing: _I needed to cut and draw it again without the changes, but I've done it now._

I had _Carole_ _____ read it, and this is what s/he thinks:

    It was very nice! It said so many things about things we do and places

    we go. It was really nice. The spelling was almost perfect! It was too

    nice and exagerated some things.

Pamala's review of the card she sent to a friend reveals an impressive audience focus generated by a clear, sensitive purpose.

Much of the analysis promoted by the conference is almost certain to be focused on language processes. You may decide to wait until the first conference to introduce and explain how you and the student will take "cooperative" notes on what you decide and that these notes will go into the portfolio. But making those notes, and looking them over afterward, will be an activity almost sure to initiate self-assessment and one that gives those notes about as much "authority" in the student's mind as anything that goes into the collection.

NUMEROUS GUIDELINES AND AIDS TO ANALYSIS CAN BE USED
Your students can use a variety of guide sheets in thinking about their work. With very young students, you can ask the student to draw a picture of or write about the thing in the collection he or she likes best, the kind of work there is the most of, something he or she would like to add, and so forth. There is a blackline master in Appendix C that can be reproduced for this, but you may wish to use it only as a model because you have other perspectives to promote.

Some teachers require students to tag everything they put into their portfolios with notes that can be quite simple or very elaborate. Since the strong recommendation here is that the student be the primary selector of portfolio contents, it is not recommended that you require students to do this. Anything that threatens to overcome the joy of keeping the collection and to create tedium is not a good idea. (Notice that the recommendation here is that you *may* want to add a rationalizing note to some things that you select for the portfolio, but it does not seem reasonable to require the student to defend a choice.)

Your students, nonetheless, should be aware that it is sometimes a helpful thing to attach a note to something they put into the collection—if there is something about it they would like to remember or would like any possible viewers to know about it. There is a sheet for this in Appendix C as well. While you ought not require students to use them, it is a good idea to hand out a sheet of three of them to each student to keep in case she or he wants one, explaining that they can be cut apart and offering more on request.

There are, in addition, numerous sheets in Appendix C that promote student analysis of individual papers in the portfolio and that lead the student to summarize and review his or her personal development.

KEEPING A LOG OF THE READING AND WRITING DONE IS THE FIRST STEP IN ANALYSIS

There are many ways to involve students in their own literacy development. A primary step in using portfolios is to have your students keep a few simple records that will involve them in thinking about what they have read and written and put into the collection. First of all, this means that students have to take responsibility for keeping their *reading and writing log* up to date. You or the student can choose if this will be two separate logs— one for reading and one for writing—or a combined log. Models for each type are in Appendix C and can be duplicated for use. The separate logs make tracing reading experiences of the students easier; the combined logs emphasize the integrated nature of reading and the importance of writing about reading.

When first introducing the log to the students, you should go over it with them carefully, helping them enter their names and grade at the top. It is a good idea to do this after the class has finished reading and writing something, so that you have something that they can enter into the log or logs. If it was a big book, you can prop it up close by, so that the students can see its name. You may also wish to print the titles and the authors' names of stories read in class on the chalkboard. If the title is long, you may want to use a shorter tag for it, as the students may do in entering it on their log; or if the author's name is long, you may decide to use just the last name and an initial. Do not criticize students if they do not get the title or author exactly correct on their logs.

For very young students, move about the room and write the names into their forms for them as they say them aloud for you. If the student is using the combined form, explain how an *R* in the middle column stands for "reading" and have the students enter it. Explain that you would like them to keep a record of *everything they read and write* on the combined log or on separate logs, even if they are not putting any other reaction to what is read or are not including the piece of writing in their portfolios.

One reaction, however, is quite simple to register for the youngest students. If you are using duplicates of one of the forms supplied in Appendix C, all students need to do is circle a smiling, neutral, or frowning face to show how they like the story or book or how they feel about what they wrote. Have volunteers point out the smiling face that shows that they like the book, the frown that shows that they do not like it, or the face in the middle with the straight line for the mouth, which shows that they are not sure. Ask the students to circle the *one* face that shows what they think of the book, and move around the room to assist as they do this. The forms for older students allow them to express how they feel about the text read or the piece of writing by writing a comment.

You may prefer to have the students create their logs on plain sheets of paper. Either way, encourage the students to record their reactions. Encourage them to make some kind of note or to draw a picture of their reaction to what has been read or written in the right-hand column on the log. Explain that their "note" can indicate what the book is about, can tell whether they liked the book or not, or both. If some students need more space than the log offers, don't miss the opportunity to encourage them to write or draw

Name __JOSh__

Teacher __mS. HAmmel__

Reading and Writing Log

Date	Title and Writer	R/W	How I liked it
Sept 14	MY hOhW	UN	☺ ☹ ☹
Sept 19	ChickeN SOWPs mjohs	R	☺ ☹ ☹ (handwritten notes)
Oct 1	SPider boOke	W	☺ ☹ ☹
Oct	JadThy mY gOOd day	R/W	☺ ☹ ☹

Teacher's Notes: Josh needs to focus more — Needs more reason + purpose + patience. He draws v. fast. Some stories don't hold his interest. He did not like writing using the Alexander ... Nat Day pattern because he had to concentrate on it too long! Josh moved here recently; likes to talk about his house + neighborhood.

Even very young students can keep logs successfully.

an additional reaction that can be included in the portfolio. When it is about a piece of writing, the paper and the student evaluation can be included in the collection.

It is not a bad idea to have the students draw or write on their own paper in reaction to the first book or story they will enter on their log before you have them initiate the log. That way, every student has something real for both reading and writing to put down; they can enter a title or tag for it. If they are using the combined log, they can enter an R for "reading" and a W for "writing." Point out that for the piece of writing they can put their name down for "author," still another indication that it is something *they* have created.

If some students do not want to put this first effort into the portfolio, do not cajole them. Rather, move about the room and praise their efforts in the hopes of encouraging them to do so; but do not say, "I think that is a very good paper. You really *should* put it into your portfolio." What you can do is to remind the students that it will be fun to look

Name Rita F.

Reading and Writing Log

Ratings:	Super!	★ ★ ★ ★
	Good:	★ ★ ★
	Fair	★ ★
	Poor	★

Page 3

Date	Title and Writer	R/W	Comments: . Why I read/wrote it? . Why I like/dislike it? . Other comments.	Rating
4/13/92	After the Rain Norma Fox Mazer	R	I think the book is very interesting. I like Rachel's personality	★★★★ (★)
10/29/92	Letter to Mr. Block	W	It lets him know how much we appreciated him visiting our class.	★★★
10/29/92	Bingo Brown and the Language of Love	R	Bingo tries to express his feelings towards Melissa by writing. I want to read more Bingo B. books!	★★★★
11/3/92	Ten Kids, No Pets	R	Their mom has rules around the house and the most unfair is No Pets! The kids feel bad.	★★★
10/?/92	Halloween Story	W	The kids in grades 1–3 should like it. I got the ideas from a bunch of scary movies.	★★★★
11/?/92	Current Events	W	I wanted it to be like a newspaper. It is very political.	★★★
4/1/9?	Horse Shy Bonnie Bryant	R	It was sad when Cobalt died after Carol got back. She was so upset I almost cried too	★★★★

Teacher's Notes: Rita reacts freely to things she reads, but they don't seem to influence her writing a lot.— except that she likes feelings. The Halloween story is fascinating and combines things from movies she's seen. She writes very fluently in letters. I think she should try
In Mazer book she was taken   a story about animals.
about feelings of death, love, + friendship.
I have asked her to write a story with letters between friends.
She loves the word epistolary!

The third page of a fourth-grader's Reading and Writing Log suggests a high volume of language use for this girl. Note how the integrated log prompted an interesting observation from her teacher.

at things in their portfolios after a while to compare things they put in early—to see how they are developing as language users.

You can also suggest that they may want to redo the reaction to the early story or book read sometime later, and you can encourage them to keep it if that seems a possibility to them. Then later, after a new drawing or draft has been completed, you can suggest that they might want to keep both versions in the portfolio to show the same process that all good authors go through. This is probably *not* a good time to exercise your right to make selections, no matter how eager you are to see the portfolio collection get under way. You should, however, encourage the students to list all things they write and read on the log because it is important to have a record of *how much* they are doing.

Right from the beginning, emphasize also that the log can show any reading, writing, and drawing the students are doing at home. Point out that this is especially interesting to you because you already have some idea of what and how much they read and write in school. Like Emily's writing above, much that children write about is based on their home lives and families; and that writing may occur at home.

Tell the students that what they read and write at home is more special because it is probably something they really want to do. Explain that sources of their ideas are interesting to you because you like to see where their ideas come from. Encourage them to bring things from home to put into the portfolio. Point out that titles and authors' names entered on the log do not have to be exact and that things they write do not have to have titles—they can use tags they make up to enter writing if they wish. As you notice entries on the log for things read and written at home and portfolio inclusions brought from home, invite the students who add these things to explain to the class how and why that was done: "Jamie, that account of your day helping with the plowing has wonderful details. I bet the class would enjoy hearing it." Note how your invitation need not seem like an order or even be a question.

Point out to your students, too, that things that they see that they want to write about can also go into the portfolio. Watch for examples of all these kinds of things in their portfolios and get students to volunteer to show them to their classmates and to explain why they wanted them in their portfolios. This interaction makes models out of peers.

ORGANIZING PORTFOLIO CONTENT REQUIRES REFLECTIVE THOUGHT

A part of the self-analysis that portfolios generate among students comes from having young writers organize and then reorganize their collections on a regular basis and from giving students the opportunity to do that at any time they wish to contemplate what they have written. It is important to this objective that the organization the student uses emerges in his or her own mind during the analysis of the materials collected.

By standing back and allowing students to take responsibility for organizing their portfolios, you will gain valuable insights into the criteria they regard as important. Students who decide to organize their portfolios according to topics reveal a great deal about their interests. Students who have difficulty organizing their portfolio content may not have thought much about their own reading and writing. Encouraging students to take responsibility for the portfolios also signifies that you do indeed trust their judgments.

Experience demonstrates that this leaving of the categories to the student will lead to structuring and analyses that are somewhat disappointing to some teachers and that test their patience—particularly the first few times the student tries analysis and organization of the collection. But you must be patient and noncritical. The students should be given the freedom to organize their portfolios in whatever way they like. After they have finished, they should make a table of contents, using the form provided in Appendix C at the back of this book, some adaptation of it you have made, or their own design.

There are several common categorization schemes that students tend to develop on their own in assessing their collections. It is important to note that while these seem quite simple—almost too obvious—students who use them often combine them in different ways. In the final analysis, such schemes are considerably more sophisticated than they may appear at first. In one class, organization schemes ranged across those discussed below to one that went from "my best handwriting" to "my worst handwriting" and another that was alphabetized by the first word of titles and tags.

At the same time, few students are readily familiar with the terms used on page 120; that is, they know they are putting their work in an order determined by when they did it, but they seldom use the term *sequential*. For the purpose of recognizing the standard organization schemes, however, the terms are useful for teachers.

SEQUENTIAL/CHRONOLOGICAL   Many students will rely on the time sequence in which their writing was created in organizing their portfolios. This is a highly sensible and useful organizing scheme because it promotes the analysis of how writing skills are developing over time during the semester or school year. In addition, this scheme also tends to keep drafts/versions of a single piece of writing in the order in which they were done, revealing what processes the student has used in writing each piece. Sequential organization also allows one to consider more readily the influences of reading on writing.

PREFERENCES (LIKE/DISLIKE)   Many students are interested in identifying the work they like best in some basic way. This leads some children to organize their portfolios with categories like "My Best Work," "My Worst Stuff," and "Other Things." This scheme suggests that self-evaluation is certainly at work, and the teacher may, in conference, encourage the student to explain why certain pieces are in particular groups. The student may be persuaded to add some notes about these rationales to the collection.

TOPICAL   The basic organization of many student portfolios is done according to topics. Some students—particularly younger ones—will sort according to their favorite subject matter: for example, one student may have a group of writing about animals, another of mysteries, and another of sports. Such an approach emphasizes the value of the portfolio for clarifying student interests to help teachers suggest future reading and writing projects.

GENRES   Many students—including young ones—decide to sort their portfolio contents by types of writing. They may put stories in one group and nonfiction in another. Some create separate categories for things like letters and journals. Some recognize the distinct difference in the way they and their teacher use logs, notes, and other less textual inclusions in the portfolio, and put those in a separate group. Within a "Story" or "Fiction" category, some students may create a single or several subdivisions, such as "Mysteries," "Poems."

> Organization Key
> 1. letters ●
> 2. Stuff that ive written ●
> 3. Reading log
> 4. Writing log ●
> 5. Things from other people ●
> 6. Pictures
> 7. Turtle times

This girl used a mixed organization scheme. The dots to the right of the tags were in different colors that matched different colored dividers in a loose-leaf notebook that held her collection.

DIFFICULTY   Some students decide to put those things that were easy for them in one major section, and those things that were harder in another. Sometimes the major categorization scheme has sections for "very difficult" and/or "very easy" and "average."

USES   Some students keep things like pictures and clippings in one section of the portfolio to suggest potential ideas for writing. This organization relies at least partially on how the contents are used.

Other students carry such organization across the rest of the portfolio contents. The most sophisticated application of this scheme would separate the logs, notes, and other references into one general category that informs on all the others, and would put writing into one group that the student considers finished, one that contains writing that needs some polishing, one of pieces that need considerable rewriting, one of things that the student is not satisfied with but does not intend to rewrite, and perhaps one of very preliminary drafts. Such a portfolio might also have a separate category for a journal, personal letters, and some poems the student is not yet ready to share. Within these functional categories, some students with amply filled portfolios might create subcategories of genres.

Clearly such a scheme is based on considerable self-analysis by a student who also has a keen sense of language use as a process.

OTHER   Individual students will create other categories that can be meaningful to them—at least for a while. This is particularly true in the many portfolios students organize using some combination of the schemes described briefly here. It is not a good idea to criticize the way a student has organized his or her collection; a teacher can, however, guide more sensitive organization during the conference:

> "What do you think you may do with this stuff that is not in the 'Good' or 'Not So Good' pile? Will you rework any of it? Which ones? Would you want to separate the ones you may work on to try to make them better? Are there any in the 'Not So Good' pile that could be moved to the new batch to be reworked?"

Some students may want to organize by topics and within topics by genres, likes/dislikes, or difficulty. However the portfolio is organized, the important thing is that the student has given the material thought while doing it and can discuss his or her reasons for the organization with you. You may want to have students work in small groups to discuss their organizations. The exchange of ideas and insights about reading and writing between students can be a very valuable outcome of this activity.

While it is possible for the teacher to provide guidelines and suggestions as to how the portfolio may be organized, the children should be given the opportunity to offer suggestions or take full responsibility for how the contents are organized. It is important that students understand the reason for organizing the contents of their portfolio—an organized portfolio allows it to be viewed efficiently by others as well as providing a means of caring for and respecting work samples. Encouraging students to manage and organize their own reading and writing samples can signify that their decisions are valued and respected.

Generally, teachers should be accepting of differing schemes and use the structure as a kind of ignition to get the student to begin discussing the portfolio and to explain his or her self-analysis that has led to the organization. Even students who resist organizing their portfolios may, in offering a rationale for their disorder, reveal something interesting about their reading, writing, and attitude toward language.

It should be remembered that establishing anything that is new will take time and patience. Don't expect miracles. Some students may be quite simplistic in their organization and may not appear to be analyzing the portfolio contents much. Encourage those students to reorganize after time. What you should look for over time is more specification in the organization.

Some students will be less able to make their own decisions about organizing their portfolios than will others. But the effort will be worth it. Taking the time to share the importance and purpose of organizing the portfolio is a vital step in encouraging students

Portfolio
Table of Contents

Name Jeremiah Gilliland

Sections/Chapters	What's in this part?	What's this part about?
1. Keeping track stuff	- Table of contents - Reading and writing log - Notes: What I think about reading and writing - Confrence Notes - Other Records - ~~Ideas~~	All these things are showing what I'm doing with the I write,
2. Shorter stuff	- Ideas - Discriptions - Opinions - Unfinished stuff - Public Journal - Reading response Notebook	A lot of this stuff I can use to write things for sections three,
3. Longer stuff	- Papers for class - Directions - Stamps - My detectice PoP co-mixs - Plays * Two last Airdales * father know west - Stuff for Exprecisional Mega ~~line plans~~	This is the most important stuff
4. Me to you stuff	- letter two freind - Journal with Mr. Knox - Journal with Bill W.	This is the stuff communication, It was in section 1 The section 2 Now 4

This sixth-grade boy has a full portfolio organized with a sophisticated focus on process, as his table of contents shows.

to be active participants in self-evaluation. Allowing time for organization not only makes the conference time more productive and efficient; it also provides an opportunity for students to reflect on and become more aware of their own progress.

Have your students organize and reorganize their portfolios before their conferences with you take place. If students organize their portfolios prior to the conference, they will have gone through some reflection about their reading and writing even before they meet with you.

When students take on the responsibility for organizing their portfolios, they will almost naturally reflect on the kinds of reading and writing they have been doing. Students may generate issues about what they have in their portfolios, including the amount of reading and writing, the types of reading and writing, as well as problems and progress reflected by their reading and writing. The focus of your conference with each student is then centered on issues that are pertinent to the student—issues that may be less significant to an outside observer who is not familiar with the portfolio content.

The importance of organizing the portfolio cannot be overstressed because it serves to focus discussions and set a direction for the conference. In order for conferencing time to be worthwhile, it is necessary for students to be prepared. Be sure to give students enough time to *thoughtfully* review the contents of their portfolio prior to the conference. They need to go through their portfolios to consider various organizational patterns. It is not important that the same organization pattern be used for each review/conference period. Indeed, it is probably more revealing to see how students decide to change the organizing themes from one period to another.

Initially some students may lack ideas for organizing their portfolios. You should discuss a variety of organizing patterns like those just described with your students, but you need to be sure that you don't push them to select a particular organization pattern or scheme.

It may help to give them some very practical assistance as well. Show them how to sort the collection into piles representing their major categories once they decide what schemes they will use. That process may point up the need for additional categories or the adjustment of others so that the papers tend to divide more easily.

Taking the major piles, the student may be able to create subcategories within each pile, dividing it into smaller piles. This type of two-layer scheme, for example, might divide the papers by topic as a major scheme; and then within the topics, the papers might be arranged by how nearly completed they are. Or such a scheme might separate as major categories genres like creative original stories, poems, papers related to things read, and personal papers like a journal, letters, and notes. Then within those categories, a two-layered scheme might break each major pile out into papers the student considers strong, average, and weak.

One technique for helping students organize their portfolio is to suggest (but not require) that they group the contents into "chapters," which they name. They can begin by selecting three major things for each chapter and writing a brief rationale as to why each was included. Having done this, they can add other items to each chapter without spelling out the rationale and let a table of contents list what is there.

At the end of the book are two sheets that can be adapted or used as is to guide your students in this activity.

TEACHER ASSESSMENT OF THE PORTFOLIO CONTENTS

Creating student self-assessors remains the primary purpose of portfolio assessment, so a major perspective of a teacher's evaluation of student portfolios is to look for evidence that this goal is being achieved. But teachers are, of course, tempted, and even eager, to review the portfolio contents; and the inclination is highly justified. As evidence of how students process meaning making as writers and readers, portfolios are much like ongoing observation.

Portfolios provide an excellent means to learn about your students' developing interests and language and thinking abilities. Coupled with your classroom observations, formal tests, and classroom activities and assessments, the information you gain from a portfolio review will provide you with a more complete understanding of how each student is developing as a reader and a writer.

There are some major general guidelines that you should follow in using portfolios to evaluate:

- The primary goal of your evaluation should be to understand the student's language development. The purpose of your evaluation of the student's portfolio is not to give it a grade or to render some label you can use to identify or classify the student. Rather, the goal is to achieve a better understanding of what the student can do and how the student feels about the reading and writing that he or she has been doing. The strength of the portfolio is that it can show what each student can actually do—containing a number of responses to classroom activities and including work from outside the classroom as well.

- One of the chief things the teacher watches for is whether the students are assessing/evaluating themselves: Are they becoming more aware of their own reading and writing development and interests? Are they becoming self-assessors? The portfolio reveals the student's attitude toward learning and thinking in general and toward reading and writing activities in particular and indicates the degree to which the student is aware of his or her own development and what can be done to strengthen language use. In evaluating the student portfolio, decide whether it is providing the student with the opportunity to reflect about his or her own reading and writing. What about the way the student has organized and reacted to the portfolio contents indicates what self-assessment activities should be encouraged or introduced and encouraged?

- A teacher should be sure to look for signs of development in both reading and writing. Your assessment should look at the student's total language development, particularly as reading and writing are integrated. The language

The Cheetah and the Snail

There once was a Cheetah named Jazz and a Snail named Pokey. They hated each other because one time Jazz's father ate Pokey's great granda pa, Merl. They always fought but Pokey layed off a little bit because he didn't want to be Cheetah Chow. When ever they saw each other, the would stick out their tongaes and not say a word. So finally Pokey got sick of it and challenged him to a competition. There was two parts to the competition. There was a brains catogory and a physical part. Pokey exercised every day. First he did minty-nine jumping jacks every day. He jogged a mile and had his father even gave him a quiz every day. But Jazz never did anything except lay around and TV all day. When it came the day of the race Pokey the Snail was ready. But Jazz didn't even wake up until 15 minutes before the competition. Everybody was routing for Jazz because they thought he would win and because they knew he would kill them if they didn't. But deep down almost everybody except Jazz's family was rooting for Pokey.

Pokey got sick of it and challenged him to a competition. There was two parts to the competition. There was a brains catogory and a physical part. Pokey exercised every day. First he did minty-nine jumping jacks every day. He jogged a mile and had his father even gave him a quiz every day. But Jazz never did anything except lay around and TV all day. When it came the day of the race Pokey the Snail was ready. But Jazz didn't even wake up until 15 minutes before the competition. Everybody was routing for Jazz because they thought he would win and because they knew he would kill them if they didn't. But deep down almost everybody except Jazz's family was rooting for Pokey. Each part of the competition was worth 100 points so, whoever got 100 points first won. They did the brain part first and Pokey scored 77 points. Jazz only scored 23. Now, it was time for the phisical part. They had a race and Pokey won 98 to 2. Pokey won! He won because he had ran and practiced every day.

Pokey had a big victory party and everybody came except Jazz and this family.

All kinds of interests crop up in this girl's original story: Obviously, she has enjoyed reading fables; and like most students, she considers family attitudes and behaviors to be important. Here they appear to be assigned to the story characters. The ever-popular sense of athletic competition is in the story, too. It gives the teacher a lot to talk to the author about in order to further define the student's interests.

modes or behaviors develop concomitantly, and research supports the conclusion that development in one area is crucial to development in another. The integrated language arts portfolio system is an opportunity for you to see a student's total language/thinking ability at work. Focus on the relationships between reading, writing, listening, and speaking. The contents of the portfolio should contain numerous and varied products that integrate reading and writing in a number of ways. Your daily observations and portfolio conferences with the student will give you some indication of his or her abilities as conversationalist and listener. As you examine the evidence directly related to reading and writing, think of how it compares or contrasts to what you have noticed about the student's thinking and listening abilities.

- Teachers should evaluate portfolios regularly and keep some record. You may want to do so shortly before or after you have a conference with the student and to keep notes of some kind. Forms can be used to speed up portfolio evaluation, or you may wish to keep more complex notes than most forms encourage.

WHAT INDICATORS SHOULD WE LOOK FOR IN PORTFOLIOS?

"All right," you say next, "I can come to my evaluation of portfolios with some articulated criteria determined by my instructional objectives. And I'm to look for *language development as a process* and for *student self-assessment*. More assistance, please! Besides my list of criteria—if I use one—what should I look for?"

Nearly every book and article that you read about using portfolios will give you a set of objectives for using the system. More often than not, they are very similar. The particular emphases in portfolio assessment proposed in this book are not dramatically unique; they too recommend that you watch for certain things. Table 4.1 lists things you, your student, and anyone else examining student portfolios can and should look for. Besides modeling and encouraging ongoing student assessment of the portfolio contents using these same criteria, the teacher will use them in reviewing the portfolio by himself or herself. Under the subsection in this chapter on teachers' evaluation, there are other lists of other indicators, often more specific, and synthesized from many sources. Think about these lists of indicators as guides for portfolio assessment as you read them, and *begin to craft a list that reflects your particular beliefs about language acquisition, development, instruction, and the like.* You may wish to keep your list relatively simple at first to see how it goes: what you learn, how difficult and time-consuming it is.

Then you can modify your list for a second period of assisting students with their portfolios and of examining the collections. Even as you try out the perspectives you decide to use, you will be able to evaluate your students' portfolios with a more meaningful focus. One approach is to very simply analyze student writing and determine one activity that your observation suggests, as in Table 4.1.

BE SURE TO ASSESS BOTH PRODUCT AND PROCESS

While creating understanding for different audiences, portfolio assessment should emphasize *student* self-assessment and focus on *process*. At the same time, one of the rich aspects of the portfolio is how it reveals student interests and thinking, and this kind of analysis depends on the products in the portfolio. Teacher assessment and product assessment are also a very basic part of the portfolio approach. This means that portfolio assessment permits the evaluation of a student's reading and writing from four different dimensions, depending on who is doing the assessment and what they do: The evaluators are the student and teacher, and each examines process and product.

This simple analysis suggests that these are discrete dimensions, but they are not. In reality, language processes are examined by looking at and discussing products. Since

WHAT THE PORTFOLIO SUGGESTS FOR DEVELOPMENT OF STUDENT WRITING

TABLE 4 • 1

What Teacher Notices in Portfolio	What That Suggests
Rosemary has written comparing her little brother to the little brother in Judy Blume's *The Pain and the Great One.*	She likes stories that relate fairly directly to things that are happening in her life. She puts herself into much that she reads.
There is little fluency and connection within pieces of writing in Keith's portfolio.	There is very little evidence in Keith's writing that he thinks much about a topic before he begins writing. The teacher needs to get him to think and plan more about what he will say.
This fifth-grade boy reads one comic book after another and does not record all of them on his log. Most are humorous types; many are about Garfield the cat.	The teacher should look for some humorous stories about cats for him to read—perhaps with a character as ornery as Garfield.
Anders has a note attached to two mysteries he has written saying that they are his favorites. He also has indicated on his log that an adventure story he wrote is his best because "it is exciting." There is not a large amount of writing in the portfolio, however.	The teacher could develop more opportunities for Anders to write. The adventure is a good story. Perhaps if Anders shared it with some fellow students and saw how they enjoyed it, he would be encouraged to write more.
Tad doesn't write a lot, but he draws well and is considered the best artist in the class by his classmates. His journal, which is spotty, is mainly about sports heroes. He also seems to write kinds of reviews about scary movies he has seen somewhere.	The teacher might ask Tad to be the sports editor on the next issue of the class newspaper. He could also illustrate one of his friend Adam's stories and perhaps write a sequel to it. The teacher decides to see if Tad would like to read *Joe Montana and Jerry Rice* by Richard J. Brenner and the mystery *Is Anybody There?* by Eve Bunting. Another book that she could recommend to him is *Scary Stories to Chill Your Bones* by Alvin Schwartz. He could review the ones he reads for the paper and/or for the bulletin board and do illustrations for them.
Heriyadi's story "A Pizzaman's Adventure" is a kind of string of things that happen to a delivery person. It is the same character name as the "Gary" in his story "The City Street." Both of these stories have stringy plots but are very rich in details that build and build until offering the reader a rather complete picture of the character.	There is keen evidence that Heriyadi is thinking about what he writes and its impact on his reader. It's as if he keeps wanting to ensure that the picture is really complete enough for his readers to see it as he does. He should be encouraged to write some detailed, descriptive pieces.
There do not appear to be any obvious reading sources for Benny's writing about bats and Thanksgiving. There are numerous accurate details about bats. He details the familiar feast in describing Thanksgiving.	Benny appears to have used background experience and knowledge in his writing. He could be asked to write about some of the interesting entries in his journal.
The student wrote "Ghost Story" about witches and cats because it was Halloween and he wanted something appropriate. He also has several cats at home.	This boy writes about familiar and immediate things. He can be encouraged to expand on writing about cats by reading a book or two about them.
Harold's "Snow Day" is about sledding, eating snow, and building a snowman. It ends with a question asking the reader what s/he remembers about snowy days.	He seems to be very audience-conscious in this piece. He anticipates that the things he likes about snow will also be what the audience likes, but he has to ask to check it out. Let several classmates react to the piece and ask questions he could answer in revising the piece.

CHARACTERISTICS OF THE FOUR DIMENSIONS OF PORTFOLIO ASSESSMENT

Student Evaluation of Product	Teacher Evaluation of Product
• Periodic—not continuous • Compares products in order to self-assess progress as a reader/writer • Judges products to determine "What do I like and why?" • May organize according to some emphasis in the product, such as particular content • May select show portfolios for particular viewers, such as parents	• Periodic—not continuous • Considers volume • Reviews student interests and attitudes • Examines products as results of instruction • Looks for progress, growth, and development • Judges quality of the products
Student Evaluation of Process	Teacher Evaluation of Process
• Continuous • Focuses on ideas first, skills and strategies second • Emphasizes what student *likes* about the reading and writing • Looks for ideas on how to improve • Is a self-reflection • Engages in organizing ideas and materials, sometimes to show how products developed	• Continuous • Focuses on process and development • Emphasizes getting the student to self-assess • Gives attention to the basic process behaviors with attention to specific student needs in constructing meaning from reading and writing • Evaluates instruction as part of the process

the product is the result of those processes, the two major perspectives are far from discrete.

WHAT SHOULD WE LOOK FOR AS *PROCESS*?   To get at language process, we must:

- Infer process by looking at written products or listening to spoken products. (What is in the expression that indicates how it was thought out, put together?)
- Observe language in use.
- Get people to tell or write what they do when reading and writing. If we interrupt their reading and writing with this *verbal protocol* and ask what they *are doing* or *just did,* it is *introspective;* if we wait until they have finished, it is *retrospective*.
- Use all of the above methods.

TEACHER EVALUATION OF LANGUAGE PROCESSING   What teachers want to know about a student's use of language is clearly related to process; and the portfolio can help them get the answers:

- What background, experiences, interests, and concepts does the student *bring to* the reading or writing experience before it starts?
- What strategies does the student rely on to help him- or herself construct meaning while the reading and writing is taking place?
- What does the student do with the meaning constructed after reading or writing? How does this use compare with the student's purpose for reading and writing in the first place?

T A B L E 4 • 3

AIMS RELATED TO THE FOUR DIMENSIONS OF PORTFOLIO ASSESSMENT

Student Evaluation of Product	Teacher Evaluation of Product
Students need to look at their reactions to reading, written expression, notes, and records they have collected and at what they have decided about it previously. By comparing evaluation of the products over time, the student can draw conclusions about his or her progress based on the analysis. The emphasis is on creating a feeling of success and on encouraging reflection. This can be accomplished by writing a story or drawing a picture that represents his or her reading and writing. It might be promoted with a letter or memo written to parents describing the progress the students sees in the products.	The teacher needs to pull things together for a kind of summative evaluation at the end of marking periods, before conferences with students (or parents), and before reporting to certain other audiences. This is accomplished by examining the products in the portfolio from different perspectives: • The volume or amount of reading and writing • What the content reflects about student interests and attitudes • What evidence there is of growth and development as a language user
Student Evaluation of Process	**Teacher Evaluation of Process**
Students need to engage in continuous self-assessment of what they are doing as they process ideas in reading and writing. This is not just a "How am I doing?" or "How good am I?" kind of evaluation. Rather, it should be a matter of determining "What am I doing? What do I like doing? What do I want to achieve?" The procedures for accomplishing this include keeping certain simple records, writing memos and other self-reflective papers about the portfolio materials, making notes with the teacher during joint assessment conferences and at other times, and organizing and reorganizing the collection.	The teacher needs to engage in continuous assessment of student language behaviors. The attempt should be to identify how meaning from reading and writing materializes, whether students are becoming reflective, and what strategies and skills students need to develop. The procedures for accomplishing this include examining the portfolio for indications of where interests come from, how they affect reading and writing, what sequences are followed in constructing meaning and what students do with it. This evaluation also depends on interviews/conferences, records and notes, and observation.

Thinking, too, is at the heart of the process of using language, so there are meaning-related perspectives that the teacher can watch for. While answering these types of questions depends quite directly on examining the products in the portfolio, the purpose for asking them is to get at the thinking processes that are tied directly to reading and writing:

- How much command does the student seem to have of main ideas and generalizations? Are the ideas expressed in writing framed in some sense of their significance to or impact on the reader? Do examples of the student's writing appear to add up to some purpose for writing or to flow somewhat logically out of stated conclusions and generalizations?

- Does the student appear to comprehend the gist of what is read—the intent of the author—or to take some other meaning adequately related to the student's purpose for reading?

- Do the captioned drawings by very young students, including those that react to reading, exhibit some sense of purpose, theme, unifying feeling or idea, or other quality that prevails as a kind of "main idea"?

The Rainy Day

By Garett P.

Mark woke up. It was raining. "Oh, man," he grumbled. It was the first day of summer and it was raining. "Oh well," said Mark. "I'll call Ryan and ask if he can come over." Mark went downstairs to eat breakfast. After breakfast Mark asked his mom if Ryan could come over. She said, "Yes." Mark went to the room with the phone and called Ryan. "Hello?" asked Ryan. "Hi, this is Mark. I was wondering if you could come over?" "Let me ask my mom if I can." "Okay." Mark heard a silence at the other end of the phone. Finnally, Ryan picked up the phone. "Mark, you still there?" "Yes." "Okay, my mom said I could come over." "Okay, see you then." "Bye." "Bye." In about a hour Ryan rung Mark's doorbell. Mark answered it. "Oh, hi Ryan. Come in." Ryan stepped in. "Hi." Mark took his coat. "What do you want to do?" "I don't know," replied Ryan. "How about some Nintendo?" "Okay," said Ryan. They played some Nintendo they played some board games. In a while Mark's moms yelled, "Ryan, time to go!" "Bye," said Ryan. "Bye," said Mark. After Ryan left, it stopped raining and the sun came out. "Yippie!" shouted Mark.

This boy's interest in realistically sequenced details is interesting, especially in the light of two comments made during the student/teacher conference: (1) that he thought his stories were not very good because they did not contain enough facts and (2) his favorite story was one about driving hogs to the river (market), a story that dispatched ten unfortunate hogs in a series of accidents. (That story had more plot and less detail than any other one he had written.) The teacher decided to stress the importance of story line, hoping to loosen the boy up a bit from his dedication to realism and detail.

- Do ideas, feelings, and contexts recur across products in the portfolio?
- How detail-conscious is the student? Does s/he rely on the details in a text in responding to what s/he has read? Are details applied in some way that appears to serve a purpose for reading? Do subsequent products add enriching details to an accruing interest in and grasp of favorite topics and themes?

- Do the main ideas and conclusions expressed in writing grow inductively out of adequate details and exemplification? Do details tend to accrue as mood or feeling? Are generalizations used to frame or to provide logical deductive flow to details?

- Are the students' retellings and original stories or drawings detail rich? Are the details harmonious content-wise or in some other way?

- Does the student's grasp of texts read rely on the interrelationships between some details? Does the expression and description in writing indicate an understanding of relationships between ideas? For example, is there an indication that the student has used or understood number/order or time sequence; cause and effect; comparison and contrast; classification? Does the student compare story characters, settings, events to each other and/or to life experiences? Are drawings and/or stories sequential in any way? Do pictures, stories, and/or retellings and reactions present an event growing out of a cause? Does the student's organization of materials in the portfolio suggest a self-determined classification scheme? Is organization related in any way to indications of purposes to read and write?

TEACHER EVALUATION OF THE PRODUCTS THAT LANGUAGE PRODUCES

In evaluating the portfolio as a collection of products, you can assess whether your students are actually becoming more effective users of language and what you might do to promote those results. Some teachers may wish to include the student as a co-evaluator in the review of products, using the product evaluation as an additional opportunity to get the student to become reflective about his or her reading and writing or incorporating the evaluation into the student conference. One problem with the latter approach is that the purposeful focus on the quality of the products can smother attempts to look at process.

Other teachers may wish to reiterate evaluations they have made before meeting with the student by focusing on product during a special session with the student in which the student's perspective is allowed to clarify and modify the teacher's. Others may wish to conduct the product evaluation without the input of the student, often after conferencing with the student so that what the teacher and student have agreed to jointly in conference informs the teacher's perspective. Any of these approaches can be useful.

Still other approaches to product evaluation by the teacher involve students by having them select or identify specific work in their portfolios that they want the teacher to evaluate. In such a system, of course, the students tend to identify what they think is their best work, a process similar to creating a show portfolio.

There is no reason that you must stick with one of these approaches across a year or even a semester. You may decide to try one and then another, or to evaluate the products with a combination of such approaches. *Just be sure that you do not end up putting such emphasis on product quality that your evaluation becomes the dominant feature of the portfolio experience for your students or that it torpedoes either your efforts to establish a sense of student ownership of the collections or to keep the focus of portfolio analysis on process as much as possible.*

Product evaluation is a summing up. Usually it is conducted near the end of an instructional unit, semester, or year. However, you may find it useful to sum up a student's progress just before a parent conference, when planning instruction, or just before you are to discuss a student's progress with a supervisor or school administrator.

When possible, it is advisable to do this product evaluation at a time after the student has added a considerable amount of material to the portfolio and has had adequate time to organize and *reorganize* what is in it. After you and the student have analyzed the contents, you should summarize what you have found—just as you encourage the student to do that. You may wish then to suggest that a majority of the contents of the portfolio be banded and moved out of the collection for storage or taken home—after the student has selected unfinished and favorite items with which to begin a new collection.

UNDERSTAND DIFFERENCES AND RELATIONSHIPS BETWEEN PRODUCT AND PROCESS

Since you conduct so many kinds of assessment in your classroom, it may be helpful to review the distinctions between the *product* and *process* evaluation that you will be using in portfolio assessment. *Product evaluation* looks at *how well* someone accomplishes a task. *Process evaluation,* on the other hand, considers *how* someone accomplishes the task.

For example, athletic events have final scores that determine a winner. Looking at those scores to decide how well a team has done is an example of product evaluation. A coach who wants to develop better players, however, will study how each player performs. The coach will study films of the game—and watch at practice—to see how each player performs, play after play, skill after skill. From these observations the coach will be able to see how the player is performing, whether his stance is correct, if he is watching the other players appropriately, or whether he is moving to a proper place on the field or court at the right time. All of these little movements (processes) will determine if the player (and the team) plays well, and, as coaches are fond of saying, the team that plays well (process) is the team that will score the most points (product) and win the game. *Even more significantly, the coach will have the team study the films in group and small sessions. His or her job becomes significantly easier—not to mention more successful—when this approach develops in the team a habit of ongoing self-assessment!*

The metaphor extends to considering athletes who compete individually. A springboard diver, for example, needs to practice aspects of diving that are part of the process, such as starting position on the board, steps taken, height attained during a dive, entry into the water, and the like. The goal is to perfect and integrate all of the parts of the process that will produce a well-coordinated dive to improve the product—the judge's scores—during competition.

This kindergartner's paper is fascinating because the words run into the picture! This child was already making a successful association of language with the things he visualized.

In a similar manner, we want students to use language effectively to succeed in life: to sustain and improve interpersonal relationships, to earn good livings, and so forth. The observation of language process, however, is quite difficult. We may see that a student is reading or writing in inadequate light, amid distracting influences, with inadequate equipment, or at inopportune times that are too short and unfocused. But we cannot see the really important but subtle aspects of how language is processed by observing.

We cannot see the magnificently complex connections of ideas in the brain—of sense of audience, of specific purposes, and so on. So we use one or more of the methods mentioned above. Generally, we must infer what happens when people process language by looking at writing products or products that represent some perspective on reading comprehension. Consequently, much of what we determine about the student's process of using language is gained by close examination of what is written. However, by asking the student how he or she did something, by observing them as they work, and by reviewing initial drafts, we will be able to develop a more in-depth understanding of the processes. On the other hand, examining the products in a portfolio is very much like studying the films of a basketball game, and in that sense, is a genuine process focus. This is particularly true when the portfolio contains materials like drafts, ideas and clippings that prompted writing, and other materials that in sequence clearly indicate what happened *in process*. A single draft of writing based on reading is indicative of thought process as language-structured response.

Another important technique that we can use is, as we have noted above, to encourage students to write retrospective notes telling about the products they examine and indicating how they processed language in creating the products. These can be retrospective summaries based on their analyses of their portfolios and on the reactions of their fellow students to them. They can be observations about particular things they have decided to include in the portfolio or they can be mere observations of ideas they had while reading and writing. All of these reflective pieces or notes are the next best thing we have to an X ray of the "little black language box" with which we think, read, write, speak, and listen.

The fact that all these attempts to generate student self-assessment tend to mix product and process shouldn't bother you. As has been noted, the interrelationship of these dimensions is so close as to nearly defy classification. It is not really possible to look at language process without examining products, and records that indicate process can aid a product perspective as well. *Since you need not stress, or even explain, the process/ product distinction to your students, you can just let the natural overlap of these dimensions support each other.*

We have noted in earlier chapters that some performance assessments create products that can reveal process. The student/teacher conference to be detailed in Chapter 5 provides another good handle for the teacher on process and one of the surest ways to promote that focus in students. During these conferences the teacher can ask the student process-revealing questions like *why* he included certain things, *how* she selected the information used, *to whom* he felt he was writing, *what* she hoped to accomplish with a piece of writing, and the like. In doing this—and by listening very carefully to and clarifying and confirming the student's responses—the teacher uses the conference to model the self-evaluation that the teacher hopes the student will develop.

The conference in which questions that promote this kind of self-analysis are asked is primed by previous analyses of the contents by both student and teacher. These pre-conference analyses, in fact, suggest many particular questions that the teacher may have for the student and that the student may have in an effort to clarify his or her analysis. At the same time, the teacher uses the conference to talk about the student's organization of the portfolio and to review any self-reflective notes the student has included. Out of the discussion comes a focus on goals to direct the student's efforts in the next period and frame the discussion for the subsequent conference.

Regular classroom attention to the collection by the student and informal interaction with the teacher have also already made the portfolio the focus of such metacognitive concerns. The student organizes the collection before the conference and prepares

NOVEMBER 13, 1992

TEACHER

- Jessica likes to read better than write, because its hard to think about what to write about.
- Likes animals, baking food, & making pottery.
- A good book for Jessica may be The Popcorn Story.
- Find a book of poems for Jessica.

JESSICA

I want to find a book a bout food
I want to find a book about poems
I would like to have more storys pictures and work

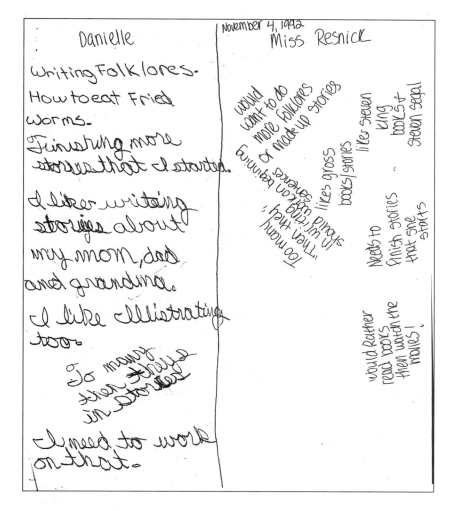

Even the first conference for elementary school children can yield self-determined objectives for the subsequent period of time, as the conference notes above indicate. The teachers used plain paper divided so that the student could write on one half and the teacher on the other.

an updated table of contents. Written synopses of the student's self-analysis of his or her work may also be done at several times preceding a conference. Thus the particular questions the teacher asks are prompted by an evaluation of the collection. In short, the acknowledged purpose of keeping and studying the collection is for the teacher and student to cooperatively understand the student's strengths as a language user and to identify some reasonable objectives and goals for the coming weeks.

All that doesn't *guarantee* that the student will have complete or totally accurate recall of why, how, or when he or she wrote specific words or reacted in certain ways. It is, after all, the *developing* self-assessor that the portfolio approach is hopefully creating, not the language *expert*. The odds are that, with the collection as the focus of a team effort between the student and the teacher, they will indeed overcome many of the challenges in getting at language use process. It seems reasonable that their cooperative analysis and attention to the products of the student's reading and writing will get enough perspective on the process to effectively inform both the student's personal goals and the teacher's instruction.

At the end of each of the conferences, the teacher and student will have conducted as reasonable a *process evaluation* as can be done of the student's language use. They will have talked about the student's reading and writing, focusing largely on what the student enjoys reading and writing and on how the student goes about reading and writing activities. It is also a time when the teacher can coach students about skills, strategies, and activities they can use to become more effective users of language.

What the teacher and student are looking for are not very different. The student is interested in what the process and product evaluation of his or her language use shows about how he or she can develop into a more effective and satisfied user. But more immediately, the student is interested in learning about, clarifying, and articulating particular topics and ideas. Much of what the student learns from and about constructing meaning from reading and writing comes from experiences structured and encouraged by the teacher's instruction. Much of the experience the student gains as a self-assessor comes from teacher-guided activities that model what both the student and teacher hope will become habitual behavior.

"THINK-ALONGS" MODEL THE READING PROCESS

An interesting teaching technique that models this process for students is called "think-alongs" or sometimes "think-alouds." Most teachers need to try this a few times to become adept at it, but what they do is to read a story aloud to the students, pausing as often as necessary to reveal what they are thinking as they read. Actually, the thinking out loud begins before the reading to reveal some purpose for reading.

Usually, the purpose is something other than to model the thinking process, but that will work, too, coupled to some purpose like, "And I thought this story was one that we would all enjoy" or "I've always thought this book looked interesting, so I thought this would be a good time to find out if I'm right." The teacher proceeds to read, pausing—in the middle of sentences, if necessary—to predict, correct impressions and assumptions, comment about words, characters, setting, other details—in fact, almost anything at all.

With the eight icons in mind, the teacher can be sure to cover with the comments all of the basic process strategies. It is a good idea to be sure to pick a text that is short enough to finish in the session when the "think-along" begins. Be sure, too, that there will be some time for the students to discuss what you have done when you have finished.

After this kind of thing has been done a few times, it is interesting to let students who wish to volunteer to try it. It would also work to conduct a "think-along" with writing—perhaps beginning with a letter that focuses on a very particular audience. Be tolerant with yourself in trying "think-alongs." They take some practice, and the best way to do that is before the students. Almost any success you have with them will be of some value to your students and will provide them with some good discussion.

AN EXAMPLE OF A "THINK-ALONG"

The class gathers on the floor around the teacher who sits before them with a "big book" open at her feet and facing them. "I want to try and show you what is going on in my head when I read," she said. "So I'm going to think out loud as I read this book.

"I knew I would like this story when I saw the picture of the kitten. I just love kittens so I knew I'd enjoy reading this story *Stolen Supper*. Poor little kitty, must have been really hungry to steal his supper. Only he doesn't look hungry. In fact, he looks very full. And he doesn't look much like a kitten either. You can always tell a kitten because they are little and their heads are big compared to their bodies and they are cute. But he looks like a nice old cat, I think.

"I do know this: Cats like to eat, and my cats could eat all the time if I'd let them. So they are always hungry. But my cats don't steal. Well, they grab things and run, trying to get me to play with them. I'll have to read to see what this cat did.

"*Portense was in trouble. Again! Again!* Well, this cat is up to something. And it must not be a tomcat. Portense sounds like a girl's name, I think. *But then . . . Portense was always in trouble—not now and then!* Oh, oh, maybe this cat is not as nice as I thought. I wonder if this whole story is going to rhyme.

"*Portense's people were having fish . . .* Well, cats always love fish, but do you suppose she took fish off the table? Oh, my mother used to get very angry at our pets if they tried to get up at the dinner table. I can see the round cat now jumping up onto the table and grabbing some fish. No wonder she's in trouble. *Portense turned up her nose, gave her tail a swish.* Strange cat, this Por-

tense. I've never known one not to like fish. And it is a female cat, since the story says *she*.

"*Did you ever know a . . .* Now what is that word . . . T.a.b.b.y. . . . Is it Tay-bee, like baby, or tah-bi, or what? *Did you ever know a [Tay-bee] who didn't like fish . . . or wasn't gabby?* It must be 'Tabby' and rhyme with 'gabby.' I think I'll look it up or ask someone. Does any of you know? It is 'Tabby,' like 'gabby,' isn't it? Has stripes. I see. Well, that matches the picture doesn't it?"

And so the teacher reads on to find that Portense loved sweet things, and the teacher guesses aloud that Portense will jump up on the table during dessert, then had to adjust her prediction when the lady of the house cannot find the dessert, *which had been left on a yellow cabinet near while Portense sat smiling from ear to ear.*

"I wonder what will happen to Portense. Will she be punished? The family looks very unhappy with her." She lets the students guess and then turns the book to the back picture showing Portense outside in the dark looking up at the door of the house with a frightened look on her face. "I don't know about this strange Portense," the teacher says. "My cat loves to go out at night."

This teacher uses three or four such "Think-alongs" to model reading process: setting a purpose, reviewing what she knows about the book's topic, looking at the story to decide what it is about and to predict, picturing and deciding what makes sense, adjusting or revising her comprehension and guesses when necessary, and getting help when she needs it. Later she lets volunteers try it, using familiar stories at first. Other volunteers follow, and the teacher and then the student models help make the process memorable for all the students.

YOU CAN EVALUATE PORTFOLIO CONTENT FROM SEVERAL DIMENSIONS

There are three broad dimensions of a student's portfolio that can initially guide your product and process evaluation: These involve considering (1) the volume (amount) of reading and writing a student has been doing; (2) the student's general attitudes about and apparent interest in reading and writing and in specific topics, genres, and so forth; and (3) evidence of growth and development in reading and writing.

A SENSIBLE WAY TO START: CONSIDERING VOLUME   By starting with a review of the volume of a student's work for a particular evaluation period, you will become generally familiar with what the student has been reading and writing for that period. In addition to reviewing the reading and writing materials the student has collected in the portfolio, you should review the reading and writing log or logs the student has been keeping. Doing that should give a succinct indication of the amount of reading and writing the student has been doing. Also, the notes that you and the student made during each portfolio conference may give some indication of volume.

It has long been accepted by educators that the *more* students read and write, the *better* readers and writers they will become. You will be able to judge how valid this

T A B L E 4 • 4

WHAT THE TEACHER LOOKS FOR IN ASSESSING PORTFOLIOS

Look for Indications of	Longer Term	Current
The **amount of reading**	Is it increasing across the weeks?	Is the student reading enough to promote development as a reader? Is classroom experience promoting much reading? What kinds of texts have been read? Was much done outside the classroom?
The **amount of writing**	Is the student writing more as the weeks pass?	How much practice is the student getting? with what types of writing? Do classroom activities appear to generate authentic writing? Is any writing done outside of class? How much? What type?
Student's **attitude toward reading**	Is it changing over time? If so, how?	How does s/he feel about reading? Is it enjoyed? Is it valued? What genres are enjoyed and valued most?
Student's **attitude toward writing**	Is the student developing a more positive attitude toward writing?	How does s/he feel about writing? How can one tell? Does s/he like to write? What types of writing appear to be enjoyed most? How is writing valued?
Student's **interests and ideas**	Is there an indication of interests that are developing? Are interests changing?	Does this collection support what you believed you knew about this student?
Use of the **reading and writing strategies** specified below	Are they evolving? Is there indication of increasing use or just sporadic use?	Is the student using metacognitive perspectives as s/he reads and writes? Which are used most?
• **Purpose**	Is reading and is writing being used across time more clearly for purposes the student selects?	Which papers and notes indicate a clear purpose in responding to reading and in writing? Which of these purposes were clearly selected by the student? Is there a difference in any discernible purposes on papers done in class and outside of class? How has the student responded to purposes that tend to be set for him/her?

maxim seems for each student by looking for signs of development and improvement in products and by comparing the degree to which a student has improved and developed to the quantity of material in the portfolio.

Your ability to do this, of course, is limited if the student's policy in selecting materials for the portfolio has been to set standards that are quite high or by limiting inclusion

Look for Indications of	Longer Term	Current
• **Use of background**	How habitually has the student appeared to rely on his/her background in constructing meaning?	Is there any indication in notes and other reactions to reading that background has informed comprehension? Do free reading choices reflect the student's background? How oriented is writing to the student's background? Which pieces appear to rely most on background? How are they different from other pieces in the collection?
• **Getting a grasp before starting**	Across time, do examples of writing reveal more control that would come from prethinking topics? Are there notes or process drafts that reveal this? Do responses to reading appear more thought out?	Which pieces of writing, if any, show an attempt to think out a topic before beginning to write? Which texts generate the most control in responses?
• **Prediction/visualizing/ testing the sense of text/ adjusting**	Is there anything across the collection that suggests that the student is using these strategies more regularly?	Which pieces have the kind of logical flow that would come from thinking ahead, picturing, challenging the sense of ideas, and making adjustments as one writes? Which show reactions to reading in which reader confirmed or rejected predictions and adjusted meaning?
• **Use of resources**	Is there any indication of increasing reliance on resources?	Which papers indicate that the student consulted which resources?
• **Self-assessment**	Do the notes and other reflections in the portfolio indicate that the student is self-assessing more than in previous time periods? Is s/he showing more insight, thinking deeper about what is read and written, expressing reactions beyond "I liked this."	Where are the indications of self-assessment most obvious? In the table of contents? In summary notes? In other writing, such as journals? What do they show about the student's appreciation of factors in this table?

in some other way. This is just one reason that the teacher maintains the right to add to a student's collection and is encouraged to keep an eye on the portfolios as they are developing—in order to get, among other indications, a handle on the screening criteria individual students appear to be developing. By adding overlooked papers, the teacher can model a broader set of criteria without enforcing them, can demonstrate to the student how process-revealing inclusions (such as idea sources and early drafts) make valuable portfolio inclusions, and can assure enough content to allow evaluations informed by overall volume.

Determining the amount of reading and writing a student has done will be less subjective than some of the other judgments you will make, but even this evaluation is somewhat subjective. Generally, you can begin by classifying the amount as *extensive, adequate,* or *limited.*

You can make this judgment by looking at the total quantity of materials in the collection, but you may also wish to separate your consideration of volume into the quantity of materials in the collection that *were not* required and the quantity that *were* required. You can note, as well, how much of the material that was not required comes from outside the classroom. If it is a considerable amount, there is an indication that the student is becoming involved in reading and writing as authentic activities.

There are several other ways to make the judgment about volume:

- **You can compare the student to himself/herself.**

You can compare the volume of a student's reading and writing during a particular period to your evaluation of the quantity in this student's portfolio in the previous period. Does there seem to be an increase? If so, what kind of materials appear to account for the increase? What does it indicate about the student's language development, attitude about language, and degree of self-assessment?

It may be that the amount for the period you are evaluating is not large, but the volume may be greater than the previous period, indicating that the student is doing more reading and writing. Or if it has fallen off even more, there may be some problem with the student's self-concept as a language user that you have not yet considered and dealt with.

The amount of nonrequired material may be increasing, indicating that the student is becoming more involved in language-related activities and/or is beginning to pay more attention to how and what he or she is reading and writing. There may be indications that the parents are getting involved or that language use is increasing at home for some other reason.

This kind of comparison of volume is a particularly reasonable perspective because it uses each student as his or her own benchmark. A student who is not as fluent or who uses selection criteria that are very rigid will not be expected to have as much quantity in the portfolio as other students. You may be working with the student on a regular basis to get him or her to include more things that can reveal interest and attitudes as well as language processing. So you note that while a particular student's collection may not be extensive, you expect it to grow because of particular attention that you have given the student. Volume can relate to how effective your instruction has been and so examining it may be a good way to evaluate your efforts with a particular student.

This comparison of a single student's volume over time periods can cue you to consider whether a student's criteria for selection are changing somehow. Are efforts that you have made to model good criteria for selection that will reveal process affecting the volume of particular students' portfolios?

If a student has less than fluent command of the language, he or she may simply not read and write as much as you wish, or the student may feel less than confident about saving things in a collection that you, and even others, may look at. You can watch for signs that your attempts to praise strengths you can identify in the student's work have led him or her to include more reactions to reading and other pieces of writing in the currently ending period than in the previous one.

Given this perspective, a portfolio that is noticeably spare should give you reason for concern: Has the student had a bad experience related to expression—a disappointing reaction from you or someone else, for example, that makes the student less willing to take risks with language use? Has the student adopted an overly rigid set of criteria for inclusion? Does the student seem unwilling to include materials that show the development and process of language products?

- **You can compare the portfolio's volume to your expectations.**

You can compare the amount of material in a student's portfolio to what you might expect, given the classroom activities during the period being evaluated. Perhaps you did not provide a great deal of time for extra reading and writing activities during the period, or perhaps you did indeed structure numerous activities that were designed to promote the integration of reading and writing and to encourage creativity and other expression that you felt would be authentic. If the latter, you can expect the students to value the products of the classroom activities enough to want to include them in the portfolios.

If your classroom objectives have tended to limit the quantity of reading and writing or to provide fewer opportunities to react to texts read, you may not expect a lot of volume. If that is the case, consider student language development carefully in relation to the limited volume. Are your objectives worth the limited practice and potential development?

If during what you had thought might be a leaner period for the portfolios, some students have added an amount that surprises you, you can look for the reason: Is there an indication that the student is becoming more expressive, more involved in reading and writing related to some particular topic, more aware of himself or herself as a language user?

- **You can compare the volume in a student's portfolio to that in the portfolios kept by his or her classmates.**

Each of your students is a unique individual, and comparisons of students are frequently conducted for the wrong reasons and are generally discouraged among educational professionals. But noting the volume in a particular student's portfolio as it compares to that in the portfolios kept by all your students can give you a sense of how the student's collection fits volume-wise in the range of material that is available to most students in your class.

If Jane, for example, is relatively adept with language but has a far slimmer portfolio than many of her peers, she may be exercising self-evaluation that is too harsh to encourage fluency and the language development that accompanies it. Or she may be unwilling to take risks with language and expression. Or she may not be priming her interests with enough reading.

Comparing the volume in one student's portfolio to that of the class as a whole—not to another particular student—may prompt you to conduct other revealing analyses of the content in Jane's portfolio and may even suggest questions you will want to ask Jane: "Why didn't you include the poem you wrote about the last story in the reader? The version you included of your paper on the rain forests is much shorter than ones you wrote before that. Why do you prefer the shorter version? Do you still have some of the earlier drafts? I would like to include them with the paper you have put into the portfolio so we can look at the process you used in finishing that paper."

This kind of comparison should *not*, however, prompt an evaluative standard like the one suggested in the following kind of comment/question: "The other students have saved a lot more of their work than you have. Why aren't you putting more into your collection?" While you can encourage students to increase the volume of their collections, volume should not be presented as some kind of standard in and of itself.

AN OPPORTUNITY TO EVALUATE INTERESTS AND ATTITUDES   After you have completed the review of the volume of reading and writing that the student has been doing, you will be ready to describe the student's interests and attitudes about reading and writing. Your analysis can begin by considering the volume you have been evaluating in the light of student interest and involvement. How much of the content in the portfolio suggests that the student is truly involved in the reading and writing done during this period?

Attempt to compare the quality of work that gives evidence of genuine student involvement to that which does not. What can be generalized about the portfolio contents that fall outside the portion that suggests student involvement and commitment?

My house is in the woods.
When we go down to
the bus stop we
hear leaves rustling.
We here foot steps.
but behind our house
there's a big field.
We ride our bikes
in the field. My dad
owns 3 acress. We
always go in the woods.
I like it when at
night when we're in the
car he shuts off the head
lights and scares my
sister.

The importance of interaction with his family is obvious in this boy's inclusion of a paper written at home and brought to school to put into the portfolio.

Besides the student's responses to reading and other writing in the portfolio, be sure to examine notes you and the student have made during any portfolio conferences you have had and any other self-evaluation the student has summarized or written out at other times, the reading and writing log, and any other inclusions, like ideas and pictures of special interest.

What topics and genres has the student seemed inclined to read and write? You will find that some students include a wide variety and range of reading and writing materials in their portfolios; the collections of other students may be considerably more limited. Does the student's collection reflect reading and writing from beyond the classroom? Does it cross different subject areas? Whatever is the case, you will find the information created by your evaluation valuable in making instructional decisions.

Whatever topics and genres are evident in a portfolio, they can be used to help the student find more material of those types and on those topics. You will need to find ways to engage students whose reading and writing has seemed limited in order to broaden their language-related activities by increasing the range of topics and genres they read and write about.

Making this kind of analysis allows you to run a check on your grasp of what interests are important to the particular student. Throughout the period that you are evaluating—

and ideally before—you should make an effort to understand the student as an individual by surveying and evaluating his or her interests. What does the material in the portfolio say and show about what you believe you know? Are there indications of new or missed interests? Are there interests that have not been developed through reading and writing? How can the student move on from those that are reflected in reading and writing activities to related and more detailed attention to the topics? What does the student's selection of genres to read and to write reveal about the individual you have tried to know? Are there authors and titles that this student appears ready to appreciate?

While reviewing what you know about the particular student's interests, it is important that you also use your analysis of the products in the portfolio as a primary source of evidence about the student's attitudes toward language. Does the student seem to be aware of himself/herself as a language user? Does s/he like, dislike, or seem indifferent to reading? To writing?

Do the reactions to reading, the conference notes, and other summaries or special notes of self-evaluation indicate that the student is genuinely involved in self-evaluation of what s/he has read and written? How clearly has the student appeared to formulate goals for improving his/her language use? Is there any indication in the materials for this time period that the student has actually held any goal or goals in mind? Is there evidence that some have been achieved? How instrumental to any self-assessment evident in the portfolio for this period does the portfolio itself appear to be? *How would you summarize the student's attitudes about reading and writing?* Have they changed in any significant way since the last time you made this kind of analysis?

This analysis may, of course, be the first you have conducted on this student. Whichever time period is involved, make some kind of notes that you can look back to when you are looking at the student's products for indications of interests and attitudes during the next time period.

When you are examining portfolios, make notes about how you can use what you have learned. Here are some examples from a fourth-grade teacher named Ms. Mallory:

- Writing products and reports on reading in several of the portfolios demonstrate that a group of students are keenly interested in the air quality of their community. Some have been reading the articles in the newspaper about how air quality relates to the local economy. I can form a study group and ask the librarian to create and lend us a display of books and articles about air pollution. (The students could help prepare it, and later do a display.) Maybe a student publication could grow out of this.

- Develop a letter-to-the-editor project out of the air issue and other local issues that crop up across portfolios.

- Billy C. is having a problem getting dialogue into his stories. Learning how to punctuate it would give him more confidence, but so would a little fluency. See if he will bring the car-racing story back to school. That may be why he didn't finish it. Can I get him to identify the problem so that I don't have to point it out?

- Some of these kids seem to be tightening up—losing their fluency. There are fewer "freewheeling" stories for this period, and those that there are appear shorter. What happened to all of the great risk-taking that was under way last time? I fear there has been too much emphasis this quarter on mechanics. One way to solve this may be to emphasize and praise fresh content and ideas as the students select what they want in the spring class magazine. Then—after the good stuff is identified—a group of volunteer peer editors could go over the mechanics with the student authors.

- What's happening over in Washington Heights? Those kids all seem up on their neighborhood. Maybe they could produce Jason's play over there.

LOOKING FOR SIGNS OF GROWTH AND DEVELOPMENT   You will, of course, want to know if your students are developing as more effective language users. An important way to judge this with a broad perspective is to ask questions like these:

- How fluent a reader and writer is the student becoming? Is he/she writing and reading more? If less, what appears to be restraining language use? Is the student taking risks with language? Are there increasing indications that the student is developing his/her own voice as a writer?

- What indication is there in the products that the student is applying or seriously challenging the ideas encountered in reading? Is there a tendency to deal with more details in topics that recur? Does the organization of the writing indicate that the student is getting a handle on valid generalizations and/or different aspects or categories relevant to the topic?

- What types of texts is the student reading and writing? How much variety in types or genres is there? Is he/she attempting new writing forms? Is there any indication that clearer purposes for reading and writing are dictating some of the forms?

- Does a development of thinking ability appear to be accompanying any development of language noted. Can reactions to reading be described and "increasingly thoughtful"? (Note examples.) Is there indication of criticism that is supported or more carefully thought out than in the past? Are details sometimes structured into categories, comparisons or contrasts, or causal analyses? Are there valid generalizations that appear to grow out of or be supported by details?

- Are papers in the portfolio related to plans for other projects and other writing? Is there evidence of this kind of preparatory planning?

- Is there evidence of increasing attention to standard language forms and conventions? Does it appear to strengthen the student's expression? Is there any indication of developing variety and effectiveness in sentence structure? Is there any direction toward incisiveness, color, or other development in diction?

You should not use these questions as a checklist to be applied to each student's collection; rather, you should be aware of these—*and other considerations that your philosophy about language use and development suggests adding*—as you examine the products in a particular student's portfolio so that you can note those that reflect particular strengths and those that suggest ways to encourage development you feel is important for that individual.

You will already have answered some of these questions by evaluating volume and student interests and attitudes, but the tendency in reapplying them should be to look more closely at individual reactions to reading and other pieces of writing and to compare particular papers in the collection. Fluency, for example, will be evident in volume, but in writing style, as well. With fluency comes a surer, better flow of ideas and more natural sentence structure.

Types and genres of text reveal progress as they compare to earlier analyses of portfolio content. The kinds of signs of development that you should look for will vary, naturally, depending on the level of your students. Similar analyses can be done of the portfolios of much younger readers by asking questions like these:

- Do the student's pictures and captions demonstrate a sense of story structure: beginning, middle, end?

- Is there evidence of more detail in drawings and any captions accompanying them?

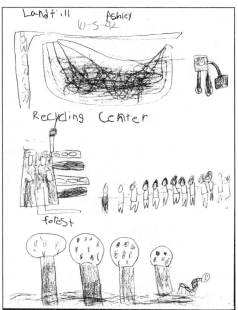

In reacting to a story called "The Dark Dark Tale," this first-grader demonstrates an impressive understanding of how stories are structured. First-grader Ashley's paper on recycling would make a wonderful addition to any child's portfolio and tells a wonderfully clear story. What an effective poster it would make!

- Do the creations of the student relate in more obvious ways to stories read and/or to classroom discussions?
- Is the student using drawing and writing more to express himself/herself than to parrot things heard?
- Is there any increasing continuity across drawings and pieces of writing?
- Do the products tend to reveal more about the student's interests and background? Are they incorporated into the writing process?

Rather than relying on these particular questions, however, it is far better that you use them in constructing your own, using your philosophy of teaching, your understanding of and familiarity with your particular students, and your knowledge of the classroom activities that you assume have contributed significantly to the development you are looking for.

A student's metacognitive awareness is a direct indication of how language aware he or she has become. So the way the portfolio is organized will be revealing. If you have looked at this student's portfolio before, has he or she reorganized or clarified or specified organization since the last time you examined the collection? What does the order and any comments on the table of contents tell you about the student's sense of how language is used, how it serves his or her needs, and whether goals set by the student are being met?

Do conference notes or other student notes help clarify this indication of student grasp of reading and writing—its strategies and its purposes? Any indications in the portfolio of the student's reflections about his or her own reading and writing should be noted in terms of how they reveal increasing appreciation for language and language-related strategies.

Once again, it is not just the reactions to reading, stories, and other pieces of writing that will inform your determination to note student language development; but particular types of student writing should be examined with special sensitivity as well. Process sequences, such as prewriting ideas and notes, early drafts, and final revisions, will be very revealing of what the student has learned *and applied* to his or her own expressions. Of key interest should be whether the student is demonstrating an inclination to revise, a vital part of the process that so many students resist.

Reactions to reading should be examined particularly carefully. Is there an indication of increasing sophistication in reacting to reading texts that is obvious in a sense of how authors and their readers relate, in attempts to incorporate styles read into the developing student voice, and the like.

The eight icons that are applied frequently throughout this book apply again in evaluating portfolio products and looking for language development. They are purposefully *process*-focused, yet they can be adapted to product evaluation as well—illustrating once again how much process and product overlap in analysis that must rely so considerably on product to evaluate process. Finding indications of these processes in products is easier, perhaps, in reactions to reading than in writing.

A reaction to reading, for example, may mention or imply that a text read fulfilled or disappointed the purpose the student had for reading it; and in doing this, the student may make assumptions about the audience he or she believes the writer had in mind. Such purposes are based on what a reader already knows about a topic and are formed, therefore, with that consideration of background knowledge. They also make assumptions and predictions about what a text will be about.

In reacting to these kinds of expectations, a reader may reconstruct evidence of visualizing the text as it was read and of summarizing its fit to the purpose for reading as the discussion progresses. It is basically in negative reactions to a text that a reader may report and detail his or her attempts to understand what did not become clear, and sometimes the sources consulted in seeking the meaning that did not become clear are revealed.

These evidences of reading processing are not often so clear in written reactions to text, and rarely do most of them occur. To find evidence of even one or two is quite worth noting, however, and indicative of a developing metacognitive prowess in a student. This is true even when such indications are not explicit in products in a portfolio and must be inferred. They might be drawn, for example, from texts such as the following:

- A drawing of a story that incorporates far more detail than was supplied in the narrative and obviously came from the student's background.

- Drawings and captions that suggest surprise or astonishment, suggesting that story events contradict a clear prediction or assumption inferred from story art, title, and so forth.

- "I new It! She couldn't wait! She sat on the chr an the paynt is stiil Wet! Big sirprise! I always said she was a stoopie cat!"

- "He wrote this for people who hate rock'n'roll, and I love it! I knew this guy was going to make me realy mad!"

- "I thought the space ship would sail right through the black hole, but the story ended with it in there! Wow! What a surprise!"

- "Now I know that raccoons don't wash their food, the way I thought. But I want to read some more stuff and find out why they sometimes put their food in water before they eat it. Maybe they aren't so clean, after all."

- "So Maria took umbrage. I thought she was cobbing some kind of spice from the cook. Even my brother didn't know. He thought she must be hiding from something. Well, I found out in the dictionary. What an odd way to have a character get mad about something. I wonder if this writer isn't just showing off."

These are just a few samples of the kinds of comments in products that can reveal process. They come from looking closely at products, but they are basically a view of process.

Such inferences are more difficult to get from a student's writing, but you may become adept at seeing them. Drafts that have words crossed out and ones that have been found in sources written above them are one example; a few texts may address a reader or very clearly invite a prediction. All such instances are delightful examples of how your attention to the eight language-processing icons can lead to spotting evidence of the processes you hope you are developing *within* products in the portfolio. They are sure signs of your students' development as language users! Here is a kind of checklist of others:

- More details in descriptions.
- Discussion of how a paper developed across several drafts included in the portfolio.
- Signs of changes written into any draft of a paper.
- Writing with evident beginnings and conclusions.
- Reports on reading that tell how something learned has been used, has changed what the student believed, is worth challenging as incorrect, and the like.
- Reference to something written or read in earlier periods, indicating a new understanding of the topic.
- Reaction to something by an author who has become a favorite.
- A creative imitation of an author's style, story structure, and the like.
- Questions to an author or about a particular text.
- Comparisons of characters, settings, themes, and styles *across* stories.
- A synthesis drawn without direction from two or more texts.
- Information located to elucidate, confirm, contradict a text read.
- Writing with clearly personal purposes, including affective pieces.
- Reports on/reactions to reading done outside of class/in other subject areas.
- Fuller, more logically flowing ideas.
- Increased mention of things read.
- More vigorously expressed and detailed opinions.
- Increasing reliance on standard English.

SIGNS OF SPECIAL TALENTS   Portfolio contents are the best indicators in the classroom of special student abilities. Look for the signs, and remember that "a gift" need not be a creative genius or super high or quickly applied intelligence across all or even many subjects, topics, and behaviors. Even students with deficits in certain disciplines, a Texas state manual on portfolios reminds us, may develop products that show resourceful use of materials or evidence of high interest and perseverance. (*Texas Student Portfolio:* See citation for Hiatt under "Advice on How to Conduct Portfolio Assessment" in Appendix B.)

Knowing about these strengths allows the school and teacher to plan instruction and experience that will maximize the student's potential to succeed. A table of identifiers in the Texas guide cues teachers to indications of gifted ability that may be found in portfolio content:

- Things written in unusual and imaginative ways—even diction or style that may seem eccentric, odd, or offbeat.
- An interest in "adult" issues with details not normally provided by the student's age group; a command of advanced or technological material not yet presented in school.
- A whimsical, sophisticated, or keen sense of humor.

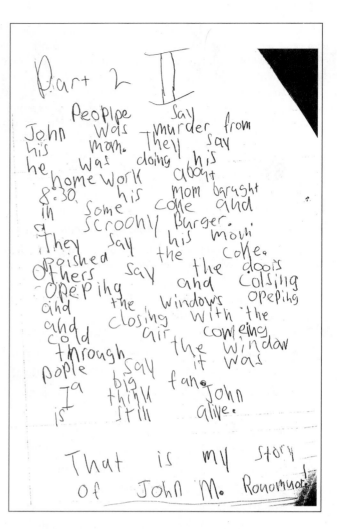

This third-grader displays a wonderful sense of humor. Note the freshness, the play on words, the teasing whimsy, and the sense of satire.

- Use of complex, asymmetric, difficult, or novel ideas or sophisticated problem-solving approaches.

- Ability to organize elaborate detail effectively and/or to judge what is important; to analyze problems; to grasp topics, ideas, or skills not frequently commanded by peers—often indicating a long-term or unusually intense interest in certain topics.

- Ability to improvise using commonplace materials.

- An innovative vocabulary.

- Ability to exemplify, illustrate, elaborate in explanations, descriptions, and story-telling; experience with exploratory research approach; use of unexpected resources; ability to synthesize information from multiple sources.

- Ability to organize and structure and communicate in unusually clear, concise, and sequenced manner—sometimes accompanied by ability to enhance presentation with unusual visuals.

- Tendency to become involved and absorbed in problems and complicated tasks; an enduring curiosity; a long-term commitment to some out-of-class activity.

ADD YOUR ANALYSIS TO THE PORTFOLIO

When you have finished evaluating (1) volume, (2) student interest and attitude, and (3) development, summarize what you have found. A very simple kind of summary encourages you to note several things about the student's use of language based on these perspectives of the portfolio collection, and then to integrate your observations into a descriptive synopsis or plan of action. Not only does this summary report encourage you to synthesize what you have found, but it also gives you a record to use in comparing what you find the next time you evaluate the portfolio.

There are numerous guide sheets for the teacher to use in Appendix C. They can be copied for use or taken as models for ones you develop yourself.

These summaries may prove quite useful in other ways. You can use them to develop class profiles to use with supervisors and administrators and other teachers as you discuss your students' language development.

The summaries of evaluations and your contribution to the conference notes are not the only notes you can add to the portfolio to aid both your and the student's evaluation. Make notes of observations and anecdotal experience that will inform on the student as a language user and add them to the portfolio. Sometimes evidence of student development, interests, attitudes, and self-assessment happens unexpectedly, or at least spontaneously, during the course of a class discussion. In a conference, the comment could go in the student's notes; in other cases, you have to make a point to do that at your first opportunity. It is useful to jot down observations of such metacognitive/reflective comments so they can be available to your and the student's analysis.

Such notations do not need to be about startling events. Rather typical observations like the following can be very useful:

> "Even though Beth is having to work very hard at developing her reading strategies to keep up with the rest of the class, she is motivated and likes to work hard. During class discussion, she is frequently the first to volunteer reactions and information; and she seems very eager to learn. Even so she gets distracted very easily."

CUSTOMIZE YOUR OWN EVALUATION PROCEDURES

You may decide after some experience in evaluating your students' portfolios, or even before you begin portfolio assessment, that you will want to examine other factors when you evaluate student portfolios. Use the guidelines suggested in this chapter to formulate the procedure you intend to use, and devise any records that you intend to keep.

There is nothing sacred or prescriptive about the approach suggested here. There are, however, some questions you should keep asking yourself as you design your evaluation approach:

- Will it protect student sense of ownership, an absolutely essential environment for successful portfolio assessment?
- Will it leave the student feeling responsible for self-assessing and not turn the portfolios into key products to be graded?
- Will it leave room for the student to focus on how language serves him or her and not impose selection criteria that will make student control cosmetic?
- Will it focus on language *process,* authentic purposes for reading and writing, and making meaning with useful, interesting ideas?
- Will it keep fluency, communication, and expression primary over language mechanics?
- Will it encourage the inclusion of reading and writing done outside of class, the development of personal voice, and creativity, as well as improved thinking?

- Will it value and promote the integration of the different language behaviors?
- Will it tell me:

How much/well the student has developed as a language user and thinker in the time period being considered?

What both the student and I can do more effectively to help the student develop as a reader and writer?

Whether the student is developing significantly as a habitual self-assessor?

There are valid options and techniques that teachers can use in evaluating portfolios to help limit the time that the kind of evaluation described above would take. Here are just a few examples:

- You can follow the three separate focuses above and eliminate keeping records on each of them, opting instead to keep only the summary record.
- You can consider the three perspectives at one time as you look at the portfolio, making notes that can inform a summary record.
- You can apply just one or two of the perspectives in a particular period, alternating for subsequent periods. This works particularly well if you are evaluating more than four times a year.
- You can have the students select from their portfolios the papers that they wish you to evaluate—as a kind of show portfolio that they may select at other times to show to particular viewers. You can specify certain numbers of certain types of papers, or you can have the students include only the materials that they feel best illustrate the process they follow in making meaning with language. This method, which uses one technique for promoting student self-evaluation, tends to require that the teacher have certain familiarity with the contents of most portfolio collections, so that if a student selects in a way that tends to misrepresent himself or herself, the teacher will be aware of it.
- You can sort portfolios as you use one or more of the first three of the four steps discussed above. For example, you could place those portfolios that have extensive volume in one group, those with adequate in another, and those that are limited in a third. This kind of evaluation works best when you are primarily interested in whole-class evaluation and want an indication of instructional impact; but you can, as you do this, make notes about individual students as well.

SHOULD YOU GRADE A PORTFOLIO?

Invariably many teachers ask, "How do I grade a portfolio?"; and there is a surprising amount of emphasis on grading and rating them in the literature. There are ways to do that, of course. Most try to compare portfolio content to a set of criteria that the teacher creates to match instructional objectives. The student is supposedly aware of how the portfolio is being judged and may even have helped articulate the criteria. The rating gains validity when the criteria grow out of (a) instructional goals and objectives and (b) student interests and purposes. The idea is also to try to make the rating more objective—more reliable.

That can be done to some degree, but the many factors that make an individual student's portfolio collection unique and powerfully revealing tend to work against the attempt to grade and rate. The student's background and developed abilities also make what he or she does with language highly individualistic, endorsing a subjectively determined rating—if you are determined to grade portfolios.

There is a very real danger of negating the value of portfolios by placing emphasis on portfolio grading and rating, however. The minute the student knows you are grading or rating or ranking his or her portfolio, the responsibility for doing that ceases to be his or

ONE TEACHER'S USE OF PORTFOLIOS

In reporting in *Portfolio News*, teacher Jane Hancock reports how she evaluated her students' collections: "Their portfolios held examples of many kinds of writing, some finished, many unfinished. As the students worked on each assignment, I read their papers but gave no grades, just positive comments as well as suggestions for making the pieces of writing better. Once each quarter students individually met with me and we reviewed

together the whole body of their work and discussed their grade, based on completeness, effort, improvement, attention to the conventions of writing, and style. At this time, the students wrote a letter to me, referring me to several pieces that they wanted me to evaluate, discussing how those pieces reflected their growth and scope as writers."

Source: "But . . . what about grades?" 2 (Winter 1991): 3.

hers. The more emphasis you put on any sort of grading of the portfolio, the more apt you are to undermine the student's sense of ownership and commitment to *self*-assessment. The more the student thinks of you as a grade-wielding audience—as opposed to a partner interested in finding out how he or she can develop as a language user—the less validly the portfolio represents the student's interests and purposes for using language.

There is another problem with grading portfolios that stems from the emphasis portfolio assessment appropriately places on the ideas contained inside it. Examining these—but not evaluating the substance of them—is an excellent way of assessing the student's developing interests and attitudes. As all teachers know, it is the support, development, clarity, and, to some degree, the consistency of those ideas that can be evaluated, not the ideas themselves. When grading a portfolio, a teacher runs some risk of

This personal note was an entry in a fourth-grade student's dialogue journal kept with her teacher. Does it seem appropriate for the teacher to grade the package it is included in?

appearing to evaluate the interests and values that a student is encouraged to reveal in a portfolio. This may be no more problematic than trying to be objective when grading a single piece of student writing, except that it puts a tag on a package that tends to represent more of a whole thinking/value system.

It is misleading to think of portfolio assessment in the way that we have thought of standardized, normed, or even criterion-referenced tests. While it is not uncommon to evaluate portfolios using criteria that reflect instructional goals, we ought not lose sight of the primary goal of portfolio assessment: to increase everyone's understanding of the student as an individual with language abilities that are developing and constructing meaning in response to unique interests and purposes. Almost everything we have agreed on about reading and writing over the past 20-some years recommends that goal; and none of the other, more traditional assessment approaches is even faintly as capable of doing that job as well!

"Well," you say with a somewhat defensive sigh, "if we're going to put all this time into developing and analyzing portfolios, it's got to have some impact on the marks that go on report cards!" Perhaps, but consider this: If portfolios increase your understanding of the individual student, they are sure to inform any evaluation you make of his or her work—be it an individual paper that may or may not end up in the portfolio, or some subjective summation of a student's effort and achievement over a grading period.

If because of the portfolio, the student comes to feel like the authentic proprietor of his or her language development, the attitude is sure to affect performance on whatever language-related efforts you are grading and averaging—raising the student's report-card grade as a reflection of instructional goals more effectively achieved.

If you start noticing those kinds of results while using a portfolio system, you should be quite comfortable with not grading the collections in an effort to protect their ability to involve your students.

"But," you add with one final plea, "the principal and supervisors see these large collections of student papers and may expect to see a grade on the collection as a project in which we have invested a lot of time." If these special audiences see a grade you have put on a portfolio, they may subconsciously feel that a good share of their reason for looking at the collections may be done for them—just as analysis will be closed off for the student once he or she sees your ranking. That's not what we want from portfolios!

Just like students, parents, supervisors, other administrators, and any special audience looking at working or show portfolios should be left to draw their own conclusions. Of course, both the student and you can assist the analysis with notes, memos, letters, and other analyses of the work that you have done daily and in conference; but the main impact of that analysis only contributes to the overall effect you want the portfolios to have: "Hmmm," you hope the administrator will think, "look at how much reading and writing these students have done. I guess I tend to forget what an integral part of learning language is. And I'm surprised that the students seem so aware of themselves as readers, writers, thinkers, learners."

Some special viewers may come to portfolios with established criteria, and some of the measures they apply may lead to expressions of concern about what they find. "I'm quite surprised," one father might say, "that you aren't marking and making my daughter correct her misspellings!" You get the chance, using the collection, to point out that misspellings decrease from drafts to final copies, across time and papers included in the portfolio; to note how inventive spelling is yielding to the convention that such parents may value so much; to talk a bit about your goal to encourage fluency; and to show how reactions to reading and creativity are prevalent in the collection to a degree that might surprise the parent. When the kind of exchange just depicted here occurs, the portfolio is serving its purpose: to create understanding of the student as a language user. And think about it: What other assessment approach can you think of that would have equal effect?

ALL RIGHT, ALREADY! THERE MAY BE A WAY   There is one recommended way to grade work that grows out of portfolio assessment, but it is not grading the *working* portfolio. If it seems essential to grade the student's portfolio assessment efforts as a kind of project that has involved a reasonable amount of time, pull from the working portfolio a show portfolio for that purpose. This can be done in a variety of ways:

- You could have the student select a sample of his or her best work to put into the special portfolio. The student could write an evaluation of the papers to introduce them, and could be allowed to grade the collection before you grade it.
- You could instruct students to select three papers or sets of papers that they think are their strongest and then you could select from the remainder of the working portfolio three other papers or sets. Then the student could prepare a written evaluation of the work, explaining its strengths and indicating how it demonstrates his or her growth as a thinker and language user.
- You could sit down with the student and together select the strongest work for the special portfolio and together assign a grade based on the strength of the material and, more importantly, on the development it reveals.

Whatever method you devise, it should emphasize that looking at the whole collection in the working portfolio is still more important than selecting and evaluating the reduced collection. That this needs to be stressed reminds one once again of the dangers involved in grading portfolios. The primary purpose of portfolio assessment—both as it serves the student and the teacher—bears repeating one final time here: To develop in the student the habit of ongoing self-assessment motivated by an appreciation of himself or herself as an ever-more-capable thinker, writer, and reader.

SUMMARY: TWELVE KEY WAYS TO ASSESS WITH PORTFOLIOS!

- Have the student build a collection of a variety of types of writing written for various purposes and audiences and provide class time for the student to critique them individually and attach notes to each piece analyzed.
- Give the student regular opportunities to keep track of the collection and its relationships to texts read in a comprehensive log.
- Help the student learn to organize the collection in categories and subcategories that are meaningful and interesting to him or her.
- Emphasize to the student that the primary purpose of the portfolio is to use in becoming a self-assessor who analyzes and is aware of his or her development as a language user and thinker.
- Promote student analysis of portfolio contents by interacting with him or her and asking good questions about the interests and development the collection portrays.
- Help the student to understand that the portfolio products portray the process of using language and that that should be of primary interest to the portfolio keeper. Encourage the student to engage in metacognitive self-questioning about that process.
- Build your ongoing informal exchanges with students about their portfolio contents around regular, more formal conferences that identify progress and goals and objectives for the future.
- Assess both product and process to identify student strengths and needs.
- Model and use "think-alongs" to promote metacognitive awareness and ongoing self-assessment among your students.
- Look at different dimensions in assessing portfolios: volume, student attitude and interests, and individualistic signs of progress.
- Correlate what you learn about individual students to your theory and philosophy of language growth and teaching strategies.
- Develop and perfect your portfolio assessment abilities by identifying and understanding an increasingly meaningful set of indicators that show in portfolios progress, talent, and student instructional needs.

C H A P T E R   F I V E

CONFERENCING

FOR SUCCESS

Minimally, you should schedule and conduct four portfolio conferences with each student each year. This may seem like a great deal of time—and it is. If each conference averages 15 minutes (about the right amount of time at the elementary level), you will be spending an hour with each student on a one-to-one basis over the course of the entire year.

REASONABLE OPTIONS FOR MEETING

THIS CONFERENCING GOAL

When you first start with portfolios and conferences, you may find that four one-on-one conferences each year are more than you can handle. That's fine. If you can't manage four, then see if you can do at least one individual conference with each student each semester.

Those two conferences will help you to gain experience in managing and organizing the time with your students. If individual conferences seem like too much to handle, then do small group conferences, meeting with perhaps three or four students each time.

Yet you should think of these portfolio conferences as one of the most important teaching and assessment opportunities you will have with your students, and we strongly urge you to work toward the four individual conferences per student per year. However, it is more important for you to get started and to learn how to plan for, and conduct the conferences. This chapter will take the position that four is the ideal number, but don't hesitate to get started because you cannot achieve that goal in your first year.

There are difficulties in scheduling and conducting conferences within a school in which students change classes and have a different teacher for each subject. This class organization is prevalent in many middle and junior high schools and even at the intermediate grades (5 and 6) in some schools.

It is almost impossible for a teacher who has five classes of 25 students each to find time to hold four conferences for each student for a total of five hundred conferences per year. One way around this problem is to take advantage of team teaching. Students who are scheduled for social studies, science, math, and language arts classes with different teachers can benefit if those teachers can plan together the kinds of things they would like to see in the students' portfolios. This would include such things as the kinds of projects as well as reading and writing that can serve the students across the curriculum.

The first conference period can involve all four teachers, each of whom would conference with about one-fourth of the students. At the next conference period, the teachers would conference with a different quarter of the students. In this way, each teacher would have conferenced with all of the students at least once by the end of the year, and each student would have had a total of four conferences.

This arrangement calls for especially careful note-taking, so that the teachers who subsequently conference with a student can know easily what a team teacher and the student decided about the collection and what objectives were set for the subsequent period. But this plan of operation can be very effective since it necessitates careful planning by the teachers and an agreement about the kind of reading and writing activities they believe cut across the curriculum. The students will come to realize that all of the teachers value their reading and writing, even though each has a somewhat different perspective in coaching their development.

Student portfolio conferences provide an opportunity for you and your students to discuss and assess their developing reading and writing interests and abilities. When you listen to your students in these conferences and in ongoing exchanges about their portfolios, you are sure to discover or be reminded that they can indeed construct meaning as readers and as writers. An overriding impression produced by talking one-on-one with your students about their language development will surely be that they use the strategies that result in comprehending—in constructing meaning, whether in reading or writing.

If portfolio assessment is a means of discovering that our students are indeed language users, what are we trying to teach? The constant theme of this book is that we want youngsters to become self-assessors of how they construct meaning. But portfolio assessment—and the somewhat formalized endorsement of the analysis it involves that we give by conducting conferences—achieves other worthwhile and closely related results worth reviewing:

- It builds the confidence of the students in their own ideas.
  The conference should demonstrate the teacher's respect for what the students think and for the topics that interest them. This acceptance is focused in the conference and combines with the student's sense of his or her increased competence in expressing ideas to build the degree of self-confidence that supports self-assessment.

- It raises their awareness of themselves as thinkers—particularly as they acknowledge and respond to the ideas of others, who may hold views that vary from their own.

T I P

SOME ORIGINAL IDEAS FOR
SCHEDULING CONFERENCES

Here are some examples of the kinds of creative ideas teachers have devised to make the scheduling of conferences a natural part of classroom activities:

1. A first-grade teacher has her students let her know when they are ready for a conference. They keep their portfolios in pizza boxes. (She utilizes deep-dish pizza because the boxes are deeper. She also has Velcro strips glued on the box tabs to make for easier opening and closing since the cardboard tabs on the boxes are difficult for little first-grade fingers to manipulate.)

   The boxes are kept in "cubbies" on one side of the room. When a student feels he is ready for a conference, he goes to a large empty paint can on the teacher's desk. In the can are three paint-stirring sticks with a figure of a child with his hand raised stapled to the stick. The student takes the stick and places it in his pizza box portfolio with the figure of the student sticking out. This is a signal to the teacher that the student is ready for a conference.

   When the teacher finds time during the day, she calls the student to a small table in the back of the room for the conference. When the conference is finished, the student puts a check mark on a large chart the teacher has constructed that lists all of the students' names and has a place to check when each conference has been completed. The students know that a second conference is not possible until each child has completed the first conference.

2. A fifth-grade teacher organizes her conferences during her author circle writing times, which she schedules every Tuesday and Thursday afternoons. During these authoring circle periods, the teacher schedules various students for an individual conference. The students look forward to this private time to discuss their reading and writing with the teacher. This schedule allows the teacher to conduct three or so conferences each Tuesday and Thursday and still have time to walk about and encourage the authoring circle activities. She has little difficulty fitting in one-on-one conferences four times a year with each of her fifth-grade students.

3. A group of primary teachers in one school organized their conferences by calling them portfolio picnics. The students sign up for their picnic, which is in reality their lunch period. The students and the teacher eat lunch together and begin to talk about their reading and writing ideas as they eat lunch. After eating, they spend time looking at the portfolio materials together and making notes about what they want to work on next. These came to be called "portfolio picnics" because this school is located in a warm climate where there are benches and tables outside the school and the teachers and students often eat lunch outdoors.

While these three ideas may not work just this way in your school, they may give you some ideas as to how you can creatively arrange the time to conference with your students.

This enlarged understanding of multiple perspectives and meanings promotes an intensified appetite for enlarged and new ideas.

- It raises student thinking to a higher level by encouraging them to consider how they are making meaning as readers and writers.

   Not only can the conference focus this metacognitive awareness, but that self-assessment encourages the practice of basic thinking skills like inference drawing and other inducing, categorizing for comparison and synthesis, and both deducing and challenging the generalizations of deduction.

- It helps students become purpose-motivated language users who are aware of targeted audiences and of the need to revise and refine ideas for those audiences—in the broadest sense of the term—for *publication*.

From the teacher's perspective, the conference provides an outstanding opportunity to learn about students' language use. The teacher gets a clear idea of how much reading and writing each student is doing. More importantly, the conference requires that the teacher focus on the student as a unique individual with particular interests and ideas—with different reasons for using language and unique approaches to using it. It is also an opportunity to coach the students as developing language users.

AN IMPORTANT STEP IN THE ASSESSMENT PROGRAM

The conference is not, of course, the only—or even the first—time the teacher and the student confer about the portfolio contents. The papers should be thoughtfully evaluated by both the student and the teacher in impromptu and planned exchanges that occur regularly.

The student does this as he or she adds papers, attaches evaluative sheets or other comments to them, and places them within whatever organization the student has structured for the collection. It happens more intensively whenever that organization is challenged and restructured. It can occur with classmates in opportunities like authoring circles. It occurs as the teacher moves about the classroom informally during times allotted for working on the collections, answering questions, commenting about new inclusions, and reacting and offering advice in other ways. All this is done regularly, frequently, and informally—on a daily basis if needed.

But in addition to this kind of ongoing communication, the portfolio conference is a regular time for the student and teacher to sit down one-on-one and discuss what they believe the collection shows. While the nature of this conference should be relaxed and informal, it is, nonetheless, more formal in the sense that it is regularly scheduled. The student and teacher anticipate it and plan and prepare for it. When it takes place, the attention of the teacher and student is more focused on the collection than at other times.

An upcoming student/teacher conference should be viewed by the student as an opportunity to ask questions of the teacher about the collection and about the reading and writing process. But it also involves an obligation for the student to review his or her work in preparation for the session—to think about the collection and to reorder it if necessary.

The exchange that takes place during the student/teacher conference is a primary opportunity for the student and teacher to examine the portfolio contents together in an effort to assess how the student is developing as a language user and thinker. Even if ongoing, more informal attention to the portfolio is less frequent, focused, and analytic than it should be, these conferences can ensure that the portfolio is more than a kind of unique file folder—more than a mere place to store samples of the student's work.

THE NEED TO KEEP IT CONVERSATIONAL

The conference should be friendly and casual, yet it can have an air of formality that holds the student accountable for having given some serious thought to his or her work. This general objective should not lead the teacher to turn the conference into some kind of "grill session." Observations that promote student response are much better than questions that seem to demand an answer. For example, the teacher may use praise and observations about the collection as attempts to get a conversation started. The teacher can say something about his or her own interests and reactions to particular texts. This approach is more apt to produce an in-depth response from a student than questioning will. And a list of questions asked of a student turns an opportunity for a conversation into an interrogation, which removes the student from the role of thinking his or her own thoughts. Here are just a few examples of the kinds of statements that may work well:

- "When I read that story about the old dog, I thought about Carrie, the dog I had when I was in the fifth grade."

  This is a better attempt at getting a conversation going about a topic and a developing paper than "Who did you want to read this paper about the old dog?"

- "I was wondering how you felt while you sat with the dog at the vet's office."

  This comment as an attempt to generate an exchange is better than "Why didn't you describe what it was like to take the dog to see the vet?"

- "There is a wonderful story here. Everyone who ever had a wonderful dog would want to read all about how you felt."

  This is a better way to encourage revision and development than "Would you be willing to redo this paper and make it a story that tells more about how you felt?"

- "Karen has a paper about her dog in her portfolio. Maybe you two could exchange papers and give each other some advice about how to make them into stories."

  This is much less intimidating than "Don't you think you should add more descriptive words to your story?"

At least you can attempt to generate conversational response during the student/ teacher conference before resorting to questioning that gives the student the feeling that it is a session that you control. The accountability that the teacher wants to establish is for the student to account to himself or herself as a genuinely involved self-assessor. That means that the conference has to be a nonthreatening exchange—primarily a pleasant conversation—during which the student comes to understand himself or herself better as a person with good reasons to read, write, and think ever more effectively. The conference may not cover all the ground that the teacher would like to review, but if it minimally involves the student to that degree, it will succeed.

USE THE CONFERENCE TO LEARN
ABOUT THE STUDENT AS AN INDIVIDUAL

A logical and challenging question that some teachers ask is, "Look, if I am doing a good job giving individualized attention as my students build and organize their portfolios, what do I gain from more formal conferencing?" This chapter provides many answers to this question, but a single benefit that makes conferencing worth the trouble is that you can discover that your students are even more interesting as individuals than you have already realized.

The portfolio conference can achieve this if it is a good conversation with each child about his or her ideas and interests, beginning with what is represented in the portfolio. As the examples that will be offered at the end of this chapter show, the conference succeeds if the teacher uses it as a genuine attempt to find out what is on the student's mind. This one primary benefit will be, almost without fail, rationale enough for whatever challenge conferences are to schedule and conduct.

The conversational nature of the conference can also reveal other things about the student that are relevant to successful instruction and learning. You may discover that you

If you have not had an opportunity to use it before, the interest questionnaire in Appendix C might be administered following the conference.

have not been able through formal and informal classroom activities and conversations to tend to particular problems students have or to answer particular questions they have been wanting to ask:

- "I wanted to put the stuff I like the best in the first section. I can't decide if this thing about the way earthworms multiply should go there. Do you think it is one of my best things?"

  Questions about organizing the portfolio and about evaluating the contents can come up at any time, but the portfolio conference promotes them because the student spends time looking over the collection getting ready to talk about it with the teacher. The opportunity arises to stress that the collection should reflect the student's assessment, not yours.

- "I wrote a thing about crystals for science. I like it, but I was afraid you didn't want science stuff in here."

  Some students may not want to risking looking "dumb" by asking about some very simple concerns when other classmates are around, but the portfolio conference gives you a chance to deal with them—in this case, stress how eager you are for the writing in the portfolio to cross subject areas.

- "I read more comic books than anything. Do they count as reading and can I put them on my log?" "I wrote a rap song. I suppose that doesn't really count as writing."

  Very legitimate questions and comments like these are more likely to be asked seriously in the conference, which gives you a chance to explain that reading involves enjoying many kinds of texts and writing crosses lots of ways of expressing oneself.

- "I want to put this story about my little brother in my portfolio, but I wouldn't want my mom to see it. You said she might look at the portfolio on Back-to-School Night. So I have to leave it out, right?"

  "I have some stuff I really like in my journal. But I don't want to put the whole thing in there 'cause I saw Martha looking in other kids' portfolios. I don't want her reading my journal."

  Questions about the privacy of the portfolio represent the kinds of concerns a student is not apt to ask about when working on his or her portfolio in the classroom. The focus and relative privacy provided by the conference is more likely to accommodate them.

LET THE CONFERENCE LEND WEIGHT TO ANALYSIS OF PORTFOLIO CONTENTS

It is almost certain that you will find from holding conferences that students somehow focus on questions and express needs for help that never would have surfaced in daily opportunities to work with their portfolios. There is apt to be something about the formality of scheduling and conducting the sessions that gives the student's portfolio and his or her analysis of it a kind of weight, importance, or endorsement that it would not otherwise have:

- The upcoming conference will seem important—even exciting—to very young students, who may begin adding more caption writing to the drawings they have collected.

- Thinking in terms of an upcoming conference brings questions about the contents of the portfolio into a clearer focus. One student, for example, may have been keeping his dialogue journal up front in the portfolio with things he continues to work on. Tempted to put it in a later section that includes letters and memos and notes to particular people, he decides to leave it up front. The decision reflects his keen interest in the ongoing exchange with a best friend and causes him to discuss with his teacher whether he should consider re-organizing the whole portfolio by how completed or finished things are, instead of by genres.

After praising the boy's interest in genres, the teacher notes that he could go ahead and move the journal but keep it in a subsection to be established in all sections of the collection for unfinished writing. The boy decides to consider that after the conference.

- The prospect of the conference may require settling on an organization that has not quite come together in time for the conference. The problem may be made evident by the need to make a new table of contents that displays the somewhat disjointed nature of the new organization on paper. The need to force the organization for the conference, where it can be discussed, can encourage students who are overly concerned about how logical their organization schemes appear to take a kind of risk that becomes a kind of breakthrough.

- Getting ready for the conference tends to promote analysis that crosses more than one paper; it prompts comparisons, summarizing, and even synthesis— even when the depth of the new intensity is not fully obvious to the student. The approaching conference tends to crystallize questions and opinions, and to clarify some ambiguities.

Comments and questions about process and evaluation of product are more apt to surface in the conference than as the teacher circulates in regular classroom situations. The conference allows the time and focus that can produce student/teacher exchanges like these:

- **Student:** "I have been trying to figure out what to do with all this odds-and-ends stuff. It's got some good ideas in it that I want to remember. But I left it at the end here because I wasn't sure where it should go. Maybe I should just take it out of the portfolio."
  Teacher: "I keep stuff like that in my portfolio because I'm sure I want to write more about it. Some people have a kind of "Ideas" chapter. I was noticing the picture of the beautiful horse and thinking how much fun it would be to read a story about that horse."

- **Student:** "It seems that nearly everything I write is alike. I saw that when I started looking through things because I knew we were going to talk about it. Maybe I need some new stuff to write about. I sure like writing about baseball, though. But I guess I've got enough stories and other stuff about that."
  Teacher: "Oh, I think that happens to a lot of writers. I was looking at things I've written the other day and I noticed that I write an awful lot about my garden. 'People will think that's all I care about,' I thought. So I took a kind of break and just wrote a letter to a friend. I didn't even mention my garden, and I wrote a lot about school. My friend wrote back and asked, 'Hey, what's become of your garden?'

  "It would be a shame for you to quit writing about baseball. I think those stories are some of your best stuff. I was thinking earlier that you could put all your baseball stories together in a kind of book about baseball. Meanwhile, I noticed that you wrote about camping in your journal. You know a lot of things about that. I have an article about wilderness hiking you could read if you want. I would really like you to tell me more things about camping."

- **Student:** "I know why I hate this stuff. I've been writing it 'cause I thought you like it, not because I wanted to. I think I should read and write about some stuff I like. What should I pick?"

Teacher: "I can't tell you what you like. You tell me. I do know what I like a lot in your portfolio, but I'm not going to tell you because I want you to pick the ideas that interest you. I also know a story of yours that I like a lot that you didn't put into the portfolio. I know what. Let's each make a list of things that we like to read and write about. Mine will be what I like, not what I want you to like. Then we can compare lists in a few minutes. I'm really eager to see what you will pick."

- **Student:** "I was going to do another picture to show what happens to the fish later, but I forgot. I think I will do that for next time."
  Teacher: "Oh, you mean Salty. I like that fish. That's a wonderful idea! I hope nothing bad will happen to him. He is a saltwater fish, right? He couldn't live in a lake could he?"

Exchanges like these can happen in daily, informal situations; but that isn't nearly as likely as it is in portfolio conferences. Even if it accomplishes little else (which is unlikely), the portfolio conference makes it clear to the student that the things in the collection—and the ideas in there—are important and worthy of discussion.

THE CONFERENCE'S POTENTIAL TO SET MEANINGFUL OBJECTIVES

By conference time, of course, you are somewhat familiar with the student's collection and you already know enough to make observations and to ask questions that can promote self-analysis by the student. This self-assessment continues after the conference with direction that the conference discussion has provided. The focus of a successful conference should help the student set some specific objectives or goals for becoming a better reader and writer during the weeks that follow.

Often these objectives are as practical as agreeing that it would be interesting to read more stories or books by a certain author or on a certain topic.

An objective might simply acknowledge that a particular story or other piece of writing is worth revising or developing. Another might use a story as a platform to develop a project of some sort.

Sometimes such objectives are basically a short list of intentions to avoid certain usage errors or to adhere to language conventions that the student may have been avoiding. It is quite satisfying when self-assessment brings a student to unsolicited and unintimidated recognition of how language conventions can assist readers. But if these are the only or primary objectives resulting from the conference, it probably has not been adequately focused on ideas. Such focuses are too infrequently accompanied with intentions to pursue developing interests and particular authentic purposes to read and write.

Several key guidelines for the conference can help produce useful objectives:

- **Communicate about ideas.** What is the point of saying something with perfect and beautiful diction and perfect grammar and spelling if the expression is not worth comprehending? Begin with a primary interest in the meaning the student has or wants to construct—the interests and background revealed by the portfolio collection. With that kind of beginning, it should be possible to consider language conventions without losing the focus on ideas.

- **Emphasize process.** One way to avoid an overly tactical focus in portfolio assessment is to make an effort to keep the student thinking about his or her language use as process. Portfolio conferences should help students understand that making meaning from language is a process.

Students' comments during a conference should indicate how process-aware they are. Suppose, for example, that a student professes that she did not really understand a text to which she has reacted in writing. It is a chance to discuss behaviors that might have resolved the problem. Did she have a clear purpose for reading the text? Did she relate the story or text to what her experience tells her about the topic? Did she predict/anticipate, visualize, adjust meaning while reading? Did the student seek help from any sources? In short, the conference can become an appropriate time for the teacher to suggest how reading strategies can contribute to comprehension.

Suppose, for another example, that a student expressed discontent with something he has written that is in the portfolio—perhaps something the teacher has selected for inclusion. It is an opportunity to discuss the student's purpose for writing the piece. The teacher can explain why she thought it a good example of the student's thinking and writing, and the student can explain why the piece fails to appeal to him. Chances are that in such an exchange, that teacher will learn something about the student that she did not know.

The result may be that the teacher will convince the student that the piece has more promise than he thought, or the teacher may realize that the piece was far less valid for the student than the teacher thought. If the former, the teacher might convince the student to rewrite, responding to some objectives they outline together: a clearer description based on better visualization by the student or on a clarification of the audience, for just two examples.

- **Focus on progress.** Another way to keep attention on process-oriented strategies and away from an overfocus on language conventions is to get the student to discuss and articulate the progress that he or she has shown as a reader and writer over the time period the conference concludes. The teacher can attempt to steer this analysis to a focus on how well the portfolio contents have served the student's purposes for reading and writing.

This kind of self-evaluation is missing in most assessments, because for most of them the teacher is the only person with access to the assessment results and to the key or guidelines for interpreting them. In portfolio assessment, the information is created and collected by the students, and they learn to interpret it according to their own needs and interests. Just examining the materials regularly will promote some of this assessment, but students need guidance and modeling to use the portfolio as effectively as possible; and the conference is one place for that to happen.

You don't have to eschew a student's self-determination to rely more on conventional spelling; you can praise the decision. But by keeping the primary emphasis on what language use is doing to serve his or her genuine interests, you present a much more convincing demonstration of why all concerns about language use are important. You also promote the assumption of responsibility for development by the student; and when self-assessing becomes a habit, it serves to promote lifelong development as a reader and writer.

THE CONFERENCE SHOULD STRENGTHEN INDIVIDUALIZED INSTRUCTION

The portfolio conference can help the teacher set goals as well. Your familiarity with the student's portfolio has taught you something about his or her reading and writing interests, habits, overall abilities, attitudes toward language, and development as a language user. You can know this before the conference—well enough for you to frame comments and questions for the conference that can clarify and increase your understanding of the student as a language user, thinker, and learner. Ideally, you should come out of a conference convinced that you know the student better than before.

The conference is an opportunity to check the intensity of the student's interest in a new topic that recurs in the portfolio. It is a chance to find out how the student's background has contributed to this and other interests. The conference is also the time to check out purposes that have not seemed clear or convincing, and, if necessary, to help the student identify some more authentic reasons to read and write.

The goal of this increased understanding is to make you a better teacher. By the end of the conference, you should be able to join the student in articulating a few highly appropriate instructional/learning objectives for the next several weeks. Ideally these should be based on compelling reasons to read. Here are just a few specific examples:

- To laugh at something new by a favorite author.
- To get the information needed to make a more detailed model of a spaceship.
- To follow an interest about some animal, a particular period in history, a sports heroine, and the like.

Objectives set for writing should be framed within purposes for which the student can generate some real enthusiasm. A few specific examples include:

- A captioned drawing to give Dad for his upcoming birthday.
- A letter to the author of a science text, explaining why the student thinks a piece of information may be incomplete or inaccurate.
- A story relying on the student's presently consuming interest in dinosaurs to select characters and setting.
- A set of instructions to a worrisome little brother on how to treat their puppy more humanely and to care for it properly.

Some objectives may focus more on strategies. Reading objectives can include, for example, using resources to look up key words that are not recognized, pausing as a story develops to relate details to the student's background and experience, or employing any of the other key process strategies.

Writing objectives may include tactical commitments, such as the intention of using more descriptive adjectives, paragraphing more frequently, or being sure to use question marks appropriately. But objectives such as these can be expressed within plans for activities, projects, and so forth that develop the use of language in ways that will serve the student's interests and authentic purposes for reading and writing.

For example, the student could determine to cope with and master the names and classifications of dinosaurs in order to make a timeline chart of when different species are believed to have lived. This could be indicated by listing particular sources or by articulating strategies for finding sources of information.

Alternatively, descriptive adjectives might be derived for an existing draft of a story or character sketch by first illustrating the characters and/or settings in detailed drawings and then finding words and phrases to describe the details in the drawings. Classmates might also be asked to draw characters or scenes based on some description as a test of how effective added details have been in helping the reader visualize what was described.

CONFERENCES CAN PRODUCE CUSTOMIZED GOALS AND PRIORITIES

The goals or objectives that are established during portfolio conferences will be different for each student because the focus of each conference should be different and personal. That means that you do not go into a student conference with a set or checklist of items that are used with all or most students. Rather you approach the conference with focuses for discussion based on your evaluation of the particular student's portfolio and your observation and ongoing instructional experience with him or her.

The portfolio helps you recognize the ways in which individual students can best develop as thinkers and learners who depend on language. Your analysis of the contents of portfolios enables you to understand how your students will want to expand reading interests in a *variety* of ways. Individuals will want to read about certain topics—or books by favorite authors. One student may want to try writing a play while another may be eager to compose song lyrics. Some students may want to become more confident oral readers while others may want to learn how to find reference materials more quickly and easily.

Few of your students will know precisely which strategies and experiences will serve them best, but you can help them identify them. While this can be done at any time, the portfolio conference is a highly effective time for that to happen. If portfolio assessment is successful, students will become more and more capable of doing this on their own; but it is in sessions like the conference where they come to understand how to do this and why it is important.

When you combine the information gained from reviewing the materials in the portfolio with what you learn from the conversation that you have with the student about those materials, you should have a deeper understanding of the student's language abilities and a clearer indication of what language experiences are most likely to increase them. This understanding allows you and the student to discuss priorities for the student's reading and writing activities over the next period that are relatively unique for that student.

PORTFOLIO CONFERENCE
PLANNING AND PROCEDURES

Like any effective teaching methodology, successful portfolio conferencing takes some planning that sets out some sensible procedures. This begins by introducing the concept of conferences when you are introducing your students to portfolios, suggesting the kind of partnership you hope to develop with your students and emphasizing the importance of both analysis of portfolio contents and the chance to discuss them in the conferences.

As the school year progresses, you will need to reinforce student awareness of the importance of the conferences without making them intimidating in any way:

- Discuss what will happen in conferences with your students not long before the first ones begin. Be sure they know when the conferences will be held and that they are to look at the materials in their portfolios, think about them, organize them, and make out a table of contents showing the organization before each conference.

- List the students who are scheduled for conferences on particular days in a prominent place.

- Try to arrange to hold the conference in a place that will provide a degree of privacy for you and the student, who should not feel that he or she is on display in front of classmates.

- Find inventive ways to work all the conferences in, demonstrating to the students the importance of conferencing through your determination to conduct them.

- Follow some sensible general guidelines and conferencing strategies.

INTRODUCE THE CONCEPTS OF
PORTFOLIOS AND CONFERENCES TOGETHER

Early in the portfolio process, explain to your students that you will be meeting with each of them several times throughout the year to discuss their portfolios. You may not want to go into much detail when you are introducing portfolios the first time, but it is a good idea at this time to mention the conferences and how important they are. Emphasize that you and the students will be able to look at their portfolios many times during class all through the school year to discuss the things they are reading and writing. Explain that they can come to you with questions and for advice whenever they feel they need it.

Tell them that there will be, in addition, special times when you will meet with each of them so they can tell you about the things they have been reading and writing and about the ways that they are using language. Point out that these conferences are a time to kind of sum up what they have been thinking about the things they have been reading and writing (or drawing).

You need to be sure that students do not view the conferences as a grading session. Students should understand that these conferences are private times to talk with you about their reading and writing. Emphasize that the conferences are an opportunity to meet with you to share their thoughts about favorite stories and the kinds of writing they are doing, to talk about good things they think you should notice about their reading and writing, and to discuss things that they find difficult. Perhaps there will be things they would like help explaining. Emphasize to your students that conferences are a time to ask questions and a time when you are eager to learn about their ideas.

PLANNING FOR FOUR CONFERENCES REQUIRES SOME SCHEDULING

You will want to be organized and systematic about establishing conference times. The schedule for conferences should be planned so that you talk with each student every couple of months—after he or she has had time to accrue new materials in the portfolio and to reorganize the materials one or several times or to subcategorize while thinking about them.

Of course, you will be talking with each student about some aspect of his or her portfolio many other times—informally during class, and particularly during times you have set aside for working with portfolios. Ideally, during these opportunities that occur regularly between scheduled conferences you will be able to move about the room as students work with their collections in order to observe, to comment about what you notice, to listen carefully as your students respond, to answer questions that the students have, and to offer advice.

Even so, it is vital that you *schedule* a minimum of four formal conferences with each student. At that frequency, student portfolios will have about eight weeks between these formal student/teacher analyses to develop. Experience has indicated that about 15 minutes is an average length of time for these conferences, although time will vary depending on many things—including your busy schedule.

SCHEDULE THE INITIAL CONFERENCES EARLY   The first individual conference should be held not long after the students have set up their portfolios and have begun collecting papers for them. For later conferences, you will want to be sure to allow

---

KEEPING TRACK OF
CONFERENCE SCHEDULES

Student names could be written on cardboard with magnetic tape attached. These could be put on the blackboard when certain students are due for the conferences. They could then be removed after the student has had his or her conference. You could also leave a note board for students to sign up for conferences when they feel they are ready to meet with you.

There is a blackline master for keeping conference notes in Appendix C. You can, however also use a plain sheet of paper, folded or otherwise divided down the center.

enough time for portfolio contents to accrue and for the student to think about them; but holding the first conference relatively early gives the students an opportunity to raise questions about what may be a new assessment procedure for them. The early conference gives you the opportunity to evaluate how clear the portfolio procedure is to each student and to prompt important questions your students may not have felt free to ask in front of their classmates.

In addition, a conference early in the year helps you get to know your students early and to learn about their reading and writing interests. The conference is an opportunity to interview the student, using what the portfolio may reveal about background, interests, and attitudes about language as a starting point for initiating revealing conversation and for framing friendly questions.

The initial conference may very well include a discussion of what is meant by the term *portfolio*. You may want to discuss professionals who keep portfolios, such as artists, architects, and photographers—and the reasons they do so. You can discuss how some portfolios are used to keep only the best work while others collect a lot of work so progress can be determined.

AT LEAST THREE MORE CONFERENCES SHOULD BE SPACED THROUGHOUT THE YEAR   The remaining three conferences should be scheduled at regular times throughout the year. The second could be scheduled around the first of December, the third about the first of February, and the final conference near the beginning of April. During these conferences, the student and teacher review the reading and writing log together. It and the work samples and other materials in the portfolio provide a comprehensive basis for talking about reading and writing.

Together the student and teacher discuss attitudes, interests, and reading/writing strategies. This is also a time to review the materials that both the student and the teacher have added to the portfolio. All this provides you with a minimum of four formal opportunities throughout the year to learn about your students' literacy progress. In addition to what you learn, the students will become better self-assessors because their exchange with you during the conference will become a kind of model of the self-analysis they can conduct afterwards. The conference should demonstrate to them how to gain valuable insights about their reading and writing interests, abilities, and development.

Finally you will have created four distinct points in the academic year when you and the student deliberately and carefully articulate some objectives or goals for that student's language development in the weeks that follow the conference.

For all these reasons, it is important to think of these sessions not as times for you to judge your students but rather as opportunities for your students to develop as individual learners as you guide them to think about themselves as readers and writers.

CREATE A RELAXED AND NONTHREATENING ENVIRONMENT

The physical arrangement for the conference should be as comfortable as possible. You'll need table space to spread out the contents of the portfolio and to allow you and the student to write on the conference notes without shifting about awkwardly.

Ideally, you and the student would have a private place to examine and discuss the portfolio, but experience shows that that is not often possible. Conferences must often be scheduled during classtime, and the teacher must retain responsibility for the other students, who may be working independently or in small groups. Be sure that the class has sufficient assignments and resources so they can work independently while you are conducting conferences. It may occur during a session regularly scheduled for the students to get their portfolios out to work on them.

Allowing the students to move about too freely can create problems, making the classroom too noisy for the conference or distracting the teacher, who feels the need to caution particular students. If the class understands the importance of the conference and the need for easy conversation between the teacher and the student being conferenced, that task may be easier. It will be good if you and the student can discuss the portfolio contents in modulated tones that the class cannot distinguish easily. You need to help your students understand that conferences are private times for each student and that they should avoid interrupting when you are conferencing with one student.

The student you are conferencing with needs your attention, so the situation you set up should try to ensure as little interruption as possible. This will give the student an opportunity to develop his or her ideas and will establish for all your students that the conference is a very important event.

BE CREATIVE ABOUT FINDING THE TIME FOR CONFERENCING

One of the most frequently asked questions at workshops covering portfolio assessment is "How do I find the time to schedule four conferences for each student each school year? I have 30 students; you are recommending 120 conferences; at even 15 minutes each, that will take 30 classroom hours a year. How do I get the job done?"

It would be foolhardy to argue that this concern is not legitimate. One might propose that portfolio assessment recaptures the time it requires by saving time in instructional planning and by guiding individualized instruction quite effectively; but it remains that with all of the other demands on your time and energy, conducting the all-important portfolio conferences will not be an easy task. Successful use of portfolios for assessment depends on successful conferencing, however, and the benefits of the portfolio approach make scheduling the conferences worth the time and effort.

The different situations for individual teachers do not recommend prioritizing specific ways to find the time for conferences in your classroom. What will assist you in doing that depends on many things, including your teaching style, the help you may have available from volunteer tutors like parents or teacher aides, and the willingness of other teachers to team teach when conference time comes around.

Portfolio conferences are much easier to plan and schedule in a classroom where authoring circles, reading/writing projects, and individual reading assignments are typical daily instructional activities. In this type of classroom, portfolio conferences become a natural part of the ongoing activities.

Regardless of your situation, finding time for portfolio conferences will be a challenge, but remember that their value far outweighs the difficulty you will have in finding the time to meet individually with your students. Depending on the way you organize your classroom and plan instruction, you may be able to use some of the suggestions in Table 5.1: 25 Ideas for Scheduling Portfolio Conferences. The authors have devised this list in a challenge from teachers attending portfolio conferences and workshops to live up to the promise that there are "at least 25 ways to schedule and carry off conferencing."

The suggestions are not fully developed here. For example, learning contracts, sustained silent reading, authoring circles, and portfolio organizing sessions are all ideas that are included below. If you decide to try any of those ideas, you will need to search out other references about those activities if they are not familiar to you.

OTHER SENSIBLE GUIDELINES AND
STRATEGIES CAN HELP ASSURE SUCCESS

Here are some other commonsense general guidelines and strategies that can help assure the success of conferencing in your portfolio program:

BE A GOOD LISTENER Your aim should be to establish the conference—and the entire portfolio assessment program—as a means for the student to learn to self-assess. Consequently, it is vital that the sense of ownership that one hopes to establish in

25 IDEAS FOR SCHEDULING PORTFOLIO CONFERENCES

General Ideas	Specific Suggestions
Getting someone to work with the remainder of the students while you conference with individual students is usually the most convenient solution. If you have assistance available, you should not turn the portfolio conferencing over to the person who helps you. Conferences are so important to you as a teacher that your personal time with each student must be protected.	1. Teacher aides are available in some schools and they provide a useful resource. 2. Parents are often willing to serve as teacher helpers. Some can explain their vocations or avocations to students in a way that provides very valuable information and broadens students' interests. 3. Some schools provide opportunities for older students (often high school students) to serve as teacher aides. If activities are carefully planned, these students can work with the class while you conduct conferences. 4. Team teaching arrangements provide ideal opportunities. You and a fellow teacher can plan some large-group activities during which the two of you can take turns working with the total group of students while one of you conducts conferences.
*Many activities in an **integrated reading/ writing program** provide conferencing time.*	5. When students are organizing and reviewing their portfolios to get ready to conference with the teacher, several portfolio conferences can be held with those who finish their organizing more quickly. 6. During student-led authoring circles, you could conduct several portfolio conferences with students. 7. The time that students are engaged in reading/writing activities such as revising and editing papers for publication is another good portfolio conferencing time. 8. Library visiting periods are usually a key part of an integrated language arts program, and while students are engaged in library research or browsing, you can meet with individual students. 9. Many teachers provide time each day for students to write in journals. You may find time to conduct one or two conferences during this journal-writing time. 10. It is very useful to have students summarize their thoughts about their portfolios in writing before they conference with you. (Kindergarten students can draw pictures of what they feel their whole portfolio says.) During this self-reflection time, you can conduct conferences.
Time outside of class can be used if you can coordinate your schedule and that of some students.	11. Some school systems provide short periods either before or after school for teachers to meet with individual students, and these times can be used for portfolio conferences. 12. If students have scheduled study periods or other flexible time in their schedules, you may be able to plan to meet with them during these times.
You can also attempt to work the portfolio conferences into your regular instructional time without looking for "extra time."	13. Some teachers utilize individual learning stations as a regular part of instruction. One of these can be developed as a portfolio station where the students come to meet with you while other students are engaged with other learning activities. 14. Portfolio conferences are often natural ongoing activities in reading/ writing classrooms and they need not be scheduled. Students in such classes seek out teachers to discuss the latest story or book they have read or to share a written piece with a teacher. However, it is important not to depend on the conferences happening by chance. You have to make sure that they do happen. 15. Peer tutoring can be organized around activities such as buddy reading or shared reading, conferencing about written pieces, or developing special projects. During these peer-tutoring times, you can conduct conferences.

General Ideas	Specific Suggestions
	16. Sustained silent reading is a time when all students (and the teacher) are to be reading silently. However, given the importance of conferences to the support of reading, you may want to use that time to schedule portfolio conferences.
	17. Many teachers plan a variety of class activities when students work independently or in small groups. These include such things as doing research for a project, preparing art materials for a story or poem, and self-selection of a reading or writing activity. During these independent class activities, you can plan to conduct portfolio conferences.
Giving students the responsibility to find the time to meet with you works well in some classes. In using these suggestions you will not be solving the time problem, but you can get the students to share the responsibility for finding the time.	18. Learning contracts can be developed where one aspect of the contract is that a student must schedule an appointment to discuss his or her reading/writing portfolio with you. 19. Post a schedule and tell students that they must sign up for portfolio conference time during the scheduled times. These times could include class periods where you have scheduled large group activities that you don't have to monitor—or before or after school.
If you have tried some of the ideas above, and you are still struggling to find the time for portfolio conferences, here are some suggestions that can help you get started when all else seems not to work.	20. Start out with small group conferences. You may have organized reading or writing groups in your class. Use these groups to conduct small group conferences, giving each student an opportunity to discuss his or her portfolio. Small group conferences are not nearly as effective as individual conferences, but they are a way to get started. 21. You can have a kind of conference without even meeting with your students. Have each student write notes about his or her portfolio and then you can collect the portfolios and after reviewing the contents of the portfolio, you can write a response to what the student has written. 22. Peer conferences are a good idea later in the school year, after you have conducted several individual teacher/student conferences with each student. Peer conferences are of limited value if the students have not experienced in-depth discussions with the teacher about reading/writing ideas. If, however, you can demonstrate an excellent conference with one or two students while the rest of the class listens in, you may be able to start out with peer conferences. 23. Have students take their portfolios to a learning center (perhaps a table in the back of the room) equipped with a tape recorder. Have the student review the contents of the portfolio and tell you (through a taped message) about all of the things in the portfolio. You can listen to the recording and leave a recorded response to the student's message. 24. Plan a two-stage approach to conferences. Have the students do peer conferences before (or after) they conference with you. If they are held before, they give the students an opportunity to get their ideas together before meeting with you. If they are held after your conference, they give the student an opportunity to expand on ideas you have started by talking with another student. During the peer conferences in this two-stage conference time, you can conference with individual students. 25. This last idea is left open for you to write. The opportunity emphasizes that classrooms are organized differently and that teaching styles differ. There are many opportunities for portfolio conferences in your class. Add them to this list of ideas.

the program in general carry over to the student/teacher conference. It can be fatal to the success of your program if the student looks on conferencing time as an accountability session. That means that you must strive above all else to keep the conference casual and conversational—as already stressed.

Try to engage the students in conversations about their work by commenting about it in such a way that your observation will encourage them to comment in an effort to confirm your observation, enlarge upon it, correct it, clarify the work you are commenting about, and so forth. It will be very tempting to resort to questioning, and if it becomes necessary to generate input from a student, keep the questions open-ended. Try to get the students to share their beliefs and understandings about the topics in their reading and writing and about reading and writing (and thinking) as processes. If you resort to a question, try going back to some observation in the declarative mood. Often an indirect question will work: "Well, that still makes me wonder where you got such a good idea for a character like that in a story about raccoons."

A key aim should be to get the student to self-assess or to describe language processing. One way is to offer an observation about your own writing: "I still enjoy writing about animals. Did you know that former President Bush's wife wrote a book that pretended to be by her dog Millie? Millie would have had an interesting view of what goes on in the White House, wouldn't she?"

If necessary, use a question or two to focus on language processing, trying when possible to link reading and writing:

- "This is the second version of the story about the raccoons, isn't it? How did you change it?"
- "Why did you want that change?"
- "Did you think about who would read this story? Who would enjoy it?"
- "This reminds me of a story in our reader. Do you know which one? What other stories have you read where animals are the characters?"

Make sure that your comments and questions open up opportunities to converse rather than closing down conversation. Comments and questions that promote only confirmation from the student or yes or no answers are not "expansive" in this way. They are not likely to teach you much about the student and his or her progress. What you hope to do is to learn by getting the student to explain, justify, clarify, and expound on ideas and opinions.

Whatever you do, be sure to listen carefully to the answers to questions and to responses to comments you make hoping to generate student reaction. Students will provide more input if they believe you are truly interested in and respect their perspectives. If you find that you are not getting much open response from a student, you have some reason to think carefully about your conferencing strategies and goals. Base your subsequent comments on what you hear, not on some note you have on a list—no matter how customized the comment is to the particular student. If the conference weaves almost coincidentally out of your exchange with the student, it is almost certainly a conversation. If it tends to be you trying to get comments out of the student in response to a series of observations and questions, the nature of the interrogation will not escape the student.

GET OFF TO A GOOD START   Many teachers find that the most difficult part of portfolio conferencing to master is getting started. Once the exchange about the student's collection and language use is under way between the student and the teacher, the session is often directed by the teacher being a good listener and the interaction of the two participants. One way to think about this is to visualize the conference as having two parts. The first part is usually concerned with establishing some sense of how the student uses reading and writing and with how the child visualizes that use in terms of purposes, audiences, and the like. It should revolve more around the student's interests.

Because beginning the conference has been reported by teachers to be difficult, Table 5.2: Help in Getting the Conference Started, offers some general comments and questions that can be used.

HELP IN GETTING THE CONFERENCE STARTED

Initial Comment/Question	Follow-Up Comments/Questions
Make a kind of summary comment about the organization of the portfolio without being complete and hoping to provoke the student to complete and clarify. "How have you organized your portfolio?"	Attempt to determine if there are subdivisions within the major divisions and make a comment noting what you have found. "This is a good organization. Why did you decide to do it this way?" "How did you decide which piece should go into each section?" Comment about one or more ideas you find interesting. "Which ideas do you think are the most important?"
Make an observation about the kinds of reading listed on the log. "How often do you stop to make entries on your log?"	"I love this story you read about the dinosaurs." "Which thing that you read is your favorite?" Make a comment about the student-selected piece. "Why do you like this one?" "My favorite thing that you have written is _____." "Which piece of your writing do you like the best? Why?"
Comment about a particular text read and listed in the log. "I haven't read this story. Tell me about it."	"How did you come to read this?" "Would you recommend this to a friend to read?" Comment about the author of the piece. "Why do you think the author wrote this?"
"I was noticing how your writing is changing." "How do you think you have changed as a writer?"	"Last week I had a decision to make and it seemed hard. I sat down and wrote a letter about it to my sister. I learned that writing helped me think it out." "What do you like or dislike about writing?" Look down the log noticing pieces of writing. "Did you try any new kind of writing?"
Comment about several things the student has listed on the log as something read. Mention something you read recently and why you liked it. "How do you think you are changing as a reader?"	"You read a lot about _____." "You read a lot of different kinds of things." "Have you read any new authors that you like?" "I notice that you wrote about this article you read." "What kind of stories do you like best?"
"What do you think you might read about next?"	"I know of one author/story/book about that." "Can I help you find it?"
"What will you write about next?"	"How do you plan to get started?" "Can anyone help you with this?"

AVOID BEING EVALUATIVE   Even when the student expresses an evaluation or opinion that you feel does not promote his or her development as a thinker and user of language, be respectful. You might try carefully to determine why the student feels that way, but do not pass judgment.

If the student feels that everything the two of you decide about the collection is to be a kind of evaluation of its quality and his or her performance, there will be little possibility of focusing on writing and reading as useful processes that can be developed. Avoiding a general evaluative attitude is different from discussing with the student, for example, the three pieces that he thinks are his best work for the time period being discussed. You may even want to pick your three favorites and discuss in a very open way any differences with the student's choice and in the reasons the pieces were picked. This should be done very respectfully, honoring the student's selection and criteria.

Nor is avoiding the overevaluative approach the same as encouraging the student to talk about how pieces of writing that have come later are better than earlier efforts. Nor does your offering a bit of praise for a revision effort violate this general objective for conferencing.

LET THE CONFERENCE GENERATE A NEW SET OF OBJECTIVES

The conference is a perfect time for you and the student to plan collaboratively. In discussing what the student has read that has been interesting and enjoyable (and that has sparked writing), you can encourage him or her to detail the kinds of reading, particular authors, and particular topics that can become a part of the student's development in the subsequent period.

The conference is also a wonderful place for the student to plan future writing. You may notice a particular enthusiasm for a type of story or a topic read and suggest—but not insist—that the student try writing in that style or about that topic. By praising pieces of writing, you may suggest that they be revised in ways that hopefully the student will be prompted to suggest.

There is a blackline master in Appendix C that can help you and the student focus on these goals.

Both prospective reading and writing can be approached from the perspectives of *ideas, purposes,* and *authors and audiences.* These objectives should be noted in writing so that they can become a framework for discussions in the next portfolio conference, which are sure to focus on self-assessed improvement.

BE SURE TO KEEP CONFERENCE NOTES
During the conference or immediately afterwards, you and the student can jot down notes about the student's reading and writing interests and activities. Some teachers have had students write notes prior to the conference as the student is organizing the portfolio and getting ready for the conference. These preconference notes are then expanded and revised as a result of the conference. Regardless as to when the notes are made, you and the student should review the notes at the conclusion of the conference. Talk about the things you learned about the student's reading and writing interests. Note the kinds of books you and the student may want to read next, what the student's plans are for writing and rewriting in the next few weeks, and the things the student needs to work on to become a better reader and writer.

This review needs to be taken seriously by you and the student. The notes should become an action plan. The student needs to see that you are using the conference as a time to help him or her plan. This brings the student into the assessment/instructional planning cycle, and that involvement is key to effective learning.

The objectives or goals for the period of time following the conference are not the only collaborative agreements that should be noted in writing. At any time during the conference, the teacher and the student should feel free to note in writing an observation, an idea, an author, a title, a suggestion or anything that can guide the student in his reading, writing, thinking, reanalysis and reorganization of portfolio contents that begin anew after the conference.

Like the conversation in the conference itself, these notes can be highly interactive. A preferred form allows the teacher to write on one side of a split record and the student on the other. This requires handing the form back and forth, and the teacher should model the interactive opportunity by making a point to write a note reacting to one already written on the student's half of the sheet. Separate sheets can also be used, and these, too, are split into columns so that the student can write on one side of the teacher's note sheet and the teacher can write on the student's sheet.

REMEMBER THAT GUIDELINES ARE ONLY GUIDELINES

There is a considerable risk in devising a checklist to carry into a portfolio conference with your students. The danger is that you may rely on it too much. The questions you ask in

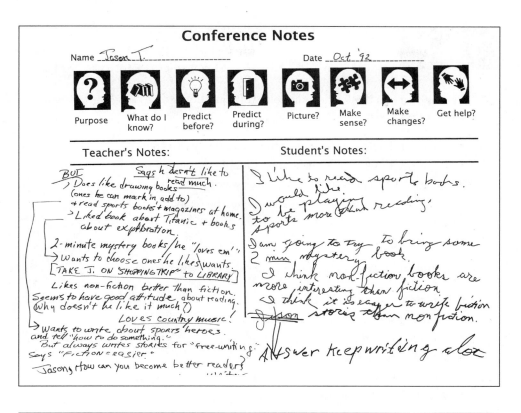

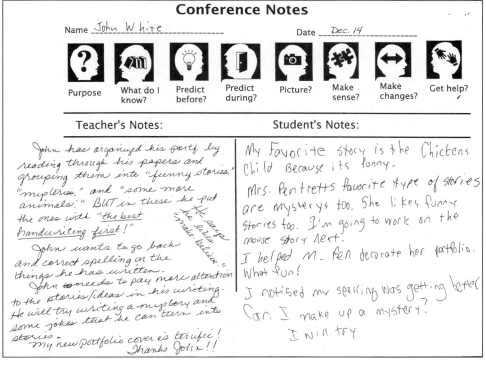

These two sheets are notes taken in two different conferences, with the teacher writing on the left-hand half and the student using the right-hand half. In the top notes, Jason is honest about preferring athletic activities to reading, but he realizes that the way to improve as a language user is to read and write a lot. In the bottom notes, both John and his volunteer tutor reveal that they have been keeping portfolios.

TIP

QUESTIONS THAT CAN LEAD TO
GOOD CONFERENCE NOTES

The teacher can think about the following questions when deciding what conference notes to take:

- What can I get for this student to read and to write about?
- What two things would make this student's writing more interesting?
- What do I like best about this student's writing?
- What does this student think about when he or she reads and writes?
- What does this student need to do to get his or her writing ready for publication?

The student's notes can be prompted by questions like these:

- What do I want to read and write about next?
- What are some things I want to find out about?
- What kinds of things do I like to read best?
- Why do I think that story is a good one?
- How can I make my stories more interesting?
- Which of my favorite authors can I write like?
- What parts of my stories are the best? Why?
- What do I need to do to get my stories ready to publish?

a portfolio conference should grow out of several sources: (1) your analysis of the student's portfolio, (2) what you have learned about the student from other sources, such as your own observation, and (3) what you learn during the conference by listening carefully to the student.

Consequently, the list offered here poses questions you can ask yourself. As a checklist, it enables you to think about aspects of student language use that may be useful and translate into questions that fit a particular interview as it develops:

- What are the student's most apparent reasons/purposes for reading and writing? Which of them seem the most important to the student?
- What evidence is there of reading being applied in some way? Why did the student write most of the pieces in the collection?
- How idea-oriented is the student? Does s/he seem to value encountering ideas in reading? How willing and eager is the student to share ideas?
- How much confidence does the student have as a thinker? Is s/he a risk-taker and willing to encounter and experiment with new ideas? How willing and ready does the student appear to be to explore his or her own interests through writing and reading?
- Where does the student tend to get his or her interests and ideas? Is the content of the portfolio traceable to other writers, to friends, to family, to classroom experience? Is the student's writing style influenced by authors and genres? Is s/he able to draw on such sources? Do preferences for authors, content, and so forth relate to the student's background and personal experiences?
- How aware does the student appear to be of the authors of stories and other texts read? Does s/he visualize particular audiences for the things s/he writes?

IDEAS FOR DEVELOPING
YOUR CONFERENCING SKILLS

Try these projects as ways of improving your conferencing skills:

- Conference with ten students at least twice each, keeping a journal about which conferences went well and which did not. Attempt to explain why.
- Work with a fellow teacher to develop a set of guidelines for teachers to use in common across grade levels when conferencing. Include in the guidelines ideas for finding time, organizing the conferences, taking good notes, establishing effective emphases, and starting conversations with the students.
- After getting permission from six students, tape-record their conferences. Analyze what you learned about the students' abilities to use the eight strategies represented by the head icons.
- Hold a student-parent portfolio breakfast during which the parents will conference with their children about the portfolios. Get the students to help you write some helpful guidelines for the parents explaining the portfolios and what can be achieved by conferencing.

- How responsive does the student's use of language appear to be? Are responses to reading indicative of author's intent, other readers' responses? Is there evidence that feedback from others has been incorporated into the student's writing and reading selections? Is this student a reviser? If so, what guides the revisions?
- How expressive is the student's language? What distinguishes or describes the diction and apparent lexicon of this student? How precise is word choice? How fresh? How imaginative is s/he? Is there evidence that this child is developing his or her own expressive voice?
- How clearly are ideas presented, summarized, reviewed, applied to individual purposes for reading and writing? How good or controlled a thinker does the student appear to be? Is there evidence of ideas connected logically? of organizational schemes? of use of or grasp of comparison/contrast, cause and effect, time sequence, and the like?
- How can the sentence structure of this student's expression be described?
- How aware is this young writer of grammatical and other language conventions, such as punctuation, number agreement, and so on?
- How aware is this student of his or her strengths and weaknesses as a language user? How supportive will his or her attitude toward language use be in directing development?

OTHER TYPES OF

PORTFOLIO CONFERENCES

In addition to the planned conferences about them, portfolios are the basis for informal conferences held throughout the schoolday with your students. These may include the following types:

ROVING CONFERENCE   Roving conferences can be conducted as you move about the room while your students are engaged in any reading and writing activities. You may

You can have a truly rewarding experience at the end of each portfolio conference if you and the student trade something in your portfolios. Of course, this means that you have to be keeping a portfolio yourself.

You might have in it a story, poem, or other material you have been writing. You don't have to have a separate item for each student. They each would like to have something from their teacher in the student portfolio. However, they have to give you something from their portfolio that you can add to yours. If you and the student want to keep these in your own collections, they can be xeroxed.

In one class, where one of the authors was conferencing with the students, the session concluded with the exchange of stories. The student, whose name was Matthew, offered his "idea sheet" as a trade. He said it was how he got his ideas and that it was important that everyone have one, and it had been praised as a "great tool" during the conference. The sheet was a list of things the teacher had been working on with the students to help them become better observers and get good ideas, how to jot down their ideas for stories, and how to think about what they were reading as ideas for writing.

Matthew asked what he would get for his portfolio. Roger Farr had a folder of writing that he worked on on airplanes to put into a portfolio he keeps at home. He pulled out a draft of an idea for a story he had been working on. It was actually based on a writing suggestion another teacher in another school had made. That teacher had told the student to think about what it would be like to be some kind of clothing. Roger had decided to write about being a shoe. He showed Matthew the notes and told him that he wasn't yet finished with the story, but that he would be sure to come back in two weeks and give Matthew the finished story. Matthew agreed that Roger could have some time to finish it.

When Roger returned, the coauthors of this book had developed a story poem for Matthew. It not only went into his portfolio, but Matthew submitted it for "publication" on the class bulletin board. It went like this:

Matthew's Shoe

Of all the things that you could do
Never try to be a shoe!
It's not a happy thing to be.
    You don't believe it?
    Look at me!
I do get outside every day.
I do get out and get to play.
I go with Matthew, don't you know.
    Where he goes,
    I have to go.
If he plays hop-scotch or kicks a ball
Or bangs his toe against a wall
Or stomps a puddle—to name a few,
    Who gets scuffed or wet?
    Guess who!
When Matthew plays where doggies do,
My tongue hangs out, and I go PHEW!
I wish he'd watch more where he goes.
    Thank goodness
    I don't have a nose!
Then, when he gets home, you know,
He goes in, but I can't go!
"Don't wear those crummy shoes indoors!"
    (Matthew's mother
    loves her floors!)

So I get left alone outside
Until I'm cleaned, or brushed, or dried.
And Matthew's silly socks enjoy
    The warm, soft carpet
    With my boy!
And then when I'm too small or worn
With holes and places where I'm torn,
Will anybody care when he
    Tosses me out
    And is done with me?
I've made Matthew's feet feel good
Like shiny new shoes never could.
He's worn me long and all about
    Until he's finally
    Worn me out.
There's not a sadder thing to see
Than some old beat-up shoe like me
In some big old box someday
    With other trash
    To throw away!
Be a boot—with a blade or wheels,
Or some soft slipper someone feels.
But the dumbest thing that you can do
    Is ever try
    To be a shoe!

spot a student who seems to be having difficulty getting started with a writing activity or seems unable to find a book that interests him or her. That can be a good time to conference with the student. You may want to review the student's portfolio to see if you and the student can find ideas that the student has written or read about successfully in the past. If you jot down a few notes from this *roving conference,* they can be added to the student's portfolio.

CONFERENCE FOR SETTING GOALS   There are times when you need to have a conference with a student other than at the regular conference time because the student seems lost and confused. Anytime you conference with a student, it is useful to have the student set goals for his or her writing and reading. However, when a student is having difficulty, you have an authentic opportunity to sit down and help him or her look through the portfolio to discuss what has been accomplished.

In this case, it is especially important that you look for positive and supportive comments you can make about the collection and the student's interests and command of language. You may be able to help the student find new ideas to explore in reading and writing and to set directions for future reading and writing activities. You and the student may want to put a note in the portfolio about what you decided at this conference.

PUBLICATION CONFERENCE   Students who are involved in publishing things that they write frequently need to meet in pairs or small groups to discuss writing submitted for publication, how it is to be edited and reproduced, and sometimes work they have in their portfolio that they feel is ready for publication.

Students can select things from their own portfolio, or they may ask another student to see if there is something in their portfolio that they like and that they think should be published. Ideas about revisions and what students value in writing are then shared.

EXAMPLES OF PORTFOLIO CONFERENCES

Giving suggestions and guidelines for conferencing is tricky business, because the key axiom of conferencing is to let the needs, purposes, styles, interests, and development of the individual student dictate the conversation, the analyses, and the directional goal setting.

One way to give you a better idea of how conferences go is to present you with accounts of some. The first thing you will note about the first two described here is that they do not seem very typical—at least of what you might expect. Yet they do demonstrate how a good conference proceeds like a natural conversation focused on the student's understanding and use of language. They also suggest how much can be learned by just talking with children about what they read and write and demonstrating genuine interest in their ideas, how they are expressed, and what they know about doing that.

ALAN REVEALS AN IMPRESSIVE
UNDERSTANDING OF HOW LITERACY DEVELOPS

One of the authors had the following conference with Alan Rodriguez in a San Antonio elementary school in an inner-city neighborhood. The students in this classroom had been keeping portfolios all year. For Alan, and for most of his fellow students, the experience was their first with portfolios. The following report was written on the flight home from Texas:

"I was a visitor in the school and had been meeting with many different students to discuss their reading and writing. The teachers had invited me to their school so that I could learn more with them about the portfolio process. Most of the students seemed to accept my meeting with them as a normal part of their class routine. Several of them told me that they had just met with their teacher the previous week to discuss their stories.

Alan Rodriguez walked slowly and cautiously toward me as I sat at the little table at the back of the room. In his hand he clutched a folder, and I could see several disheveled papers sticking out from its sides. On the front of the folder I could see that Alan had pasted a picture of David Robinson of the San Antonio Spurs. He had also drawn pictures and symbols on the folder, but I couldn't see exactly what they were.

As Alan slumped down into a chair at the table next to me, he said, 'The teacher told me to show you the stuff I got in my folder. What do you want to see?'

'I really don't have anything special in mind, Alan,' I replied. 'I'd just like to learn about the stories you like.'

'I don't like too much,' said Alan, 'but I did read *Willy Wonka and the Chocolate Factory.* That was pretty good.'

'I liked that story, myself,' I told him. I knew better than to start asking lots of questions about the first book he mentioned. 'Are there any other stories you like?' I asked. I was hoping to get some idea of the range of Alan's interests.

Alan looked around to see if anyone was listening in on our conversation. When he saw that no one was within earshot, he kind of mumbled that he liked 'some of those girl stories.'

'What girl stories?' I asked.

'*Blubber,* and some of the other stuff that person wrote.'

'Those aren't girl stories,' I told Alan. 'Those are just stories about what happens to a kid. The kid happens to be a girl, but it could have been a boy.'

'Yeah, that's what I liked,' said Alan. 'The stories were all about getting shoved around and hollered at for all kinds of stuff.'

'Did you read any other stories by Judy Blume?' I asked.

'Who's Judy Blume?' Alan asked as he looked at me quizzically.

'She's the person who wrote *Blubber,*' I said. 'She wrote a bunch of other books that are sort of like *Blubber.* I bet they have those in the library. Maybe we can take a look later.'

'Hey, Alan, what's that picture about?' I asked as I noticed a picture in his folder that seemed quite well drawn for a fourth-grader—even though the picture seemed a bit gruesome. The picture showed one person with a dagger stuck in his chest. Other people were carrying clubs and seemed to be swinging them at one another.'

'That's a picture that goes with my story. I'm writing a story about gangs. Do you know anything about gangs? Were you ever in a gang?' he asked.

'I was in a kind of a gang, but we called them clubs when I was a kid. Our club was called the Tiger Men.'

'What did you do in your gang?' Alan asked.

'All kinds of things,' I responded, 'but mostly we just sort of hung around together.'

'Yeah, that's what gangs do where I live.'

'You know why I'm writing a story about gangs? It's 'cause I'm thinking about being in a gang. My mom doesn't want me to be in a gang, but you ain't nothin' if you ain't in a gang,' said Alan, suggesting with his expression that I might not know much about the world. 'I don't know if I should be in a gang 'cause some of the gangs get in trouble. I dunno,' he said. 'I'm thinking about it and this story kind of helps me think about it. The pictures kind of help with the story.'

'Yeah,' I said, 'the pictures help tell about what you're writing.'

'Nah,' said Alan, 'my pictures don't tell about my words. I do the pictures 'cause I don't know how to write my ideas. Pictures tell lots of my stories.'

I was amazed at the insight about reading and writing that this fourth-grade boy from an inner-city school was revealing to me. I knew that even the youngest children could explain with disarming simplicity some of the concepts that reading theorists and researchers grappled with in their professional books and articles. Here was Alan Rodriguez telling me that he wrote because he wanted to think about things in his life. And he had told me that had read stories about pretty average fourth-graders who seemed to be having a tough time fitting in. When Alan told me about his pictures, I had to pursue the extent of his understanding.

'Your pictures are really very good. They sure give me a good idea about gangs.'

'Oh, don't think that gangs just fight.' Alan seemed to want to correct any impressions I had about gangs. 'Gangs do lots of good things for people, but sometimes they get mad at one another and fights start. That's the part my mom says is so bad.'

'Show me some of the other pictures, Alan. There's lots I don't know about gangs.'

'Look at this picture.' Alan held out a picture of lots of people who seemed to be crawling all over a house. 'That's a picture of a gang that I know that helps people fix up old houses.'

'This is a great story, Alan. The pictures make it seem so real.'

'It is real,' Alan retorted. 'I just write and draw about the stuff I see and think about. Do you think people who draw pictures for books are people who don't know enough words so they draw pictures?'

'I don't think so, Alan. I suppose some of them do, but I think lots of them just like to tell their stories with pictures rather than with words.'

'Yeah, but words is better,' said Alan. 'At least you got to have *some* words. You know how I think you can get more words?' Alan asked. And then he immediately answered his own question with a statement that showed complete understanding of the connection between reading and writing. 'If you read more, you get more words. You get ideas about how to say stuff. I bet if I read more, I'll get more words in my head.'

The conference didn't end there. It went on for another ten minutes or so with Alan telling me about his stories, about his life, and about how he saw himself as a reader and a writer. I listened intently and continued to share some of my experiences with Alan. I focused on the ideas that intrigued Alan, on the things that he wanted to read about, and write about, and think about."

COMMENTS ABOUT THE CONFERENCE WITH ALAN   *The author made the following observations about the meeting with Alan:*

"This conference was not typical. However, there are probably no portfolio conferences that are typical. The goal of such conferences should be to allow each student to talk about the ideas that interest him or her. The teacher learns what the student wants to talk about, write about, and read about.

If there were such things as typical portfolio conferences, we might soon conclude that we do not need to hold them with each student, for we could predict most of what we would "learn." It is the uniqueness of each student that we are attempting to understand. More importantly, the conference is an opportunity for each student to express his ideas and to talk about his view of reading and writing.

Alan was typical in that most students, given the opportunity, can be thoughtful and insightful as fourth-graders. The conference helped me to understand that Alan knew a great deal about literacy. We did not spend time talking about spelling and punctuation errors. We talked about ideas and what it means to be literate—even though I never asked Alan such a question. We talked about ideas and life, and Alan and I saw literacy as a chance to talk about "stuff" that was important to us. Had I been making notes about Alan's portfolio, I might have written:

Ownership: It was clear from the start that this was *Alan's* portfolio. He brought it back for me to see. He had decorated it, and its dog-eared look indicated that he had used it frequently.

View of Literacy: Whether it was the classroom teacher or just what Alan had learned on his own, Alan focused on ideas. He used literacy (pictures, stories, and writing) to think about ideas. He had a very mature view of reading and writing.

Focus: Alan's focus—and the focus of our conversation—was on ideas rather than on writing conventions. We shared our ideas, and, without stating it, we talked about the value of language in enabling us to share ideas.

Planning for Instruction: I knew some of the things that I would want to work on if I were Alan's teacher. I knew some of the books and stories I would help him find. I thought I even knew some ways to capture Alan's interest in drawing as a lever to getting him to write more. However, far more important was that Alan had developed his own insights about his reading, writing, and drawing. Alan was a terrific self-assessor. I felt that if the teachers he encounters in the coming years would help Alan to continue to develop the insights he revealed about language, he would become an excellent reader and writer—and thinker."

A SECOND-GRADER CONCENTRATES ON DEVELOPING HER STRENGTHS

In another visitation to a classroom, one of the authors got an opportunity to learn from a second-grader. The girl's teacher had authorized the visitor to use the conference with Judy to set instructional objectives:

"Judy, a second-grader in Miss Oleon's class, had been feverishly sorting her reading lists, stories, pictures, and other materials into various piles. Judy had a very outgoing personality and had always seemed to want to please the teacher. I noticed that she seemed to be studying each of the stories and each of the various reactions to things she read, carefully considering which pile it should go on. When she had gone through all the papers, she carefully wrapped a piece of paper around each pile and wrote something on it. I was anxious to see how she had organized her materials.

When she came to the table for her portfolio conference, she immediately showed me the largest pile of materials. 'These are my best things,' she said. 'I put these in this pile 'cause I knew the teacher would like them.'

'Do you like them, Judy?' I asked.

'Oh, yes,' she said. 'They are all my best writing and they look very neat.'

'Is that what makes writing good,' I asked, 'good handwriting and neatness?'

'Oh, yes,' she said vigorously, 'my mom always says I am too sloppy. She says my writing's a mess, and I need to be better in writing—and I think in cleaning my room, too.'

I didn't want to make that note on our conference notes because I might have to register some disagreement with Judy's mom. I have noticed in some of the many conferences I have had with students that their focus on neatness, handwriting, spelling, grammar, punctuation, and usage comes from parents who mean well and are eager to help their children develop as acceptable language users. They seem to think that the value of writing is in the mechanics rather than in the development of interesting ideas. (The same evaluation foundation surfaces with a few teachers who find it safer to point out mechanical errors in writing than to get involved with the ideas the student is discussing.)

'What do you like most about stories?' I asked Judy.

'Oh,' Judy said as if she were grateful for the question, 'I like monster stories best. I read Clyde Monster and I think that was the best story I ever read,' she quickly added. She was more than eager to tell me about her interest in monsters.

'Why do you like monster stories?'

'Well,' she said, 'when I was a little girl I always was afraid that there might be a monster in my room. My mom got a nightlight, but I was still scared sometimes. I sort of got over being scared—but I still get scared sometimes.'

'I think we all do,' I told her. 'I know that I'm scared of the dark sometimes, especially when I hear strange noises.'

'You are?' she said with a strange look on her face. 'Like Clyde Monster,' she added. 'He was scared of the dark and his monster mom had to leave the door of his cave open just a crack so he couldn't be scared.' Judy giggled a bit. She found it very funny that a monster was scared of the dark.

'You know what I do to get over being scared?' she asked. 'I make believe I am talking to Clyde. When I talk to him, it is sort of like he is a friend.'

'And I write stories now about monsters,' Judy quickly added. 'They're my favorite stories.'

'Do you have one you could read to me?' I asked. She pulled a paper out of one of her piles. On the wrapper it said 'Monster Stories.' It was then that I realized that Judy's organizational scheme might be more sophisticated than just 'Best' and maybe 'Not so good.' At least some of her monster stories were separated from the other writing that she considered her best.

'I did this story last week,' Judy said. 'I like it 'cause the monster does a lot of talking.' She read the story aloud, and the monster did indeed do a lot of talking. I was very interested in Judy's ability to write dialogue. I made a note to see what might be done to take advantage of this strength.

I also peeked over the edge of the paper and was impressed to notice that most of what the monster said was inside quotation marks. They framed every successive sentence, and when another character talked, the words were in the same paragraph with what the monster said. I made no note about that. This was not the time, I knew, to damper Judy's fluency with dialogue by making her self-conscious about punctuation that she appeared to basically understand.

When Judy had finished reading the story, I was eager to reinforce its designation as a 'best monster story.'

'That was a wonderful story!' I told her.

'Oh, no,' she said. 'I thought it was good when it was done, but now I don't think so.'

'Why not?' I asked.

'Well, did you hear me? All I said was HE SAID, HE SAID. I used too many HE SAIDs.'

'What could you do to change that?'

'Cross some out,' she responded and started to do just that. Suddenly, I had an idea of how to encourage Judy's keen interest in dialogue—in the case of her jabbery monster, monologue.

'Judy,' I said, 'how would you like to write a play to put on for some of the kids in your class? It could be a monster story, and you could use a lot of this story you just read. You could be the monster and a friend could be you. The play could show what it's like to talk to a monster.'

'Oh, yeah!' Judy exclaimed, sort of holding out the monster story. It was looking better to her suddenly. 'That would be fun! Could I stand on a chair and put a big coat around me so the kids can't see the chair? I could look like a really big monster!'

'In a play,' I said, 'you don't need to say HE SAID at all.' Judy was looking askance at me. 'All you do is write MONSTER and then one of these.' I made a colon on a piece of paper. 'Then you just write what the monster says.'

'I know,' Judy said coyly. She was obviously perturbed with me for not knowing that she knew.

'When would you be ready to give your play?' I asked.

'Oh, this is important,' she said softly. 'Can my friend help? We need to decide what the monster will say.'

'Of course,' I said. 'But you can use your stories, you know. A lot of what the monster says can come out of your monster stories.'

'I know,' Judy said again, beginning to wonder if I really did believe in her.

We went on with the conference and Judy and I made notes about getting ready to write a monster play. We made one, too, about how talking to someone about being scared was one way to get over it."

COMMENTS ABOUT THE CONFERENCE WITH JUDY "The session was a bit heavy on monsters, perhaps. But I was amazed when I stopped to realize that I had been conversing with a second-grader, who:

- Had read an original story that she wrote aloud.

- Had written a story heavy with dialogue but was concerned about how many times she had repeated HE SAID.

- Was about to embark on revising her talking monster into the main character of an original play.
- Was nonchalant about the whole business, including the prospect of producing the play she would write.

I had to wonder if her mother wouldn't have been impressed with her seven-year-old author. Surely, she too would have been caught up in the actual content—in the actual poise and confidence of a young language user more excited about a project and its content than self-conscious about how neat she was.

Not that Judy was not self-aware. She was rather tough on herself as a *self-assessor.* We need to allow students to self-assess and to focus on content, style, and form as ways to improve the writing.

You will no doubt see rewarding student performance of this quality in daily classroom situations, but the portfolio conference tends to provide the focus that reveals with regular frequency how really capable youngsters are as self-assessors of their own language use. It's a payoff that makes portfolio assessment worth any challenge and effort it takes to make it successful."

A Young Author Gets an Opportunity to Discuss Stylistic Details

Elaine Guelli, a third-grade teacher in Palm Beach, Florida, videotaped an unrehearsed conference with student Brennen, demonstrating how stylistically sensitive and satisfying portfolio conferences can become.

"Let's take a look at our last conference notes and let's see what we talked about the last time and what kind of things we agreed to work on," she begins.

"All right." Brennen digs into a black backpack that contains his portfolio collection. When asked later how it was that he picked the backpack, Brennen explained that it was old, that he always liked it a lot, and that he didn't want to throw it away. He was very pleased to find an ongoing use for it. It is obviously quite full and he is having to carefully thumb through papers to find the notes. "Got a lot of stuff here."

"Have you done some organizing in this portfolio?"

"Oh, yes, but not for a while. I thought those notes were here on top. I just haven't had the time to. . . ." It becomes clear as the conference progresses that Brennen spends every minute he gets writing and rewriting stories for his collection rather than organizing it.

"You have some ideas on how you want to organize it this time?"

"Yeah. I think I want to put numbers on the sections and make a new list of all the things I have in each part. There will be one about history, and it will have all the stuff I write about history." Brennen reaches into a separate pocket on the backpack and pulls out a table of contents, but he mumbles in embarrassment because he can't find the notes.

"Oh, that's a neat way of using your portfolio holder, keeping the table in that pocket," the teacher says.

Brennen smiles and produces two pages of notes stapled together. "Here they are," he says proudly, mumbling some explanation of why he didn't find them the first time through his stack of papers.

"Well, I've pulled out my copy," Mrs. Guelli says. They lay the two sets of notes side by side. "You and I can look at our copies together and see what it was you said you wanted to work on before this conference."

"Ummmmm," Brennen says, "I wanted to redo the one grasshopper story and organize my portfolio, but I haven't done that too well yet."

"But you did publish the grasshopper story, right? Do you have a copy of that?"

Brennen finds the published grasshopper story quite easily.

"Well, that's one out of two goals," the teacher says. "Not bad."

Brennen pulls out still another paper. "I've got another story, too," he says, "but this one has not been published in the newspaper."

"Oh, well, we can take a look at that, too," the teacher says.

"Now, here is the one about the grasshopper," Brennen says. "I did some of it over at home."

"Do you have the other copies of it in there?" the teacher asks. "You had some notes and when you were first writing on it you did a first draft. Do you have any of those papers in your portfolio?"

"I took that home."

"Could you bring it back so we could put it in here?"

"I think so."

"It's important when you are looking back to have those things sometimes. You might want to do another part of this story, and it could help to have the first draft. How do you feel about this story now?"

"I'm happy about it."

"Do you remember when we talked about this story last December? What were some of the things we discussed that you said you were going to do to it for publication?"

Brennen doesn't remember off the top of his head, so he and the teacher refer to their notes from the previous conference. "Remember how it kind of left us hanging at the end, and we thought it would be good to have some different organization there."

"I took it home and worked on that," Brennen says. "You said if I finished it by January, you would give me a car book, so I got it done."

"Well, I ordered that. This was just published last week and you will get the book tomorrow. I am really proud that you got this published in the school paper."

"Can you find something in your portfolio that we can look at for you to work on before the next conference?"

"I like the *how* story, but it's not in here."

"That one is in the processing area." She has another student go and get it.

They look at it together. "I've been working on this one," Brennen says, "and have kind've been messing it up."

"Well, that's okay," the teacher says, "it's a rough draft. Can you tell me about it?"

Brennen begins a story about a cobra that gets its teeth stuck in a tree. A crocodile, a lizard, and another snake come by and tease the cobra by offering it food. But the tree is very strong, Brennen explains, and the cobra has to pull hard to get its teeth free so it can eat. And that, he explains, is how it got its long fangs.

The teacher expresses interest in the kinds of characters and asks Brennen how he picked them. "They are all reptiles," Brennen explains, "and I couldn't think of too many, so I had to use a second snake."

"Do you know a lot about reptiles?"

"Kind of, but not enough."

"Do you know the difference between reptiles and birds and other animals? What makes them so special?" She is making a note about getting some reptile books for Brennen.

"They are cold-blooded. They can get heat only from the sun. The other animals are warm-blooded and can get heat from themselves." Next the teacher and Brennen discuss amphibians and review the characteristics of "how" stories. "They tell how something happened or how some animal got something," Brennen says. "Usually an animal. It's part real and part make-believe."

Next the teacher invites Brennen to read his story aloud. The young author beams. He is in total control of the conference now, and this is exactly what he wanted to do: show his creative stuff. The sentences about Charles Cobra are precise and very clear and so is the boy's voice—unlike it had been in the friendly, unpressured conversation. Clearly, Brennen likes to write because it gives him more control of his ideas. The causal chain of how the cobra gets his fangs is very carefully established in logically flowing sentences. They are brisk but written in a varied style. They have a cadence and tend to march along.

The teacher tells Brennen that his writing made it very easy for her to visualize what was happening in the story. She asks him if there are any other details he might want to add in rewriting. The story can be redone, she reminds Brennen, before the teamed editing exchange with members of the fifth-grade class the next week.

"Yeah," Brennen says. "When I read it, I changed this *well* to a *when,*" referring to a nicely turned sentence with an introductory time clause. "I already have a couple wells," he says laying pencil to the paper. "This will make it more interesting."

The teacher compliments Brennen on the title of his story, pointing to the word *the* at the beginning of it. "I forgot to use a cap," Brennen says. "I can fix that, too."

The teacher notices the word *indent* written in one margin. "I didn't indent that paragraph," Brennen says. "And I want to do that."

"You must have already read this over at least once," the teacher says, noticing some insertions as well.

"A couple times," Brennen says.

"How do you feel about this story?"

"I think I'm going to try and get it published," Brennen says earnestly. "I'll keep workin' on this and get it published."

The teacher gets Brennen to describe the pictures he will draw to illustrate his cobra story. "What do you really like most about this story, Brennen?" They agree that the detail in the cobra story demonstrates that Brennen accomplished still another goal since the December conference, as noted in their notes.

They decide that Brennen needs to think about new goals, agreeing that he can carry over his objective of improving the organization of the portfolio. And he will get the cobra story published, he decides.

Brennen asks if the teacher has read a long, six-page, illustrated story about another grasshopper who needs a home. He had pulled it out earlier for attention. She assures him she has. He says he wants to get it published. He wants to read it aloud, and he gets to do that. He explains how he has rewritten it three times and thinks it is ready to be published, like the other grasshopper story. They lay out the versions of this story, and note the care with which it has been revised. She praises his habit of revising, his creativeness, and his attention to his goals.

While they review Brennen's goals for the ensuing weeks, he tells about his friend Aaron who goes to another school. "He writes stories, too," Brennen says. "We play together, and I want him to be my editor." The teacher agrees to go with Brennen to visit Aaron's teacher to see if they can make that arrangement.

COMMENTS ABOUT THE CONFERENCE WITH BRENNEN   Here is a teacher who uses ingenious and flexible methodologies to promote the one vital writing/thinking process that is virtually absent in so many other classrooms in the United States: *revision*. Note that she has arrangements for her third-graders to work in editing teams with students in the fifth grade. Note how powerful a motivation the opportunity to publish in the class newspaper is. Note how she agrees to try and establish an editorial team across schools.

Her nonjudgmental and flexible attention to Brennan's powerful creative urge feeds his developing talent, concentrating on reasonable objectives that appear to ensure Brennan's success. More important, perhaps, than the fact that this boy may well be on his way to becoming a successful author is the clear confidence and satisfaction he gets from the opportunity to write and read his clear, precise, and logical prose descriptions.

And, it bears repeating, the attention to style and revision speaks to the highly admirable success of this teacher's methodologies, which include a conferencing style in which these processes can emerge.

SUMMARY: REVIEWING A DOZEN GOOD GUIDELINES TO SUCCESSFUL CONFERENCING

- Schedule a conference with each student at least four times a year—and more often if possible. Devise a means for conducting the conferences that works for you and in your classroom.

- Let your students know that the conferences are coming and are important. The reason for talking about them is to get the students thinking about them and about their collections, which will be the focal point of the conferences. Get the students to plan and prepare for the conferences; establish this as their responsibility without being intimidating. Advise the students to "Get your things organized so we can share our reading and writing ideas."

  Give the students time to think and write about their portfolios. Suggest that they can write about "Why you saved some things, what you like best and why, and what you want to write and read next." Advise the students to "Keep these notes in your portfolio so we can look at them when we meet. And be sure to write down some questions to ask me."

- Explain and demonstrate how the conferences will work before you hold the first ones. Establish a kind of conversational equality for the conferences, during which you and the student will chat as two readers and two writers talking about how they make meaning with language. Offer observations about yourself as a language user.

  Make sure that the students know that the conference is their opportunity to talk about the texts that they are reading, the papers that they are writing, and ideas that are important to them. Stress that it is a time to plan for new stories and other things that they will write and read. Be sure to emphasize that the conference has nothing to do with grades. The aim is to avoid having students think of the conference as some accountability mechanism of the teacher—as a time when they are "called on the carpet."

- Think of conferencing as the most important diagnostic opportunity you will have, but remember that the primary things you want to learn are how this student thinks and feels about his or her own reading and writing, how this student habitually constructs meanings, as well as how much reading and writing the student is doing.

  Your analysis needs to be systematic and developmental: Where has the student been as a language user? Where is the student going? Begin the second or subsequent conference by taking a look at the notes you and the student made during the previous conference. How have the objectives set out there been achieved?

- Look on conferencing as your most important teaching time. Decide ahead of time what aspects of the individual student's language use and development that you would like to emphasize.

  Focus on a few areas for each conference. Pick no more than three of the icons for language processing and devise questions and comments about them that you might use during the conference: Does the student know what he or she wants to know when beginning to read or write? Does s/he build on a recognition of what is already known about a topic? Does the student think ahead about what a text or story will tell? Does s/he predict while reading or writing? Does the student visualize while reading and writing? Does the student recognize when something is not making sense? Does the student re-read and revise to strive for good sense? Does the student know where to get help and seek it when it is needed?

- During the conference, make an effort to focus on language use as a process by paying attention to evidence of prewriting activities and revisions.

- Treat the conference as a time when you can become more of a real person to the student—as the opportunity to demonstrate a genuinely sincere coaching stance that is built on understanding and appreciation of the student as a unique individual.

  Tell about a story you have written, for example, or about one of your favorite authors. Then advise, "Now you tell me about this story you wrote. How did you put it together?" Or ask, "Who is your favorite author? What do you like about the way that author writes? I often write like my favorite authors. Are there any papers here where you have written something like yours?"

- Avoid turning the conference into even a friendly inquisition. Develop a technique of commenting to supplant questioning. For example, ask the student to pick out one or more things in the portfolio and ask the student to "tell me about this."

  You can begin with "What have you been doing since the last time we looked at your portfolio together?" Comment sometime during the conversation, "I was looking in here for any changes in your reading and writing. What would you pick?"

- Let the student take control of the conference. Keep the portfolio materials in the student's hands. In being conversational, talk less than the student. (Tape-record some conferences and actually check the amount of time you talk compared to the amount of time the students talk.)

- Make a point to examine and discuss materials that have been read or written outside of class and in more than one discipline.

- Encourage students to identify and to consider multiple meanings—including perspectives that are new to them, opinions that they do not necessarily agree with, other readers' potential reaction to texts and what they write, etc.

- Be certain that both you and the student take interactive notes during the conference, ending with agreement and a record of several achievable and reasonable goals for the student to follow in the weeks following the conference. These particular notes can be the initial focal point of the next conference.

SOLVING THE

ASSESSMENT PUZZLE

Over the years, language arts assessment has become a genuine puzzle. It has many parts that may seem confusing and frustrating to someone who examines them separately, but after decades of debate and confusion, it has become clearer how a school system can fit them together and solve the puzzle. The solution involves putting the pieces together thoughtfully and with an understanding of the information needs of different audiences. The solution requires recognizing how these different needs can be met by the assessment of reading and writing. It also requires understanding what types of tests and other assessments are needed to do that.

UNDERSTANDING THE INFORMATION

NEEDS OF DIFFERENT AUDIENCES

One of the major reasons that assessment of the language arts appears so puzzling is that different assessment audiences need and want different kinds of information, and in

The developments treated in this chapter and the interpretations discussed here have been considerably controversial. Thus a fair amount of referencing seems appropriate. Typical or exemplary sources have been cited throughout and the bibliographical information is listed in the "Reference and Recommended Reading" list at the end. The reader is encouraged to read for himself or herself and to develop opinions about assessment types and needs based on that background and his or her professional experience.

T
A
B
L
E

6
•
1

ASSESSMENT AUDIENCES

Audiences	The Information Is Needed to	The Information Is Related to	Type of Information	When Information Is Needed
Students	Identify strengths, strategies to develop, learning activities	Individual	Related to specific, developing, and emerging goals and objectives; criterion-referenced and descriptive	Daily, or as often as possible
Teachers	Plan instruction, strategies, activities	Individual, small group	Related to specific goals and objectives; primarily criterion-referenced and descriptive	Daily; or as often as possible
Parents	Monitor progress of child and effectiveness of school; identify assistive role	Individual	Related to broader goals and to specific objectives; criterion- and norm-referenced and descriptive	Periodically (five or six times a year)
School administrators/staff	Judge effectiveness of curriculum, materials, teachers	Groups of students and individuals	Related to broad goals and more specific objectives; criterion- and norm-referenced and descriptive	Annually or by term/semester
General public and the press and other decision makers	Judge if schools are accountable and effective	Groups of students	Related to broad goals; norm- and criterion-referenced and descriptive	Annually

demanding what they need, they are not sensitive enough to what other audiences want. The two general types of audiences are teachers and students, on the one hand, and the people who are interested in knowing what kind of job our schools are doing—how accountable schools are—on the other.

Students and teachers need information to plan daily instruction that will serve each student's unique set of needs and interests; they need to know how the individual child is developing as a reader and writer, and what strategies and experiences will strengthen that development. Teachers, of course, often consider the effectiveness of instruction by looking at how all the students in their classes are doing.

The people interested in accountability would quickly argue that they are interested in having the information needs of teachers met, but their more immediate need for educational information is for easily digested data that reports on the effectiveness of their schools. Any interest they have in more detailed information about how individual students are doing is secondary and often reflects their eagerness to compare test results to make decisions or form opinions.

They tend to want to know how today's students in their particular schools, systems, districts, and states perform compared to those from earlier time periods and other groups of students. Teachers are interested in knowing what data about effectiveness says about how they are doing, too; but that data is not often directly applicable to helping them teach more effectively.

Parents form still another general audience because they want both the accountability data and assessment information that details their child's achievement.

So the accountability audience is made up of several general groups:

- School administrators, directors, and other key professional educational decision makers.
- Parents and other taxpayers eager to get the best schools possible for their dollars.
- The public, including some tireless critics of the schools.
- The media (often referred to as *the press*), which professes to look out for the interest of the public.
- Persons outside of the schools who make key educational decisions, like approving budgets and funding to run the schools—school board members and members of state legislatures.

THERE TENDS TO BE A WALL THAT BLOCKS UNDERSTANDING

It is not surprising that teachers and decision makers see the use of assessment differently. Teachers want to help students learn, to guide their understanding of the world, and to involve them in thinking about their own development as language users and learners. Although not always as primarily as some of us would like, decision makers are concerned about guiding students, too; but their most immediate need for assessment is to determine whether students are learning. Decision makers' concerns are most directly about the results of the education system while also focusing on the factors and objectives that enable those results.

Indeed, the most recent national efforts to improve education have been on establishing standards that presumably will result in the development of assessments to hold educators accountable. At the same time, the differences in how these two general groups look at assessment has resulted in the call for more authentic performance tests (Cloer, 1994; Pearson, 1993; Robinson, 1996; Salinger, 1996; Standards for the English Language Arts, 1996).

The assessment needs of these two general groups tend to be different and even contradictory, and if they do not recognize each other's needs, it is because these distinctions create a kind of wall depicted in the chart A Lack of Understanding/Acceptance on page 188. It is essential that we breech that wall if we are to get our assessment act together! (Hayes and Camperell, 1994).

ACCOUNTABILITY HAS LONG RELIED ON STANDARDIZED, NORM-REFERENCED TESTS

The information needs of these different accountability audiences may vary somewhat, but generally what all of their members want is data on student achievement that will tell

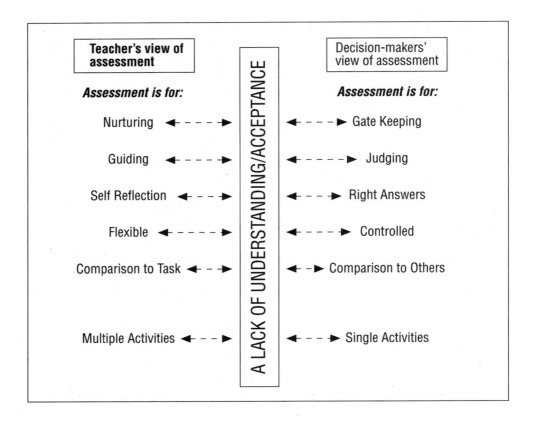

them how well the schools and school systems they are interested in are doing. Over the years, the best way of creating assessment information that reports on school performance has seemed to be to use norm-referenced standardized tests designed to allow accountability audiences to compare how their students perform to the performance of a broad and diversified national sample used to norm the test. These tests have generally been developed as multiple-choice assessments, since such tests can be quickly and economically scored.

Such assessments have had to include test items that have correct answers, since test-scoring machines cannot make judgments about student alternative answers that students might develop. Thus, we refer to these assessments as "right answer" tests. This does not mean that there is always only one right answer; the IGAP assessment developed as the Illinois statewide assessment has test items that include one or more correct answers (Wang and Ackerman, 1994). Despite this change in test format, some answers are correct and others are incorrect and they can be scored by a machine.

Most accountability audiences have been interested as well in trying to compare their students' performance to that of other groups in significantly different settings, from other time periods, and even on different versions or editions of the test. Such comparisons are not advisable or dependable, but people often make them because they are so intensely interested in trying to find out how their schools are doing.

Critics do this surprisingly often. Even well-intentioned members of the media and important decision makers have made these kinds of comparisons. The only justifiable comparison that should be made using the scores of groups of students on a standardized test, however, is to the score reported for the sample used to norm it.

As criticism of our schools and concern about their effectiveness has mounted over the years along with the rising cost of financing them, use of norm-referenced tests has become more and more "high-stake" (Catterall, 1990; Linn, 1994; State student assessment programs . . . , 1993). This kind of assessment came to dominate school assessment some years ago. The scores of groups that did not compare well to those of the norming samples brought pressure on the schools and teachers of those students to do a better job; they were being pressured *to be accountable.*

Naturally, many teachers examined the kinds of questions and behaviors the tests measured and were inclined to be sure that they taught those kinds of things, and in the same format that was used on the tests. Critics noted that the tests might focus the curriculum narrowly, but some educators came to assume that these tests would generate all or most of the information needed to make good educational decisions—both in the classroom and beyond it (Aronson and Farr, 1988; Farr and Carey, 1986; Farr, Carey, and Tone, 1986; Johnston, 1986; Farr and Olshavsky, 1980; Farr and Roser, 1974; MacGinitie, 1973).

All this resulted in heated criticism of the tests themselves. Many educators have criticized these norm-referenced tests over the years for not really informing the instructional process. Since the test is meant for use across the country, neither its content—nor the behaviors it requires and professes to measure—can be based on or can reflect *a school's particular curriculum,* the instructional objectives of any particular school or teacher, or the learning and development needs of a particular student. More importantly, these tests place a premium on "selecting" a correct answer rather than having a student "construct" an answer. The end result is a set of scores that provide evidence about how students have learned to select correct answers, and no information about how they come to construct meaning.

Other examples of criticisms of standardized tests have included:

- The short passages used to measure reading are not representative of the kinds of stories and other texts that students normally read. (The test content is not valid.)
- There is no validity in the discrete skills tested; no one knows how they actually add up to reading or writing.
- The student is not required to *apply* the knowledge tested.
- There is no real chance on the tests to *construct meaning* or to employ background and prior knowledge. The behaviors required on the test do not reflect what the best theory tells us about language use.
- The inferential thinking required is too limited.
- The students used to norm the test do not represent the particular balance of students in many schools and districts that will nonetheless be comparing their students' scores to those of the norming sample.

As the standardized tests have been revised periodically, an attempt has been made by their authors and publishers to construct them so that they can serve instructional and other needs. Standardized reading tests have added criterion-referenced interpretations, special interpretations for teachers, special reports for parents, individual score reports, and instructional support materials of various kinds.

For some time, the tests were fractured further into more subskills to be "diagnosed" to inform teachers who might set them as instructional objectives—so much so that on a test that takes 40 minutes to an hour, these designated but never validly established parts of language behavior are often measured by a mere three items each. In more recent years, the nationally standardized tests have decreased the number of subskills and focused more on general reading comprehension assessment. Some of the nationally normed tests in reading have added optional student constructed response items.

"What," you might well ask, "should one do differently in instruction for the student who misses one of the three than for the student who misses two or three?" (The test manual will probably give you someone's arbitrary decision as interpretive advice.) All this has made these standardized tests longer, more expensive, and somewhat confusing; but they have been promoted as the one-test answer to the reading assessment puzzle, adding to the confusion with the misconception that this can be so.

As Chapters 7 and 8 will demonstrate, using such tests successfully requires dictating the purpose for writing so that a rubric and anchor papers for rating can be created; and the purpose must be selected to be as authentic as possible.

To solve the assessment puzzle, it will be necessary for teachers and other educators to admit that norm-referenced test results can be of some value to the public and other decision makers, including parents. But these standardized tests should not be as they have evolved in response to the criticism of them. Large single-test batteries that promise to meet all of a school's assessment needs from classroom diagnosis to accountability tend to dictate instruction that narrows the curriculum.

What such large-scale reading assessment can and should do is to report a global comprehension score, with no special subtests on traditional skill focuses like word recognition and vocabulary. Without the time-consuming battery of accompanying tests, reading tests can be shorter while using longer passages of a variety of types. These passages can yet evoke different purposes for reading that reflect the real reasons students read in and out of school. Thus the reading test will be more authentic.

Without the burden of reporting on a host of specific reading and thinking subskills, test makers can write items that truly reflect the balance of a passage, the students' probable purpose for reading such a text, and the aspects of the writing that make the text one of quality and worth the students' time.

The change in writing tests has been mainly to have the students *write*, not identify usage errors in someone else's sentence-long copy. While language conventions will be considered as part of the criteria for rating a student's performance, the emphasis will be on whole content, organization, use of detail, and the like.

DECLINING TEST SCORES AND MORE CRITICISM PROMOTED CRITERION-REFERENCED TESTS

As criticism developed of the limited relevance of standardized testing to instruction and particular schools' curricula, criterion-referenced tests became more popular (Farr, 1987; Hambleton, 1994). They could be written by teachers for their classrooms, for a whole school, for the district, and, as became evident, for a state (Popham, 1993).

The criterion-referenced tests that standardized reading tests have tried to emulate compare student performance to particular reading tasks. The tests can be written so that these tasks cover particular teacher and curricular objectives and the material in particular textbooks.

Performance is reported by score interpretations that are not comparisons to the performance of any sample. The number of questions a test taker should get correct to perform on the measure adequately is usually determined somewhat arbitrarily by persons considered to have the expertise and experience to make that judgment. While the tests may be tried out and revised after use, the scoring interpretation is usually determined by the teachers and authors and publishers who design the tests. Using their experience with students, they decide, for example, that most sixth-graders will be able to answer correctly 15 of 20-some multiple-choice questions on a test. That sort of decision making tends to place the test in the norm-referenced category since it is the expected scores based on one's knowledge as to what students might score on the test that determines the criterion performance level that is suggested.

One of the key reasons for the increasing concern about school accountability and for more testing was declining scores on standardized tests. While this was true about many tests given across the nation, it was most apparent in tests that attempted to predict a student's ability to succeed in college, like the Scholastic Achievement Tests. Reported with a unique scoring scheme that tended to inflate the severity of the decline, SAT scores and scores on other standardized tests continued to decline from the 1960s through the 1980s. Consequently, the demand for more accountability testing found strong support among school board members and legislators.

Sensitive to criticisms of standardized tests that expressed concern about a national and narrowing curriculum, most of the educational decision makers who mandated new accountability tests decided that such tests should be criterion-referenced to particular objectives set out in the city, district, or state curriculum or to objectives agreed upon by a panel of teachers from the area. Yet there was a general unwillingness among the public to determine accountability with tests that had objectives that vary significantly from school to school and teacher to teacher. There were those who would argue rather convincingly that this was not a bad thing; Willard Wirtz (1978) was optimistic about the interest that generated a movement that would reflect local priorities and help sustain "pluralism" in our schools.

What developed, nonetheless, were sets of tests that could be given each year to students at designated grade levels, most often across a state. More and more states began writing and administering *minimum competency* testing programs, most of which were criterion-referenced to state-determined objectives. Along with some standardized tests that have been adapted to state needs, criterion-referenced exams are now mandated by a majority of the states. This phenomenon has raised a host of as yet unresolved issues (Afferbach, 1990).

The tests are used to compare student performance to tasks that are often put on the test by committees of curriculum specialists, sometimes with review of their work by a lay committee. They also arbitrarily set cutoff scores as criteria representing minimum competency that is acceptable. In a sense, criterion-referenced tests came to resemble the standardized tests.

Although minimum competency tests are not *normed* in the technical sense of the term, frequently they are revised after use and their content reflects the skills and strategies that had long been tested on the standardized tests. Both the standardized tests and the broadly administered criterion-referenced tests are being used as evidence of a school's, school district's, or state's accountability. Yet minimum competency programs have not replaced a prevailing demand for nationally normed testing.

The data to determine how seriously scores on reading tests were actually deteriorating over time have always been sketchy at best and tend not to substantiate claims of dramatic declines (Farr and Fay, 1982). Nonetheless, the public has remained convinced that performance has dropped rather dramatically. Nor has the prevalence of minimum competency programs significantly altered the conviction of the public and the press that student achievement—particularly in reading and writing—continues to deteriorate.

This concern with national accountability led to the National Assessment of Educational Progress (NAEP), an ongoing federally mandated assessment program that now provides some of the best large-scale reading and writing performance data available (Results from the NAEP 1994 reading assessment . . . , 1996; Langer, et al., 1995; Wirtz and Lapointe, 1982). It reports on several age groups over several time periods and by geographic areas and other demographic factors. Although it tends to evolve each time it is nationally administered, it supports comparisons across time—of one gender in one age group in the most recent administration to the scores of the same age group in the previous administration, for example.

Whether any declines that the ongoing NAEP study has depicted justify an alarmed public's assumptions about student performance is questionable. Careful analyses of the SAT score declines by the Advisory Panel on the Scholastic Aptitude Test Score Decline (*On further examination . . . ,* 1977) cited several reasonable causes other than poor schools (including a significant change in the type of student population taking the test, a young adult population disillusioned with public and educational values during the Vietnam War, and the demotion of the importance of the scores by some college admission offices, for example).

This kind of qualification had been suggested before (McCandless, 1975). There were challenges to this interpretation (On further examination of *On further . . . ,* 1977; Kinder, 1977), and the qualifications of the SAT score decline did not mitigate the public demand for accountability testing (Shane, 1977).

In recent years, the continuing debate about the quality of U.S. schools has given rise to a new focus on standards and assessment (Ravitch, 1995; Standards for the English language arts, 1996). George Bush's administration called for "voluntary national tests" for fourth-, eighth-, and 12th-graders in five core subjects (Bush, 1992), and Chester Finn (1992) echoed the call from the White House for new national achievement tests to compare the performance of U.S. students to "world class standards." By 1996, the Clinton administration echoed the call for accountability as a primary interest (Clinton, 1996).

The new tests helped some teachers settle instructional emphases, but they tended to restrict the teacher in setting objectives and instructional emphases based on individual student needs. Most important of all, perhaps, criterion-referenced tests yet failed to measure writing by having the student actually write and did little to measure reading that had authentic purposes.

Criterion-referenced testing had not answered the prevailing criticisms levied on norm-referenced testing, and raised new objections, intensifying and confusing the assessment puzzle.

More Assessment Led to an Emphasis on Alternative Assessment

Teachers have always used informal assessment, including anecdotal and more structured observation. They have always constructed their own quizzes to match their instructional goals. Often they have tailored the assessment goals measured to match individual student development—criterion-referencing in the best sense. Laboring under the increasingly oppressive dictation of more and more accountability testing, those concerned about the emphasis on language skills isolated from real reading and writing experiences began to look for "learning experiences or opportunities" and to place new faith in their own subjective judgment (Miller, 1995).

There has emerged with the dramatic increase in accountability testing a quest for instruction closely aligned with more holistic views of language development. But some curriculum theorists who suggest that assessment priorities almost always win out in a mismatch between curriculum and assessment have determined that if curriculum is to change, tests of reading and writing must change (Smith, 1991). This has brought about the development of new assessments—both formal and informal.

Included in this mix have been modifications of conventional tests with new item formats and the addition of the assessment of behaviors not often included on traditional tests, such as those that openly reflect background knowledge, student interests and attitudes, and metacognitive strategies. In general, reading passages have become longer, student products to be evaluated frequently involve more sophisticated thinking strategies, and some items try to emulate some application of what is comprehended (Wang and Ackerman, 1994; Fremer, 1991; Dutcher, 1990). The think-aloud or think-along technique has gained more and more favor as a research and instructional methodology (Powell, 1989; Meyers and Lytle, 1986).

The collection of student work samples in portfolios is an assessment process that departs rather dramatically from the multiple-choice format of standardized norm-referenced and short-answer criterion-referenced tests (Meisels, 1995). Perhaps the best way of tagging these and other observation-based forms of assessment is to call them *descriptive*. They produce student products that depict his or her language use, thinking, and meaning building. And with its inclusions of self-direction and self-assessment, of idea planning and revisions, the portfolio also describes/depicts the process the student has used (Birrell and Ross, 1996).

As the discussion in previous chapters has indicated, portfolios themselves have taken different forms, from *show portfolios* built from carefully selected samples to *working portfolios,* which provide the show portfolio with a much wider sample of student work. In the working portfolio, planning papers, revisions, and other products revealing the *process* of language use are deliberately kept together.

The popularity of alternative assessments such as portfolios has been coupled with an emphasis on performance assessment. In testing language-related abilities in particular, this has seemed important, for the acquisition of language skills is evident in their application. The selection of the correct response from among the options on a multiple-choice test had long been considered so atypical of the way that students use language that it was argued to be virtually no application at all. Even the attempt to test student awareness of process by asking so-called metacognitive questions has not gotten at process very well.

Performance tests, on the other hand, are tasks in which students have to apply what they have read in a written response. A second type has the student write what are essentially short essay answers to questions based on what they read and then write a longer response that is related to the text read in some way—usually topically. Unlike the responses on a multiple-choice test, the written product of the performance test can be analyzed from perspectives that are more directly revealing of both the reading and writing process.

Again, unlike typical standardized testing, the kind of emerging performance tests that integrate reading and writing are evaluated by comparing the responses to rubrics that tell what numerous teachers involved in a standardization of the test have agreed will indicate good, average, and weak responses and to actual sample or anchor papers that exemplify responses rated from 1 to 3, 1 to 4, 1 to 5, or using some other scale. The anchor papers are selected from the agreement of a group of teachers and make the test somewhat like many criterion-referenced tests in this regard (Murphy, 1995).

Developing reading/writing performance tests that are reliable across raters of student efforts is a difficult challenge. If the tests are to answer criticisms of standardized testing, they must require—or at least appear to require—realistic or *authentic* purposes involving audiences that the student might normally address. This *face validity* has to survive:

- The selection of a text or texts for the student to read.
- The prescription of a task as to how the students are to apply their comprehension of the text selected (or in case of the second, nonintegrated type of performance assessment, the writing of the item questions).
- The use of criteria to structure and carefully define the ways that raters will look at the results—the students' performance.

Doing all that is a big order; doing it while maintaining convincing authenticity is a genuine challenge that can be a fascinating and valuable professional experience. Thus teachers in numerous school systems across the country are tackling the job of constructing integrated performance language tests customized to their beliefs about language development, their curricula and instructional goals and objectives, and texts they select as appropriate for their students.

Another factor has promoted the development of reading and writing performance tests: the success of portfolio assessment. Many teachers have accepted portfolio contents as demonstrations of student language development. Among parents, administrators, and others interested in school effectiveness, portfolios are often found to be very informative of how students are learning to use language.

All this seems to recommend an attempt to harness the type of authentic response to reading and the writing that can be found in portfolios in some assessment instrument that can be reliable. If student responses to a reading text can be generated by assigning an authentic task that requires understanding it, perhaps they can be rated using the same descriptive scale and anchors. If so, comparisons of ratings of the responses can be made to inform accountability interests.

The rating process, of course, must be guided adequately, so that different raters would arrive at the same score or not give significantly varying ratings to the same student efforts. This kind of instrument, which will be described more thoroughly in Chapters 7 and 8, attempts to bridge the advantages of the portfolio to those of norm-referenced, standardized testing. Yet it can involve reading and writing performance that can be described as criteria.

A reader who has bought into all of the claims for the potential value of portfolio assessment and who identifies with the confusion and debates that have surrounded educational assessment in the past several decades might be inclined at this point to hail

Chapters 7 and 8 of this book are a detailed description of how to engage in that activity, explaining how teachers can begin with consensus-building discussions of their language-related values and instructional emphases and work through the selection of reading prompts, writing/thinking tasks, and the rubrics and examples of student responses that can guide reliable rating of student efforts.

portfolio assessment as *a panacea* that can eliminate all of the puzzling confusion. If portfolio assessment can meet many student and teacher needs and can serve needs for the other audiences, it must be a suitable replacement for the kinds of nonauthentic assessing we have done in the past.

Everyone should, some enthusiasts might conclude, stop using tests altogether and embrace portfolio assessment as the primary way of finding out how well our students are achieving and how well our schools and teachers are doing. After all, the contention is that the student reactions to reading and the other writing collected and analyzed in portfolio assessment are indeed products that result from authentic uses of language and thinking. They are far more authentic, it is contended, than the responses generated by norm- and criterion-referenced tests; so an advocate of portfolio assessment might argue that its widespread use should eliminate criticism and tend to solve the assessment puzzle.

Too often the debate about assessing the reading and writing behavior of our students has focused in this way on the latest panacea someone is touting. Yet none of the new types of assessment tried over the years has provided a single solution to the puzzle. The more you learn about the history of testing U.S. students—particularly the testing of reading and writing—the clearer it should seem to you that one of the least productive attempts to clear up the confusion about assessment is to jump on the newest bandwagon and try to crowd out the other options.

HOW, THEN, DO WE LOOK FOR A SOLUTION TO THE PUZZLE?

In order to bring some sense to the proliferation of assessment, we need to understand that all assessments have one general purpose: They are nothing more or less than attempts to systematically gather information. The information is used in education to help improve instruction and create better opportunities for students to learn and to grow in their ability to use language. A primary aim of portfolio assessment is to get the student to watch for that growth and those opportunities. But overall, assessment information gives teachers and others concerned with students' development the information they need for decision making relevant to education, including that needed for curriculum and instructional planning. While considering and respecting the informational needs of various audiences, it is a good idea to keep that seemingly obvious fact in mind. The bottom line in selecting and using any assessment should be whether it produced information that helps students.

NEEDS THAT STRUCTURE PLANS   In order to think more clearly about overall assessment plans, we need to know why we want to assess. If the assessment package we use is to meet the needs of different audiences efficiently, we need to know what they are. Without considering the information needs of the different audiences and then selecting assessments that will fill those needs, the assessment program in any school system will remain a set of jumbled puzzle pieces, and more often than not, it will not be adequate.

The three general types of assessment are diagrammed in the chart Fitting the Pieces Together on p. 195 to show how they serve three general types of audiences. It depicts how performance assessments can provide direct linkage among the main users of assessment and how the three major types of assessment are linked. The chart is a plan for pulling the pieces of the assessment puzzle together into a solution that can inform all decision makers involved in a student's development into an effective language user.

The analysis represented by this chart contends that norm-referenced standardized test scores will continue to be of interest to educational decision makers and the general public. These audiences will need some measuring stick to hold against the performance of particular groups of students taught within a particular curriculum, using particular methods and materials, and so forth. The public and its media will continue to want some kind of indication of educational effectiveness that shows how students compare to national samples they believe are scientifically selected in the test-norming process.

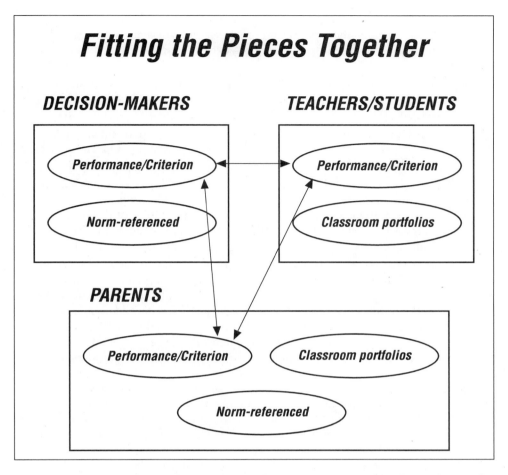

At the same time, they will continue to rely on criterion-referenced tests that can be customized to reflect the particular curriculum, goals, and objectives valued in a school, district, or state. Among those criterion-referenced tests are the increasingly popular performance tests, which the chart shows uniting the general types of assessment audiences. All users of assessment information, the chart stresses, are interested in criterion-referenced performance tests that profess to offer them the best of both worlds. They offer the authenticity and validity that critics contend are missing from nationally normed standardized tests and the dependability and reliability that is so difficult to achieve with the portfolio without contaminating it (Reed, 1993). So a solution to the assessment puzzle takes shape, and it recommends a key role for integrated language performance testing.

None of this discussion of the solution to the assessment puzzle should suggest that critical analysis of reading assessment should stop. Nor should attempts to improve tests in response to the criticism cease. Efforts that have experimented with multiple *correct* responses within each multiple-choice item and with much longer passages followed by numerous items have been interesting, if not conclusive. Numerous states, such as Vermont and Kentucky, are now trying using portfolios in competency testing ("This is my best . . . ," 1992; The primary program . . . , 1995; Harnack, 1994).

Most publishers of standardized tests have attempted to construct items that will assess what are generally accepted as strategies involved in higher order thinking or to create and use items that reveal students' awareness of how they are processing texts (metacognition). Although longer reading test passages, different question formats, and the like will not solve the assessment puzzle, they might reshape the parts we pull together for a better fit.

Pulling the assessment puzzle together will require tolerance and compromise on the part of many critics of particular types of assessment. The process would be facilitated if:

- Critics of the schools would become aware that assessment must serve more than school accountability. Ideally, critics will inform their concerns with a better understanding of their schools' curricula and will seek information that indicates how effective it is.

- Teachers and other educators would admit that norm-referenced test results can be of some value to the public and other decision makers, including parents.

- Decision makers would become more interested in new performance assessments—especially those that integrate reading and writing—that attempt to report student performance with data that will seem nontypical at first.

- The most idealistic of the critics of assessment would become more realistic and flexible, tempering their insistence on authentic performance assessment. It seems fruitless, in particular, for some critics to insist that all assessment revolve around observation of activities that are not apt to involve fewer than all children and that will reveal language use in highly varying degrees.

- Producers of assessments would acknowledge that no one assessment is going to suffice as a school's examination of reading. This would mean that they would no longer promote any of their products as such a test. It would also mean that future revisions of standardized reading tests would undo much of their complexity. What are not needed are large single-test batteries that promise to meet all of a school's assessment needs from classroom diagnosis to accountability and that consequently lead to the narrowing of the curriculum.

Revisions of standardized reading tests, for example, would eliminate the designation of language subskills and report a global comprehension score derived with items that truly reflect the balance of a passage, the students' probable purpose for reading such a text, and the aspects of the writing that make the text one of quality and worth the students' time.

More assessment specialists and publishers would provide the assistance that teachers and schools need in preparing portfolios, planning performance assessments, and integrating assessment information. School districts need help with developing assessment programs that link audiences instead of dividing them. They should be supplied the assistive tools to encourage discussion among administrators, teachers, parents, and students about what they hope to learn from assessment; to select assessments that will supply that information; to develop workshops in which teachers learn how to use portfolios and to conduct effective observation, and so forth; and to report assessment information to various audiences effectively.

NEEDS TRANSLATED TO USES Perhaps most important is an understanding of the use of the assessment results. Decision makers and those who plan instruction should understand that they will need to use test results in very different ways. The effective use of test results are described below for the three general types of assessments that have been discussed in this chapter: (1) short-answer tests, which are usually multiple-choice or brief student-constructed response items—and which are either criterion referenced or norm referenced; (2) longer student-constructed response tests, which involve an authentic purpose and an audience—and which are only criterion referenced; and (3) student collections of a variety of classroom projects and activities. We will refer to those three respectively as (1) right-answer tests; (2) my-answer tests; and (3) self-assessments.

The right-answer tests are used by decision makers as evidence of how a school or school district is doing. The scores should be used primarily on a group and not on an individual basis. The emphasis is on the group performance, and these scores are then compared to a criterion or norm that has been established.

On the other hand, teachers already know who their best readers and writers are and the right-answer average scores tell them very little about "how" to teach. Teachers who want to help students achieve higher scores on these right-answer tests need to work with students about how they answered the questions. They need to help students to learn how to identify main ideas, select pertinent details, and accomplish the other right-answer tasks on the tests. This means that the teacher must have the questions and the student responses and engage in discussions with students getting them to think about how to select right answers.

It is not adequate, nor is it desirable, to have students merely complete more worksheet activities that look like the right-answer tests. They must learn how to select answers by thinking about the material that has been read. This need to have the answers and the questions presents a dilemma: the test norms necessitate that the questions be kept confidential since they represent a sample of possible questions that could be asked. It would be counterproductive to have students and teachers drill on only a sample of the domain that needs to be mastered. In addition, releasing the questions to teachers would, almost certainly, invalidate the norms for the tests since some teachers would actually drill on those test items.

What is needed, therefore, are assessments that are like the right-answer tests and that provide teacher guidance on how to help students learn the skills and behaviors that are required to determine and select correct answers.

In brief, the difference between the use of right-answer tests by decision makers and teachers is that decision makers are asking "How well are we doing?" while teachers should be asking and teaching "How do students learn to select right answers?"

For the my-answer assessments, the concerns are the same. Decision makers want to know how well the schools and school district are able to accomplish the kinds of tasks that are included on these assessments. Teachers, on the other hand, want to know how students go about solving the problems that make up the assessments. Decision makers are interested in the final scores while teachers are interested in determining how to make the students into better performers. As in coaching athletics, a good teacher understands that if I can teach them how to do it, the final product will be improved.

This means that teachers, like good coaches, need to look past the scores. They need to observe students as they are engaged in completing performance assessments, and they need to discuss with students how they went about doing the performance activity. Most importantly, they need to nudge, to coach the student to think about how the activity can be done.

The third general type of assessment, the self-assessment activity, results in two different kinds of products, the show portfolio and the working portfolio. The show portfolio, which will be discussed more fully later in this chapter, includes materials selected by both the teacher and student. The show portfolio can be used as an adjunct to the more traditional right-answer and my-answer assessments. It can be used to give decision makers a more in-depth idea of what students are doing by selecting a random set of portfolios and making them available for review. It can also be used as a backup system when the right-answer and my-answer assessments seem to have provided an inaccurate evaluation of a student's accomplishment.

Since all tests are to some degree unreliable and since the right-answer and my-answer assessments are usually relatively brief assessments administered under one set of conditions, a show portfolio can provide another look when a teacher feels these other assessments are not providing a true assessment of the student's accomplishments. This does not mean that the right-answer and the my-answer test results should be ignored in lieu of the show portfolio. It does mean, however, that the show portfolio results should be given at least equal weight. It means that ongoing teacher and student assessment will be considered.

The teacher's use of the self-assessment materials in the working portfolio is a primary focus of this entire book. In brief, the working portfolio is the tool that the teacher and the student use to constantly review and plan. Portfolios are not a new idea in education. Educators should consider portfolios as a concept and not a particular physical thing with specific procedures as to how the working portfolio should be used.

The portfolio concept is exemplified by the teacher who has said to a student, "Billy, go and get the stuff you are working on and let's sit down and look at the stuff together. I'd like to learn about how you think you are doing and what you'd like to do next." That in its simplest form is the concept of a portfolio and the concept that has driven much of the thinking in this book.

Portfolios, Performance Tests, and Large-Scale Assessment

Numerous schools, districts, and even states around the nation are now experimenting with the use of portfolios and integrated language performance tests in order to better inform audiences interested in educational accountability. A few are using portfolios as a primary assessment approach, adding portfolios as a supplement to more traditional assessments. Some others are including portfolio assessment in their school district or state assessment plans, with the portfolio serving primarily as a classroom assessment rather than as an accountability assessment.

The results about how adequately these programs appear to serve the full information needs of parents, school administrators and specialists, other educational decision makers, and the media and public are not yet conclusive.

Can Portfolios Serve Both Instructional Needs and Accountability?

Most educators who support the value of portfolios are concerned about attempts to make them more reliable as tools to inform these audiences. It is feared that this use will dictate the contents of portfolios and the criteria used to evaluate them and that this will preempt most decisions the students should be making and destroy any genuine sense of ownership essential to developing student self-assessment (Irwin-DeVitis, 1996). If you are going to ensure that different raters will look at different students' portfolios and come up with similar evaluations, it is assumed, you will need to tell them what to look for and how to rate it. To do that fairly, teachers would need to know what raters will be looking for in the portfolios and to advise them to have their students include these things.

To be fair to students being evaluated, the argument continues, you will need to tell them what the raters will be looking for. So in a rather sudden and dramatic shift, the student must begin thinking of the portfolio in terms of those criteria, not his or her own. Analysis is dictated to the student, who is not left to induce it through his or her own analysis. If that happens, the student has lost the primary control of what goes into his or her portfolio—and probably of the way it is arranged and analyzed as well.

Performance Tests Try to Reflect the Best of Both Worlds

Integrated language performance tests are intended to absorb the impact of controls for reliability while maintaining the authenticity of portfolio contents. Many of the integrated language performance tests, some of which have now been in place for almost a decade, are *intended* to combine controls that provide reliability with student performance that is more typical of the kind of meaning construction the student would create in the classroom and other language-related activities—the kind of work that would be selected for inclusion in the portfolio.

Performance tests try to frame the kinds of language experiences typical of those that produce portfolio products, and they appear to succeed when compared to the student responses required by short-answer reading and writing tests. At the same time, to ensure that different raters' evaluations of particular students' performance on the tests are similar and that ratings assigned to different student efforts are somewhat comparable, much that would inhibit portfolio collections is prescribed to the student and raters.

Theoretically, at least, the test would provide information that is more consistent than one would get when the kind of portfolios being recommended in this book are rated by different teachers or educators. The structuring for reliability limits what the test can tell us when compared to what we might learn with our own relatively subjective analysis of the portfolios of the students who took the test, but they may tell basically what several audiences of educational assessment wish to hear.

THERE ARE SERIOUS CONCERNS ABOUT THE ALTERNATIVES IN ACCOUNTABILITY ASSESSMENT

It is encouraging when audiences we may have assumed are primarily interested in accountability seem eager to understand student language development by looking at alternative assessment. Actually, it should not be too surprising that most people can interpret portfolio collections and performance test products better than they can fully understand the data produced by standardized testing. Most of us have a better, more responsible grasp of language than of statistics.

The bulk of concern about the ability of these alternative assessments to inform accountability in a dependable and effective way comes from within the educational community and from some measurement/assessment specialists (Stewart et al., 1995). It would be irresponsible to recommend the use of integrated reading/writing performance tests and of portfolios in reporting to audiences other than teachers and students without noting a few examples of reservations in the field.

Mike Beck, who has extensive experience with the construction of all kinds of educational assessment, believes that performance tests—and presumably the criteria for evaluating portfolios—are not yet well enough developed or defined to endorse their use for accountability:

> Performance tests have an important, even critical, role to play in a well-conceived, instructionally informative school-based testing program. However, that role is NOT on a state-level accountability testing program. The appropriate goals of a state test are breadth, not depth; reliability, not instructional utility; assessment of product, not process; and efficiency of measurement. (Beck, 1991)

Beck notes that the analysis of performance test responses—not to mention portfolio collections—is very time-consuming and expensive. He argues, too, that when performance tests are administered on a district- or statewide basis, they fail one of two criteria for authenticity: For a test to be authentic, he argues, it must be more than realistic. It must also be administered at a time *when the teacher and student deem it is an important thing to do.*

While Beck endorses the use of alternative assessments as *adjuncts,* he argues that they are just not cost-effective in meeting the information needs of the audiences that have depended on large-scale testing. Beck feels that decision makers and educational evaluators should rely on as many good kinds of information as they can afford and can get. He points out that no assessment format—including multiple-choice—should be used (as Beck admits it has) to the exclusion of others.

Beck's second test of authenticity is an interesting one, and it tends to argue that performance tests should be developed by teachers locally to match their classroom or school objectives. Certainly, the teacher/student control he calls for applies to portfolio assessment. When controls and criteria that appear to be necessary if portfolios are to serve accountability interests are imposed on collecting and evaluating them, the portfolio is no longer a clearly student-owned collection. It is most apt to be put together in response to a recipe from someone somewhere outside the classroom; it does not emerge from a combination of a student's unique interests, background, classroom experiences, and needs to use language.

Pamela Moss (1992) expresses this concern very clearly:

> A number of districts, states, and national committees have begun to explore the feasibility of using large-scale, standardized performance assessments to complement or replace standardized multiple-choice assessments as a means of educational accountability and reform. . . . Implicit in typical models of assessment serving accountability purposes is the need for centralization of authority within a given context to decide specifically what is measured and how it is measured; tasks, scoring procedures, and administration conditions are standardized in order to enhance comparability of scores from task to task, scorer to scorer, and subject to subject. This model, which separates assessments "that count" from ongoing day-to-day activities, has been criticized for disenfranchising teachers and students from setting their own intellectual problems and debating the criteria and standards that will be applied to their work. The potential negative impact of such a model has been noted in the context of both student development and teacher development.

Beck's and Moss's are not the only cautionary voices. A pilot study attempting to use portfolios to describe student performance was begun by the National Assessment of Educational Progress (NAEP) in 1990. Initially reported results (NAEP study casts doubt . . . , 1992) seemed oddly mixed. Even though the samples of writing in 2,200 portfolios collected for the study represented "disparate examples of writing," those evaluating them *were able* to come up with general scoring rubrics. At the same time, they expressed concern about setting objective standards for "the myriad of student writings, which reflect different teaching techniques and classroom conditions."

A member of NAEP's governing board was quoted as saying, "It seems uncertain that this process can ever provide a sound, practical way to compare schools, districts, states, regions, genders or ethnic groups." Apparently, however, analysis of the portfolios did afford one rather disturbing conclusion: The board member added, "We don't have a hidden treasure trove of wonderful student writing out there. . . . the quality of even their best efforts is often pretty poor."

From a quarter to one-half of the students who submitted portfolios for this pilot NAEP portfolio study had scores on the timed NAEP writing exam that were "quite different" from the scores given their portfolios. It is not clear whether they were higher, but that seemed to be the suggestion.

The same brief report, however, quoted the Education Department's assistant secretary for Educational Research and Improvement, who in 1992 hailed the project as a step that will "break the iron grip of the multiple-choice test."

The mixed and unclear messages from this preliminary report on a pilot study became somewhat clearer when the NAEP collected and studied 5,000 portfolios in 1992 (Gentile, 1995). These "portfolios" were actually three samples the students selected themselves to represent their best work. Again there was little correlation between the ratings given the portfolios, which were not exceptionally high, and the students' scores on the NAEP writing test. Again the implication is that the students did better on the test than their writing samples would have led one to expect. And again it is not clear which assessment method is deemed to be more dependable. The report on this portfolio study proves interestingly descriptive of student writing, however—a seeming recommendation for looking at actual student writing.

These somewhat conservative perspectives on the use of performance assessment and portfolios in reporting on accountability underline the importance of understanding the assessment puzzle. The assessment audiences interested in accountability will certainly let us know if they are being adequately or better informed. The inclination here is not to write off the possibility that integrated language performance assessment may ultimately replace, or become an equally important balancing instrument with, standardized norm-referenced tests.

Who would suggest that portfolios should not be shown to decision makers or the public, if they will take the trouble to look at them? (No one has so far.) It seems reasonable, however, to question whether portfolios can *replace* the assessment instruments traditionally used to determine accountability—at least without limiting what portfolios can be and what they can do for student language development.

THERE IS A CLEAR ROLE FOR PORTFOLIOS

Meanwhile one can enthusiastically recommend that portfolios be used as an accompanying source of information that can enrich the understanding that accountability-focused audiences seem eager to have—of how our students are actually using language, and of how they are developing as language users across time and exposure to instruction.

Ideally, a sampling of portfolios would be offered to administrators, legislators, and the media along with the scores from norm- and criterion-referenced tests *as a matter of policy*. At the least, portfolios can be available as a backup system.

Often portfolios that are shown to viewers other than teachers and fellow students are *show portfolios* selected by students from their *working portfolios* and with the particular audience, such as parents or the principal, in mind.

This activity is an excellent way of getting the student to give additional reflective attention to his or her collection, but it may lead the viewers to distrust how representative the collection really is. Several factors that weigh in this problem can be solved at least partially by convincing the student that the show portfolio must be an honest representation and should show as much of the reading and writing process that he or she used to create the pieces selected as possible. But overculling can blunt the portfolio's potential.

Portfolios can even become a key source of information when the reasonable interpretation of data from standardized assessment is less than obvious, when conflicting conclusions have been drawn from the test data and other information, and when test results seem not to represent the ability of a student that the daily experience and observation of a parent or teacher suggests is greater than the scores imply.

"Look," says the teacher, who knows from experience that includes looking at Johnny's portfolio collection, "these low test scores misrepresent this boy's ability. Perhaps he had a bad day the day he took the test. He never seems to grasp the mechanics of picking from among multiple-choice options with much efficiency; his test scores are often low. But here are numerous samples that show he can indeed construct meaning adequately, even effectively—that he comprehends things he reads well enough to react to them substantively, that he has a better command of language conventions than the test shows, and that when he is motivated by his own needs and interests, he is highly original, has a refreshingly incisive lexicon, and can think critically."

Any reasonable analyst should at least consider giving the portfolio samples collected over weeks or months priority weight over a one-hour performance on a test. At the very least, the conflicting indicators in such a situation should persuade the decision maker to retest the child, preferably with a performance instrument that will set a more authentic purpose for reading and writing than a standardized test can.

What is recommended here is the use of many kinds of assessment information to inform different audiences with different information needs. And it is contended that for this to happen, these audiences will need to appreciate each other's interests and needs more fully. The school system building an effective assessment program can then put it together without the different audiences trying to impose the assessments that serve them best on each other as the only ones that are needed.

It is especially important that the teacher who would hope to use portfolio and performance assessment to broaden the perspectives of the accountability audiences understand their needs—those that often get expressed and those that seem to get identified as they are met. The ones that require the efficiency of the standardized or short-answer criterion-referenced test can be accepted. Those that emerge as people examine actual student responses to reading and student writing in portfolios and on performance exams can be primed by making those alternative assessments available in effective ways. The rest of this chapter gives some examples of ways to do that.

How to Use Portfolios as Part of the Solution

Solving the assessment puzzle will take some time in any school system as the information needs of various audiences are defined, appreciated, and used to develop and select assessments. Meanwhile teachers, who carry a large portion of the responsibility of reporting assessment results to the other audiences, often have questions that need resolving as soon as possible.

The questions that educators who have the opportunity to put together a comprehensive assessment program should ask themselves are logical and sequenced. They may vary from classroom to classroom, department to department, and school to school; but when they are laid out appropriately, they will look like a logical and sensible plan. The sequence suggested in the chart below, A Sequence to Guide Assessment Planning, is typical of the kind of thinking that should be done.

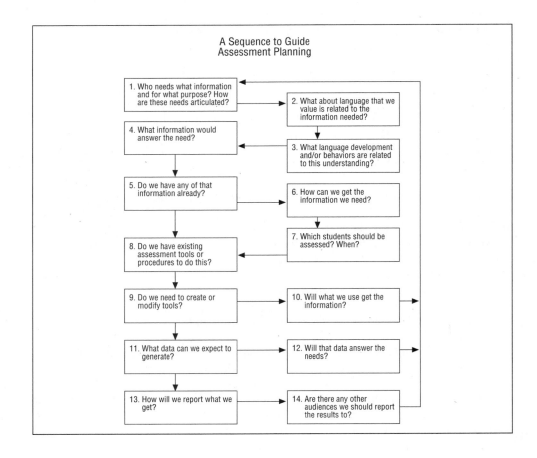

A Sequence to Guide Assessment Planning

1. Who needs what information and for what purpose? How are these needs articulated?
2. What about language that we value is related to the information needed?
3. What language development and/or behaviors are related to this understanding?
4. What information would answer the need?
5. Do we have any of that information already?
6. How can we get the information we need?
7. Which students should be assessed? When?
8. Do we have existing assessment tools or procedures to do this?
9. Do we need to create or modify tools?
10. Will what we use get the information?
11. What data can we expect to generate?
12. Will that data answer the needs?
13. How will we report what we get?
14. Are there any other audiences we should report the results to?

In addition, there are other general questions that relate to designing and executing the plan.

"How Can I Grade the Portfolios Responsibly?"

Elsewhere in this book, there are admonitions about the dangers of grading portfolios: Primarily the danger is that doing that robs the student of his or her sense of ownership of the collection and shifts the emphasis from *how language serves the development of interests and the need to communicate* to *the teacher's criteria for assigning the grade.*

It would be unrealistic and unfair, however, not to acknowledge that many teachers will be under considerable pressure to assign grades to portfolios. "We spend a considerable amount of time on the portfolio," a teacher may point out, "and my principal expects me to evaluate the student's performance on the project. So do most of the parents, and many of the children. So don't tell me arbitrarily that I must not respond to these expectations."

Another argument that supports grading portfolios goes like this: "The portfolio is so central in my classroom that there is no way to deny its potential impact on the grades I must assign for report cards several times a year. Is it honest to do that subjectively and not in an open way? Wouldn't it be fairer to the student to explain why I feel I must assign the grade and to give the student an idea of the criteria that will be used in determining the grade? And what if I have to support or rationalize the grade I assign to a student? I'm going to go straight to the portfolio; I'm certain of it. And I'll be articulating and using some criteria then."

Still another argument goes like this: "The alternative to grading the portfolio as a whole project is to assign grades to the individual products that the student can select to put into it. I've done that, and most of the kids select the things that got the best grades. Not only did this work against the development of a working portfolio and promote the development of a show portfolio, but worse yet, it also took the selection process out of the hands of the student. My grading criteria decided what was 'best,' and the students didn't have to do any of their own thinking about why *they* thought certain pieces belonged in their collection. I've decided that coming up with a grade on the whole portfolio allows me to let many classroom activities go ungraded and forces me to synthesize responses to considerations like these:

- How has s/he improved as a reader/writer/thinker?
- How much self-assessment appears to be taking place?
- How well do the things in this portfolio serve what appear to be genuine purposes for reading and writing?
- How much evidence is there of synthesizing of reactions to different texts, what is read to interests and background knowledge, etc.?
- How much has reading appeared to reflect writing?
- Do interests, beliefs, attitudes appear to change and develop with accruing language experiences?
- How much indication of revision and other process is there in the writing?"

There are other sets of criteria that you can consider and select from in composing portfolio grades. In addition to the list above, they include:

- How fluent is the student as a writer and thinker?
- Does the student write in a variety of genres and make meaning from a variety of texts?
- How much does the student appear to enjoy reading and writing?

For a more extensive discussion of how the teacher can evaluate the contents of portfolios, see the latter part of Chapter 4.

- How effectively does s/he employ appropriate reading/writing/thinking strategies?
- How effectively does the student take and give instructions?
- How creative is the collection?
- How relevant is the collection to the student's life?
- How clear/logical/sequential is the student's thinking?
- How effectively is the material organized? How much self-analysis does the scheme reveal?
- Is the student developing a personal voice and style in writing?
- Is there improvement in terms of his or her grasp of language conventions?

If it is necessary to do so, portfolios can be graded while limiting negative impact on the sense of student ownership and the all-important goal of developing self-assessment. Here are a few suggestions of ways to limit the damage:

- Teachers like the one who listed the criteria above often do several important things as part of the grading procedure:

  a) They keep their criteria as broadly focused and process-oriented as possible, carefully avoiding the articulation of values that will preempt the necessity of student evaluation and judgment.

  b) They make sure that the student knows from the outset of portfolio development what criteria the teacher will use or select from in assigning grades, wording the criteria so that they serve as a list of guidelines that the student can follow.

  c) They sometimes allow themselves some latitude or room for judgment by making it clear that they will use *some and not necessarily all* of the criteria they provide for the student.

  d) They "individualize" criteria to fit the strengths and needs of individual students.

  e) They let the student partake in the formation of criteria—in effect, grading the student in terms of how well s/he has met his or her self-determined objectives.

- Some teachers use multiple grades—not on individual pieces in the collection, but on different aspects of, or perspectives on, the portfolio; *and they couple the set of grades to narrative evaluative comments.*

- A few teachers grade the portfolio solely on the basis of how well the student has achieved the goals set out after self-analysis.

- A few teachers grade selected papers or the whole portfolio with the student's input and self-analysis *during a portfolio conference.*

- Many teachers who grade portfolios have their students pick from the collection a certain number of papers near the end of each grading period that they want the teacher to grade. (In a sense, they are pulling a show portfolio of what one would presume they think is their "best stuff.") Depending on how much written evaluation the teacher intends to give the student about each piece or the group of papers, the number may vary from 6 to 12. Some teachers attach a written analysis to each one. Other teachers have the students write the analysis of each piece, the group, or both. The portfolio grade is a sum of reactions to the separate papers and includes the teacher's evaluation of the student analysis.

- Some teachers list at the beginning of a grading period the papers that will be graded and averaged as a portfolio grade, but it is advisable that this calculation also include a grade for degree and quality of self-assessment and/ or one for progress in achieving self-articulated objectives.

- Some teachers give the portfolio an overall subjectively determined grade and list several key reasons for it in writing. The rationale(s) for the grade can be discussed with the student during a conference. If the student makes a good case for criteria the teacher has overlooked, some teachers adjust the grade by the end of the conference.

- Some teachers have the students assign a preliminary grade to their own portfolios and write a rationale for the grade. After looking at the self-evaluation, the teacher meets with each student to explain why the grade seems too high or low and to negotiate a final grade.

Other teachers, of course, are able to steadfastly resist temptations to grade their students' portfolios, whether they have assigned grades to some of the papers in it or not. This recommended practice is wisely accompanied by the habit of summarizing in a written description what the portfolio tells the teacher about the student's language use, self-assessment, improvement, attitude, and other such factors, which can vary depending on each student's individual strengths, needs, and effort. These summaries are put into the portfolio, where the student can read them *after the student has written any such evaluative summaries of his or her own that are encouraged or required.*

Some teachers send these evaluations home for parents to see, and (if the student has been told that this may happen) the summary may be given to the principal or some appropriate school supervisor. But such analyses are not always clearly meaningful and are sometimes frustrating for the person who receives them if not accompanied by the portfolio itself. This tends to be particularly true for the parent.

You will need to work out some practice that responds sensibly to your particular situation. Whatever you decide to try, be open with your students about what you will do. They are, as you are no doubt aware, rather savvy about grades; and they can probably handle having their portfolios graded as long as they believe the process is open, fair, and intended to help them grow as a language user.

If grading the portfolios has a negative impact on your students' attitudes toward the portfolio assessment process, think carefully about whatever procedure you have used and about how it can be changed to eliminate any cynicism or distrust it creates. You might want to have an open discussion with the students about it and what they would recommend be done.

"WHAT IS THE BEST WAY TO SHARE PORTFOLIOS WITH PARENTS?"

There are numerous ways to get parents involved in the development of the portfolios their children build. Some present some problems you need to consider, and most are common-sense approaches that you have no doubt already thought of yourself:

- Begin the portfolio procedures in your classroom by sending a letter home to the parents explaining what portfolios are, how they will be used, and *how parents can encourage their children to include things related to what they read and write outside of class.*

- Instead of a letter—or as a follow-up to it—have your students put together a portfolio newsletter that can be distributed to parents as well as to other audiences. Minimally, the newsletter need only fill one or two sides of an 8-by-11-inch sheet of paper. Have the students plan and write different stories for it about what they are doing with their portfolios.

- Send the portfolios home with the students and tell them that they must invite their parents or guardians to look at the collections. Point out that some parents may want the student to go through the collection with them and to discuss the contents as this is done. Send a letter with the portfolio—even if you have sent such explanations before—telling what the portfolio is and how it is used and inviting parental comments about it. You may also want to include a simple questionnaire that solicits reactions from the parents. Keep the questions simple and open-ended to encourage uniquely revealing and directive comments. Make sure that the students understand that they are to bring the questionnaire back, or include materials that facilitate the parent in mailing them back.

The letter that goes home with the portfolio should stress the importance of the portfolio being returned to school! One serious hazard of sending portfolios home is that they will be lost or mishandled or that the parent will misunderstand and think that the material is being sent home permanently at a time when they are still needed in the classroom.

- Of course, you can do just that. You can send most of the collection home for good after you have the students pick particular records, unfinished work, ideas, work to be revised, summaries of previous periods of collecting, and a *few* favorite things to seed a new collection. Be sure, too, that you and the student have conferred about the collection being retired, and that any analyses to be written about it by you and the student have been completed and included. (You may decide to copy summaries of your analyses and the student's self-analyses so that they can stay with the collection sent home and still be included in the newly developing collection.)

Have the student put a rubber band around the things not selected for the new collection or package them in some other way. Then have the student take the culled material home for parents to see and keep. Be sure that the papers are accompanied by a note or letter explaining exactly what they are and inviting parents to come to school to see the active collection. You can have the students write these letters, but you may need to dictate a few of the inclusions by writing them on the chalkboard for copying.

An excellent idea already mentioned elsewhere in this book suggests having the students decorate boxes near the beginning of the school year to be taken home and kept on a shelf as a storage box for these sets of papers. At the end of the school year, most of the remainder of the portfolio can be sent home to add to the packages already in the box. Both parents and students will enjoy perusing this collection in later years and may long be grateful to you for providing the incentive to save the papers.

- Make sure that the portfolios are out for parents to browse through on back-to-school night or similar occasions. Remember that you will need to explain one more time what the portfolios are and how they are used. Be sure to allow adequate time for the parents to look through the portfolio, and move about so you can answer any questions they have.

- Plan a *Portfolio Workshop* for the parents of students in your classroom. Plan about a half-hour explanation of how the portfolios have been developed, how they are maintained (who selects, etc.), and why you believe they are important. (You may decide to have students help you make this presentation.) Then give the parents another half hour to look through the portfolio their child has collected and to answer questions.

- Be sure to offer parents the opportunity to look at the portfolio anytime they visit school. Do not hesitate to get it out if you know of something in it that will illustrate a point in the discussion about whatever concern brought the parent to your classroom.

- Near the end of the school year or a period when you want students to begin new portfolio collections hold "Portfolio Day," in which parents and students get together. Let your students help prepare a presentation explaining how they built their portfolios and what they have done with them. (You may want to have the students show how they use some of the forms, such as the Reading and Writing Log, on an overhead during the presentation.)

After the presentation, the students should take their parents to a place where they can share in an examination of the contents of the portfolio. Invite the parents to write a response to what they have seen to help close out the collection, and try to guide them to write a positive response. At the conclusion of Portfolio Day, let the students and parents take the portfolios home to keep as a memento of the school year.

Special conferences with family members, similar to several suggested above, can be very useful in getting your students more involved in the portfolio process and in encouraging them to think more about their reading and writing. At the same time, this process will help the family members learn more about their children than they ever could from homework assignments or tests.

In the final section of this book, there are models of the kinds of letters and other materials you can use to inform parents about portfolios suggested in this section.

The impact of portfolios on parents and their attitudes about their children as language users is sometimes quite surprising. Consider these comments actually written by parents who were given a chance to look at portfolios their children had collected and were invited to respond to on an open-ended questionnaire:

- "I reviewed everything with Leslie on Friday. We both had fun!" [kindergarten]

- "I think it's good to point out a child's strengths and reinforce his goals. However, I would like to know what to do when I notice errors. How can I point out JB's mistakes and help him correct them without hurting his self-esteem?" [kindergarten]

- "I am proud of Melonie and her progress. She seems so self-assured!" [kindergarten]

- "I see this kind of writing and drawing and stuff all the time. Some of the things in the portfolio were done at home, so this doesn't stand out to me at all." [first grade]

- "I am very impressed with Anna's writing. I enjoyed all of her stories. She expresses herself well and has some great ideas, especially if she were president." [first grade]

- "I loved reading Billy's work. I did not think him to be as creative as he is." [fifth grade]

- "Greg's improvement from the beginning of the year to the present is noticeable and impressive. I enjoyed reading his bear story and will encourage him to continue using his imagination." [sixth grade]

- "I understand that Portfolio Assessment is an individual method of evaluating, but how can I know if my kid is reaching all the objectives of the third grade, and what are the subjects where she is having problems, and what I can do to help her? How can this portfolio do all of these things?" [third grade]

- "I enjoy seeing the progress that my child is making. As a parent, I can honestly see and understand it, when it is right in front of me. From start to end of the school year." [fourth grade]

- "Beth's actions at home seem to parallel her accomplishments at school. She is dedicated and conscientious but easily frustrated if she doesn't do as well as she thinks she should. Her writings show, to me, an organized mind, but her penmanship tends toward the messy side. I think her enjoyment of reading has helped her writing and I am supportive." [fourth grade]

Traci G. Jones, an elementary teacher in Palm Beach County, Florida, explains how her student's portfolios developed and became the focal point of highly successful student/parent conferences. Along the way, Traci used numerous successful instructional methodologies:

TAKING PARENTS BEHIND THE SCENES

Blake sits side-by-side with his dad and shares his story of how he will train whales at Sea World. Erin and her mom snuggle close together as she shares her first poem about friends. Michael and his mom read his booklet about what plants need in order to grow. Steven sits between his mom and dad to proudly share his first published book called *The Ways We Jump*. Are these children sharing stories at home before bedtime? It may seem that way, but they are actually first-grade children conducting conferences with their parents at school. They are sharing their personal reading and writing ideas with their moms and dads.

As a primary teacher, I have struggled with how to assess the children's abilities for some time. I wondered, What do I assess? When do I assess? and What should I use to judge my student's work? Then Dr. Farr came to Palm Beach County to introduce teachers to using portfolios and performance assessments in the classroom. Schools were invited to become part of a lead team to pilot this methodology in their classrooms, and my school elected to become part of this team.

I began to see this as a possibility to find some answers to my assessment questions. That summer I worked through the book *Portfolios and Performance Assessment* and began to visualize how this could happen in my classroom. I sensed that it would work more easily for me because I would be having the same children in first grade that I had in kindergarten the year before. These children and I already knew each other and had a running start. As I envisioned the program functioning in my classroom, I saw it as a "triangle" where the child, their teacher, and their parents would need to communicate about the language development of the children.

In the past, parents of my students had acted as passive recipients of assessment information, but this approach opened the whole assessment process up for parents to examine. Portfolio assessment would give me an opportunity to invite them to become participants in their children's language development. A key objective would need to be to bring them into the classroom where "it's happening."

FIRST STEPS TOWARD CONFERENCING

In September, each child began to compile his or her own portfolio in a self-chosen container. Many holders were jam-packed with every piece of writing the child had done, but some students had been much more selective about the pieces chosen for the portfolio. I encouraged the children to keep their audience in mind as they added to the portfolio. They decided their audience would range from peers to teachers to family and friends.

Now that the portfolios were growing, I began to ask myself, "What do we do with them now?" I reviewed Dr. Farr's information on portfolios and began to see that the ultimate goal was getting the child to talk about his or her work and become a "self-assessor."

Getting children to talk about their work may seem like a very natural process, but it's not always that simple. It took time and practice for some children to become fluent in this process. I began by conferencing one-to-one with each child. About three conferences a day was all I could fit into the schedule. Each child came to the conference with approximately two pieces of work to share with me. My job was to be knowledgeable about each child and to be an active listener. The conference needed to be filled with "natural" talk: with exclamations, suggestions, ideas, and feelings. I also hoped that the writer would learn something from our conference that would help him or her another day with another piece of writing. I wanted them to leave the conferences wanting to write more!

AUTHOR'S CIRCLES

Besides conferencing with me, the children were also conferencing with their peers in Author's Circles. There each child would sign up on a clipboard as he or she completed a piece of work. Every fourth child to sign up would go to gather the first three children with their finished pieces. The four sat knee-to-knee, each with a particular job. The first child shared his or her work; the second tells two things he or she liked about the piece; the third tells what he'd like to know more about; and the fourth asks two questions about the piece. Then the roles rotate, until each person has had all four jobs.

CONFERENCES BEYOND OUR CLASSROOMS

All of these activities were taking place in preparation for conferencing with a third audience for the portfolio: a parent, guardian, or other adult with whom the child wishes to share his or her portfolio. We first surveyed the parents to determine a convenient day and time for them to come in for a conference. We looked at scheduling them just before the first report card to help give parents a visual picture to go along with the report card.

In October, the students helped to plan our first conferences with their parents. As part of the preparation, the students designed invitations to take home to their parents. This became a great opportunity for a lesson on the "W" questions: Who? What? When? Where? Why? Then the children filled in each answer as it pertained to the conference day. Parents were requested to RSVP so I could help those children whose parents could not attend find another adult on campus to come conference with them. No one was to be left out!

I found the staff and administration more than willing to come in to conference with a child about his or her work.

GUIDELINES FOR CONFERENCING

The day came and parents began to arrive. We had greeters at the door to welcome everyone. The children really began to get a sense of how important their work is and how important that time with their parents would be. In their minds they had already chosen a few pieces that they planned to share. At this point, I did not feel we could let everyone loose to rampage through the children's work. Just as the children had spent time developing sharing guidelines for their portfolio, the parents needed these guidelines as well. A parent's first tendency would be to take the child's work and thumb through it all, never really knowing what they are looking at. My job was to give a few guidelines for sharing their child's work:

1. Allow your child to handle his or her own work as they share: This allows the child to feel a sense of ownership of the portfolio.

2. Give the child the freedom to choose what he or she will share; rather than trying to see every piece of work, ask "why" those pieces were chosen.

3. Try not to probe with a million questions. Try to get the child to talk about his or her work, the ideas in it, and where the ideas came from.

4. *Praise your child's achievements!*

Now imagine 30 children, each with one or two adults, discussing their work all at one time within our first-grade classroom. It may sound chaotic, but it works. Every corner, table, and center was filled with children, adults, and writing samples! My job was to stand back and let the children take over.

CONFERENCING SURVEY

It was impossible with 30 conferences going on for me to be part of each one. But I felt I needed to know how productive this time was, not only for the children, but for the parents as well. The way to do this was to create a survey that would allow the parents to tell what knowledge they gained about their child. Following are the six questions given out, along with a few sample responses:

1. What new thing did you learn about your child through the sharing of his or her portfolio?
   I learned how Lynnie picks up on our home life and what she feels is important by reading the entries of her journal.

2. What kinds of changes have you seen in your child's reading and writing?
   Kelsey's reading skills have improved 200%. Writing skills have also improved. Kelsey has a lot of great ideas for stories. Kelsey also recognizes when she has read a word incorrectly because it doesn't make sense in the sentence.

3. Was your child able to discuss his/her work with ease?
   Yes, she explained what she was doing and why. She explained how different things related to each other.

4. What pieces of work did your child seem most proud of and why?
   Tiffany was most proud of her Funny Girls story, because she wrote it herself and some of her favorite people are in it.

5. Did this time help open the lines of communication between you and your child about what he/she is doing at school?
   I don't always have time for the two of us to share. I enjoyed being there just for him and the fact that he didn't have competition from his siblings was important to him.

6. Do you feel like you learned more information about your child's progress from the portfolio than you would have if you had only received your child's report card?
   Yes! A report card wouldn't be able to begin to share the progress she has been making. The portfolio allows us to see "hands-on" how she is doing. The portfolio explains more to us by just looking at the papers. What can a check mark or an X tell us? The portfolio is an incredible learning tool for me as a parent. I have learned many things about my child through her work.

When I designed this survey, I never imagined I would get such an overwhelmingly positive response from parents. We have now had three parent/child portfolio conference days this year. Each time there are more parents, family, and friends who come to see the pieces of writing the children are producing. Each time we have had a survey similar to the one above, and each time the reactions are more and more positive.

THE GIFT WE GAVE OURSELVES

For many of the children and parents this time together is like a "gift." In today's hustle and bustle many children never receive that quality time that they are yearning for. It's not that parents do not want that; they are just unable to make the time. That seems to be what these parent/child portfolio conferences do: They make that quality time for children to share their thoughts, ideas, and questions from their world into which parents rarely get to venture. Taking parents "behind the classroom scene" brings them into this grand world of learning that teachers and children create every day!

- "*Bees Knees* and *Hatchet* showed that Patricia can write clear, colorful sentences. She indicated in the writing that she clearly understood the stories. We were so impressed with her enthusiasm for those pieces." [fifth grade]

- "I can see improvement in Andrew's work. More importantly, I have noticed improvement in his self-confidence. He seems more comfortable with the work load at school now. He's much more willing to argue a point when he's certain he's right." [fifth grade]

- "I have seen remarkable improvement in Nina's writing skills this year, and she seems to enjoy writing. My only concern is her spelling and punctuation." [fifth grade]

- "It is pretty evident that James is enjoying school this year and that he feels both productive and challenged. His work has become much better organized and his work habits have improved. We especially enjoy his stories and pictures." [fifth grade]

The use of portfolios for informing the parent audience is becoming more and more attractive. The following author/date notations represent just a sample of the articles published in recent years on the topic: Huffman, 1996; Santa, 1995; Austin, 1994; Paulson and Paulson, 1994; Kasse, 1994. The bibliographic information for these sources is in the reference list in appendix B.

Don't expect, however, to get only favorable reviews. The comments above are typical of most of the comments from parents in the single school from which these samples were selected. But there were also comments like these:

- "I think portfolios are a waste of time and money. You should be having them work on their ABCs and phonics. There's plenty of work to be done without having them waste time on this thing."

- "No comments!"

- "I cannot see how the sample writings are his best work when the words in the sentences are not spelled correctly. Is this normal for a child of his age? He needs to focus more on the form of each letter and the correct spelling of words."

- "We feel that these folders take away from the teacher's valuable time with the children. We would rather see it spent on more worthwhile things."

But generally, the response from parents is very supportive. You are apt to suspect that we concocted the following letter because it voices the very claims made in this book. But it is an actual letter that a parent wrote to his son's teacher, linking portfolio assessment solidly to teaching effectiveness:

> You requested feedback from our family regarding your teaching efforts for the '96–'97 school year.
>
> We have been very pleased with the progress of Anthony both academically and personally. One of your greatest strengths as an educator is the way you lead kids through the process of self-evaluation. In addition to the feedback you provide them, they are learning the importance of assessing their own strengths in areas that need more attention.
>
> We hope that our children will become life-long learners. By providing them with a foundation for continual self-evaluation, you are helping them gain a skill that allows them to gauge and critically evaluate their own progress. The student portfolio is a wonderful vehicle to help students recognize their own growth and achievement and challenges across the school year.
>
> Your presentation of learning opportunities kept Anthony interested and motivated to do his best work. He particularly enjoyed reading, creative writing, and projects related to books.
>
> Thank you again!

"HOW CAN I USE PORTFOLIOS IN REPORTING TO FELLOW PROFESSIONALS?"

Portfolios make an excellent backup system in reporting to some audiences. The way that they can inform and even settle seeming assessment discrepancies has been discussed earlier.

Suppose, for an extended example, that students in your school are selected for programs for students with special abilities using some kind of standardized test as a screening device. Patricia is not to be considered for a project that will allow students considerable time and resources to research one or more topics of their choice. She is not eligible because she did not score high enough on the norm-referenced test used to select students for the program, and you are both surprised and disappointed. You know from teaching the girl for months and from looking at her portfolio that she is uniquely creative and that while her interests may seem unusual and quite limited in number to some adults, they run unusually deep.

She is, for example, an avid bird-watcher. You know this because she has written about it several times and because she has read numerous books and articles about birds, some of them quite advanced for her age. You know that Patricia knows a great deal about numerous species, can imitate many bird calls (which she has included on a tape in her portfolio), and is expressive about numerous issues related to the protection of species and the like. She is also a doll collector, and while her personal collection is limited by what she and her parents can afford, Patricia's knowledge about the history of dolls is quite impressive.

It's time for you to take Patricia's portfolio collection to whoever has the authority to make an exception regarding her eligibility for the program. You may decide to select from it some showpieces or to let the principal or whoever will look at it discover Patricia's strengths within it on his or her own. That will depend on your knowledge of the audience and how eager you think the person will be to look at the evidence supporting your request that Patricia not be overlooked for an opportunity that seems almost customized for her.

This example of how a teacher can use the portfolio is typical of many other situations:

- A parent or administrator expresses surprise that a student's response on a performance test is judged weak by outside raters. You and the questioner spend some time looking at the writing in the portfolio, including another product resulting from a performance test. The principal compares the writing in the collection to that of several other students, whose portfolios are selected at random. It is agreed that this student does not write as well as some adults have expected and that she talks much more fluently than she writes.

  You take a longer look at the work and the analyses you and the student have done before. You make a plan to try and strengthen the student's writing: Perhaps you decide that she is more fluent as a talker because she lacks confidence as a writer. You think of some writing projects that will promote more fluent writing. You decide to have a special conference with her, discussing the things in her writing that you and the parent or principal have noted are good. You praise things she says and suggest that she write about them.

- The school psychologist's testing of a boy who has not been learning or developing as much as you would like suggests that his capacity to learn may be impaired in some way. You have seen signs in the portfolio of an attitude problem about school and school experiences. They are revealed in unenthusiastic analyses that display nonetheless some command of language.

Before parents are called in to conference and the psychologist's report is filed, you ask the psychologist to look through the boy's portfolio to see if she feels that it throws any light on the problem.

In using the portfolio in ways such as these—*or to describe any particular student as a language user*—one can use the criteria suggested and discussed in Chapter 4 of this book. Keep in mind that the portfolio does a better job than other assessment techniques in supporting the following general kinds of analyses:

- The amount of reading and writing a student is doing.
- The student's interests as they are revealed in language experiences and his or her attitude toward language, learning, and thinking.
- The amount of risk-taking a student is doing as a thinker.
- The student's growth and development as a reader and writer over time.
- A deep and subjective evaluation of the student's language abilities that relies on the many strategies and factors that cannot be validly segregated, prioritized, or sequenced.

You will also find that portfolio conferences are invaluable for explaining your language arts program to the principal or curriculum leader in your school. Sample portfolios can give an administrator valuable insight into the kinds of things you are doing and the progress your students are making. Most administrators realize that a collection of work samples in a portfolio gives at least as good a representation of student achievement and progress as a set of test scores.

The goals for a conference with an administrator should be:

- To help the administrator understand what you are attempting to achieve.
- To provide concrete evidence of your students' development.
- To discuss specific problems and needs you may have in making your program more effective.

"HOW CAN I USE PORTFOLIOS IN REPORTING TO OTHER AUDIENCES?"

The portfolio can also be used to enlighten audiences outside of the school and family. Here are just a few examples. Suppose that one of the following persons came to you and asked for assessment "data" that would serve his or her needs:

- A newspaper reporter is preparing a feature about the things that students read and wonders how he can determine how they use the information they get from books.
- A local candidate for the school board who is very critical of the school and who feels your fourth-grade children should be delving into 17th-century English history instead of reading adventure stories, mysteries, or even the textbooks she contends are full of errors. She challenges the thinking that your students engage in as "frivolous, inappropriate, and inaccurate." She has approached your principal and asked for an opportunity to select samples of student writing to prove her point.
- A graduate student from a nearby university is interested in studying the styles children use in writing. He is not sure what he will be looking for and wants to do a pilot examination of student writing at several grade levels, beginning with your class.

Portfolios could accommodate the needs of all three of these persons, although you will want to ensure the objective evaluation of the school board candidate. Here are just one of several ways that each situation could be handled using portfolios.

- You suggest that you identify a half a dozen portfolios *for the reporter* that will demonstrate how your students react to reading in different and authentic ways. You want to be involved to this degree to be sure that the reporter sees a truly representative sample. You volunteer to tab pieces related to texts read with colored Post-its with notes that tell what you think the examples show, but you would like the reporter to see the entire collection in each of the six portfolios as well.

  You note just a tinge of concern in the reporter's voice that you might be controlling the situation too much. So you add: "After you have looked through the six samples I select, you can come to the classroom and pick any number of the portfolios at random and examine them as long as you like. I will stick around so you can ask questions, but I won't kibitz while you are working. I will also arrange for you to interview any child you like if you give me time to get parental approval and will come during a subsequent school day." You also promise to round up any of the texts referred to by the student writers that the reporter would like to see.

  A superb article is in the making here, and it will be informed by portfolios in a fashion that no other assessment procedure or instrument could.

- You and the principal discuss the request of *the school board candidate* and decide to handle it in this way: You will ask the person making the request to select at random 10 portfolios to be examined by the candidate and any other school board candidate who accepts an invitation to participate. You also arrange for several other individuals to form a committee with the candidates to examine the portfolios. It will consist of a widely respected local historian, a highly regarded retired teacher, and a psychologist from a nearby institution of higher learning. Each is to examine the portfolios *to focus on the ideas* contained and referred to in them. Each must agree not to make any public references to individual students in any way that will identify them, and each agrees to report what he or she has found at an open symposium you and the principal arrange to follow a PTA meeting. Finally, each participant agrees to write a 500-to-1,000-word summary that can be distributed.

  The school board candidate is too busy campaigning and declines, but several other candidates accept the invitation and the evaluation takes place. The committee reports that the fourth-graders are greatly involved with their siblings, parents, and home; are highly interested in sports, space, and animals; are concerned about protecting the environment; and have a surprising number of special individual interests, including those of a boy who reads a lot about the Civil War and writes occasionally about it, a girl whose fascination with medieval times has led her to write stories that take place in a full-size version of the model castle she has constructed, a boy who likes to consider all of the potential discoverers of the New World, two students intensely interested in Native American culture, and a girl who knows the names of most of the English monarchs she often reads about.

- You discuss the *graduate student's* project with the students, and most of them agree that he can examine their portfolios and analyze the style of their writing. After a call to the chair of the student's doctoral committee, he is allowed to visit the classroom at will and to browse through and study portfolios to which a blue permission slip has been stapled by each cooperating student.

  He starts out selecting about a dozen at random but ends up looking at every portfolio in the class, since each student has ultimately expressed an interest in becoming a part of the study. He holds at least a brief conference with each portfolio keeper and writes at least a paragraph about the writing style found in each collection. The students have agreed to keep the college researcher's comments in their portfolios.

Before he leaves, the researcher gives a presentation to the class explaining some of the things he has found. He says he is surprised at the amount of "front-shifting" he has found in their style, demonstrating on the chalkboard how that is putting modifying words, phrases, and clauses at the beginning of sentences. He is also interested in how much dialogue is used in their stories and in how effective it appears to be. He admires the creativity in their fictional writing and the sensitivity of the poetry he has found, but he is surprised there isn't more poetry. He suggests that the students look at their nonfiction writing to see if they are using enough details in it and to see how the details are used and organized.

The student has identified what he calls 20 "style features" to look for in the next pilot phase of his study and gives each student a photocopied list of them so the students can use it if they like in assessing their own writing. He thanks them with great sincerity and departs rather reluctantly. "Reading portfolios," he tells the teacher, "is very close to making new friends."

"CAN PORTFOLIOS BE USED FOR LARGE-SCALE ASSESSMENT?"

As indicated earlier in this chapter, this is still a debatable question. But certainly, portfolios are being used for many purposes: to evaluate instructional programs, to document academic growth, to validate assessment programs, to inform decision making, to provide the basis for appealing educational decisions, and to measure outcomes identified by teachers, schools, districts, and states. The procedures for conducting accountability assessment based on portfolios can vary across the places where it is being done. Aggregation of the collections can involve only certain parts prescribed for the portfolios or different levels of students—by grade, schools, cities, and so forth. Many are done by using some sampling procedure. Such programs may vary as to how much they prescribe the contents of the portfolio and if so, on what must be in them; they can vary as to who picks portfolio contents, what time period they cover, and who evaluates them.

Some districts, schools, and states have panels of teachers or outside reviewers assess randomly collected (but mandated) portfolios with what is actually a rubric—an *analytic trait* chart, which can be quite detailed and rigid or may be an attempt to guide holistic analysis. Across such situations, teachers are invariably involved in setting the criteria, and students may also be involved. Any such evaluation of portfolios should set criteria after defining the objectives of the assessment program, specifying how the portfolios will be collected and describing how the results will be reported.

At the same time, such a study should describe and analyze the procedures, results, and reactions to the use of integrated performance tests in large-scale assessments of reading and writing to learn whatever emerges from such an analysis, but to note, in particular, how well they appear to serve the needs of audiences seeking information related to educational accountability.

Perhaps your classroom and/or school will have produced some of the data that will be analyzed and synthesized in some of the studies suggested here.

SUMMARY: A DOZEN APPROACHES TO HELP SOLVE THE ASSESSMENT PUZZLE

- Take a careful look at the different audiences who want and need information about your schools and about how well your students are doing. Who are they? What do they need to know? Why do they need to know this and what will they do with it?

- Take an inventory of the kinds of assessment going on in your classroom and school. What kinds of information does each produce?

- Try to match up the needs of the audiences to the information you are now producing. Which needs of which audiences does each type of assessment meet? Do those audiences have access to it and understand it?

- Consider the assessment package related to your situation in terms of how well it is serving information needs. Are there gaps? Is there duplication? Are there types of assessments that are not being used that could respond to the gaps?

- Consider in particular how well assessment is serving your instructional needs and the needs of your students to develop as language users. Which type do you value most and why? How could you explain that to fellow teachers, parents, administrators, and the public?

- Focus on audiences interested in accountability in particular. Who are they? How well is assessment information serving their needs? What could be done to improve the situation?

- Consider the parent audience as a direct focus. Which assessments can tell them what? What role can you play in delivering that information and in developing understanding of what assessment can show among the parents of your students?

- Analyze the audiences you have considered in terms of their understanding of the needs of each other and of the types of assessments and what they can show. Think about what can be done to create more understanding across audiences about assessment and what it shows and suggests.

- Consider in particular the role that portfolio assessment is playing or could play in your classroom and school. What could you do to make it more effective?

- Articulate for yourself the role that performance assessment could play in meeting information needs of the audiences you have identified. Study what you have spelled out: How well do you understand performance assessment? What kind if any is being used in your educational situation? In your opinion, what kind should you be using?

- Think about what you would tell your students about the assessment they experience when they begin asking about them in free discussions.

- Consider the debate about the effectiveness of schools and how assessment can enlighten the debate. Pretend that you are in one or more of the following situations, and think about what and how you could explain to mediate:

  a) A group of school critics is using national score decline data but no data pertaining directly to the local schools to criticize the situation in the press and in public meetings.

  b) A group of your fellow teachers is criticizing other teachers who are spending time in their classes developing and using portfolio assessment. Those on the attack are pointing out how only standardized tests are reliable enough to be used in directing more effective education.

  c) A group of fellow teachers in your school wants to develop a performance test in your school to cover several grades, but they are not sure how to convince the principal and their supervisors that the project is worth the time it will take.

  d) A group of highly articulate teachers is attacking any use of standardized measures in use in your state as a waste of time, money, and effectively placed emphases.

CHAPTER SEVEN

CONSTRUCTING AND SELECTING PERFORMANCE ASSESSMENTS

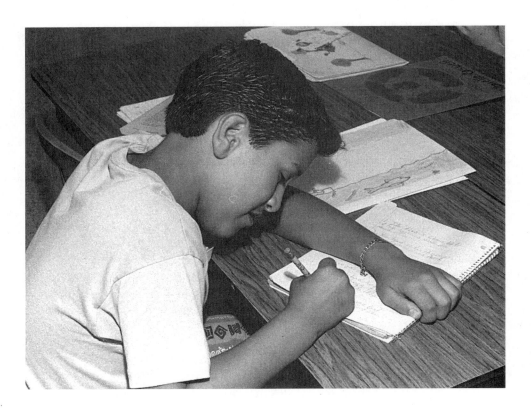

Several sources typical of those which ground these contentions are referenced in the reading list in Appendix B. These include Wilson, 1981; Wiggins, 1989; Valencia, 1989; Smith, 1990; Farr and Tone, 1994; Courtney, 1965.

The newest language arts performance assessments respond directly to long-held concerns about the validity of the norm-referenced and short-answer, criterion-referenced tests that have been used predominantly in our schools. Performance assessments are better reflections of the curriculum of most instructional programs, which now emphasize an integrated approach to developing language skills. It is one in which reading and writing are taught in combination, not as separate subjects. At the same time, performance assessment reflects language development theory that has emerged over the past two decades or more and that has stressed language use as the construction of meaning.

Some language arts performance assessments now reveal student reading and writing behaviors in a single student response designed to integrate them. This response is generated with an activity that establishes a clear audience focus and purpose. In this discussion, this type of performance assessment will be called *fully integrated.*

On a fully integrated performance assessment, a situation, problem, or task is presented. The student is asked to read a text, which is called a *prompt,* and to respond in writing. The same student response is used to evaluate both reading and writing and sometimes to rate perspectives such as response to the task. After discussing some general objectives that apply to both, the discussion of performance assessments here will focus on this type.

A second type may be referred to occasionally in this discussion and will be illustrated more fully following it. This other type of performance test will be referred to here as *analytical*. This term has been manufactured here solely for the purpose of distinguishing the two types. It must be noted that the fully integrated assessment is highly analytical and that the second type is also considered to be an integrated assessment. But the latter separates the responses generated into focuses on the two language components: those rated for reading comprehension and that rated for writing.

In the "analytical" type of integrated performance assessment, a prompt is followed by questions or comments that generate student-constructed written responses. These short essay-type responses are rated *as a unit* for reading performance. Then the student writes on a topic related to or motivated by the passage. This longer written response is used to rate writing. This second type of performance assessment will be described in more detail following a discussion that focuses more directly on the fully integrated type.

Completing the tasks on each of these types of assessment is considered a relatively realistic (authentic) experience for the student. This is especially true in the fully integrated performance assessment because it focuses on a problem or issue that the student is to read and write about. An audience and purpose is defined for the writing the student is to construct. This is quite different from the typical multiple-choice items on standardized tests, where there is often no problem to be solved nor any audience to consider in selecting responses.

As they read the prompt on the fully integrated performance assessment, students understand that they will apply the comprehension they construct while reading when performing the *writing activity*. The student's response is then analyzed to determine how effectively the student read, wrote, and used one or more other thinking processes in *responding to the task*.

Two examples of such *prompt/writing activity* assessments illustrate how a fully integrated performance assessment does this:

- Sixth-graders are given a story "We Want the Show!" from the book *Lenny Kandell, Smart Aleck*, by Ellen Conford. It tells about the show that two friends, Lenny and Artie, present for the other children in their neighborhood. The students are asked to read the story and to write a review of the show for their neighborhood newspaper.

   The student response is scored on *Reading* and *Writing* from *1* to *3*, with *3* being high. The categories considered in determining the reading score are *Degree of Understanding*, *Selection of Information*, and *Accuracy of Information*. The categories used in determining the writing score are *Accomplishment of Task*, *Organization*, *Development*, *Sentence Structure*, *Vocabulary*, and *Mechanics*. But the student is not rated on these separately. The ratings *3*, *2*, and *1* for reading and for writing are described using these considerations in a *rubric*, a chart that helps teachers arrive at a single score for each of the major ratings: *Reading* and *Writing*.

- First-graders respond to a shared reading of *Mushroom in the Rain* by Mirra Ginsburg. It tells how a series of animals take shelter under a mushroom when it rains. (There is a clear implication in the story that the mushroom is able to accommodate all its guests because it changes significantly during the story.) Students are asked to demonstrate their understanding of the story and its implication by drawing (and captioning) two pictures: one of the mushrooms at the beginning of the story and one at the end. The pictures are to explain to other students how the mushroom changed and what changed it.

The first two performance activities described briefly here are part of the *Unit Integrated Performance Assessment* that accompanied the Harcourt Brace Jovanovich, Inc., *HBJ Treasury of Literature* (1993). They are typical of the integrated performance assessment available in some language arts and reading series.

The third test described is from Harcourt Brace's *Integrated Performance Assessment,* which accompanies their *Signatures* series (1997).

Several other examples in this chapter are drawn from the *Integrated Assessment System,* Language Arts Performance Assessment—Reading/Writing, by Roger Farr and Beverly Farr, The Psychological Corporation, Harcourt Brace Jovanovich, Inc., 1990. This system is an example of several published performance assessments on the market that rate reading and writing using the same student response and that incorporate rating scales for other factors that involve the integration of reading and writing.

Still other samples are from the *Indiana Performance Assessments '92.*

The authors are grateful to these publishers for the permission to describe particular activities in their products as a means to exemplify the kind of performance assessment you can construct for your classroom.

Again, the response is evaluated on *Reading* and on *Writing,* using a general rubric that explains ratings ranging from *3* to *1* and also using specific questions about responses to this particular text and activity.

The rubrics for the two examples above are general or generic ones designed to evaluate student responses across various purposes for writing about a variety of types of texts. The scoring of responses can also be guided by criteria that fit particular purposes for writing, types or genres of text, or combinations of these; and rubrics can also be designed for particular texts.

In the case of these examples, the teacher is provided with guidelines in the form of questions they can ask themselves while rating the response. These help the teacher consider (1) how well the particular text was understood and used and (2) how well the particular writing task was accomplished. Examples of actual papers that exemplify each of the three possible scores in both reading and writing are offered as well. These *anchors* are particularly helpful in assigning the ratings.

Assessments similar to these have been accompanied by a 4- or 5-point scale and/or have included a third major category that evaluated how well the student responded to the task overall or could focus on *descriptive* and *evaluative* writing and response to reading, and on *persuasive* writing.

The *analytical* type of language arts performance test in which the student's responses to the reading are rated separately from those intended to reveal writing ability may require more, if somewhat less targeted, responses. The following is an example of such a test:

> The theme of a grade 4 assessment activity is to develop an understanding that people with disabilities are not different but are enabled in different ways. The students read Barbara Seuling's story "I'm Not So Different" about a girl who uses a wheelchair. She learns to accept the curiosity and frequent insensitivity of her peers, and adults as well, and to understand how she can triumph.
>
> A series of five questions designed to reveal the student's comprehension of the story and to promote rather extensive writing about it develop responses to be rated for reading. Then the idea of how each of us is unique but not so different is used to motivate a writing activity to rate the student as a writer. Students are asked to pretend that they are new to a school and are giving a talk to introduce themselves to their new classmates.
>
> As in the fully integrated performance assessment, the rating of these student responses is guided by both rubrics and sample or anchor responses actually collected from trials and rated by actual teachers.

Both of these general types of performance assessment are described here as they exemplify the kind of assessments that teachers and groups of teachers can construct for use in their classrooms. The development of performance assessments is an excellent instructional activity for teachers. They begin by reviewing what they believe to be true about the language development and use of their students. They consider what applications and skills are vital to that development and what classroom experiences are most apt to contribute to it.

The next task is to develop or find a reading selection or selections that will require the kinds of comprehension that the teacher hopes the students will develop. This must work well with the kinds of applications of that understanding that seem authentic to the teacher and that can be translated into authentic types of writing for realistic audiences. The kind of responses that the teacher expects need to be described in terms of some scale as a rubric that helps explain the ratings assigned.

When—as is often the case—such tests or test programs are developed for a school, a district, or even a state, the teacher is working cooperatively with fellow professionals. What he or she believes as essential to defining targeted student development and to picking topics, tasks, reading prompts, and writing tasks must be carefully articulated so that they can apply across classrooms, schools, and districts.

The process is a highly clarifying, enlightening, and involving experience. But it is also exhausting and time-consuming. The designed tests must be tried out, the results analyzed, and the various aspects of the tests revised for subsequent application. This can affect prompts, tasks, the instructions and administration, and certainly the rubrics, and the all-important sample or anchor papers that will guide the rating.

In a test to be used by more than one teacher, those rubrics and anchors must evolve from actual student responses collected during the tryout of the test. The quality and clarity of the guidance they provide future raters using the test is essential to any trust one puts in the assessment's reliability—the belief that the scores that one rater gives a student's efforts would be the same or nearly the same as those other raters would assign.

What has become clear in many places where such a development project has been conducted is that many teachers and systems will want to look for models for their assessments to one or more of the published performance assessment batteries that have been developed in recent years. These products have grown out of considerable teacher input during the development and the initial rating stages that have provided the rating rubrics and anchor paper guides. Their tryout/revision stages are often quite extensive.

The reason that this reality is underlined here is that this section of the book has a second purpose. Not only is it intended as an initial, introductory guide to developing performance assessments, it is also a potential training introduction to the selection of published performance assessments. Both the more integrated type and the one that integrates the reading and writing activity but generates separate responses for reading and writing evaluation will be described. But first, we want to review some factors that recommend either type.

The general procedure for constructing and using rubrics and example papers is described in Chapter 8. Chapter 7 focuses on developing the authentic reading/ writing activity.

RESPONDING TO CONCERNS
ABOUT ASSESSMENT

In identifying new strategies to complete the assessment puzzle and to complete information needed to guide the language development of their students' needs, educators should begin by committing to tests that will respond to the long-articulated criticism of norm-referenced tests. As Chapter 6 pointed out, we are not recommending here that you set out looking for a replacement for your existing methodologies, but for methodologies and instruments that will enrich your program. There are several general maxims that effective performance assessment can endorse.

PERFORMANCE ASSESSMENT SHOULD
EMULATE A VARIETY OF REALISTIC ACTIVITIES

Your students' lives are rich with a variety of language applications. Students need opportunities to write for different purposes and in different forms; they should be given choices as to what they read and write. The portfolio is a place where that work can be collected and analyzed. Periodically, however, teachers should have students respond to a common and more controlled reading and writing task. This is where performance assessments fit in. It is useful, for purposes of evaluation, to have all students respond to the same task using the same reading text.

Like portfolios, performance assessments can reveal a great deal about the language development, thinking processes, and interests of the students who take them. What they reveal about these things, however, is apt to depend on how genuine the experience presented by the assessment is for each child. On a language arts performance assessment,

PURPOSES THAT MAINTAIN AUTHENTICITY!

Have your students read and then write to:

Convey feelings and aesthetic experiences and responses:

- Writing a story that incorporates personal experiences that can be compared to the prompt—shaping an experience with words.
- Writing about and relating to the feelings of characters in the prompt.
- Playing the role of a character in the prompt and writing entries in his or her diary or journal, or writing a letter to someone in their family or to one of their friends, clarifying thoughts and feelings significant to the prompt.
- Writing a letter to one of the characters or to the author.

Inform a familiar audience:

- Writing a report on a topic of interest to both them and the audience.
- Writing directions or instructions for someone they know to follow.
- Writing critiques of something peers might read or watch or buy.
- Preparing records of something for other students to use.

Persuade and to analyze other points of view:

- Writing a letter of advice to a friend or peer.

- Writing a critical essay about a topic important to students.
- Writing an editorial for a school or town publication.
- Writing a letter applying for a job or other opportunity.
- Exploring and evaluating the issues to solve a problem.

Entertain:

- Writing a story parodying the unique style of the prompt.
- Writing new story endings or beginnings to share with friends.
- Writing poems and rhymes modeled by the prompt.
- Retelling a story for a younger brother or sister.

Learn:

- Writing a retelling as a record of a story, its characters, and events.
- Writing an outline or summary of a fictional or nonfictional prompt.
- Taking and organizing notes about a relatively detailed topic so that they can be used as a personal reference.

students should actually use language in a way that they would use it in a realistic activity in school or outside of class. What they are asked to do should not seem like taking a test.

The students are directed on these language arts performance assessments to complete a writing activity, which must be prescribed but is carefully selected as the kind of writing that students actually want and/or need to do in their everyday lives. Since the writing activity needs to be *authentic,* so does the text, which provides the content that the student must use in writing the response. It is selected as something a student at this age and grade level would be likely to read—and to select on his or her own.

There are, of course, limits in this consideration. The assessment creator will need to assume, for example, that children may enjoy certain tasks that are improbable—that they would, for example, become involved in imagining that they can actually write a letter to a turtle. It cannot be assured that their unique imaginations would have cause to spark this particular task, but the test maker assumes that it may be typical of the imaginative purposes children might create for themselves.

If your assessments truly involve the student in reasonably authentic reading and writing, the student responses will vary as those realistic purposes for using language would vary from student to student. Individual responses that incorporate unique background experiences and interests into what is gained by reading and applying the prompt should be promoted by the instrument.

By having the student construct a response by writing, the integrated performance assessment engages the student in more authentic language behavior than is required on more traditional reading and writing tests in which students choose from among a set of choices. The performance assessment asks the student to *apply* both reading and writing strategies essential to meaning construction.

PERFORMANCE ASSESSMENT
CAN AVOID ARTIFICIAL RESTRAINTS

Since the prompt, which can include one or more related texts, is the only reading task on the assessment, its length can be greater than the typical reading passage on a traditional test. It can be a complete story or article or a set of articles that take different perspectives on the same topic. This answers another major criticism of standardized reading tests—that the only place students encounter stories and nonfictional texts that are complete within 200 to 500 words is on the traditional tests themselves and on exercise sheets designed to emulate them.

In addition, performance assessments can be designed so that they can be administered over more than one class period, crossing two or more school days if necessary. Usually there is no rigid time limit for administration. All this means that the length of the prompt is not an issue as it is in designing the traditional tests, which usually must be completed in time units approximating class periods. This flexible administration also means, however, that performance assessments cannot be norm-referenced, since the administration of the tests are not standardized.

Many performance assessments have other unique features and answer to the criticism of more traditional testing in other ways. They can accommodate and even encourage student collaboration, and they are scored holistically for a comprehensive view of student performance. Above all, *they model good instruction,* placing an emphasis on the process of writing and reading.

The key idea that drives performance assessment is to assess in the same way that you teach! The teacher is encouraged to move about the room and work with students one-on-one during all phases of the assessment. Usually students are encouraged to think about their responses and to get organized to write with a prewriting activity. Also, most performance assessments provide the students with an opportunity to revise their initial drafts and to create more polished final drafts.

Many student writing experiences are, of course, structured by a school's curriculum for teaching reading and writing at the various grade levels in a school system. The natural result of placing increased importance on accountability testing has been to lead some teachers to emphasize what is on tests at the expense of other instructional objectives and goals that may be valued. Short-answer tests are better designed to cover lots of different objects, but since the test items are usually short answer or selection of answers through a multiple-choice format, the assessments have little depth. They focus on broad coverage or breadth of the curriculum and problem solving and longer student-constructed responses that could get at a deeper understanding are neglected. Thus, the school that focuses only on short-answer assessments tends to develop a curriculum that focuses on breadth of curriculum coverage at a fairly shallow level rather than depth of understanding.

The deeper, more complex problem-solving reading and writing behaviors are less apt to be tested; and when many administrators, the public, the media, and critics are inclined to use these short-answer tests to judge how effective the schools are, teachers are understandably pressured into focusing on what they do cover. As a result, the tests may begin leading the curriculum, which becomes shallower. Since the total time allowed for the tests limits what they can cover from a curriculum, attention to the test also tends eventually to focus on shallower recognition at the expense of deeper understanding.

Performance assessments can answer to this concern by evaluating student's deeper understanding and problem solving. So these assessments can be developed to match those deeper and problem-solving goals of the language arts curriculum of a particular teacher, school, district, or state.

It is easy to see how the short-answer tests with their specified right answers can be balanced with longer performance assessments, which generally allow a student to develop his or her own unique response to a problem situation. This has caused the authors of this book to suggest that the short-answer tests can be thought of as *right-answer tests,* while the performance assessments can be thought of as *my-answer tests.* Together these two approaches to assessment can provide a more comprehensive coverage of the curriculum. Right-answer assessments (short-answer) can cover a lot of curriculum objectives (breadth), but they do not effectively get at deeper understanding, problem-solving objectives (depth).

On the other hand the my-answer assessments (performance assessments) cannot cover a broad range of specific objectives (breadth), but they do a better job of assessing deeper understanding and problem solving (depth). We certainly need the assessment of both breadth (right-answer) and depth (my-answer) if we are to assess the total range of objectives we hope to have students accomplish.

THE ASSESSMENT ATTEMPTS TO ASSURE THE RELIABILITY THAT ACCOUNTABILITY DEMANDS

This point is explained more fully in Chapter 6, which discusses the importance of reliability to audiences interested in educational accountability.

If one admires performance assessment because it has many of the qualities that portfolio assessment offers, why have the performance assessment? Why not just put whatever time and energy the teacher and student put into preparing, taking, and rating the results of a performance assessment into keeping and assessing portfolios?

The answer is simple. A performance assessment attempts to provide the *reliability* that the portfolio cannot offer without content restrictions, rigidly defined evaluation criteria, and panels of raters—all of which can limit the strengths of portfolio assessment by making it so cumbersome and time-consuming that it loses its feasibility and appeal to many educators and students.

The language performance assessment maker is in a position to turn the control achieved by supplying the text and selecting the writing activity into a more structured and feasible process for rating student performance. And that controlled rating process can provide assurance that different raters will give a particular student response the same scores on the same factors. The assessment audience can then know that a student who gets a 3 on a factor called "Reading," for example, wrote a response that most raters would agree fits the assessment's definition for a 3 on that factor.

Audiences who want to evaluate schools and educators and who make educational decisions on the basis of assessment want some assurance that they can rely on the information assessments produce. The performance assessment has more facility to deliver this assurance than does portfolio assessment.

The criteria that guide raters of performance assessment responses can be much more focused than any that could be applied to the variety of materials in the portfolio. They can focus on several factors that are considered important in constructing meaning from reading and writing. The assessment cannot cover the breadth of language use that the portfolio can include, so how authentically it represents the *reading* and *writing* behaviors depends, as noted above, on the selection of the activity, the text (prompt), the factors used to rate the responses, and the definitions that distinguish a 2 from a 3 on each factor, for example.

HOW TO DEVELOP OR SELECT YOUR PERFORMANCE ASSESSMENTS

The development or selection of a performance assessment activity is followed in this chapter from the perspective of developing one. This ensures the consideration of most key factors that make up a good performance instrument. It gives the teacher who may never intend to develop one the understanding, nonetheless, to critically examine those that are available on the market.

In following the perspective of the test developer (in order to inform the test selector as well), the discussion in this and the next chapter follow the process from inception through the initial administration of the assessment as a tryout. This development involves five general steps. Some of these, particularly the second and third steps, include major issues for the developers to consider and important decisions that must be made, at least initially.

The tryout of the new assessment, Step 5, produces the papers that allow the developer to proceed with the development of a rating system for evaluating the papers and then to use and report the results. Although the test selector will be inclined to accept the rubrics and anchors that the publisher of a selected test presents, this discussion can inform you about what to look for in these tools, which accompany the instrument you select. You might even decide on the basis of what you know about performance assessment to modify these rating systems and guides in some way that seems to fit your instructional situation more appropriately.

The five steps that can guide you to the initial development of an integrated reading and writing assessment are:

- **Identify your goals for language development:** Think seriously about what it is that you believe the students at the grade level you teach should be able to do well as readers and writers. See if you can come up with *a set of key behaviors* that you would want them to be able to do. These will guide you in the next step.

- **Use the goals that you have identified and articulated to select texts for prompts and writing activities that apply them:** The activities should encompass or reflect the set of behaviors you have identified as those you want to develop in your students. What kind of reading and writing do your students do that these language behaviors will serve? What types of thinking are most often involved?

  Check the goals you articulate against those of any curriculum that is supposed to guide the instruction of the students who will be assessed. Be sure that the texts are appropriate for the grade levels. The single performance assessment will probably require only one kind of writing, will have the student read only one or a few genres of text, and may emphasize particular types of thinking. Thus, it will be important that you consider developing several assessments that will cover as many of the genres and writing and thinking types that you value for a particular grade as possible. These can then be used throughout the school year to ensure that a variety of reading and writing genres are assessed.

- **Make some key decisions about the assessment and its administration:** How will you develop the interest among the students that will ensure their commitment so that they try to do their best work? Do you want to allow collaboration among students? What prewriting and postwriting activities can you present with the assessment to promote a response that grows out of good *process?* Will the students be required to do these or will they be optional? This chapter makes strong recommendations for many of these decisions, but what the assessment developer or selector decides will affect the general amount of time required to complete the activity.

- **Prepare the assessment for administration:** If the assessment is to be administered by other teachers, it should be accompanied by directions that spell out the decisions made in Step 3 and that tell the teacher how to proceed. This major step also includes presenting the writing activity and the prompt in such a way that the students understand very clearly and easily what they are being asked to do, who they will be writing for, and the purpose for the writing. This audience focus and purpose were key considerations in Step 2, but must be clearly and simply articulated for the student. The student's assessment package should also include the prewriting activity, the postwriting activity, and any aids that you have decided to present with them to facilitate the student's use of them.

The steps for developing the evaluation system and for using the results will be discussed in Chapter 8.

- **Try out a preliminary edition:** The ultimate assessment package should grow out of extensive field testing that includes administering it to a group of students. The student responses that are collected in this tryout are *essential* to the subsequent development of a system for evaluating the assessment results for this and all subsequent administrations.

The following major sections discuss the five steps just summarized.

1. IDENTIFY THE INSTRUCTIONAL GOALS AND OBJECTIVES THAT YOU WANT TO ASSESS.

It only makes sense in beginning a project of this scope to spend time determining what it is you want to assess. Remember, the performance assessment will be a criterion-referenced measure that should reflect goals for reading and writing in your language arts curriculum and thus it should report on your students' learning experiences. First of all, the assessment ought to reflect what the teachers who develop or select and then administer it believe about helping students develop as readers and writers.

It is possible that this step may be omitted because it is assumed that the goals and objectives that will be measured will be taken directly from the curriculum guide teachers are presumably following. Even so, it is essential that the assessment designers spend time brainstorming what they believe about the language development of their students. Curriculum guides, you may need to point out, are often notoriously inclusive; and no series of singular writing activities can cover all the objectives in most of them. What the assessment should do, then, is reflect what the teachers who will be asked to use it are emphasizing in their classes.

Over the past several decades, many teachers have found it has been very worthwhile to take part in the identification of the criteria to be measured with criterion-referenced minimum competency tests. Many have selected objectives that represent what they believe is important in language development. That has meant articulating their beliefs and experiences while listening carefully to what other teachers believe and feel they know about reading and writing. The traditional multiple-choice assessments often used have allowed these committees or task forces to be relatively inclusive. More often than not, the objectives identified were very specifically defined subskills, were quite numerous, and had to be covered by numerous multiple-choice items following a group of passages. This made the job a bit tedious, perhaps, but it was easier for committees and task forces to agree on objectives because you were focusing on breadth of coverage. The goal was to assess every little objective anyone could come up with.

Imagine, however, what it must be like to seek agreement with and among your fellow professionals about depth of understanding, about applications of language abilities that will demonstrate your students' abilities to *process* language and that will reveal the kind of development you want to verify in your students. If one is judging integrated *performance*—the actual thinking and writing a student does in responding to a text—what does one look for to rate or measure? If students are truly constructing their responses on the assessment, and are not just making marks that either are or are not in the right places, how do we rate their efforts? What sort of ways should they use reading texts? What and how should they write? What kind of thinking is most important to target?

Groups of educators attempting to answer such questions must do more than list tags for skills and subskills; they have to *articulate* what they believe actually constitutes good reading, writing, and thinking as a single holistic behavior. Then they have to identify the kinds of activities and texts that will promote that kind of behavior. Equally challenging, they have to come up with the criteria that should be used to evaluate the results.

Constructing an assessment like that means thinking carefully about what a good writing product that responds to reading looks like and how it can reveal the processes you hope students are using. If what is emphasized in the guide and many of the classrooms around you is a list of very tactical objectives—reading skills and subskills, writing usage rules, and the like, you will have an opportunity to use what you learned in Chapter 6. Point out that the breadth of those objectives are probably a close match for any standardized, multiple-choice testing that is done in your system and perhaps are already covered by minimum competency testing in the state, city, or district. Explain that those instruments should serve such purposes well; and that since performance assessment is not really designed to do that, why try to make it duplicate the information that is available from sources that are better suited to gather it? You can also point out that performance assessment can reveal what you want to learn about the depth of your students' language abilities.

Try to direct the conversation to those broad goals and objectives as expressed in the curriculum, particularly as they relate to applications of language in the lives of your students. These kinds of goals are in almost any curriculum guide, but when all the brainstorming is finished, you and your fellow teachers may decide that the teachers and administrators in your system need to consider revising the curriculum—perhaps to bring it more in line with what has been spelled out by good theory during the past several decades.

Take the opportunity in discussions with fellow teachers to point out that a performance assessment needs by definition to focus on reading and writing process, and try to direct the discussion to reveal what your fellow teachers believe about student *purposes* for reading and writing, what *audiences* they feel their students actually write for, and what *kinds of things* they believe their students like to read and write and should be reading and writing.

Here are just a few samples as examples of the goals that you might hope will come out of such brainstorming:

- "I want my students to be able to predict as they read; I think it is the key process strategy for readers in the early elementary grades."
- "Students should learn to analyze and evaluate as they read and after they read. They should be able to use comparison/contrast, sequence, and other thinking skills to decide if they like or admire characters in stories, whether they are persuaded or remain skeptical about authors' arguments, when they need more details than the text gives, and the like. Even getting a really good joke in a story can involve analyzing what a character says or does."
- "I think one way to tell if very young readers are able to apply what they read is to see if they can extend a story."
- "The secret to learning is synthesizing and applying. Students should synthesize what they read into what they know, have experienced, and have read before. The real test is whether they can then apply this new synthesis in some way."
- "Problem solving. We can judge how well a student understands something he reads by presenting him with a problem and asking him to solve it. To do that, he has to organize what he reads and consider possible solutions, beginning with any that are stated. We can see how well he writes by examining the resolution he produces in writing."
- "I like my students to be looking for cause-and-effect sequences and to be categorizing using comparison/contrast. Cause and effect connects everything in a sequence and explains a lot of relationships between events and

---

TIP   NEVER UNDERRATE A
                         THINKING ACTIVITY!

Thinking activities are a vital part of the language integration. Keep them in mind as you look for good writing activities for language performance assessments.

- Predicting
- Evaluating
- Extending
- Comparing/contrasting
- Looking for causes and effects
- Problem solving
- Applying/Synthesizing
- Persuading
- Challenging/accepting

Integration in Language Arts Assessment

Thinking

Reading   Writing

---

details. What the student learns and remembers is kept in some complex categorization scheme that relies on noticing details that tend to group things (comparison) or separate them to be grouped somewhere else (contrast)."

You probably will not agree with all you hear about what reading and writing are, but that in itself is a kind of articulation of your own beliefs. It's a worthwhile experience: learning what your fellow teachers believe and how to integrate your beliefs with theirs. And remember, you want to get to a point where you can help teachers who agree with your goals steer the project toward performance assessment that you believe will be useful and enlightening. To do that, you will have to listen, ask good questions based on what you hear, and be tactful. Here are some examples of the kinds of questions that teachers can use in discussing what they believe reading and writing instruction should develop in young language users:

- What kinds of texts do your students read? What would you like them to read more of?
- What purposes do they have for reading things they select themselves? Do the things your students read tell you much about their interests and backgrounds?
- Can you tell if many of your students read much outside of class? Does this reading differ much from what is read in class? How? Which do you think is the most legitimate reading activity? Why?
- Have you noticed students using things they have read? What kind of texts were they? How were they used?
- How often do your students write in reaction to reading? Is this usually/always a classroom activity? What do you have them do? What reading/writing activities have you always wanted to have your students try? Why?

- What kinds of writing do your students do? What kinds of free writing do they do? Are you aware of any difference between free writing and that done in the classroom as a part of instruction? What causes any differences noted?

- What do your students write the best? Why is that? What reasons do they have to write that we don't create for them?

- If you were on the school board, what would you want to look at to see how well the students in this school system are writing and reading? Why?

- How do you mark or grade student writing? Why do you use this system? What are your criteria for identifying a good reader or writer?

- What writing and reading strategies should our students be learning now so they will be more successful as learners next year and thereafter?

As you engage in such discussions, watch for statements from your fellow professionals that suggest things that students could write which:

- Rely on one or more texts.
- React to fiction as well as nonfiction.
- Are not alien to authentic purposes students might have for writing.
- Promise to be interesting to most students.
- Will have students write for particular purposes.
- Involve various thinking strategies, but particularly the synthesis of more than one text.
- Are naturally addressed to a clearly defined audience.
- Are apt to generate responses that can be appreciated as language process as well as product.

By listening carefully and noting what your fellow professionals have to say, you can also get ideas about particular authors, titles, or genres that they mention when revealing their appreciation for authentic uses of language by their students. Ask questions

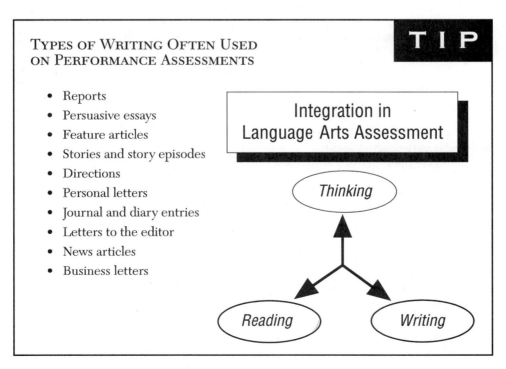

TYPES OF WRITING OFTEN USED ON PERFORMANCE ASSESSMENTS

TIP

- Reports
- Persuasive essays
- Feature articles
- Stories and story episodes
- Directions
- Personal letters
- Journal and diary entries
- Letters to the editor
- News articles
- Business letters

Integration in Language Arts Assessment

Thinking

Reading   Writing

to promote specific examples, which can provide wonderful guidance in picking writing activities for a battery of performance assessments. If these meetings or conversations are genuine and open, they are also apt to reveal some prewriting and postwriting strategies that can be useful in designing an instrument or that can guide selection of a published test.

As you initiate your assessment development or begin the selection process, it could be helpful to make a list of:

- Possible titles, authors, and types of texts that may work well.
- Writing activities that will seem authentic to students.
- Prewriting activities.
- Postwriting activities that encourage unforced revision.
- Criteria that may hold up in rating the student responses to your assessment.

Many teachers are still in situations where they feel they must move with some caution in developing and using performance assessments. You may not feel quite ready to broach the prospect of developing or acquiring performance language assessments in a system where they are not yet being considered very seriously. This should not deter you from developing your own performance assessment, however. Check to see, too, if the text or any reading series you are using offer them.

The experience of developing or trying a performance assessment may give you the direction and familiarity needed to suggest broadening it to the school or system. Or you may have one or two fellow teachers who will be interested in your results and might enjoy working with you as a team to try performance assessment across several classes or grades.

Even if you find you must pursue your interest in performance assessment alone—just for your classroom—it can be a professional experience that you may ultimately rank very highly. The remainder of this chapter and the next chapter give a description of how to go about designing or selecting one and rating the results of a single integrated language activity, which could be administered once with each group of students for which it is written.

A full performance assessment program, however, would need to include several such assessments for each grade level and would cross several or all grade levels. The different assessments administered at a single grade level would be designed so that, as a set:

- They cover different purposes for reading and writing.
- They ask the students to read different types of texts.
- They set the students to responding with different kinds of writing.

As a set, this variety of language performance would reflect the language development goals of the curriculum.

If you are developing or selecting a performance assessment on your own, this initial step is *both* easier and more difficult. You have only your own values to reckon with and will have the final say on what you have the students do on the assessment. On the other hand, you won't have the benefit of the ideas of fellow professionals to spark more of your own—unless, of course, you can involve some of your faculty friends in conversation about your project—if not in the project itself.

2. NEXT DETERMINE THE WRITING ACTIVITIES AND TEXTS THAT WILL WORK WELL TOGETHER.

This step will vary somewhat, depending on whether you are most interested in the kind of performance assessment that is fully integrated or the type that will produce student writing to be evaluated separately in terms of reading and writing. In that type, you will be perhaps more concerned about the kind of writing task that depends on making meaning with that text. In the second type, you will have more opportunity to guide the student through aspects of the comprehension that you can factor a bit, and the text will not have to figure so directly in the generation of the student response that will used to be evaluate writing, but only to motivate and spark it in some topical or more general way.

The selection of the writing activity for a fully integrated reading/writing assessment or the questions that call for the student-constructed responses in the analytical type must depend on how well you can match them (or the publisher's test maker has matched them) to a text that is appropriate for each grade level. Obviously, it should be a text you feel that students in your class or at the grade level where it is to be used will be able to read without difficulty. The next logical step is to initially determine what you would like to ask the students to do, based on the kinds of considerations recommended in Step 1.

You may want to begin with a checklist of ideas from your discussions and considerations in Step 1—texts, type of texts, types of writing. Your prompt/writing activity combination should have a clear and reasonable enough purpose to be accepted by both teachers and students as authentic. As you identify writing activities and texts, ask yourself:

- Is this something I believe is a worthwhile and interesting thing to do?
- Is this something my students would consider a worthwhile and interesting thing to do?

That means that the combination should involve important language behaviors that you feel should be developed in your students. It means that doing the activity will be something your students feel is reasonable and interesting. It needs to be an activity that will promote the integration of their backgrounds and understanding with important details in the reading prompt that are needed to respond.

Here are some ideas culled from numerous sources that could be used in the fully integrated type of assessment or be modified to generate the writing sample for the other type. Also on these and the following pages are boxes with some examples of assessments that are representative of those actually in print. Hopefully these can help you develop your own and/or help guide you in selecting an instrument.

The task might be to have the student write:

- A letter to:

    A character in a story, offering advice, sympathy, tactful criticism.

    The newspaper, taking a position on a school or city issue.

    A celebrity, complimenting or criticizing behavior.

The examples are taken from the *Unit Integrated Performance Assessment* accompanying the Harcourt Brace Jovanovich, Inc. *HBJ Treasury of Literature* (1993); the *Integrated Assessment System,* Language Arts Performance Assessment— Reading/Writing, The Psychological Corporation, Harcourt Brace Jovanovich, Inc., 1990; and the Holt, Rinehart and Winston *Integrated Performance Assessment* accompanying the *Elements of Literature,* 1994. In addition, several examples are from the *Indiana Performance Assessments '92.*

TRY TO SELECT TOPICS THAT:

- Are familiar to the students.
- Have the authentic appeal to engage the students.
- Invite personal reactions.
- Encourage differences and promote discussion.
- Allow the use of references, incorporation of personal experiences.
- Solicit explanations.
- Rely on textual information/ideas and their interrelationships.
- Can be handled in a reasonable amount of class time.
- Represent different genres across assessments in a school or district.

AVOID TOPICS THAT:

- Can be answered with yes or no.
- Seem to state or invite the recital of universal truths.
- Ask for consensus opinions: "What do people think about . . . ?"
- Assume more background than your students may have.

In responding to "Turtle's House," second-graders read a letter from a turtle "in such a dither" because he can't decide if he should look for a new house, and if so, what kind of change he should make from his present abode (his shell). Turtle presents several categories to be considered (color and appearance, size, upkeep) and asks the reader's opinion. The students write to Turtle, giving him advice. The task involves the selection and use of details to be persuasive.

Source: *Integrated Assessment System,* The Psychological Corporation, 1990.

Obviously the prompts accompanying such activities for the fully integrated assessment would have to provide the background that the student would need to write as directed or some aspect or feature that would tend to promote or model the writing sample in the analytical type: a story with a character who has a problem and needs advice, the details on at least two sides of some school or civic issue, several reports about the celebrity, preferably painting a varied picture of him or her. The letter to a character has been shown to work well with students in the lower elementary grades.

- A carefully considered decision on something like:

    Which brand of new bicycle, skateboard, or Rollerblades should be bought.

    What public use an old school building should be put to.

    Which of several vacation spots to pick for a family trip.

The prompts could each contain two or more ads, brochures, reviews, personal accounts (in a letter, for example), or some combination of these. The civic issue could be presented with two articles or letters to the newspaper, for example. In the fully integrated response the student would be synthesizing the material to support the decision he or she has made. In the other type, the need for the student to synthesize the meaning made from all the texts would need to be covered in the open-ended responses to the questions intended to evaluate reading performance. The writing response could be motivated topically or in some other fashion that gives the student some leeway in writing.

- The resolution to a problem:

    What to do with a bratty little brother or sister.

    How to preserve the Antarctica environment.

    How to promote safety when rollerblading.

Again the prompt would need to present the problem in adequate detail to invite selection and should suggest a range of solutions. In the fully integrated type, the writing activity should invite the student to select or come up with his or her own solution based on the facts comprehended. In the analytical type, the questions generating responses to reveal reading comprehension would need to promote recounting the options, while the writing response could be personal, thematic, or topical in some very general way.

Second-graders read Arnold Lobel's *Grasshopper on the Road* to decide whether they would prefer to travel with the main character or with some dragonflies who "bug" him about his values. The students are asked to defend their decision. The task in this fully integrated assessment involves comparing and contrasting to explain an evaluative choice.

Source: *HBJ Treasury of Literature:* Unit Integrated Performance Assessment, 1993.

High school students read three texts as part of a prompt before writing a "Purchase Recommendation Memorandum" to a company official about types of bicycles that should be carried by a growing retail department store chain. One of the texts to be synthesized in this fully integrated task is a memo from the boss, explaining that bicycle sales have dropped. A second source consists of notes and tables based on three reports from a consumer magazine. The third is information from a business magazine about the bicycle marketplace. The student, assuming the role of an employee, is to analyze the material provided and make recommendations about products that should be added to the inventory. The activity requires supportable selection, use of comparison/contrast, and synthesis.

Source: *Indiana Performance Assessments '92.*

- A report on something of interest:
  Dinosaurs that lived in North America.
  Some natural catastrophe.
  Alternative forms of energy.

In order to avoid having the writing activity be merely the recitation of facts, say, as a synopsis, they would have to be presented in multiple texts (probably three different texts) that are organized in unusual ways or that are of different genre—forcing the student to synthesize to get the report, and the student would need to be instructed to be sure to use as many of the sources as possible. In addition, the introduction of the writing activity should add a question that will force some order other than juxtaposed synopses: *How different were the dinosaurs that once lived on our continent?* The analytical assessment would look for the same reading comprehension and allow a much freer hand with the response to be evaluated for writing.

- A persuasive essay:
  To get the reader to recycle.
  To urge people to contribute to some charity.
  To promote bicycle safety.

The prompt could be a single report or article, but it would need to stress the problem and at least imply that people have to help solve it. The writing activity should be introduced in a way that ensures more than a recounting of the problem: *Persuade the students in your school to practice bicycle safety by telling them what they should do.* The article or report might, for example, contain a paragraph on the number of accidents caused by people riding double, give a brief personal account of a driver who came upon a cyclist at night with no light on the bike, and detail other problems for which the solution that should be mentioned in the persuasion is implied. The reading part of the analytical type of assessment might press for the same details and let the student try to persuade anyone to do anything that comes to mind or to just write something about a bicycle, for example.

High school students read an unusually long prompt on the water shortage problem in California. It consists of a rather technical article typical of those that might appear in a science newsletter, a descriptive article not unlike that which would appear in a news magazine, and an encyclopedia article on water use. Embedded in these are several tables, maps, and captioned photographs—as well as some solutions that have been considered. The students are asked to write to the California Water Commission with a long-term plan to solve the water problem. This sophisticated and fully integrated activity encompasses a wide range of thinking behaviors, including cause/effect, synthesis, selection and organization of data, and the creative incorporation of background knowledge.

Source: *Indiana Performance Assessments '92.*

A dinosaur prompt for third-graders presents information in different categories: size, type, diet. It asks the students to write a report selecting and comparing and contrasting two of the five types discussed. The task calls for selecting information, synthesizing, and using comparison/contrast effectively.

Source: *Integrated Assessment System,* The Psychological Corporation, 1990.

- An article for a paper:

    On students with interesting hobbies.

    On teachers who have traveled.

    On athletes who had athletic brothers and sisters.

The prompt could consist of at least three texts about separate students and teachers and could consist of student essays, letters to someone, an announcement from the principal, and other types of information. Each set should suggest synthesis by having content in common: all the teachers went to the Near East, all of the hobbies have to do with entertaining, all of the older brothers and sisters were also students in the school at the same time. Other details within the sets should invite other comparisons and contrasts. The reading part of the analytical type could press for synthesis, too, while letting the student write about something he or she has read in a newspaper that is interesting.

- The directions for doing something:

    Coloring a picture of zoo animals.

    Building a bird feeder out of a plastic milk jug.

    Playing roque.

The first idea above is suitable for lower elementary children, and the prompt could be a list of the animals' names with brief descriptions to help the reader identify them in the group picture and with notes on their colors and markings. Perhaps it could be a chart. The student could be steered to some synthesis by the directions: *Tell which crayons someone should use to color the picture.* The analytical type could supply the colors and have the student match them and then let the student draw and caption creatively—a favorite animal, for example.

The roque prompt could describe the game by comparing it to croquet and with no particular sequence but with abundant details that invite sequencing. After describing a roque "playing field" and the game in general, the article would drop back to how it begins, then how it is won, and then discuss some playing strategies. The writing part of the analytical type could be as simple as telling about a favorite game.

- An addition to a story:

    A new beginning or preceding episode.

    A new ending or succeeding episode.

A good and appealing story is the secret here, with initial action that invites imaginative addition of the causes of it and with attractive characters that suggest particular

Fourth-graders read "Bugs Beware" from *Highlights for Children* by Pat Kite, to learn about plants that trap and eat insects. Then they are asked to pretend to be adult insects informing their young about the dangers and persuading them to be cautious. The task requires reorganizing details to explain and persuade.

Source: *HBJ Treasury of Literature:* Unit Integrated Performance Assessment, 1993.

A fifth-grade assessment activity developed for a school in the Midwest has used school records, a news story from the "School Press" of the local newspaper, and oral reports from several teachers. The prompt is about three girls who were outstanding runners at the school.

One part of the prompt is an interview; another is a table; two are descriptive. The student is asked to write a feature story for the school paper. This fully integrated task involves comparison/contrast, synthesis, and the careful use of descriptive details.

---

actions and dialogue; or a story that is somewhat less than resolved and invites a new ending as an effect. (The assessment maker should be cautious about using stories that are apt to be highly familiar to the students, for some students may have read or have had the story read to them and would construct what they recall.) In the fully integrated assessment, the presentation of the writing activity should stress the importance of the addition being logical—that it "fit" with what is given. The analytical type of test might let the student create any story he or she wishes for the writing part after answering questions and explaining reactions to the story in the reading part of the test.

- An adaptation of nonfiction to fiction:

   A story about the great San Francisco earthquake.

   A fictional story about the whale that swam upriver.

   A story about cowboys.

The textual prompts could be a long, descriptive entry from an actual diary the day after the earthquake, an article about Humphrey the whale, an actual journal kept by a cowboy. In the fully integrated assessment, the students would need to depend on the details in the prompts to flesh out their stories. In the analytical type, separate essay-type responses would respond to questions about the texts and then would serve as a model for the student to tell about an experience of his or her own.

- An adaptation of fiction to nonfiction:

   A news story about a dangerous mountain climb.

   A police report of a solved mystery.

   A journal entry of a character in a story.

The texts should each be fictional stories: one about mountain climbers, one a short mystery, and one with a character who has had an eventful day. The analytical type of assessment could ask for responses that reveal comprehension but would avoid dictating how the details are adapted or reworked in the writing part.

- A synthesis of texts:

   A synopsis of what characters did at a party.

   A discussion of ocean currents or the selection of a pair of sneakers.

An article describes the effect of different ocean currents, which are shown on a map of the world; a table specifies the effects with numbers. The student is asked to "discuss the effects of ocean currents on the world, using information from all of the sources."

In a fully integrated assessment, third-graders read "Baking Day" from *Tales of Oliver Pig* by Jean Van Leeuwen and are asked to draw from the description of what Oliver and his mother did in the narrative to write directions for making cookies. The task requires selec-

tion and careful sequencing of details and considerable synthesis of information in the story and a recipe that is published with it.

Source: *Integrated Assessment System,* The Psychological Corporation, 1990.

Fifth-graders finish a story about a family camping when the son and daughter awaken to strange "Heavy Footsteps" outside the tent. They see that their father is not in his sleeping bag. The task involves using details in the story to write a logical extension and sequencing for the story to explain the footsteps. Although this assessment is fully integrated, it could have served the type where reading and writing responses are separate as well.

Source: *Integrated Assessment System,* The Psychological Corporation, 1990.

The unique and common features of three fictional brands of sneakers are described in an advertisement, a fashion article, and a poster; the student must pick a pair and explain why that choice was made.

In the type of assessment where responses rated for reading and for writing are generated separately, the reading part could focus on the comparison and contrast and cause and effect using details, and then the student could be simply asked to write something about his or her favorite piece of clothing or something about experience with weather.

- A patterned story or story extension based on a prompt story with a very distinct pattern.

The two types of performance assessment would probably appear a great deal alike with this kind of prompt, except that the less integrated type would have a set of questions aimed more directly at aspects of reading comprehension. The prompt is a piece of fiction with a highly distinctive style, usually with a repetitious structure, almost like a refrain or catalog that varies, develops, or grows in some way, adding new details as the story progresses. Children find such patterns easy to emulate while presenting original material.

THE "ANALYTICAL" ASSESSMENT TYPE KEEPS READING AND WRITING SEPARATE

On the type of performance assessment that analyzes separate responses to arrive at reading and writing scores, the questions that generate the responses to be rated on reading ability are not so unified or compact as those on the tests that integrate the response used to assess both reading and writing.

While the answers to the reading part of the test are indeed student-generated and open-ended, they intentionally call for and focus on several more specific perspectives on the meaning. Consequently, multiple samples of these tests would take nearly as much space as a manual—unlike the more integrated tests, where the task and its relationship to the prompt can be relatively simply stated. These tests in which *the evaluation* of the student performance is not integrated actually tend to generate more writing than the other type. Although the responses to the various reading questions are normally rated as one combined effort, the presentation of anchors and rubrics to inform the rating process is a bit more complex.

Seventh-graders read an account of the *Titanic* disaster that includes details about some of the passengers in this fully integrated assessment. The students are asked to assume the role of one of the passengers and to write a diary or journal entry about the sinking of the ship from that perspective. The task requires the selection of details from a particular perspective and a great deal of inferential empathy. An assessment of the other type using this prompt might have asked the student to recount some details of the accident and to react to some of the content (to get responses to analyze for reading) and then have them tell about some experience of their own for the writing part.

Source: *Integrated Assessment System,* The Psychological Corporation, 1990.

Sixth-graders read Laurie Lawlor's *Addie Across the Prairie,* a narrative about the adventures of a pioneer girl when she faces a prairie fire while crossing the United States. The students are asked to write an entry that Addie would have put into her journal, describing what happened and how she felt. The task requires selection of details from a particular perspective and the inferential empathy necessary to assume the character's feelings. Again, the other type of performance test might have focused on aspects of comprehension, such as sequence and cause and effect, and on character reactions (for the reading part) and then students would have been asked to write an account of something that has happened to them at home, when on vacation, or while traveling.

Source: *HBJ Treasury of Literature:* Unit Integrated Performance Assessment, 1993.

Since the response used to generate writing is not to inform reading comprehension, the prompt is used only to spark ideas in the student's mind and to help generate some fluency. The rating of the writing response is not so complex to guide as the reading. In batteries of the type with these separate responses and ratings, however, the type of questions asked students about what they have read then have to be structured the same across prompts and even grade levels.

The Holt, Rinehart, and Winston instrument described here as an example has six questions with room for the student to write nearly a page response to each. They cover an initial "reaction"; a question designed to promote some thinking skill like comparison/contrast, categorization, sequencing or the like and guided by a matrix for the response; several about author intent or theme; and several that try to generate personal reader response and application. See the two boxed samples for illustration of how this works.

SOME SPECIAL CONSIDERATIONS IN COMPLETING STEP 2

There are several special considerations in selecting prompt/activity combinations for use on the assessment:

PLAN FOR SOME SCOPE   If you are developing a battery of these assessments for use across your school or district, you will, of course, need at least one prompt/activity pair for each grade; ideally, however, you would have from two to four for each grade. In selecting published tests, one should look for a battery that assures that kind of coverage as well. Because of the demands of such a task for teachers constructing their own battery, it might be a good idea for a school system just considering performance assessment to begin with one grade—say grade 3—having all the teachers with students in that grade work together to develop several of the assessments.

Then, after the administration of two or more activities and the analysis of the results, teachers in the other grades could begin to prepare their own assessments, using those in the trial grade as models. For this to work well, the first teachers to develop the assessment should keep journal-like notes about their experiences, intending to share them with teachers in the other grades. These notes should:

First-graders do a shared reading about how "Bill's Hat" is rescued when it flies off his head on a fishing trip with his father and sister. The student reads and completes captions with details from pictures and must infer from a final picture that a fish has got caught in the hat. In the second type of performance assessment, the inferencing meaning making might have been solicited as drawings to use in rating reading comprehension, and another, captioned drawing about losing something could have revealed how the student makes meaning by creating or writing.

Source: *Integrated Assessment System,* The Psychological Corporation, 1990.

IN SELECTING A STORY, BE SURE IT:

- Appeals to student interests, values, and backgrounds.
- Is not too complicated.
- Invites reactions.
- Allows a variety of interpretations.

- Describe what is done at each step.
- Detail problems that arise.
- Explain the way problems were handled.
- Record the results.
- Include copies of each draft of each assessment to show how it evolved, explaining what happened to recommend each change.
- Explain how things might be done differently another time.

The teacher who is working alone in developing a performance assessment may wish to keep similar notes for himself or herself, and this scientific approach is sure to pay off when subsequent prompt/writing activity sets are developed. The notes could also provide an excellent basis for a professional publication on what was learned from the experience.

HELP YOUR STUDENTS KEEP AN AUDIENCE FOCUS Create or select activities for which the audience the student is asked to address is as specific as possible. This is less important in having the student write in the analytical type of test, but even there, it can help guarantee better writing. For example:

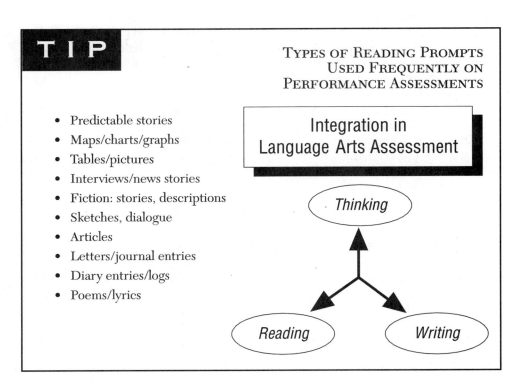

TIP

TYPES OF READING PROMPTS USED FREQUENTLY ON PERFORMANCE ASSESSMENTS

- Predictable stories
- Maps/charts/graphs
- Tables/pictures
- Interviews/news stories
- Fiction: stories, descriptions
- Sketches, dialogue
- Articles
- Letters/journal entries
- Diary entries/logs
- Poems/lyrics

Integration in Language Arts Assessment

Thinking

Reading   Writing

After reading the story *When I Am Old With You* by Angela Johnson, second-graders are asked to continue it. The story is patterned as a lovely catalog of all the things a grandchild enjoys doing with her grandfather, expressed as things they will do together when they are both old. The student is invited to add to the catalog in the style of the author. The task requires assuming the mood and style of the author. An instrument using the second type of performance assessment might have asked questions about the details in the catalog and then asked the student to use the style as a model.

Source: *HBJ Treasury of Literature:* Unit Integrated Performance Assessment, 1993.

- It is much less important for a student to write what s/he thinks of the way a character in a story behaves than it is to write a letter to one of the specific characters in the story (perhaps the character whose behavior is being evaluated) or to write what s/he would say to the character in giving him or her advice.

- It is less important for a student to write an article for fellow students in a school paper explaining some phenomenon than it is to "write a report" about it.

- It is less important to "describe the costumes and setting of a story" than to write instructions to the set designer and costume designer of a play the student is involved in producing about the story.

- It is less important to summarize an event while selecting its most relevant aspects by writing a news story for the people in the town where it occurred than it is to "tell what happened in this story."

- Writing a journal entry about a historical event is less important than when one is advised to think about the reader who will find the journal and read it generations later. More importantly in this case, however, is being directed to retell the event from the perspective of a particular individual mentioned in the account used.

If you are selecting a battery, consider whether tasks can be changed if you should decide to without losing the value of the rubrics and anchor example papers that will guide your rating and make it more reliable.

A sixth-grade package gets the reader going quickly with only a very general and brief introduction to "Being Japanese American," a personal account by Yoshiko Uchida that is approximately 2,200 words long from the book *The Invisible Thread.* Space is left in a wide margin in the test booklet for the student to write "My thoughts about reading" as a kind of metacognitive "think-along."

After reading the student is asked to write an initial response to the story, then a guided sorting of details that make the author feel Japanese and those that make her feel American. Then an opinion question has the student pick what he or she thinks the author likes most about her Japanese heritage. The next question asks the student to apply the general theme of feeling different to his or her own life, and tell how that has happened to him or her. A more difficult fifth question calls for a kind of metaphorical interpretation of the book title in light of the selection.

The entire "reading" response is rated as a unit, and the student is not penalized for a very short, weak, or completely absent answer to one or more of these questions if there are stronger responses that reveal comprehension. An optional group activity prepares the student to write a response to be rated for reading. (It should be noted that prewriting activities—also optional—are almost always available with the other type of performance assessment as well.) The writing genre is dictated—here a letter—as is the audience, in a general way. So is the general purpose of the letter.

Source: Integrated Performance Assessment for the HRW Language Arts Program.

An essay on nonviolent resistance by Martin Luther King, Jr. is the prompt for a ninth-grade assessment that rates reading and writing responses separately. The reading responses, which are rated as a unit, are nonetheless guided by six questions: one seeking an initial general reaction, one that asks what the essay reveals about Dr. King, one in which the student picks a person or event that influenced the author and explains how and why it was selected, a personal application of the understanding of the text to a conflict the student knows about, an evaluation of Dr. King's strengths, and a question for additional student-selected understanding of the essay. The pattern of the reading questions across grades can be seen when comparing these focuses to those in the other Holt, Rinehart, and Winston sample described here. An optional group prewriting activity prepares the student to write about what he or she thinks makes a good leader—a response used to evaluate writing.

Note here that the objective is not primarily to make the activity *easier*—though there is nothing short of frustrating results to be gained in assessment by making it deliberately difficult. The main reason to specify audience is to make the activity less abstract, and thus more authentic. The results will be stronger, as well. Perhaps writing tests sometimes yield results that are not as strong as we wish because we leave the young writer in audience limbo with an inauthentic writing task and his or her primary challenge is to deal with the somewhat meaningless unreality of the situation.

Note too, from the examples above, how specifying the audience for the performance assessment writing activity also specifies and clarifies the purpose for writing. We may not be evaluating that task-fulfilling behavior in the second type of performance assessment, but we take a giant step toward involving students and assuring that they will do their best when we help establish a clear purpose for writing—*other than the understood "because my teacher says this is something I should do."*

3. MAKE SOME KEY DECISIONS
ABOUT ADMINISTERING THE ASSESSMENT.

Next you will need to make some key decisions about how the assessment will be administered.

BUILD INTEREST

Just as you would for effective instruction, you will want to build interest among the students in the topic around which the reading/writing activity is centered. If you are constructing your own assessment, you will need to prepare ahead of time the kind of introduction that will get the students to think about what they know about the topic and to anticipate what they will learn from the activity. If you are selecting a published test or battery, you will want to consider this to judge how effective the instrument's instructions and assistance are in this regard.

At the same time you will want to maintain the informality of a normal classroom learning experience. Following is a general outline of the steps you can use, and they suggest the kind of criteria you can use in selection. What is offered here is only a model, however; there are many variations you can use that respond to the particular content of a prompt, the nature of the writing activity, or other features of a particular assessment.

You should begin by telling the students what they will read about and what they will be asked to do in writing. Does the published test you are examining for possible use do that clearly? For example, you might say:

> You are going to read about a boy who is bored and is looking for adventure, but some might say that he got more than he bargained for. Others might argue that despite getting in a jam and being grounded for a month, Oban learns a lot and had an adventure he will never forget.

When you finish reading the story, you will pretend to be Oban or his friend Marquita and write several journal entries about Oban's voyage to the mysterious island of Adhurvia.

These instructions will vary with the type of test you are making or selecting. The tests that begin with questions to generate responses for the separate rating of reading, for example, may say less than that, and depend on the questions to structure the student responses just a bit.

Next, however, you may want to get the students to start thinking about what they know that will contribute to their efforts to complete the writing task. The most common way to do this is with a good questioning technique. Prepare for each prompt/activity set questions that will promote class discussion in which the students share their knowledge, background, and interest in the topic. These questions can also relate to the writing activity, the identified audience, and the purpose for writing. How extensively you do this will be up to you. Even if a published test tended to do a great deal of this, you would have the control.

In the case of the example above, you could ask if the students have ever heard of the island Adhurvia—to establish that it is a make-believe place. Then you might ask questions such as these:

- Have you ever gone hunting for an adventure? Tell us a bit about it.
- Can you think of a time when you were bored and longed for something exciting to happen? How did that feel?
- Who has had an adventure that turned out to be more frightening or exciting than you expected or wanted it to be?
- Have you ever been grounded for a whole month? What would that be like?

Questions related to the task could include ones like these:

- Who can remind/tell us what a journal is? What kind of writing does someone do in it?
- Who reads a journal, anyway? What are some of the audiences that journal writers might think of?
- Why do persons write in journals? What is the purpose?

For some questions like this one you may want to suggest some answers: to remember experiences, people, and details; to have a source that can be used for other writing; for the satisfaction of thinking through a problem or an experience. Point out that some journal writers claim that they are their only audience—that they expect no one else to ever read the journal.

- If Adhurvia doesn't exist, how are you going to get details about it to write in Oban's or Marquita's journal? [from the prompt]
- Have you ever been on a small island? What was that like?

Whether you have other ideas in mind for building interest, it is a good idea to write some questions designed to promote discussion and interest. Someone else administering the assessment at another time might prefer them to the other approach or want to use both.

There are other ways to build interest, of course. One way is to call attention to any art you are using with the prompt and get the students to examine it and to discuss details they find there. This is particularly important with students in the lower elementary grades.

You may also decide to advise teachers to use any outside materials about South Sea islands they have in introducing the passage, but keep in mind in making this decision that some teachers' students then may have some advantage. But since so much of the assessment environment is open to instructional approaches, that should be no problem.

In suggesting interest-building activities, use any other techniques that have proven successful for you in building prereading interest in your students. For example, have the students predict what will happen in the story, using any art, the title, and the topic as indicated so far.

One word of caution, however: Don't overdo the amount of these activities offered, or if you do, point out that they are just options. The examples given here, for example, would take too long, and might even wear on the student's interest after a while instead of building it.

DECIDE IF YOU WILL ALLOW COLLABORATION

In many writing situations for students in today's classrooms, collaboration among the students is permitted, even encouraged. In the examples in this chapter of tests where the reading and writing responses are kept separate, group planning and discussion is encouraged as a prewriting activity. After all, when the best writers write in real life, most look for reactions, suggestions, guidance, and encouragement from people—and editors—they know and respect. If we want the performance to be the product of as natural and authentic an experience as possible, we should be allowing collaboration.

Some teachers may feel that unlimited collaboration is distracting for a few student writers. Certainly, the idea of allowing students to work together is uniquely different from the test environment many of us are familiar with. You may decide to control collaboration somewhat by limiting it to a half-hour period near the end of the first-draft writing phase of the assessment, or you could make it an optional activity in the postwriting activities offered to promote revision. But remember, teachers who use interaction among young writers successfully have found it highly effective indeed in emphasizing writing as a process.

PREPARE A PREWRITING ACTIVITY AS PART OF THE ASSESSMENT

Many activities can promote the consideration of the details and ideas in the prompt in the light of the writing activity the student is asked to perform. The objective in selecting such an activity for a particular prompt/activity pair is to offer one or more that will set the student to reexamining the text while thinking about what he or she is being asked to write. The prewriting activity can extend past this, however, to the organization of the ideas and details to be used in writing the response.

Some published performance assessments offer *several* such prewriting activities so the teacher can choose the one that best matches the kind of prewriting activities used in the classroom to develop writers as idea processors. If you are working alone or with just a few fellow teachers, you may know which activity you prefer and can concentrate on preparing just one. It is also a good idea to allow students to substitute and/or make up their own prewriting activity.

It is also important that the prewriting activity match the prompt and writing activity as effectively as possible. What you want to do is to think of an activity that will help your students get ready to write, but keep them focused on the text of the prompt. Sometimes it helps to try the task yourself:

- Do you begin with a focus on ideas or a focus on details? How do you organize either? It is important to note here that the prewriting activity should not be so demanding or complex that it kills the student's genuine interest in the whole assessment activity.

Reporter's Fact Sheet
Kate Shelley and the Midnight Express

What?

Who?

Where?

When?

Why was the train in
danger?

How did Kate help?

In preparing to write a news story based on Wesley Porter's *Kate Shelley and the Midnight Express,* fifth-graders are supplied with a story map and a Reporter's Fact Sheet.

Source: *HBJ Treasury of Literature:* Unit Integrated Performance Assessment, 1993.

- What activity could drive the student back to the prompt to reread and to note the content that applies to the writing task before him or her? Some teachers may feel that the best way to create the focus they want is to extend the class discussion used to develop interest before reading.

- This prewriting activity may be as simple as listing a few engaging questions that the teacher can ask to initiate the discussion. Other approaches may recommend a kind of jot-note activity that gets the students to group details they

Who Was Doing What?

Character	What the character was doing as the story left off

In writing an ending for Gloria Whelan's *Silver,* a story about a puppy that is lost in a snowstorm, third-graders are assisted in prewriting with a story map and then a simple ready-made note sheet like the one to the left.

Source: *HBJ Treasury of Literature:* Unit Integrated Performance Assessment, 1993.

A Comparison/Contrast Chart *Growing Up in the Old West*		
Details to Compare/Contrast	Native American Children	Pioneer Children
Games		
Chores		
Skills and Customs		
Animals		
Clothing		

Categorical note-taking schemes, like this one from a grade 8 assessment, are usually very useful for activities that ask students to compare and contrast. In this case, the prompt, *Growing Up in the Old West* by Russell Freedman, gives many details about the lives of Native American and pioneer children. The students are asked to write a comparative description.

Source: *HBJ Treasury of Literature:* Unit Integrated Performance Assessment, 1993.

can use in a kind of crude outline. Sometimes the categories of the outline are presented as several cells in a kind of table into which the jot notes are written.

Whatever activity you create, keep its purpose clearly in mind. It is basically a kind of ignition and organizing feature to *help,* not harass, the student as s/he gets ready to write and a guide the student can then follow when writing. Some ideas for prewriting activities that match types of prompts and writing activities are suggested below. A few of them are illustrated with actual note-taking aids supplied to students in published performance assessments to give you an idea of the kind of aids you can create. In general, on the type of assessment where several reading questions are asked, a prewriting activity for each would be too interruptive. Much of your motivating may need to be done one-on-one as the students work. Prewriting activities for first-graders may frequently consist of guidance you give the students as they respond to the activity, drawing, drawing and captioning, or writing.

All of these suggestions are offered at your peril. Remember, using even two of them to motivate one performance assessment may be too much and overtax the students' interest in the topic or activity. If you have selected a published test with its own suggestions and they are optional, you should feel free to substitute ones you may like better.

- For activities like writing a news story, it may serve the student best to make notes about a piece of fiction by *characters* (or *people*), *places, events*—or in response to the questions *Who? What? Where? When? Why?* and *How?* This note-taking guidance may also work when the student is to write an informative article selecting descriptive information from several supplied texts of different types. The next step might be to put checkmarks in front of the notes that are important to finishing the writing activity.

Telling About a Story

Name _____ Date _____

Name of the story _____

_____

Written by _____

_____

Who (Main Character): _____

Story Problem: _____

_____

_____

1st Major Event: _____

_____

_____

2nd Major Event: _____

_____

_____

3rd Major Event: _____

_____

_____

4th Major Event: _____

_____

_____

Solution: _____

_____

A typical story map looks like those used in *HBJ Treasury of Literature:* Unit Integrated Performance Assessment, 1993. This form is in the back of this book in Appendix C and can be copied and used as is or adapted.

- Represent the writing task as a question if it is not already presented as one. Then ask the student to go through the prompt looking for as many answers to the question as possible. For example, you might ask: *How would you decide which puppy to take? What would help you make up your mind?* Finally the student needs to group the answers found and to select those that he or she will use in writing the response.

- You may want to encourage the students to use a completely inductive approach, advising them to read through the prompt a second time while making "jot notes." As noted in the tests from one company above, the test booklets allow for think-along notes right in the margin. The students can look at the jot notes and group them into ideas that can be used in writing the response. This approach, for example, can help when the activity is to write a report about something described by several kinds of text collected as the prompt.

- You can provide a very brief list of the key ideas the students will want to consider and advise them to follow three simple steps: (1) go back over the text and list very brief notes about details that fit under each idea; (2) put the details in order within each idea; and (3) put the main ideas in some kind of order that can be used in writing. This is similar to providing the students with a categorization scheme for their notes. For writing activities that are effectively directed by having students sort out prompt details categorically, it is occasionally helpful to give them a note sheet with categories already identified.

- When younger students are asked to write using the details from a story, it often works to have them list the characters down a left-hand column and put details about each in a right-hand column.

- When the writing activity stresses feelings or other sensitivities, it may work to have the student quarter a page and put category titles in each box. The categories might be chosen from "Things she felt," "Things she did," "Things she said," "Things other people said about her," "Things she saw," "Things she heard." Details from the prompt are then entered below these. This approach will also work when writing an evaluation of a person described in an article or a major character in a story. You might include a prepared note sheet in the materials given to the student.

- Some activities that require reporting or redescribing for a particular audience—in a variety of types of writing—suggest their own categories, which students can put on note sheet sections in order to review the prompt and record details under the category titles. Some students may be able to induce appropriate categories themselves, but you may decide to provide them on a note sheet the student can use.

- Various kinds of maps can be made and provided for noting details about character feelings, actions, attitudes, and other factors appropriate to particular prompt texts. For activities that turn stories into accounts in letters, diaries, or journals, for example, you can have students who have experience doing story maps do one for the story.

- For activities that call for writing the explanation of why something occurred or of a mystery, you could ask the students to begin by analyzing the text sequentially—as a cause-or-effect chain that traces what happens in the story or account, when it happened, and what happened next.

- For activities that call for writing the solution to a problem, including giving advice to story characters, you may wish to suggest that the students begin by restating a key problem presented in their own words, then listing all solutions discussed in the prompt and making notes on them. From that point, the student can select the solution he or she likes best and support it by comparing details across the different solutions.

- The technique used for activities that require solving problems can also be used for assessments where the activity is to make a decision or selection: The options should be listed, the details given for each possible choice under it. To facilitate comparison/contrast, the student can draw lines across the details in the options that describe the same aspect of it. For example: "Cost the most," "Cost less," and "Average Cost" could be connected across three sets of ice skates even though they appear in different rows in the three columns for three different brands.

- For young students, it is a good idea to keep the prewriting activity quite simple. You may ask the students to pick or draw their favorite character, making notes on why they like him or her. For a writing activity that asks the student to draw or write what happens next, have them draw or write what happened in the prompt and list the characters who will be involved.

- For activities that require writing about something described in the prompt using a different point of view, ask the student to reread the prompt, pretending to be someone (perhaps a particular character) with a point of view different from that used to tell a story or event and to list details which would seem different to that person or character.

    Another simple but logical approach for activities that require comparison and contrast is to use two note sheets, simply listing details about the two characters or whatever are being compared under columns for each and then transferring the details to a second sheet with two columns headed "How They Are Alike" and "How They Are Different."

- To create a focus on the feelings of characters or persons who figure in the text, suggest that the students make a simple chart of events down the left column of a page divided lengthwise and the way that key characters or persons felt about each event in columns to the right of the event column.

Water problem(s) faced by California: _____

_____

_____

Factors Contributing to California's Water Problem

Factor	Extent of Impact		
	minimal	moderate	extensive

Potential Solutions to California's Water Troubles:

Solution:

	Benefits	Drawbacks
Short term		
Long term		

Other Observations: _____

_____

_____

_____

In using extensive text to suggest solutions to the "California Water Problem," high school students completing this Indiana Performance Assessments '92 *activity are guided by an optional two-page note-taking structure, which is at the more elaborate end of the range of help that can be provided.*

Potential Solutions to California's Water Troubles:

Solution:

	Benefits	Drawbacks
Short term		
Long term		

Other Observations: _____

_____

_____

_____

> In order to fully weigh the potential of each possible solution, you will probably need to use your own paper for additional solution boxes.

Connections between contributing factors and possible solutions: _____

_____

_____

_____

_____

_____

_____

_____

_____

> Now is the time to write your first draft. Please use your own notepaper. When you finish it, you may want to look at revision suggestions on the next page.

©1992

- For activities that call for writing diary or journal entries from a story or article, you may want to review what a diary or journal is and have the students list the sequence of events that one of the characters or persons in the article experienced and might write about.

- For an activity that calls for writing a review of a production described only factually and accompanied by a program, you can suggest that the student list the acts in a left-hand column, give details about each in a middle column, and make notes about how s/he liked it or disliked it in a right-hand column.

- For an activity that asks a young reader to use the style and structure pattern of a story to extend it, ask the students to list the descriptions given and then to think of other events that could follow. Depending on the age of the student, you may need to direct this prewriting with the group, using the chalkboard.

- A very simple note-taking technique can serve the activity of writing a new or additional ending for a story. You can suggest that the student make notes using interesting details down a left-hand column and brainstorm in a right-hand column about what these details suggest would happen at the end of the story.

An important thing about prewriting activities is that they *must actually serve the students in doing what is asked of them. They must not appear to the student to be just busy work!* Also, they should not be more complex, or as complex, as the writing task itself. We all know that really careful planning can make a much easier job out of writing, but in the case of the performance assessment, we want to save the enthusiasm and creativity for the actual task, not spend it on the prewriting activity.

For this reason, it is not a bad idea to supply the student with the predesigned kind of note sheet needed. Depending on the experience and abilities of your students, a note sheet that has been divided into sections for separate categories and with a detail or two already in it can model the kind of process activity that you are promoting and ensure the value of the language arts performance assessment.

PROMOTE REVISION WITH A POSTWRITING ACTIVITY

Not all of the published assessments available on the market stress taking the time to have your students analyze their first drafts and revise them; and after looking at thousands of responses to performance assessments across all grades and in many places in the country, one might conclude that even *with* optional postwriting activities, most students do little revising on the assessments.

The low priority that revision gets in writing instruction is a shame, since revision is the purest evidence of the writing *process* as well as of *self-assessment*. "I haven't used it as much as I like in instruction," some teacher might say, "so I am not inclined to stress revision on an assessment." But the revision process on the performance assessment will be graded only as it affects the final draft, which will be stronger for any degree of revision

---

T I P   LET THEM BE
                                      EACH OTHER'S EDITORS!

When the activity is to write a news story or feature, collaboration can include student pairs, working as each other's editor—reading, marking on, and making suggestions for revising the first draft.

When the students are writing stories or sketches, it is very helpful to get peer reaction. Let the editors be considering the story for a creative writing magazine.

TIP

REVISION, THE PATH TO BETTER PERFORMANCE!

Unless teachers stress and praise revision activities highly, it appears not to be a regular part of the writing process of U.S. students. Analysts of student portfolios report the same phenomenon, despite their emphasis on self-assessment. And even with an instructional approach using the best facilitator of revision ever created, there is little: Reviewing the literature on the use of computers to teach writing, one finds that students are rarely taught the ease of printing out, revising, and reprinting. (Students are apparently lucky to get on-line to a printer once.) It is like using a VCR in instruction with a TV that has no picture, only sound!

A bit of advice: If your students' writing products are being compared to those of other groups and you want them to excel, persuade them to practice revision. Develop the habit with partners who exchange papers, with editors for in-class publications, and with portfolios. *Prepare good postreading activities for each performance prompt/writing activity,* and encourage your students to use them. Add a half hour to the time for giving the assessment if necessary.

Then sit back and watch for the results. You are apt to become a candidate for *Teacher of the Year,* if you aren't already.

---

that your students do. And remember, integrated language arts performance assessment is basically indistinguishable from good teaching; so here is an opportunity to help instill the habit of self-assessing and revising in your students.

To ensure that you are taking advantage of the opportunity, create a specific post-writing activity for each performance assessment prompt/activity combination. If you're selecting a published battery, look for one that effectively promotes revision.

These activities can be matched to the prompt and writing task just as the prewriting activities can, but they tend to be more generic. It is very important, however, that post-writing suggestions offered relate to the purpose and the audience presented for the activity so that any revision the activity recommends does not dull the effectiveness of the response.

Write a set of questions about the response that the student can ask himself or herself. These would relate to the particular writing activity, but some could be generic in the sense that they could be used with or adapted for all such activities. For example, if the student has been asked to write a news story, you could use questions such as these:

- Have I included all the major details/facts that people reading the newspaper will want to know? Do I tell Who? What? Where? When? Why? and How?

- Do I get the most important facts in at the beginning of the story?

- Are all my facts accurate?

In warning their offspring about the dangerous plants described in Pat Kite's *Bugs, Beware!,* fourth-graders are advised to review their draft by asking themselves these questions:

- Do I convince the young insects that the plants are dangerous?

- Do I tell the young insects which plants to watch out for and why?

- Do I explain what will happen to the insects if they get trapped?

- Is the information used from the passage correct?

- Are my ideas organized clearly? Will the young insects understand my warning?

Source: *HBJ Treasury of Literature:* Unit Integrated Performance Assessment, 1993.

- Will my story give the reader all that s/he needs to know to understand what happened?
- Is my story interesting?

If the task were to write a journal entry, the questions might include:

- Do I tell it the way that _____ , the person keeping the journal, experienced it? (Do I have the right point of view?)
- Did I make it sound as though _____ is talking/writing?
- Did I leave anything out that would be interesting to remember ten years from now?
- Do I tell enough? Do I have it reported accurately? Did I make it interesting?

For each of these examples, there would also be a few questions related to the particular topic. In the example used earlier, you could have the student ask himself or herself:

- Did I describe the island enough that it will be remembered?
- Did I tell how the children felt on the way to the island, while on the island, and after they got back home?

Devise your own methods for getting the students to use their answers to improve their writing. But generally it begins by encouraging them to take notes and asking somewhere in the process, "Have your answers made you think of anything you can do to your story/writing to make it better?" Here are some other ideas for postwriting/revision-directing activities:

- One way to encourage the students to use the answers to such questions in revising is to present them in three columns headed like this example with the first notes suggested:

Ask yourself this	Make notes about your answer	What could you do to improve this writing?
Do the characters in my story seem like real people?	They seem sort of stiff or stilted or something.	I could add more dialogue and let them talk like real kids.

- The idea of having editorial pairs who can react to each other's work in the postwriting phase has already been discussed above.
- Use other revision-encouraging ideas that have worked in your classroom.

Skim the first drafts your students have completed as you move about the room and phrase several questions that can guide revision. For example:

- This part is really funny! I wish you had more about that.
- Do you think someone who hasn't read the story you read will understand what you wrote here?
- Who is saying this, and this? Maybe you could make that clearer for readers like me?
- Which of those ideas tells Christina's feelings? It would be good to add more like that.
- What happens to the birds after they fledge? Does the article you read tell anything about that?

- Who is this in the picture? Could you add her name? How about putting what she is saying on it?

After you have administered a few of these assessments, you will have stronger ideas about the options you have in terms of the considerations discussed under Step 3. You can go back and revise assessments and make different decisions on future assessment sets you create. It is always a good idea to review both the prewriting and postwriting activities after you have designed the criteria as described in the next chapter, so as to be directing the students toward the perspectives that will be used in scoring their work.

4. PREPARE THE ASSESSMENT TO ADMINISTER IN A TRYOUT.

Basically the last two steps are for teachers who are devising their own performance assessment, but reading and knowing what ought to be done can give you a sense of what development processes any published test you select should have gone through.

Now it is time to put all of the parts of the assessment together and to make copies for the students who will take it in the tryouts that will produce the papers you can use to devise the rating scheme in a process described in Chapter 8. The student booklet for many such performance assessments will consist of the following parts:

- Brief, uncomplicated statements to the student about what will be read and what he or she is to write after reading the prompt.

- The prompt: a story, essay, passage, article, or combination of texts to be synthesized—accompanied by appropriate illustrations or "art" if at all possible. In some of the assessments for lower levels, the art is an essential part of the prompt. On assessments for early first grade or kindergarten, for example, *only* the art may appear in the student book, with or with out some key words as captions. The prompt is read to these students by the teacher—often in segments with pauses to let the student respond by adding to the pictures and by captioning them.

- A statement about what to do in the prewriting activity, accompanied by any note-taking forms to assist the student in the activity. (On the early first-grade assessments, there may be no prewriting activity.)

- Many such assessments have lined pages on which the student can write the first draft—in a sense, the equivalent of the blue book so many of us knew in college. For very young students, this section of the assessment can be very important. It may have pictures and supply some text to which the student is to add lines. The student may also be instructed to add things to the picture.

- A statement to the student about what is to be done with the postwriting activity and any accompanying note-recording forms that come with it. (Usually, there is no postwriting activity on very low levels of such assessments.)

- Some assessments contain follow-up activities that are optional for the student, but they are not an essential part of the assessment.

You may decide to make two booklets out of these sections with the second beginning with the prewriting part. That way students can be asked not to mark on the booklet containing the initial instructions to the student, the prompt, and its art so it can be used again in another administration.

The teacher's copy of the assessment must be prepared, too, if it is to be administered by teachers other than those who developed it. It is a good practice, in fact, for you to do this if you can find the time—even if you are the only person who will use it. You will find this copy very helpful later in recalling exactly what was done and in answering questions about the assessment after you have used it to report to different audiences.

The teacher's copy will be essentially the same as the student's, except it will be preceded with a cover sheet with a brief set of directions explaining the decisions you have made: that the assessment can be administered across more than one day; that it should take about two periods; that the teacher is to see that students put their names, their teacher's name, and the name of their schools on the parts of the booklet they will write in; that there will or will not be collaboration; that the teacher is to play an assistive, instruction-like role; that the pre- and postwriting activities are or are not optional. Next, the teacher should be instructed to read through the statement about what will be read and written with the students and to answer any questions they have.

Finally the cover sheet should instruct the teacher to pick up the booklets when the students are finished or if it is necessary to break between periods or school days. The teacher will be cautioned that all loose student notes should have their names on them and be inserted into each student's booklet, which should be collected, then handed out to be finished at the next opportunity.

Somewhere before or right after Part 1 in the teacher booklet, there should be a statement of the rationale for selecting the prompt and writing activity. This statement should be boxed or highlighted in some way to catch the teacher's attention. It need not be long or complex but should tell what the assessment focuses on. After the criteria for rating the results have been developed, this statement can be made to correlate more exactly with them.

Another important addition to the teacher's version of the assessment will be the section with questions or other suggestions for building interest in the activity before the students begin.

5. TRY OUT THE ASSESSMENT WITH AS LARGE A SAMPLE AS POSSIBLE.

If you are developing the assessment by yourself, it will no doubt be given to just your students. If one or two fellow teachers have agreed to try the assessment, it would be a good idea to hold off using their classes until you have done the tryout with yours and have developed the criteria for rating the student responses. (If you are selecting a published assessment, the more the publisher tells you about the tryouts—especially the kinds of students who participated and the number—the more you should place your trust in the product.)

If the assessment is being developed for a school district or a larger geographic system, the tryout should include some classes in different schools with varying socioeconomic areas. Making arrangements to pick up the results of these papers is very important, as they become the heart of the next steps to finish the development of the assessment. These steps are described in Chapter 8.

SUMMARY: A DOZEN GUIDELINES TO CONSTRUCTING/SELECTING USEFUL PERFORMANCE ASSESSMENT

- The assessment should fulfill information needs to learn about the depth of your students' meaning making when reading and writing. If the results of the performance assessment appear to basically reiterate what you can learn from standardized multiple-choice tests, you should challenge its potential to demonstrate how well your students can actually read and apply what they comprehend as writers.

- Your objectives for the test should match your instructional objectives and should guide you in selecting the texts that will be read and the purposes of the writing you seek from the students.

- Make sure that you can articulate your aims for the assessment. Be able to justify and rationalize its cost in time and other expenses in terms of how it can guide and improve your teaching and reporting to particular audiences. Constructing or selecting the test along with fellow teachers would guarantee this.

- Make sure that what the students read and write is as authentic as possible! If it can't be something they would actually read and use in a particular way, be sure, at least, that it is highly interesting for them.

- The types of reading and purposes for reading and writing should vary across time and the administration of different prompts so that they tend to cover the different reasons for reading and writing that your instruction addressed.

- Make sure that the reading prompt fits the kind of writing the students will be doing. Make sure, too, that comprehension and its application promote thinking behaviors such as synthesis, comparison/contrast, and sequential and cause/effect relationships.

- Be sure to build interest in the text and task. One important way to do this is to offer prewriting brainstorming opportunities that the student can use to plan and accelerate the writing required.

- The assessment should work with flexible administration that avoids constraints associated with more traditional testing. It should not matter how long it takes to complete or whom the student talks to or consults with.

- If the type of test you will build or use is the "analytical" type (in which different responses are used to rate reading and writing), be sure that the questions and tasks that promote the responses that will rate reading are as open as possible. This assessment should not be just an extended right-answer test masquerading as a short-essay assessment. The responses should clearly be student-constructed.

- Promote revision of the student-constructed responses as a postwriting activity. This needs to be an activity that will hold the students' interest and not be enforced as drudgery. With prewriting activities, this step can help assure that the test will reflect language use as a process.

- It should provide good guidance to whoever will be rating the student responses. Clear rubrics for scoring and helpful sample or anchor papers should help assure that the ratings given are reasonably reliable.

- Make certain that the rubric and anchor papers that will guide the rating of student responses have been developed along with analysis of an adequate tryout of the instrument—that the anchors are actual papers from those tryouts that have been selected by actual teacher as representative of particular ratings.

CHAPTER EIGHT

DEVELOPING RUBRICS AND ANCHOR PAPERS

"So now what do I do with the results?" you may ask after reading about how to develop and try out performance assessment prompt/writing activity sets. "Do I evaluate them the way I evaluate other student writing? What have I assessed and how do I determine what I have learned?" The answer is that you are but halfway finished in developing or critically examining the reading/writing performance assessment.

After you have developed a performance assessment activity tied to a prompt and have administered it to a sample of students as a tryout, you will need to structure a scoring or rating system. It needs to include (1) rubrics that articulate what each score means and (2) sample, or anchor, papers that demonstrate them. While the information in this chapter relates almost directly to the construction of performance assessments, understanding how rubrics and anchor paper sets are created will also help those who are selecting performance assessments and everyone in using those they create or select.

As in Chapter 7, the emphasis here is on the type of performance assessment arbitrarily labeled *fully integrated* to distinguish it from another type labeled *analytical*. In the fully integrated performance assessment, a prompt is presented with an assigned task that dictates the audience and purpose for writing in response to it. The single student-constructed response is used to rate both the student's reading performance and his or her writing performance. Often it is also used to rate a third and overriding factor called something like *task performance.*

In the *analytical* type of performance assessment, the reading prompt is followed by a series of questions or tasks designed to generate student-constructed responses that will be analyzed as a unit for reading performance only. Then the topic or some other aspect of the prompt is used to generate a response that can be rated for writing performance. The two types are not as different as the need for the two terms implies. The *fully integrated* test is analytical in its rating of student performance, and the *analytical* type integrates reading and writing to a considerable degree.

DEVELOPING A SCORING SYSTEM

The general objectives and the steps for developing scoring systems presented here apply to both types of performance assessment. Seven steps for the developing the system are described after several basic considerations.

LIKE THE PROMPT AND TASK, THE SCORING SYSTEM SHOULD REFLECT YOUR TEACHING

The job of developing a scoring system for your newly constructed assessment is not simple. But like the demands for getting this far, it is a rewarding experience that causes those who undertake it to review what they believe about reading and writing development and about the kinds of thinking involved in constructing meaning with language. Even if your interest is in learning how to select, not construct, the assessment, it is important to judge whether the rating system it offers reflects what you believe about language development.

As you articulate what you would prefer in scoring criteria, you also should be matching them to your curricular and teaching goals, objectives, and emphases. Once again, this process may require fitting what you believe into the structure that has also been used to develop the curriculum guide you are using. This point once again emphasizes the importance for the alignment of assessment with instruction.

THE SYSTEM SHOULD HELP TO ENSURE CONSISTENCY

The criteria that will prevail in evaluating student responses should be applied as consistently as possible from student to student, by different raters, and in different administrations of the same assessment. Even if you are developing or selecting the assessment for only your students, you should be interested in demonstrating that your evaluation of the student responses is systematized and can be rationally explained. That provides a degree of reliability that will complement the validity established by matching the test activity to your instruction and to authentic student needs.

Having constructed an authentic task based on a prompt that your students will find useful and having determined to make your scoring system match your instruction, there are seven steps that can help you make the test reliable. "But what if I am selecting, as opposed to creating, a performance test?" many readers may ask. "What good will considering this sequence of steps do me?"

If you are selecting a performance assessment instrument, you need to examine its scoring or rating system: Is it one you can use easily? Do you understand the criteria it uses to rate responses? Do they emphasize what you would emphasize? Is that true across the

PERFORMANCE ASSESSMENT RESPONSES BELONG IN THE PORTFOLIO!

Before describing the process for developing a system of scoring student responses, a very important point needs to be made. What you have after administering the assessment to your students is a very valuable example of how each student processes language. For this reason, the package—consisting of any prewriting notes, a first draft, postwriting notes, and the final draft—is a perfect inclusion in the students' portfolios.

In really worthwhile performance assessment, the whole activity has been structured like an excellent instructional experience, and you could, if you like, react to the students' work as you react to and evaluate the results of other writing activities. While it is not being recommended here that you stop reading now, even if you were not to follow through with the second half of this development process, the papers you could develop by administering the assessment would be worth the trouble.

All the notes and drafts related to the production of the final draft, which is the only part of the activity that will be evaluated with the scoring system you will be developing, should be added to the portfolio for analysis. They should make a near-perfect model of the type of process-centered sets that reveal how your students process language for a particular application.

Admittedly, the task and text have, in effect, been assigned, but you have attempted to make them as authentic as possible. By comparing them to other process-revealing sets in the portfolio, you may learn something about both what a particular student sees as authentic language use and your handle on what the student finds interesting and involving.

different teachers who will use it in different years? Will it produce reliable ratings across the different times that you use it by yourself? Understanding the steps with which the publisher could have created a reliable scoring system will give you the know-how to make that judgment.

Before discussing the steps involved in constructing the scoring system, however, it is important to consider an important caveat related to both its validity and reliability: The use of the term *system* in this discussion should not suggest to you that student-constructed responses to any performance test can be rated in any absolute way. They are sure to vary a great deal; the strength of the assessment methodology's response to concerns about assessment, in fact, is that it can allow for responses influenced by individual students' backgrounds and interests, as well as their grasp of the task and their reading abilities.

In short, the students' application of the meaning they are able to construct from the reading prompt will be varied, personal, and even unique—much like meaning they make of text in the classroom and outside of school. It cannot be narrowed and controlled as responses to short-answer/right-answer test questions can. Consequently, rating these varied responses is a somewhat subjective job compared to marking those on a multiple-choice standardized test.

But you can seek reliability within reasonable limits. An important goal in developing performance assessments is to limit variance in scoring. A key objective in selecting the prompt and writing activity (constructing the questions on the *analytical* type) has been to direct the student's response to a degree that allows the rater to look for certain expected things. These can be expressed as criteria to be used in scoring, and they should relate directly to the objectives that led the assessment maker to select the prompt and define the activity.

THE SYSTEM SHOULD BE CLEARLY EXPLAINED

The criteria that guide the scorer of your performance assessment should be presented and described as simply and directly as possible. This can be done in a table called a rubric. The *scoring scale,* the number of scores that the rater has to choose from, will determine either the number of columns *or* the number of rows in this table.

A simple rubric for an integrated language performance assessment, for example, might be based on a rating system where the assessment designers have decided to evaluate just *Reading* and *Writing,* using the scale *1–3.* The rubric used in the *Unit Integrated*

General Scoring Rubric
(Abbreviated Version)

READING	3	2	1
Degree of Understanding	Excellent	Fairly good	Minimal
Selection of Information	Relevant	Generally relevant	Parts may be irrelevant
Accuracy of Information	Accurate	Moderately accurate	Inaccurate; misunderstood
WRITING	3	2	1
Accomplishment of Task	Successful	Reasonably successful	Not successful
Organization	Logical, focused, clear	Minor flaws; may lack focus	Confusing; no direction
Development	Well developed, explained, supported	Fairly well developed and explained	Minimally developed
Sentence Structure	Correct; varied	Some errors; limited variety	Many errors; lacks variety
Vocabulary	Clear, precise, expressive	Appropriate; not vivid, precise, or expressive	Limited; unsuitable
Mechanics	Few significant errors	Several errors	Many significant errors

The abbreviated version of the General Scoring Rubric used across the grades in the Unit Integrated Performance Assessment of the HBJ Treasury of Literature reading series is a six-cell table—two dimensions by three possible scores. But note how each of the dimensions, Reading and Writing, consists of key aspects or factors that the scorer should consider in arriving at an overall score for that dimension. The student is given just two ratings: one for Reading and one for Writing.

Performance Assessment of the *HBJ Treasury of Literature* series published by Harcourt Brace is an example of such a rubric, which has just six cells.

The considerations used in arriving at a score might be subfactored and listed in the rubric, but the structure would remind the rater that the response is not to be rated separately on those considerations; rather, it is to be lumped into one overall score for the behavior. This forces some subjective balancing in arriving at a score, but the seemingly simplistic design makes the rater's work both simpler and more reliable.

Additional dimensions or factors to be rated can easily be added to a scheme such as this: For example, a third column or row (depending on the presentation) could be added for "Fulfilling the Task" and the descriptions for the scores added in the cells created.

It can be noted here as well that this model can apply to both types of performance assessment. The single student-constructed response on the fully integrated type can be scored in such a framework; and so can the analytical type for which the different responses used for reading are lumped into a single score.

The expanded version elaborates on this general rubric. The cell that describes a 3 in Writing, for example, demonstrates how the Accomplishment of Task, Organization, Development, Sentence Structure, Vocabulary, and Mechanics can be considered as a single unit in arriving at the single score for Writing. On the student paper which gets a 3:

The response successfully accomplishes the task.
Ideas progress logically; a clear sense of purpose and focus is evident. The response is well developed, with ideas explained and supported through specific details and examples. Sentence structure is correct and varied. Word choice is clear and precise or vivid and expressive. Few significant errors in grammar, usage, and mechanics appear.

A third aid to scorers that can be developed with the assessment is optional, but is very helpful. It consists of two additional papers gathered and scored in the tryout. These have marginal notes of raters' comments keyed to particular places in the papers that the rater noted as strong or weak. Usually, an "Excellent" paper, with the top score in all dimensions, and a much weaker response, with the lowest scores in each dimension, are selected. These marginal notes provide details that explain why raters gave the paper the scores they did, and these comments are connected by a line to words in the response that signal the strength or weakness.

In the latter case, guidelines for each question can be subfactored within the cells where the scores are described. In many such assessments, a student can skip one or more questions and yet score a 3 if the responses to the questions that are answered fully reflect the criteria on which the scoring is based.

Ratings	Behaviors	
	Reading	Writing
3		
2		
1		

Behaviors	Ratings		
	3	2	1
Reading			
Writing			

EXAMPLES OF SCORES IN THE RUBRIC GIVE THE SCORER ESSENTIAL GUIDANCE

Given the rubric, the rater needs still more guidance if performance assessments are to be reliable. An even more useful tool consists of samples (or anchor *papers*) of actual student responses that have been selected to represent each possible rating in the rubric. These *anchors* are drawn from actual student-constructed responses collected during the tryouts. They were awarded the same rating by all or most of the raters participating in the tryout.

Usually, two (but sometimes more) papers with each score on each dimension rated are selected to represent uniquely different responses that have earned the same score. With the six-cell rubric, then, there would be 12 student papers—two for each of the possible three scores for each of the two dimensions. One of the papers representing a 3 for Reading, for example, might reveal that the student can apply most of the important details from the prompt text. Another 3 might not have all of the key details and yet apply those that are used to draw effective inferences. On balance, each of the anchor 3 papers must represent the criteria; however, one 3 may be stronger on one point in the rubric and another may be stronger on another point. It is the balance that must be considered in judging a paper.

An *annotation* should accompany each paper explaining what raters saw in the response that led them to give it a *3, 2,* or *1.* In some collections of anchor papers, a single sample may illustrate two different scores on two different dimensions.

A LOGICAL AND INDUCTIVE DEVELOPMENT OF THE SCORING SYSTEM

It might seem reasonable to you to create your scoring system rather arbitrarily or deductively. You know and can articulate what you value rather clearly, and you feel you can move from that to the selection of the anchor papers. But to do that would be to over-look a prime opportunity to verify—to reiterate—the criteria your experience has recommended with a scientific and inductive process. Not only that, the method suggested here for developing a scoring system for your new assessment is easier to follow.

Even if your task is just to select a performance assessment instrument, reviewing the process that most test constructors follow should help you exercise better judgment.

Creating the scoring system and the aids for raters discussed above begins with the development of *range papers* using the student responses you should have in hand after the tryout, and the process proceeds with the steps listed below:

1. Develop range papers.
2. Decide on scoring scale.
3. Decide on the scoring dimensions.
4. Develop scoring criteria.
5. Select anchor papers.
6. Develop annotations.
7. Modify scoring criteria.

In addition, these steps should lead you to one additional and very important consideration: How will the scores that the system produces be reported to decision makers, parents, and students? Following the description of these steps, this chapter will conclude with a discussion of how the results of the performance assessment can be reported effectively.

1. BEGIN BY SORTING THE RESPONSES TO THE TRYOUT AS "RANGE PAPERS."

Sit down with the student responses from the tryout and evaluate them rather subjectively as you read them. If the system is being developed for schoolwide or district-wide use, several raters should be involved, and each would need copies of the student responses.

Basically all you are doing in this step is creating piles of papers that you feel are "good" or "strong," those that you feel are "poor" or "weak," and those that fall somewhere in the middle. These are, then, groups of *range papers*. As in any such effort, you may have some papers that tempt you to create piles between. While you should be encouraged to keep this development simple and to keep the distinction between the papers in the three piles as clear as possible, it may prove interesting to lay a few papers that create problematic decisions aside temporarily—as long there are not very many of them.

If you are creating a fully integrated assessment, this task may be a bit more complex, but you can do this exercise first to identify strong and weak reading responses and then to examine them as writing efforts. If there is a third dimension, you may need to do this three times. If your test is to be the analytical type, you need only to let exceptionally fresh or clever writing in the reading responses keep you from focusing on the reading criteria or an accurate or inaccurate application of detail from the prompt keep you from focusing on the writing criteria that is of interest to you. (If making that distinction bothers you, you might want to reconsider the type of performance assessment you are creating.)

After each rater involved in this process has created the piles of range papers, he or she should read back through them a pile at a time, asking:

- What is it about the papers in the one range that makes them strong? What do I like in them? What do they have in common?
- What specific things can I point to that make each of the papers in the low range weak?

- Why can't I cleanly put the papers in the middle pile into either the "good" or "weak" pile? What attributes keep them from being "weak"? What short-comings keep them from being "strong"?

As you do this, you may decide to relocate a few papers, and you should go ahead and do this, clarifying for yourself your reasons for doing so. Make some notes about attributes that you find in many of the "strong" papers. Do the same for the weak papers. Note any similarities that you find among the papers in the middle pile. Make sure that these notes are going to be clear and understandable when they grow cold because you will be using them extensively in the next steps of the process.

These kind of notes can be made initially on the papers themselves, and such papers should be saved to integrate with those of other raters and to select papers that can display the marginal notes discussed in the box above as a third kind of rating aid.

Eventually, you should try to synthesize these observations. You should go back over the piles, and on another sheet of paper, note differences among papers in each single pile. These notes may be useful to you as you help decide on the scoring distinctions that will be articulated in the rubric.

Finally, the different raters should bring their still separate piles of papers and notes to a session where they share their results. Particular attention should be given to papers that raters have judged differently. The raters should attempt to articulate their reasons for assigning such a paper to its pile, referring to their notes and rereading the paper—aloud if necessary. Resolving differences should clarify the rubric and the anchor-selection process.

The raters should compare their notes and discuss what they have decided is strong about the pile of best papers, weak about the pile of weakest ones, and better than weak but not quite strong about the ones in the middle pile. When all raters have identified a particular strength, it should be carefully noted on a sheet of paper. It is helpful, too, to identify papers that exemplify the strength, using stick-on tabs or notes and/or highlighters to make the examples easy to find later.

When one or some raters have noted a strength that another or others have not identified, that rater should try to articulate the value involved and it should be discussed. In each case, papers that exemplify the characteristic should be cited and read aloud and discussed. If all raters can agree about the quality, it should be added to the note sheet. A separate list might be kept for qualities or signs of weakness that a few, but not all, raters agree on.

2. NEXT DECIDE ON THE
SCORING SCALE THAT WILL BE USED.

The raters and assessment developers should next discuss the spread of scores that will be used in scoring the student responses to the prompt/writing activity. Will a rater choose between a 1, 2, or 3? Will the scoring scale be *1–4, 1–5,* or *1–6*?

Each scale has advantages and disadvantages. With the wider ranges, there will be more of a challenge to describe what distinguishes one score from the other. Unless the descriptions in the cells of the rubric can make each rating distinct from the others, there will be less likelihood of reliability—of different scorers ranking a paper the same on a particular dimension. Less reliability will mean that those who look to score reports cannot put full faith in them and in the assessment.

The shorter the score range, the less meaningful a score may be in reporting it, so the intended uses of the assessment may have bearing on the scoring scale selected. The assessment developers and raters involved in developing the scoring system have to ask themselves questions such as these:

- Will accountability audiences be able to distinguish effectively between a *1* and a *2*?

- Is a *1–3* scale sensitive enough to support the decision making that may rely on this assessment? Will it force too many students into a category that recommends mandatory extra instruction, summer school, or potential retention?

- Will a *1–5* scale offer teachers any more instructional direction than the *1–3* scale? Will a *2* on *Writing Effectiveness* be more meaningful in terms of suggesting instructional emphasis than a slightly inflated *3*?

- What would distinguish a *3* from a *4* in terms of *Management of Content* or *Completion of Task* on a *1–5* scale? Can we adequately distinguish between the different scores in defining them for raters' use?

- Will a *1–6* scale force us into splintering our dimensions to a point that suggests subskill focus? In looking for ways to distinguish the ratings, will we lose some of the emphasis of a holistic look at student performance?

All of these are good questions, particularly the last set. And there is another consideration that recommends against too wide a rating scale. Remember, you will be multiplying the number of anchor points by the number of dimensions that you will want to have scored. As the next subsection will note, it is not uncommon—or unwise—to consider three dimensions in rating integrated performance assessment responses. With a *1–6* rating scale, a three-dimensional system would require 18 cells—18 descriptions to be studied and considered by raters—a considerable challenge for professional raters and probably an unnecessary burden for many teachers.

Notice, too, in the questions above that there are several references to the rating *dimensions* and how they figure in selecting the scale. It is quite possible that the assessment developers will want to reconsider the scale they have selected as they complete steps 3 and 4 of this process, deciding on the dimensions and developing the criteria as a rubric.

3. PICK SCORING DIMENSIONS THAT EMPHASIZE YOUR PERSPECTIVES ON LANGUAGE.

Although you may have made this decision earlier, you may yet need to confirm the dimensions that you will evaluate and score. Your careful consideration of what led you to arrange examples in creating the range papers may already have suggested the clear perspectives you believe should be rated. If not, they can again figure in your consideration and in any discussions you have with other teachers working on the project.

The dimensions you select should also reflect what you believe about language acquisition, development, and use. The scoring rubric given earlier in this chapter rates only *Reading* and *Writing*, but if you are constructing a fully integrated assessment, you may wish to score some combination of the two that considers the application of what is comprehended from reading in the writing. This kind of consideration tends to focus on the thinking involved in constructing meaning while both reading and writing. It emphasizes the commonalties of constructing meaning with language when both reading and writing; it is, in effect, the prime rationale for trying the fully integrated assessment.

In its Scoring Rubric for the assessment activities in its *Integrated Assessment System: Language Arts Performance Assessment (IAS)*, The Psychological Corporation presents three dimensions: *Response to Reading, Command of Language,* and *Management of Content.* This system scores student responses on a four-point scale, ranging from a low of *1* to a high of *4*, and thus creates 12 cells in the rubric table.

Note that with this third dimension, presented in the rubric between *Response to Reading* and *Command of Language,* the focus of the latter is more on language usage and style: *sentence structure/variety; word choices; grammar/usage/mechanics.* Elements like *organization, focus,* and *development,* which are included in the *Writing* half of the HBJ rubric accompanying its *HBJ Treasury of Literature,* are evaluated in the assessment system from The Psychological Corporation with *accomplishment of task* under the dimension *Management of Content.*

General Scoring Rubric

Response to Reading	Management of Content	Command of Language
amount of information accuracy of information selection of information	organization/focus development accomplishment of task	sentence structure/variety word choices grammar/usage/mechanics
4 The response presents a substantial amount of information from the passage. The information used is accurate and relevant to the task.	The response is clearly organized and focused. The ideas flow logically from beginning to end. In expository responses the main points are elaborated upon or explained through the use of specific details or reasons. In narrative responses the events are well developed. The response successfully fulfills the task.	Sentences are correctly written, and they display variety. Expository responses exhibit clear and precise word choices. In narrative responses word choices are vivid and expressive. Few if any errors in grammar, usage, or mechanics are present.
3 The response contains a moderate amount of information from the passage. Some minor inaccuracies may appear. Some of the information selected may be irrelevant to the task.	The response may contain minor organizational flaws (digressions or repetitions), or the focus may be somewhat unclear. Ideas flow logically through most of the response. The response may not be fully developed or explained. The response reasonably fulfills the task.	Sentences are correctly written but lacking in variety, or there may be a few errors in sentence structure with greater variety. Word choices are appropriate to the response, although they may not be especially vivid, expressive, clear, or precise. There may be some errors in grammar, usage, or mechanics.
2 The response presents a minimal amount of information from the passage. It may contain frequent or serious inaccuracies. Irrelevant information from the passage may outweigh relevant information.	Attempts are made at organization, but the overall plan may be confusing or illogical, and/or the focus may be unclear. Disruptions in the flow of ideas may be frequent and/or serious. The response may be minimally developed or explained. The response may only partially fulfill the task.	There may be several errors in sentence structure, and little variety is demonstrated. Word choices are generally appropriate but limited. There may be several errors in grammar, usage, or mechanics.
1 The response may present no information from the passage, or it may only briefly mention the topic or some key words from the passage. The response may reflect serious misunderstanding of the passage.	There may be little or no evidence of a logical plan or focus. The ideas do not flow logically. The response may not be developed or explained. The response does not fulfill the task.	There may be many errors in sentence structure, with little or no variety. Word choices are limited or unsuitable. There may be many errors in grammar, usage, or mechanics.

NOTE: In the **Response to Reading** dimension, a distinction needs to be made between verbatim *copying* of information from the passage and judiciously selecting passage information to use in the response. The student who responds to the passage by merely copying "wholesale" would receive a 1 in this dimension. In cases of verbatim copying, evaluate only the original writing in the **Management of Content** and **Command of Language** dimensions.

This rubric is from the Integrated Assessment System: Language Arts Performance Assessment, The Psychological Corporation, 1990. It appears in the Scoring Guide that accompanies each prompt/writing activity in the system. It is discussed in the surrounding text.

As in most scoring rubrics, each of the dimensions consists of several factors that are listed in the first row under the dimension headings in the rubric table in the box presented here. *They are not rated separately.* The holistic nature of the assessment is stressed in instructions that tell the rater how to use these factors or features in a "weighing and balancing process."

Within each dimension all three features need to be considered before deciding on the score the student should receive for that dimension. A subtle balancing of the features is necessary. In *Response to Reading,* for example, it is not enough that students cite much information from the passage they read. It is also necessary that the parts they have chosen to include in their writing are relevant to the task. In *Management of Content,* a student might write a splendidly organized, fully developed paper. However, you must also take into consideration whether the student has accomplished the required task. You must be sure that all features in a dimension have been considered and balanced. Then the assigned score will more accurately reflect the student's performance on that dimension.

This customized approach is used in *Indiana Performance Assessments '92,* which combines its attention to the reading/writing/thinking interaction in a third dimension for scoring called *Accomplishment of Task.* In this set of assessments, the factors that describe the three dimensions also are specified to the particular prompt and writing task.

For example, in the assessment called the "Water Problem Essay," which provides students with several texts related to water use and shortage in California, high school students are asked to write recommendations for solving the state's water problem to its Water Commission. The factors describing the three dimensions for this assessment are:

ACCOMPLISHMENT OF TASK

- Organizes an essay that presents a clear and reasonable long-term plan to best solve California's water problem.
- Provides a well-reasoned solution backed by evidence from the text.
- Offers a plan of action that can be implemented by the California Water Commission.
- Adds own background knowledge to effectively support arguments.

WRITING

- Organizes the writing to guide the reader through a unified, holistic essay/plan.
- Uses a variety of sentence structures appropriate for an essay to the Water Commission.
- Uses words that are clear, concise, and reflective.
- Facilitates the reader's understanding by avoiding errors in spelling, punctuation, and grammar.

READING

- Provides a long-term plan that explains its benefits and feasibility.
- Includes material that supports the solution and allows the benefits and costs of various solutions to be weighed.
- Links the solutions to the fundamental causes for California's water problem.
- Discusses accurately important issues such as irrigation, conservation, water rights, and technology.

Notice how the first of the factors in *each* of the dimensions takes a broader perspective that looks at the whole plan, tending to create some deliberate overlap in the dimensions and emphasizing additionally the holistic nature of the evaluative analysis.

This kind of descriptive rubric works well for the analytical type of performance assessment, where reading and writing responses are separate. There is often a separate rubric presentation for each dimension, and a table is not needed. The example shown here is from the *Holt, Rinehart and Winston Integrated Performance Assessment* for grade 7. It shows the rubric guidelines for scoring writing and is customized to the task of writing a story. Accompanying it and similar rubrics for considering cause and effect, writing a bibliography, and writing an evaluation is a general rubric for language conventions.

This response and student-constructed responses to questions about the prompt used to assess reading are rated on a *1–6* scale that runs from "Minimal Evidence of Achievement" through "Exceptional Achievement."

In defining the dimensions that are to be considered by using factors or features, do not pick more than four, or, at the very most, five factors. If you can suggest a holistic description of the dimension with three, so much the better for your scoring system. Reliability across the scorers or raters who will use it will depend on it not being too complex. In the next step of the process, you will need to spell out the distinction between each of these ratings and any just above and below it for the dimensions. If the factors that make them up are too complex of a mix, that will not be a reasonable task.

As you settle on the dimensions that you believe should be scored, keep a guiding checklist like this in mind:

- The dimensions should, in a real sense, add up to and cover what you really believe the meaning-making process of language use is all about.

ASSESSMENT 1: SCORING RUBRIC FOR RHETORICAL EFFECTIVENESS IN STORY

SCORE 1
MINIMAL EVIDENCE OF ACHIEVEMENT
The response is a sketchy, undeveloped story or a loose collection of incidents. The setting is likely to be absent; characters are not developed or named; conflict is not included; and a context has not been established. No sense of pacing is evident. Dialogue, if used, is extremely simplistic.

SCORE 2
LIMITED EVIDENCE OF ACHIEVEMENT
The response is an undeveloped story. The setting is likely to be absent; characters may be named but not developed; and details are lacking. There may be an attempt to use conflict, but it is vague and undefined. There is no sense of pacing.

SCORE 3
SOME EVIDENCE OF ACHIEVEMENT
The writer may introduce the basic narrative elements of setting, character, and conflict, but one of these is likely to be missing. Characters tend to be stereotypic, not well developed, and lacking in motivation for their actions. Relationships among characters are vague. There may be shifts in point of view and problems with pacing.

SCORE 4
ADEQUATE ACHIEVEMENT
The writer places the action of the story in a meaningful context. The elements of setting, character,

and conflict are somewhat developed. Characters are well developed, believable, and motivated. A single point of view is maintained throughout the story with only brief lapses. Dialogue is usually present but not used as effectively as in papers at the higher achievement levels.

SCORE 5
COMMENDABLE ACHIEVEMENT
The action of the story is placed in a meaningful context. The elements of setting, character, and conflict are firmly established. Characters are well developed through the use of several strategies. Dialogue is used effectively and integrated into the flow of the story. Sensory details help readers visualize the story.

SCORE 6
EXCEPTIONAL ACHIEVEMENT
The response represents a compelling and engaging story that captures the interest of the reader. Setting, character, and conflict are firmly established. Characters are well developed, more complex, and less stereotypic than those found in responses at lower achievement levels. The writer uses a variety of strategies to develop characters. A single point of view is established and maintained throughout the story. Pacing is skillfully controlled.

In this grade 7 test activity designed for Holt, Rinehart and Winston's Integrated Performance Assessment, 1997, children are asked to write a story with a main character who shows courage. There are various opportunities to incorporate prewriting activities, including making think-along notes on the story read, guided note-making, classmate interaction, and practice expressing key ideas. Only the final response, however, is used to rate the student on writing, guided by these rubrics.

- The factors under each dimension should add up to the dimension you have in mind.
- While factors in the dimensions may tend to overlap, they should otherwise be cleanly distinguished perspectives that you can explain in brief written descriptions.
- They, and their factors, should not be so numerous as to fragment an intended emphasis in performance assessment on holistic language/thinking behavior.
- They should accommodate a variety of text types and writing activities that reflect what your students actually do and need to do with reading and writing.

Remember, you can go back to the *range papers* that helped you decide on dimensions at any time for clues about what makes good, average, and weak papers.

You will also note how the factors, which must be rather subjectively summed in arriving at a single score for the dimension they help describe, will dictate the criteria descriptions in a good rubric. This kind of parallelism links the selection of dimensions to the clarification of criteria, setting the assessment developer naturally to the next step in developing the scoring system.

4. DEVELOP THE CRITERIA FOR SCORING AS A RUBRIC.

If you have selected your dimensions thoughtfully and have defined them with several factors that tend to describe them when summed holistically, you are well on your way to developing the criteria that you will present in your rubric. The rubric must describe each number in the rating scale under each dimension in a way that distinguishes it from the score number above and the one below.

It tends to help at this point to have in mind some general terms for the numbers across the rating scale, even though you will probably not use them in the descriptions. For example, in a 1–3 scale, a 3 might be "good-to-excellent," a 2 might be "average," and a 3 might be "weak" or "in need of special instructional attention." In a 1–4 scale, as in the *Integrated Assessment System,* you might think of a 4 as "excellent" or "elaborated," as the *Scoring Guide* suggests, a 3 as "adequate," a 2 as "minimal," and a 1 as "unacceptable" performance. Or you might decide to label them *4 = excellent; 3 = good, but room for improvement; 2 = acceptable;* and *1 = in obvious need for improvement.*

It is up to you or the group of educators you are working with in developing the scoring system to determine how you are going to use the assessment results. This will be the most significant factor in determining the labels you use. You are going to be thinking of them as ratings in describing the factors across your rubric, so it is important that you, and everyone you may be working with, be consistent in how they are applied in writing the descriptive definitions.

Next, take your dimensions one at a time and consider the factors under them one at a time—in terms of the rating scale you have decided to use. For example, with a 1–4 scale:

- Begin in the upper left-hand corner of your rubric and ask yourself: What would a "perfect," "good," or "exceptional" paper have to get the top score in regard to this factor or feature? In terms of this factor, what cues a rater that a paper is a 4?

- What would a response lack in regard to this feature to be "less than perfect" (just "good" or "quite adequate") (a 3)? What would distinguish it from a 2 and signify that it is significantly better than just "average" or "adequate"?

- Considering just this factor, what makes a response "adequate"—a 2? What would an adequate or average response lack to keep it from being "good"?

- What makes a response "inadequate"—a 1—in regard to this factor? What would need to be added to it, in terms of this factor, to make it a 2?

Express your answers to these questions in writing, as clearly and succinctly as possible. This whole process is repeated for the other dimension(s). Remember, each cell of your rubric should tell why a response gets that score when considering each of the factors that make up the dimension. When you are finished, you will have the draft of a rubric describing the scoring distinctions you think are important—across dimensions of reading/writing performance and on a scale from unacceptable to strong. It should look a great deal like the rubrics shown above in boxes with the other steps.

If, in describing the aspects of a paper that would be rated with a certain scale number, you are suddenly tempted to add a factor or feature, you should rethink the factors for that dimension. The one you are tempted to add should be added in the cells for the other scores in that same dimension, or perhaps one of the factors needs renaming.

Note that in the Expanded Version of the General Scoring Rubric for the *Integrated Performance Assessment* with the *HBJ Treasury of Literature* the same factors are considered across all score levels. Note how the distinctions are made in this rubric between the degree of *understanding* to distinguish the scores.

This kind of parallelism structures the consideration of all factors in the description in the score cells. It is essential in a rubric, and most often, it is what distinguishes a good and successful rubric from a somewhat confusing one that does not generate reliability (similar scores) across different raters. You cannot expect raters who use your system to shift conceptual gears as they decide which rating to give a student response.

Notice in the General Scoring Rubric from the *Integrated Assessment System* presented here that the discussion of what distinguishes the dimension *Management of Content* is parallel across the four possible scores in considering the three factors: *organization/focus, development,* and *accomplishment of task.*

Consideration of how a student responds to these factors is handled with parallel terms/concepts/considerations:

- From an organization that is "clearly organized" (a *4*), to "minor organizational flaws (digressions or repetitions)" (a *3*), through "attempts are made at organization" (a *2*), to "little or no evidence of logical plan" (a *1*).
- From a response that is "well developed" (*4*), to "not . . . fully developed" (*3*), through "minimally developed" (*2*), to "not developed" (*1*).
- From *Accomplishment of Task* that is "successfully fulfill[ed]" (*4*), to "reasonably fulfill[ed]" (*3*), through "partially fulfill[ed]" (*2*), to "not fulfill[ed]" (*1*).

Again these are not actually scored separately but subjectively summed for a single *Management of Content* score.

You may be concerned about the use of terms such as *partially fulfilled* or *minimally developed,* since these terms do not suggest specific criteria. What, you may wonder, does *partially fulfilled* mean? The use of anchor papers is what makes the criteria specific. Annotations that accompany the anchor papers provide a discussion as to just how the criteria are demonstrated in the anchor paper.

A note added to the *Integrated Assessment System* suggests an interesting aspect of score system development. It arose in the development of that series of assessments. It became important in discussing how *Response to Reading* would be scored, to distinguish between responses that included a great many details from the prompt through verbatim or "wholesale" copying from the passage, which is to be rated low, and "judicious selection" of details.

The customized questions/considerations in each series are quite useful in guiding the scorer. In responding to *Baking Day,* a section of Jean Van Leeuwen's *Tales of Oliver Pig,* a third-grade assessment in the *Integrated Assessment System,* for example, the student is asked to write directions for baking cookies based on the description of what Oliver and his mother do in the story and on a list of ingredients that is supplied. In the *Scoring Guide,* the following questions help the scorer apply the descriptions in the general rubric to this particular assessment prompt and activity. For *Management of Content,* the scorer is advised to consider the following questions:

- Is there a title, heading, or introduction that indicates what the directions are for?
- Is there a set of directions for making cookies?
- Are the directions complete?
- Are the directions in logical order?
- Are the steps numbered or introduced with transition words such as "then," "next," and "last"?
- Does the student show control over the writing—does it have a sense of purpose and direction?

In a grade 2 prompt about a stray cat who comes to stay with a family that already has a pet cat not too eager to share its territory, the scorer is advised to consider the following questions in selecting a score for *Response to Reading:*

General Scoring Rubric (Expanded Version)	
Reading	**Writing**
Degree of Understanding Selection of Information Accuracy of Information	Accomplishment of Task Organization Development Sentence Structure Vocabulary Mechanics
3 The response indicates an excellent understanding of ideas in the passage. It is apparent that ideas have been interpreted in the light of the student's prior knowledge and experience. Information selected from the passage is accurate and clearly related to the purposes for reading and writing.	The response successfully accomplishes the task. Ideas progress logically; a clear sense of purpose and focus is evident. The response is well developed, with ideas explained and supported through specific details and examples. Sentence structure is correct and varied. Word choice is clear and precise or vivid and expressive. Few significant errors in grammar, usage, and mechanics appear.
2 The response indicates a fairly good understanding of ideas in the passage. Interpretation of ideas may be only on a literal level, with little evidence that the student has used prior knowledge and experience. Information selected from the passage is generally related to the purposes for reading and writing, but some irrelevant information may also appear, and there may be minor inaccuracies.	The response is reasonably successful in accomplishing the task. Ideas progress logically, but may lack focus; minor flaws in organization may appear. The response may not be fully developed or explained. A few errors in sentence structure may appear; structure may show little variety. Word choice is appropriate but not vivid, precise, or expressive. Several errors in grammar, usage, and mechanics may appear.
1 The response indicates only minimal understanding, or serious misunderstanding, of the ideas in the passage. There is no evidence that the student has used prior knowledge and experience to interpret ideas. Information selected from the passage may be unrelated to the purposes for reading and writing. Frequent inaccuracies may appear.	The response fails to successfully accomplish the task, or it addresses the task in a severely limited way. Ideas are unclear or confusing; no sense of direction is apparent in the writing. The response is minimally developed. Sentence structure is flawed and lacks variety. Word choice is limited or unsuitable. Many significant errors in grammar, usage, and mechanics appear and interfere with meaning.

This rubric guides the scorers of a prompt/activity in the Indiana Performance Assessments '92.

- Are the characters accurately identified by name?
- Are references made to events in the story? Is an understanding of the problem reflected?
- Do details relate to the proper time and place for the story (e.g., awareness that it is winter; references to the glass door and/or the field by the house)?
- Do the characters behave in a way that is consistent with the passage (e.g., Does Andy [the family cat] show negative feelings toward the white cat? Are the parents concerned and helpful)?

You can, if you like, prepare and present only a set of criteria customized to the particular text and writing task in an assessment. The rubric for *Accomplishment of Task* in the *Water Problem Essay* assessment of *Indiana Performance Assessments '92* is a good example. Note that this system does not present the rubric as a single table, but rather features the dimensions one at a time.

It is difficult to describe your scoring criteria too carefully. The descriptions that appear in your rubric should be descriptions that:

- Cover each of the factors that make up the dimension under or beside which the cell appears.
- Use parallel or uniform terms across the score scale and within each factor.
- Clearly distinguish that rating for that dimension and factor from the next higher and/or lower rating, if there is one.
- Are clear and as simple and precise as the above objectives will allow.

In short, if some teacher who has not been involved in either the development of the activity or the scoring system administers the assessment and sits down to score the results, s/he should be able to relate all the papers resulting from the administration to a particular score for each dimension without confusion, a lack of confidence, or unnecessary concern or use of valuable time.

Equally important, when the assessment is reported to different audiences, it will be clear what aspects or dimensions of performance the students were scored on and how those scores were determined.

The confidence with which teachers and other raters should be able to use your criteria should help assure that different raters will give the same paper the same—or nearly the same—score; and this reliability should give the audiences interested in accountability some confidence in the assessment because it appears to be constructed to produce reliable results.

5. SELECT SAMPLE PAPERS FOR EACH CELL IN THE RUBRIC AS "ANCHORS."

With the criteria you have constructed before you, go through the papers collected from the tryout and select examples to match each of the cells on the rubric. These papers will serve as anchors for future scorers. If you have been developing the scoring system as a team, each member should do this selection separately at first. Then you should get together and compare and discuss results. In the end, you should try to have at least two good examples of each score for each dimension in the scoring system.

These anchor papers should not be rated "best" and "second best," but rather it would be a good idea if they were somewhat different. For example, two papers are both "excellent" or "good" in terms of all the factors considered in evaluating *Writing* in the rubric, but one of them is exceptionally original and "fresh" while it is only "good" on mechanics, including a few minor errors. The other does not have a usage, spelling, or punctuation error in it; its organization is very clearly logical, and its sentences are varied and exceptionally readable. There is not much in it that is creative. The summing of the parts on the rubric led all raters to score each of these papers 4 on *Writing*. Together the two anchor examples give raters of future responses on the assessment an excellent idea of what *4* papers can be on that dimension.

In selecting anchor papers, you should not pick the two papers that developers feel are the very best in terms of a particular dimension as your anchors for *4s* or the two weakest examples for *1s*. One approach to selection is to attempt to pick two *mid-range* samples for each cell; another is to pick two that represent a *bracket range*—a very strong 3 and a 3 that is not as strong.

Even if the assessment developers think that one of the two papers selected with the same score is better than the other overall, this should not be indicated to those who will use the papers as a guide in scoring. In distinguishing between the two samples it will be helpful to label the papers in this fashion: "Writing 4a" and "Writing 4b," "Writing 1a" and "Writing 1b"; but the one the developers feel is better is not necessarily the *a* paper. In the instructions to the scorers, the point is made that the letters do *not* signify rank in any way.

If you are developing the assessment on your own, you may not have two examples for each cell in your rubric, but for school or district assessments, you should end up with 24 anchor papers for a 12–cell rubric.

As you discuss and select these examples, you may discover things about your criteria that are not as clear as you would like; often it is a simple matter of copyediting the

Examples of actual anchor papers from three different test series appear with the following discussion of Step 6— writing annotations for the anchor papers.

descriptions. Whatever you learn from this step that reflects on Step 4, make careful notes to use in Step 7: *Modify scoring criteria.*

When you are finished with the anchor papers, they should be bound together for scorers to refer to in applying the scoring criteria in the future. If the assessment is to be used across a school or district, you will, of course, need to arrange to copy these papers.

6. DEVELOP ANNOTATIONS TO DESCRIBE THE ANCHOR PAPERS.

Before the anchor papers are copied and bound, however, it is important that you develop annotations for them. Perhaps because the development of performance assessment has

Southern California is in need of water extremely bad. Something needs to be done quickly and it will last in the long run. California's population is expected to swell from 30.3 million to 39 million people in 18 years. The main problem is that ¾ of the population lives south of Sacramento and about ¾ of the rain falls north of Sacramento. A few ways have been devised to help this problem. One is desalting water from the Pacific ocean. Another way is to build a pipeline thousands of miles long from Alaska to California. The last way is transporting icebergs from Antarctica to California.

Desalting the water extracted from the Pacific Ocean seems like a good way to help this problem. There is an almost unlimited supply of water in the ocean. They can build plants to desalt the water. However, desalination plants have operated in Middle Eastern countries and in Florida. These plants use a lot of energy and are very expensive. The cost would range from $60 to $120 billion for the building and running the plants and water would cost $1900 per acre-foot. A couple of places have already begun to use this method. Santa Barbara is one of these places. The cities' two main reservoirs are only

Accomplishment Of Task 3 (Paper 3B)

Though not specifically stated, the plan provides for long and short term solutions. A combination of desalination plants and a water pipeline would provide "water now and for years from now," explains the writer. The plan is confused by unrefuted criticisms of the water pipeline idea followed by its recommendation. Some weak reasoning is evident ("bring in a lot of unnecessary water."). However, some clear inferences are also made; "slow[ing] down the flow from disaltation plants" once the pipeline is complete will save costs, for example. What elevates this essay above a two is the overall support for the plan, particularly for desalination plants.

twelve to fourteen percent full. Officials say that construction will begin on these plants by midsummer.

Another way is to build a pipeline from Alaska to California. The idea was proposed by Robert Finch and CWPNA (Citizens for Water and Power in North America Inc.) was to dam three rivers in Alaska and Alaska's Yukon Territory, and direct water through a vast chain of reservoirs, dams, and trenches into the largest water catchment ever attempted — a 500 mile long reservoir. This project will take about thirty years to complete, which is one reason why this is not such a good idea. Another reason this is not such a good idea is because it will cost 300,000 million dollars to build. The people of California would have to put up with the lack of water for longer than they would have to with another way.

The last idea is to transport icebergs by three tugboats from Antarctica to California. One reason I don't like this idea is because it would be a multibillion dollar plan. Another reason is it would bring in a lot of unnecessary water. It would bring in about 300 billion gallons of water a year.

If they would build just one pipeline and use the disaltation method to a slightly less amount than planned now, then they would have water now and for years from now. For the time being, they could use the disaltation method until the pipeline would be finished. Then in 30 years they could slow down the water flow from the disaltation plants and use the pipeline to get the needed water for less.

Score of 4: Model Paper RR–4B

Although this response is not quite as complete as Model Paper RR–4A, a substantial amount of accurate information about Amelia's problems is presented, and the information is related to the task. One of Amelia's problems (getting bossed around) is not identified. However, specific details from the poem are included when discussing the other problems (e.g., the student knows that Amelia has had a falling out with her friends and knows that she is bored because she doesn't do her homework or read books). Again, comprehension of general situations described in the poem is demonstrated.

> Dear Amelia,
> I heard about all your problems. I thought I'd write you and give you some advice. First of all, you should go to your friends and apologize. And also I heard about you being so bored. You should do your homework at home after school. And when your at school, do your work and read a book. And if you feel too bored to do that, talk to your teacher. And also, I heard about you being tired. You should try to exercise and eat right and run more. And also, you should try harder at playing the horn and try to follow the rules at being an athlete and put in more time at skating and dancing.
>
> Charlie

taken a fair amount of time to this point, this task is often sloughed off, seriously limiting the value of the anchor papers.

Annotations are a very important part of the scoring system and the complete assistance package you should provide future scorers, so take the time to develop them as carefully as you can! Simply described, they are brief explanations of the practical application of the criteria rubric to student-produced responses to the assessment prompt/writing activity combination.

To write good annotations, take each rubric paper and using the description in the cell for the dimension and score it represents, explain—factor by factor—the considerations made in rating it as it was rated. The annotation should explain why a *4* and not a *3* was given in *Thinking/Response to Task;* why a response received a *2* instead of a *3* or a *1*. These kinds of metacognitive comparisons and revelations are extremely valuable to future raters and will help ensure that the scoring system you are creating supports a reliable assessment—one that different raters can be expected to use to come up with the same scores on the same papers!

Do not shortchange the factors in your rubric in analyzing how the score was selected. It is a good idea to discuss them in the same order that they appear in the rubric and to use the same evaluative terms used in the rubric. But don't let the analysis in the annotation go at that. Weak annotations often just repeat a few key phrases that cover in order each of the factors for a dimension in the rubric.

Some good annotations may not follow the rubric line by line, however, but may indicate how they came into play as the rater examined a particular paper selected for an anchor. This may result because the actual analysis of the paper has, by interrelating the factors, shifted their order.

Discussion of factors in strong, useful annotations are expanded by explanations that tell *why* the organization was judged weak or strong. Even if one factor has figured less than might be expected in the scoring (because the strength of the paper in regard to other factors more than compensates) the annotation should mention that fact and tell what was strong about the overriding factors. *Above all, a strong annotation will point out parts, phrases, and details in the paper that exemplify and support the evaluations that determined the score!*

A few examples of annotations on actual assessments may help stress how they can be helpful and why they are important.

Water Problem Essay: *Indiana Performance Assessments '92*—Accomplishment of Task: Write a recommendation to the California Water Commission describing a long-term solution to the state's water problem.

The anchor paper reproduced here was scored as a *3* (out of *4*) and was annotated as shown. The responses were rated guided by the rubric, which appears on page 265.

What's Up, Amelia? *Integrated Assessment System, Grade 4*—Response to Read-

The annotation shown at the top of page 1 of this anchor paper reads: This child's story has a beginning, a middle, and an end. Ideas are expressed in complete sentences that are semantically and syntactically acceptable. The spelling is almost entirely conventional, and the child has even attempted to include dialogue.

One day Panda met a cat. The cat said, "You look funny! You don't have a tail." So Panda made a tail a put it on.

Then Panda saw a dog. The dog said, "You look funny! You don't have ears." So Panda made some ears and put it on.

Then Panda saw a Panda friend. The Panda friend said, "You look funny! You are a funny Panda." So Pand took off his tail and ears. He was so happ.

ing: Students read a 70–line poem about a girl who feels mighty sorry for herself because she feels that she is lonely, bored, bossed around, tired, and not successful at different things she tries. The narrative reveals that she is much to blame for each problem. Students are asked to write to Amelia with good advice. The responses are rated using the rubric presented on page 260.

The anchor paper was scored a *4* and appears in the *Scoring Guide* with the annotation shown.

You Look Funny! by Joy Kim; illustrated by Patti Boyd. In HBJ Treasury of Literature Unit Integrated Performance Assessment, Grade 4—Writing: After reading a story about a panda who meets other animals that think he looks funny and tell him so, students are asked to extend the story about other animals the panda might meet and about what he might do to try not to "look funny."

The anchor paper shown appears in the Teacher's Edition of the assessments with a score of *3* (out of *3*). The caption repeats the annotation appearing on the first page.

Again, this activity of annotating the anchor papers may lead to considerations and discussions about revising the criteria, and if so, careful notes should be made about the possible change so the notes can be used in Step 7.

7. MODIFY YOUR CRITERIA IF NECESSARY.

As you have worked with your assessment prompt/writing activity combination to develop the scoring system for it, you have given it continued close scrutiny. In picking anchor papers and annotating them, you may have decided to change some of the criteria in your scoring rubric. It may be as simple as clarifying descriptions, or it could involve combining, eliminating, or adding factors. Before you finalize your assessment for reproduction or a second tryout, now is the time to polish the criteria. You will need to check your rubric and annotations carefully to be sure that all changes are properly reflected.

This may not be the last time you adjust this assessment and its scoring system. After using it again, after reporting results—especially to your students—you may have some substantive changes to make. But even understanding this possibility, you have every right to take some satisfaction in your effort to create a reading and writing assessment that is authentic, compatible with current theory about the way that language is acquired and used, and can be meaningful to numerous audiences, including those basically interested in accountability.

REPORTING THE RESULTS OF THE PERFORMANCE ASSESSMENT

Chapter 6, "Solving the Assessment Puzzle," discusses in some detail the emerging and vital role performance assessment can play in the whole assessment picture—along with portfolio assessment and standardized testing.

There are many advantages to carefully developed integrated reading/writing performance assessments when it comes to reporting. It is, as the chart on page 195 in Chapter 6 shows, the one kind of language development assessment that links all the major audiences: students and teachers, parents, and educational decision makers. This is so because good performance assessment incorporates the kind of reading that students enjoy and are apt to do in and outside of school and because it applies the meaning constructed while reading in an equally authentic writing activity. It also assures a reasonable amount of reliability to go along with this validity.

THE RESULTS OF PERFORMANCE ASSESSMENT SHOULD BE DISCUSSED WITH STUDENTS

The reading/writing performance assessment is of high instructional value, and it is, therefore, of genuine interest and value to the teacher and the student. First of all, it is as valid a reflection of the student's use of language as we have been able to get in a relatively controlled situation. The student is directed to apply the meaning comprehended from reading as s/he constructs relevant but new meaning in a written response. Just as all real language use does, the experience invites and profits from the incorporation of individual student backgrounds and interests.

This aspect of performance assessment is a refreshing answer to the unresolved concern about the influence of background and the attempt to eliminate it when constructing standardized tests. At last it is reasonable to acknowledge that it is impossible to eliminate background and experiential impacts on assessment results. The more we attempt it, the more divorced from real student experience—the less authentic—the testing experience becomes.

In its attempt to be as real a reading and writing experience as possible, the performance assessment acknowledges and even courts the impact that background may have in individualizing the student's response. If it affects the results, it is because some students are more open and adept at incorporating their backgrounds into what they read and at articulating them when they write. It follows that they are incorporating what they are reading as a part of that background and are shaping it in some way within their structure of knowledge as they write and articulate the combination. That is what we believe reading and writing to be about; so it ought to be a reasonable thing to reveal in assessment.

THE OBVIOUS INSTRUCTIONAL VALUE OF PERFORMANCE ASSESSMENT

Performance assessment is a valuable learning experience. The incorporation of individualized reactions to what is read and used in writing as a part of assessment reinforces the assessment makers' attempts to construct a reading/writing experience that will seem real and interesting to most students. That involvement makes the students' performance an appealing and convincing focus for self-analysis, so what the student writes during the assessment belongs in the student's portfolio with the other papers that are being collected and analyzed.

The performance assessment is an effective learning tool for at least three other major reasons:

- Good language performance assessment should help the student focus on particular purposes and audiences when writing, and this is, increasingly, being recognized as a key goal for assuring effective use of language. Scoring criteria that are framed with a dimension or at least a key factor related to task performance give the student a chance to see what a rater thinks about his or her attempt to meet an audience's particular needs and to fulfill a targeted and articulated purpose for both reading and writing. Coupled to self-analysis, this can be very helpful to the student in thinking about what s/he needs to do to become a more effective reader and writer.

- If you are using the prewriting and postwriting activities provided with a performance assessment, you ensure that the student is modeling the kind of *process* that we now believe is at the heart of meaning construction from reading and writing. Used together, the notes and drafts that include the final response on the assessment allow the student to analyze the thought processes that were involved as s/he read and wrote. The set of papers is also an ideal opportunity for the teacher to analyze this process and to discuss it with the student.

- If the criteria for scoring have been carefully selected, thought out, and articulated, they make a good checklist to suggest to students criteria they may wish to incorporate into their self-assessment. When discussing the performance assessment results with your students, have the rubric or rubrics available to both of you so that you and the student can consult the factors that make up dimensions scored and the descriptions of what constitutes strong responses.

THE VALUABLE REACTION OF STUDENTS TO THE TEST   Both the teacher and the student have a clear and vested interest in the results of performance assessment, as other audiences will view them. For this reason, the student has a right to know how raters feel s/he has done on the assessment and what it may report to other audiences.

It is a good idea to go over performance assessment results with a student during conference time, one-on-one, if possible. This should be a time for encouraging student responses to the assessment itself and to the rater's evaluation of it. Begin with questions like these:

- Did you like this story? Did you like reading about . . . ? Why or why not?

- Do you ever write anything like this? Did you like writing this more than some other things you write?

- Do you think someone could follow the directions you wrote? Do you think your friends would like the ending to the story you wrote?

- Did you understand what you were supposed to do? What did you think you were supposed to do?

- The rater thinks you did not use as many details from the story as you could have used. What do you think about that?

The object of this interaction is to listen carefully to any genuine reactions the student has to the test and the assessment. The student has the opportunity to know himself or herself better than anyone else and may have some insight that could have significant bearing on the dimension scored on a particular reading/writing activity.

Student responses to an assessment may reveal ambiguities in the directions, possible interpretations of the text, or writing tasks that have escaped the assessment and score system developers, or a prompt/writing activity that is considerably less authentic than the assessment designers assumed it would be.

The potential to learn from this kind of exchange with students about their performance on the assessment is so promising, in fact, that you may wish to build it into the assessment development process—between Steps 6 and 7—so that the criteria for scoring can be modified on the basis of what you learn. A negative reaction from a number of students to the text or writing task may indicate the need to revise the assessment.

You may decide in developing future assessments to give the students a chance to respond to the experience right after they complete the task during tryouts. How much did they enjoy it? How important do they think it would be to read or write what they were asked to read and write on the test?

Finally, it may be that some students will, in effect, challenge the scores assigned to their efforts by the raters. In such a case, you have the opportunity to invite the student to look through his or her portfolio to select examples of reactions to reading and/or writing that might be shown to someone who looks also at the performance assessment results. This use of the portfolio as a backup to the performance assessment and to other assessment results is discussed in both Chapter 6 and below.

The importance of sharing assessment information with parents is discussed in more detail in Chapter 6.

PERFORMANCE ASSESSMENT RESULTS SHOULD BE SHARED WITH PARENTS

Reading/writing performance assessment results should definitely be made available to parents. The appropriateness of the prompt and the authenticity of the task should be easy for parents to relate to. Often, in fact, they express appreciation that their children are being evaluated on performance more closely related to the ways they use reading and writing both in and outside of school. This can be considerably easier for a parent to digest than a group of scores that must be interpreted in percentiles, stanines, and the like.

In discussing the student's performance assessment scores with his or her parents, give the parents a copy of the rubric if possible and explain how the factors under the dimensions are used in a somewhat subjective way to define and add up to the dimension scored.

Just as you do when discussing performance assessment results with the students, listen carefully to the parents for indications of their opinion of how real or authentic the assessment experience was, experiences they report that support or seem to contradict the results, and challenges—direct, couched, or otherwise veiled—of the scores. The latter can and should be examined in the light of additional samples of the student's work, as discussed in the final subsection below.

DECISION MAKERS SHOULD BE INTERESTED IN THE RESULTS

Educational decision makers and all audiences interested in educational accountability should find the results of reading/writing performance assessments of significant interest. A key purpose of developing such an assessment system, after all, has been to make the kind of analysis that performance assessment permits more feasible and credible to such audiences.

That has been the major reason for developing the prompt and writing activity so carefully. The object has been to contend that the assessment reflects what theorists and educational experts have learned and explained about language acquisition and use. It has been equally important that your assessment reflects the goals of your curriculum, and in trying to accomplish both of these goals, you have been able to assess the curriculum to see how well it reflects the best theory and understanding of why people read and write and of how they learn to do so effectively.

Reporting assessment results to audiences interested in accountability is also discussed in detail in Chapter 6.

Most audiences interested in educational accountability are interested in how reliable a test is. This includes the people in school administration, on task forces, on school boards, and in legislative bodies—people who must make decisions about our schools. It includes critics of our schools. In a broad sense, this group of people interested in accountability expands—through the media—to the taxpayers and population at large.

Very few of those persons understand exactly what assessment reliability is, and that is understandable; it is a somewhat technical term. What they do appreciate is that when experts who do understand the term consider a test to be reliable, it probably can be trusted because it has been developed in a controlled, scientific way. That is what most people tend to believe about standardized, norm-referenced tests; and they have come to extend that confidence to many criterion-referenced tests. The assumed validity of many criterion-referenced tests that the public puts stock in comes chiefly from the fact that the items on them have been selected by a committee of teachers or other educational specialists who are believed to be representative of the educational profession.

The approach that has been suggested in this book for developing performance tests is at least equivalent to the care with which most criterion-referenced, right-answer tests have been developed. Experience suggests that administrators, legislators, and members of the press are equally willing to accept the credibility of performance tests once they get a sense of the system used to develop them.

But most individuals in these audiences are no more willing to absorb the details of the whole process than they are to sit down with hundreds of student portfolios to analyze them and then to synthesize results. It is up to the developers of performance tests to explain the system they have used in a palatable and succinct way, and to back this up with a detailed, but highly readable, explanation of the procedures.

Basically, what most of the accountability audience and the decision makers will be highly interested in knowing is that:

- What gets rated strong, weak, or adequate would always be rated that way— no matter who is doing the rating, who the test takers are, or when the test is administered.

- Many teachers were involved in the process of developing the assessments.
- The assessment's contents have been carefully correlated to the curriculum.
- The assessment reflects our best current knowledge and understanding of how children develop as effective readers and writers.
- The assessment has gone through relatively extensive tryout and revision stages.

It is worth noting, and encouraging as well, that some of the points just reviewed refer to the validity of the test as well as to its reliability. These audiences will be interested in the assessment's authenticity—although they will not be inclined to call it that or to refer to it as validity. They will use words like *practical, sensible,* and *useful.* What will impress a group of journalists who specialize in covering schools, a group of businessmen who are concerned about our schools, or even a group of professors worried about whether the schools are properly preparing the students they will someday teach is the fact that performance assessment has students reading texts that they encounter in school and outside the classroom and asks the students to write something that people might write in real-life situations. Nor are such audiences insensitive to the kinds of thinking involved in the meaning-constructing activities on assessment tests.

One of the great surprises across the United States has been how accepting these audiences have been of attempts to add performance assessment to the scheme of sources that produce the information they need. Administrators and legislatures, for example, have not demanded that scales of *1–4* be somehow translated into percentages or letter-grade ranges that are more familiar to them. They appear ready and eager to examine student performance—and at the same time, school performance—on the basis of reading/writing tasks that appeal because they make a great deal of sense and are evaluated in holistic ways that relate to the kinds of thinking that everyone seems to value.

So the message to educators who are reporting the scores of students on performance assessments is quite simple. While explaining the results and what the scores mean, they should reveal the actual contents and prompt/writing task combinations that are representative of the test. If they have been done well, their appeal is almost guaranteed. These are the kinds of remarks that this kind of reporting can generate:

- "This is great! These are the kinds of things I want to be sure our kids can do. Why haven't tests focused on this before?"
- "I'm relieved. I had been led to believe that students were incapable of this kind of thinking. I'm eager to see how ours do on this assessment."

In reporting to decision makers and similar audiences, be sure to reveal, too, examples of student responses—not just the best ones, but indications of other degrees of performance: students whose work is adequate or good but that can be strengthened by using the factors on the rubric as goals or objectives and students whose responses indicate that they need careful attention and instruction. This approach is apt to generate comments like these:

- "I had no idea that third-graders were capable of this kind of work. The thinking and creativity here is encouraging."
- "I wish the papers were error-free and I wonder how we can emphasize spelling and grammar more with these tests, but I have to admit—the papers that are rated average and above get their points across effectively."

If you want to take advantage of the persuasive powers of the assessment you have been involved in developing, prepare a package that explains performance assessment and the way student responses are scored, being sure to include examples of the tests and samples of typical student response papers. Such a package might include a list of the kinds of texts and of writing or the writing purposes on the test.

Members of a team developing such tests can be ready to make presentations to special groups who express interest. A school or district adopting performance testing should put together a volunteer panel of teachers familiar with the assessment and its development to make short presentations before professional and civic groups, stressing the nature of the tasks required of the students and introducing briefly written descriptions of the development process.

Of course, all of this does not guarantee that your students will look good to accountability audiences on the assessment you develop. That will depend on their performance, which must be scored and reported objectively. Should they not perform to the satisfaction of audiences you are reporting to, there is one consolation: The resulting pressure for educational change and emphases should be on the development of language applications, not the skill-drill of numerous subskills.

USE THE PORTFOLIO AS A BACKUP SYSTEM FOR THE PERFORMANCE TEST

If decision makers and the public at large appear willing to accept performance assessment results, why not try to get them to examine and accept portfolios for large-scale assessment? That approach is actually being tried in a few places, and the audiences who have been willing to take on the highly subjective and cumbersome task of evaluating randomly selected portfolios have indeed seemed willing to accept what they indicate about student performance as representative.

See the Chart *Fitting the Pieces Together* in Chapter 6.

But the problems inherent in this approach to assessment may be too difficult to overcome. As has been stressed in earlier chapters here, the evaluation of portfolios for accountability purposes has tended to lead to dictating the contents of the collections—at least to some significant degree. This robs the portfolio of much of its potential to establish and nurture the habit of self-assessment among students. That is the major reason that the portfolio is not recommended here as a standard source of information for the decision maker, accountability audience.

This does not mean, however, that the portfolio has no role in informing such audiences. Whenever there is reason to question the results of any assessment—norm-referenced, criterion-referenced, or performance—the portfolio can be consulted immediately to confirm or deny the challenge of the results. Any teacher can contribute to the following scenarios of instances in which this occurs:

- Decision makers are considering the placement of a student in a special program on the basis of his or her performance on a standardized or performance test. The teacher believes that the student will experience fewer challenges and opportunities to be creative in the alternative classroom. The teacher's familiarity with the student's writing—much of it in a portfolio—tells her that the test is not a good indication of the student's true abilities.

- With the student's help, the teacher develops a show or demonstration portfolio from the student's working collection and arranges for the administrator with the final decision on the placement to examine it and discuss its contents with her.

- This same situation could work in reverse, as well. When a student's tests scores do not support his or her selection for a special opportunity the teacher feels the student should have, the portfolio can demonstrate the student's promise and potential to whoever is making the selections.

- The student has failed a minimum essentials test screening and is targeted to repeat a school year or must attend special classes. The teacher feels that the student has had one or two bad days when taking the test or is just not adept at answering multiple-choice items. The student's work in the portfolio supports this contention and is used as one of the items in the discussion of the best placement for the student.

- Parents are discouraged by a student's test scores and are dealing with the situation with requirements the teacher feels will not encourage the student's language development. In an arranged meeting, the teacher uses the student's portfolio to provide a realistic picture of their child's accomplishments and to support numerous suggestions of things the parents could do at home to develop good reading habits and writing practice that grows out of genuine interests.

In all such situations, the portfolio becomes a backup system for audiences that teachers feel may be misinformed by test scores. It comes into play then as a key source of assessment information for specific individuals in the decision maker and accountability audiences.

SUMMARY: A DOZEN GUIDELINES TO RELIABLE SCORING

- Keep your teaching and language development philosophies and theories in mind as you structure and articulate your scoring rubrics and select your anchor papers. You want the test you use to match your teaching. If you are selecting a published instrument, you can compare what you believe to what seems to have guided its preparation.

- Strive for an easily understood and easily implemented scoring system that will add reliability to the validity of the test you construct or select.

- Look for dimensions to rate that you think are important perspectives on the way that students use language and develop as language users and thinkers.

- Design a rubric that will cover the dimensions you want to measure with a scale that balances sensitive reporting with ease of use. Make sure that it is not so complex that you lose assurance that different users will tend to assign similar scores to the same student efforts.

- In developing your system by creating piles of range papers—very good, average, and weak student responses—be sure to promote open discussion with fellow teachers or articulate the values that are leading to your ranking decisions.

- Develop a set of highly relevant factors that can help define each dimension and apply them in a parallel way in describing scores across each dimension.

- From student-constructed responses from your tryout, find two good examples of papers with the same score in the same dimension to offer to those who will use the test as anchor papers. Select them to represent different ways of meriting the score and papers that are not atypically high or low quality.

- Explain in an annotation what about each sample or anchor paper led scorers to give it the score it represents. Refer to specifics in the sample as the strong or weak aspects that tended to generate the particular score.

- Select tryout papers that represent an excellent and a particularly weak response and create marginal annotations noting the particular aspects of the content that relate to the high or low score.

- Make sure that the construction of your assessment is a reiterative process. Talk about the scores based on it with students, their parents, and others and gather reactions to the assessment that can effect changes in it. Revise to perfect the product.

- Develop techniques of reporting the results of the performance assessment to your students, their parents, and various audiences interested in educational accountability. Consider this a kind of test of the efficacy of the instrument. If it does not serve as a kind of bridge between various audiences—offering information of interest to most of them—you may not have the kind of instrument you need.

- Another good test of the instrument is to look at the results as a process-revealing package that can make a valuable inclusion in the student portfolio. If it does not do this, consider revamping the prewriting and thought-provoking activities it offers or perhaps the questions or task or even the prompt.

PORTFOLIO AND PERFORMANCE ASSESSMENT

Appendix A
Questions About Portfolio and Performance Assessment

1. What is the moral of the tale of *The King and the Carpenters*?

You may have written or thought about a moral to the Prologue parable "The King and the Carpenters" that is as meaningful and useful for you as the one we believe completes it, and yours may even be more eloquently articulated. But here is the way the moral is spelled out in our official version:

The moral of this story ultimately became obvious to even the most faithful subjects of the King:

There is a big difference between naming hammers and pounding nails in a wall!

However, lest anyone believe that naming hammers is not important, just ask someone to get a particular type of hammer and see what happens if the person fetching it doesn't know the types of hammers. On the other hand, and more importantly, standing with a hammer in one's hand and knowing its name doesn't make one a builder or tell one how to use it.

Could there be a place for both knowledge and application?

2. Is portfolio assessment really new? Haven't educators been doing this a long time?

Many good teachers have always used analysis of collections of student papers to reveal progress and to identify instructional goals. Some have involved their students in the analysis as self-assessors in one way or another. Perhaps some teachers may have been disinclined to do this because of the growing importance of more traditional assessment focused on educational accountability.

What appears to be somewhat new about the current growing reliance on and attention to portfolios is their dedicated emphasis to the reading/writing connection and the focus on activities that span all curriculum areas. Also, certain aspects of the portfolio assessment approach stressed in this book may be relatively new. The emphasis on the importance and necessity of the regular teacher-student conference is one example.

3. How widespread is the use of portfolios?

There is considerable evidence of interest in portfolio assessment in the literature published primarily for the practitioner audience. Its use appears to be widespread but far from "universal" within many school districts. A few schools and districts have numerous teachers who are using it, but the "density" of the portfolio experience students get may not always ensure

that they keep and analyze portfolios for several consecutive years. (Appendix B lists reports on some different applications of portfolio assessment.)

4. Can portfolios really show me what a student needs help with?

In portfolio assessment, the help a student needs to improve as a reader must be spotted in his or her actual use of language—in what the student writes and particularly in reactions to material read. That kind of analysis is surely a more dependable indicator than counting responses to multiple-choice test items. The portfolio collection should clearly indicate the questions you and the student can consider about why comprehension may have been limited. For example, this can lead to revelations such as "I just didn't know what a lot of the words in that article meant. . . . And I didn't want to take the time to look them up." More important, it can reveal strengths to build on.

In writing, the variety of writing samples should give you a far better perspective on what the student needs to attend to in order to improve better than any single piece of writing. And if the problem is related to concerns such as writing with a clearly focused purpose or for an authentic audience, the portfolio gives you the opportunity to discuss these concerns with your students: "Oh, I just wasn't interested in that story. And I would never write to someone like the girl in it. Besides I don't give a hoot about stamp collecting. I hope we read something about football next time."

The analysis of the portfolio may be more subjective, but it can get to the heart of a student's reading/writing strategies. More importantly, if portfolio becomes the natural assessor of his or her own development.

5. What do teachers who have used portfolio assessment seem to think of it?

The response—at least as indicated by publications—appears to be quite positive, expressing appreciation for the richness of the picture that portfolios give of a student's growth as a reader and writer. They testify to the focus of attention that is brought to bear on language use, particularly on authentic purposes.

The reports frequently praise portfolio assessment for contributing to the learning process; they note the effect that a student's sense of ownership invariably seems to have on his or her attitude and appreciation of language; and some depict a "renewed belief" among both teachers and students generated by the need to trust the judgment involved in portfolio assessment. (Appendix B cites some of these testimonies.)

6. Different people seem to recommend different kinds of portfolios. Which is best?

Very generally, a portfolio is a collection of one's work over a period of time. Some uses of the portfolio concept (in certain professions, for example) imply a definition of it as a collection that shows its owner at his or her best. (Chapter 1 discusses the portfolios of artists, photographers, businesspersons, and others.) Many proponents of language arts portfolio assessment recommend collecting just the student's best efforts.

The definition of the kind of portfolio recommended in this book—*working portfolios*—is a broad collection of a student's work selected by the student with the teacher's input. It eventually includes many samples of the student's writing, including the planning and revisions that should be encouraged. It includes writing done in response to reading; it contains other materials that record, analyze, and support the student's interests and uses of language. This collection, then, is analyzed and ordered by the student to identify strengths and goals for development as a better reader and writer.

7. Is there, then, a certain way that a teacher should conduct portfolio assessment, or can the approach be personalized to fit the teacher's particular teaching preferences?

Portfolio assessment can and should be designed to fit the teacher's instructional emphases and theoretical beliefs. We have emphasized some particular features in this book, such as requiring certain records that we believe will promote self-assessment and including drafts, notes, ideas, and other materials in a working portfolio. We have articulated these preferences and convictions quite strongly in places. But none of this is set in stone.

Perhaps you may wish to establish portfolios that reflect the definition that might be derived from this book to see how the approach goes in your classroom. If you don't like some aspect of what is recommended here, try it differently. You may, for example, decide to create and use a separate Reading Log and Writing Log. You may want to incorporate the selection of "Best Papers" somewhere in the analysis procedures and to require that students develop their own criteria for selecting them.

The system suggested here allows for all kinds of personalization, such as the ultimate development of show portfolios for particular purposes. What you will want to do is to experiment over a period of time and to find the more exact kind of portfolio assessment approach that you feel fills your needs and serves your students best.

8. What is the main objective of portfolio assessment?

Without any qualification, the main objective of having students keep and analyze portfolios is to develop self-

assessors! The idea is to develop readers and writers who know what they want to achieve with language. The goal is to get students to look at the way they are using language and to identify goals and objectives for improving as readers and writers. We won't be guiding and encouraging them forever, so if they are to continue to grow as readers, writers, and thinkers throughout life, they must become their own coaches!

Portfolios are useful to other audiences as well—especially to teachers. This is true because they make such an excellent instructional approach and because they help teachers identify student needs as developing language users. (Chapter 4 discusses at some length how portfolios develop self-assessors and serve instructional needs.)

Portfolios can also be used to give administrators, other educational decision makers, parents, the media, and the general public a sense of the amount and variety of language that students use and an appreciation of student interests, attitudes, and ideas. (In some places in the United States, portfolios are being randomly collected and analyzed to indicate student achievement; but the degree of success and results of this use are not yet clear.)

For these audiences, portfolios make an especially good backup when it appears that other assessments used are not truly indicative of the reading, writing, and thinking ability of a particular student. (Chapter 6 discusses the role of portfolio assessment in the whole educational assessment picture.)

9. So how do I get the student to do all this self-assessing?

First of all, you use working portfolios, which will create enough materials to demand some kind of organizing. In addition, the arrangement of idea sources and preliminary drafts with final drafts creates a focus on writing as a process.

Equally important, you make sure that many of the writing activities from which the student can pick inclusions for the portfolio are generated as reactions to something the student has read—ideally, something that relates to that student's interests and background. Such reactions constitute analyses in and of themselves.

Self-analysis is also promoted by requiring that the student keep records like the Reading/Writing Log, which includes reactions to things read and written, and the Table of Contents, which cannot be completed without organizing the contents. You should encourage the student to attach reaction notes to particular pieces in the portfolio, and you may encourage or require the student to write a kind of periodic synthesis that identifies his or her strengths and that sets goals and objectives for further improvement. You can also promote self-analysis with good questions during conferences and in informal exchanges with a student on a more frequent basis.

There are other things you can do, such as having the student identify his or her best work from among the contents of the portfolio and articulate and write out the criteria with which the selections were made.

You can model self-analysis by keeping your own portfolio that you can discuss with students and you can model your own reading and writing with think-alongs. (Think-alongs are described in Chapter 4.) You can also encourage self-assessment by having students form partnerships in which they react to each other's work. (Ways to develop self-assessment are discussed at some length in Chapter 4.)

10. A lot of reading instruction and assessments today claim to emphasize "higher levels of thinking." How does portfolio assessment cover that?
Portfolio assessment and its emphasis on language processing are all about thinking. While much traditional assessment tries to eliminate the impact of a student's background knowledge on the results, portfolio assessment emphasizes it by encouraging students to discuss their reading and writing and relate them to their background of experiences.

It is advisable for a teacher to create numerous thinking-dependent activities among those that will generate the potential work that can be selected for a portfolio. Two sure ways to do this are to:

- Have your students write a response that requires synthesizing the material from two or more different sources.

- Create writi ng analyses that require comparing and contrasting (to select and/or categorize) or require recognizing cause/effect and sequential relationships.

This can be done as well in constructing the performance assessments described in Chapters 7 and 8.

11. What teaching philosophies is portfolio assessment compatible with? Do portfolios seem to work best in certain kinds of classrooms?
Since the portfolio collection will be made up at least partly of work generated by classroom activities, the collections your students put together are sure to reflect your teaching practices.

Studies have indicated that portfolio assessment seems to work best in classrooms where instruction relies on trade books and magazines more than, or as much as, on a basal reader; yet it is now emphasized effectively in most basal programs. It appears to be more successful in classrooms that promote cooperative learning and that rely on small-group instruction, and it is more apt to succeed in schools that permit more localized decision making.

One practical consideration seems appropriate in this regard: If you believe that reading and writing are defined by a host of particular skills and subskills, portfolio assessment may broaden the scope of your instruction and increase the development of your students as language users. But as a singular assessment type, it may not be the most effective approach you can use. There are numerous norm-referenced and criterion-referenced assessments on the market to analyze student language use from such a perspective

and they are complemented by a host of exercise/workbook activities to help maintain the focus.

Generally speaking, portfolio assessment is most suited to a philosophy that is meaning- and thinking-oriented. In this regard, it is nicely attuned to the theories that have emerged in the past several decades and that place considerable emphasis on language process.

In addition, portfolio assessment promotes and facilitates an emphasis on using texts, writing topics, and activities that are authentic—that is, that are apt to be of real interest and concern to your students. Thus it promotes the identification of genuine purposes for reading and writing, and directs considerable attention to one's audience in writing.

12. Can I really evaluate students effectively with portfolios?
What do you want to know? Presumably, determining how effectively they are reading and writing is among your major concerns. This should involve determining whether their abilities to construct meaning while reading and writing are serving purposes that are important to them. The portfolio—being close to the ultimate performance assessment—should allow you to determine that. It should help reveal the interests, attitudes, and background that determine the genuine purposes a student has for reading and writing. It should allow you—with the student's substantive input—to determine what the student should try to do to become a better reader and writer.

Most important, the portfolio should allow you to do this while convincing the student that you value his or her work. It helps you develop the student as his or her own assessor—not because a grade depends on it, but because the whole analysis has been focused on processing language and on genuine reasons for using it. (Chapter 4 discusses the teacher's evaluation of portfolios at some length.)

13. What is performance assessment and how is it different from portfolio assessment?
Portfolio assessment is a collection of performance activities. Portfolio assessment involves looking at a whole collection of student work and interests gathered over a period of time to determine how effective the language processes related to the material are.

Performance assessment also analyzes a person's language behavior, but in response to a particular task. In the case of integrated language performance assessment, the student is usually supplied with a text to read and is assigned a particular writing task to complete in responding to it. The result, then, is analyzed or scored using a specific set of criteria. (Chapters 7 and 8 describe how to make and use such a performance assessment.)

14. Portfolio assessment and performance assessment sound somewhat similar. Why have both?
Analyzing portfolios to evaluate the language processes used by the students who collected them is a highly subjective task. Even when we control the contents of the portfolios to some degree and evaluate them using an articulated set of criteria, there will be

considerable variance in a quantity of material. While this is fine for teachers who know their students and for students who know themselves, analyses of these collections are not objective enough in the eyes of many persons who want assessment data that will guide educational decisions and/or that will tell them whether their schools are doing a good job.

Performance assessment is more controlled than portfolio assessment and can use criteria that are more specified—so much so, in fact, that when different scorers each read the same papers written by students of varying ability, they give particular papers the same or nearly the same scores. In the eyes of many audiences, this makes the results of the performance assessment more reliable. Performance assessments, then, are basically attempts to assess for results with reliability something like that reported with scores for short-answer tests, which can be normed. In addition, the controlled performance assessment allows the assessment of more particular tasks that are deemed to be important. (All this is discussed in more detail in Chapters 6–8.)

15. If portfolios are not made an acknowledged part of assessment that reports to people interested in school accountability, won't their popularity wither and die?

The blunt answer to that question is, "Very probably!" Teachers are busy folks, and if they are made to be accountable to assessments that measure language behavior as a host of skills and subskills covered with multiple-choice items, some teachers are highly apt to teach to those skills. Although portfolios can allow some focus on the mechanics of writing, for example, their power to involve the teacher and student in ideas and purposes for reading and writing may seem almost distracting to the purpose of preparing students to do well on the tests that tend to serve accountability interests. As is explained in Chapter 6, short-answer tests can be a part of a solution to what has seemed like an assessment puzzle. Another part of the solution is for teachers and schools to develop performance assessment as described in Chapters 7 and 8. Its intention is to provide enough reliability to win the confidence of audiences interested in accountability. And it is highly compatible with the contents of portfolios—so much so that it makes an excellent inclusion in the portfolio collection.

SOME PRACTICAL CONCERNS

16. How much time is this assessment with portfolios going to take?

It is true that portfolio assessment sounds as though it will take a considerable amount of time, and to be sure, it's not like blocking out one period several times a year to administer standardized tests.

On the other hand, portfolio assessment is good instruction, so that the time it takes is really a valuable investment in teaching. The aim of good reading and writing instruction is, after all, to develop students who are aware of the importance of developing as readers and writers and of what they need to do as individuals to become more effective users of language. That is the key goal and potential of portfolio assessment, so teaching and assessment become one and the same activity.

The amount of time needed for portfolio activities will vary from teacher to teacher, class to class, and day to day; but minimally you need to allow time for these activities:

- You will need to block out the better part of a couple of periods to introduce and explain portfolios to your students. You may decide to dedicate an evening to a portfolio workshop for parents and the time necessary for you and your students to plan it and get ready to participate in it.

- Obviously, students will need ample time to read and to write the pieces that will make up the core of their portfolios. They will also need time to revise what they write on the basis of their analyses of their collections.

- Students need regular opportunities to look over and analyze their portfolios. Once a day is not too often, and several times a week ought to be minimal. Also, these opportunities need to be long enough for the students to get their portfolios out, add pieces to them, update records in them, think about their contents, and reorganize them and/or write one or more analyses of things in them. It is difficult to see how this can happen in less than half an hour.

- There should be opportunities for students to choose to work on their portfolios when some of their classmates may choose to do other things. These elective sessions with their portfolios may be as short as 10 to 15 minutes or as long as the opportunity permits.

- Brief times during other class activities will need to be dedicated to portfolio assessment as you confer with students one-on-one or in small groups while they are completing instructional reading and writing activities.

- You will need to block out a minimum of four one-on-one conferences with each student each school year to discuss his or her portfolio.

- Both you and the student will need time to do a little concentrated analysis of his or her portfolio in preparation for the scheduled conference.

- You will need to create opportunities for parents and some administrators to look over the portfolios and for you and some students to talk with them about what they find there.

Notice that every one of these activities is a valuable way to use school time. If you think of them as strictly portfolio requirements, the approach does indeed require too much time. If you think of them as the excellent kind of instruction and experiences you want to provide for your students, you may decide that portfolio assessment requires very little time distinctly its own.

17. Where am I going to find the time it will take for thirty-some one-on-one conferences four times a year?

This is, perhaps, the most-asked question of all by teachers interested in initiating portfolio assessment. While acknowledging that this all-important aspect of portfolio assessment is challenging, let us hasten to suggest that you needn't schedule all of these in the same week. Some students will be ready to discuss their collections before others, so the conferences can be scheduled over a period of two to three weeks, allowing you to work them in among other activities.

There are other things you can do to facilitate conference scheduling. They involve using volunteer aides to work with the other students and taking advantage of other possibilities. (Twenty-five such suggestions, one of which is to use ideas that you may have, are made in a table in Chapter 5 of this book.)

18. How long will it take for me to really get going with portfolio assessment?

If you are beginning a new program of portfolio assessment, it may be several months before you feel fully comfortable with the system. If, however, you are working in a school where many other teachers are using the system, your students may already be familiar with the approach, and there should be little delay before you begin to see the benefits of portfolio assessment.

Suppose you are the only teacher in the school using this approach to assessment. Next year, your students will be new to it, but you will be more experienced. So the development time should be shorter than it was this year. Suppose the teachers with the students in the grades below and above yours are also initiating portfolio assessment this year. Beginning next year, you should experience little "lag time" at all.

19. Doesn't keeping a portfolio pretty much eliminate the probability that students will take their work home to show their parents?

This is a valid concern, since a working portfolio may well contain most of the written work of a student; but there are policies you can incorporate in portfolio assessment that will respond to it and even help assure that representative work is viewed regularly by parents.

Some teachers send the portfolios home several times a year with their students, but some of those who have tried this have reported an inherent danger in the policy. We all know that some students will lose things such as portfolio collections in getting them home and back to school and that important papers and books may get misplaced at home. Siblings, pets, and others who do not understand the importance of the collections may get into them and damage or destroy them. The loss of a student's portfolio can be a serious setback to the ongoing analysis of portfolio contents necessary to develop self-assessment. Consequently, many teachers are understandably reluctant to send portfolio materials home until they and their students have analyzed them adequately.

What many teachers have done is to set up policies that ensure that parents will have an opportunity to review portfolio contents:

- First of all, they announce and explain the portfolio approach being used in letters, newsletters, and presentations to parents. These include repeated invitations for parents to come to school to see the portfolio collections of their children.

- After the portfolios have been analyzed and discussed by the teacher and student in a periodic conference, some teachers have the student cull the collection, picking records, unfinished work, and work to be revised to retain in the collection. The rest is banded and sent home to the parent with an explanation of what it is and how it was selected. At the end of the year, some work may be selected for a show portfolio to move with the child to his or her next classroom and teacher and the rest is sent home. Strong examples that are kept can be copied so that they can go to the parents as well.

This book details an idea that has students prepare a special box to take home to their parents with an explanation to keep it on a shelf. Batches of papers sent home to stay can be bound and put in this box after parents have examined them and discussed them with the student. Most persons value such a collection more and more as years pass and are very grateful to the teacher who helped assure that the papers would be saved. There are other ideas in Chapter 6.

20. If I let students put whatever they want into their portfolios and encourage them to include all drafts and other materials that indicate process, how will we handle the bulky collections that result?

The initial response to this is, "Anticipate the problem and find a way." The distinction between working portfolios and show portfolios is so vital to promoting self-analysis of portfolio contents that dealing with the larger collections is well worth the trouble! The major point is this: If a student selects only his or her best to go into a portfolio, most of the analysis and thinking that portfolios can generate is eliminated or is over after the selections for inclusion are made. A certain amount of bulk is necessary.

There is also one very reasonable solution to dealing with the bulk. After you have had a conference with a student that follows your joint analysis of the portfolio contents, have the student cull from the collection those things that are still developing or are unfinished to go, along with some key records, into the portfolio for the next time period. Include with this material a copy of the student's analyses of the contents of the collection before it was reduced and a copy of the notes from the conference. Send the rest home with a note inviting the parents to inspect it, discuss it with their child, and save it.

21. Who will be allowed to see the student's collection?

While it is important to maintain a student's sense of ownership of his or her portfolio, you should be honest from the beginning and explain to your students that others will be looking at the portfolio. The students must understand that you will be looking at it—sometimes when they are not present so that you will be familiar with the contents and will be able to discuss the contents with them.

In addition, the portfolio should be open to the examination of parents who come to school. Ideally, it would seem fair to notify the student that his or her parents are coming to look at the portfolio, but this may not always be possible. The student should understand that adults like his or her parents, you, and the principal or a supervisor may be looking into the portfolio from time to time.

Also, you should tell the students that it may be possible that other students will look at their portfolios without being invited to do so. This seems to happen almost invariably when portfolios are kept out where their owners can get at them often and easily. Understanding this may be important in terms of what the student says in things she or he writes—particularly in journals that are kept as part of the portfolio. These need to be the kinds of journals that are kept with the intention, or at least the awareness, that they may be read by others.

OPERATIONAL CONCERNS

22. How can I get started with portfolio assessment?
Begin by thinking about what you want your students to achieve as readers and writers and have them begin collecting the kind of work you believe will show that. Be sure to include some basic records and analysis sheets that will promote self-assessment by the students. These should include a Reading/Writing Log and a Table of Contents that will promote organization of the collection.

Explain to your students what you expect of them, and tell administrators, supervisors, fellow teachers, and parents what you are doing. Early on, decide what kind of holders your students will use for their collections and where they will be kept so that they are accessible to the students. Once the portfolios are under way, plan the essential periodic one-on-one conferences with your students. (Chapter 2 discusses numerous considerations in getting started at some length. Chapter 3 is pertinent to answering this question as well.)

23. What's the best kind of holder for portfolios?
A portfolio holder needs to be large enough or expandable enough to house a sizable collection. Yet it should not be so big that you cannot store 30 of them in an accessible place. It should be durable and something that can hold at least 8½-by-11-inch paper without folding or rolling it.

Beyond that, the best holders are ones that the students select and decorate themselves. Allowing that is a sure way to establish a sense of ownership. On the other hand, keep in mind that if you have your students find their holders at home, there may be a few children who will not have access to anything suitable. You should have some holders in the classroom that they can choose.

24. How can I get my students really interested in their portfolios?
The key way to do this is to be sure to establish a genuine sense of ownership. One way to do this is to give the students a voice in picking the kind of holders they will use and in making operational decisions like where the portfolios will be kept. Let students decorate their portfolios in unique ways. As use of them begins, make sure that they are accessible and then create the opportunities for the students to get to them regularly and whenever they think it necessary.

Giving the students a voice in deciding what will be kept in the portfolios is the primary way of establishing ownership.

In addition to these very basic concerns, Chapter 2 suggests some ways of introducing portfolios that may make the concept meaningful and appealing to your students.

25. What should I tell parents about portfolio assessment?
Announce to parents early on that you are using portfolio assessment, describe what it is, and outline your objectives in using it. Explain the importance of including in the collection things written and read at home and tell parents how they can play a role in their child's development as readers and writers. Be sure to explain that it is the child who has the primary say about what goes into the portfolio and who will be the first analyst of its contents. Keep parents posted as the portfolio assessment process proceeds, using letters sent to the home, newsletters, and talks to parent groups. (Chapter 6 discusses at length using portfolios to report to parents.)

26. Who picks what goes into the portfolio?
Primarily, the student should, but it should be understood from the beginning that you will also have the right to select some things for the collection (in case you feel that a student is not picking his or her most indicative work or is being careful not to allow anything unfinished or representative of process into the collection). Also, you need to require that some basic records that promote self-assessment are included.

It is possible that if portfolios are being used in your school or district to assess achievement for audiences interested in accountability, particular pieces or types of writing will be required as well. One way to keep this from overpowering any genuine sense of ownership that the student feels is to let the student know about this from the beginning, to make sure that the collection is a working portfolio—at least until it is submitted for the assessment—and to limit your demands and selections as much as possible.

27. What besides a student's best writing should go into his or her portfolio?
Besides showcasing the best writing products a student generates, the portfolio should reveal the student's reading and writing processes. The collection should be a working portfolio, not just a show portfolio that presents only his or her "best stuff." This means that portfolio contents should trace the development of a student's good efforts from the ideas that generated

them through any drafts that were subsequently revised. It is vital, too, that the portfolio includes as many reactions to reading as possible. It should also reveal the interests, attitudes, and background of the student, since these influence language use dramatically; and it should contain ideas as seeds for future reading and writing.

Finally, the portfolio should contain records and analyses that promote self-analysis of the contents by the student. Some of these are by the student, some by you, and a few by classmates. Some are periodic syntheses that identify development and that set goals for future language development. (Chapter 3 is dedicated to discussing what goes into effective working portfolios.)

28. What portfolio components are usually recommended?

For a working portfolio, the components are quite broad: lots of original writing with any idea sources and drafts that show how it developed; lots of writing in reaction to things read, particularly that which requires synthesizing more than one text; records of things read and written; notes and other analyses of portfolio contents; and notes and other papers that reveal interests and attitudes and that recommend future reading and writing. While you may require that all students include a few classroom activities that you think are quite important, you should not require too many of these for fear of taking control of the portfolio.

29. When should the students work on their portfolios?

Your students should be allowed to work on their portfolios as often as possible. You should structure time at least several times a week for everyone to get out his or her portfolio to add things and analyze and organize what is in it. In addition, students should have options to go to the portfolios at other times—preferably every day. This is one reason that you should keep the portfolios in a place where the students have easy access to them.

30. What do the teacher and student talk about and do during a conference?

They discuss things they have noted when analyzing the contents of the portfolio. The student has done a final preconference analysis and reorganization just before the conference, and hopefully the teacher has had time to examine the results. This analysis should have suggested comments and questions to each of the participants.

The teacher's part in the conference will rely heavily on good questioning technique that attempts to get the student to analyze further. (All of Chapter 5 is dedicated to descriptions and examples of conferences.)

31. How do I grade portfolios? Are there criteria somewhere one can apply?

Ideally, you don't grade portfolios because that tends to lead the students to think that it is you who really sets the criteria for what goes into them. That can limit the student's sense of ownership of the collection and, in turn, the student's interest in self-assessing.

Realistically, however, one must recognize that many teachers will be—or at least feel—obligated to grade the portfolio as a project in which a considerable amount of class time has been invested. If this is the inescapable situation, level with the students from the beginning and clarify the criteria you will be using. Chapter 4 may suggest some criteria you can use, but be careful. If your criteria are too explicit and too inclusive, you will have taken command of what goes into the portfolio, no matter who is selecting it. Thus, you will also have completed most of the analysis of what gets in it. You will, at the very least, be dictating whatever analysis is done. Try to make any criteria you use as process/development-oriented as possible.

You can also take some other approaches:

- Let the students select a certain number of things they have included in their portfolios to be graded—along with your estimation of how they are developing as self-assessors.

- Require a limited number of inclusions each grading period from all students, announcing that these will, as a group, constitute the portfolio grade.

- Arrive at a grade with the student contributing to the evaluation in conference. (Chapter 4 discusses the grading of portfolios at some length.)

32. How will my students feel about any grade I put on their portfolios? Won't they consider that the "final" assessment? Will it seem any different to them than other assessments and evaluations of their work?

The answer to the question above has expressed this very concern. The danger is, of course, that your students will feel that any self-assessment they have done is cosmetic in the real scheme of things, where what you think is what really counts. The only way to avoid this is to follow some of the suggestions offered just above and in Chapter 4. Try to emphasize that your grade is focused on criteria that reflect process and language development and involve the student in the grading process in some meaningful way.

33. Do grades from norm-referenced tests go into portfolios?

They could be included, one supposes, but why? They are sure to detract from the analysis of student reactions to reading, other writing, and student thinking—even when their scores tend to support what that analysis might suggest. If anything, the portfolio can help qualify and enlighten the test scores, but test scores can add little to the meaning and value of the analysis of the portfolio collection. One value of the portfolio, in fact, is as a backup that can be consulted when the test scores seem to the teacher's observation of a student's ability to be off the mark.

34. Do performance assessments go into the portfolios?

Performance assessment results make some of the best inclusions a student or teacher can select for a portfolio! This is particularly true when the assessment has involved the student in prewriting and revision activities. When these are included with the final draft, one has an excellent set of papers revealing process; and the fact that other students have completed the same activity gives the teacher some perspective about how a student's processing, reading, thinking, and writing are defined by what other students of his or her age and with the same or similar current instructional experiences have done.

35. Should my students never do show portfolios?

There may be numerous, very valid opportunities for students to pull show portfolios from their working portfolios. For example, they may be instructed to select a show portfolio that they believe will demonstrate to the principal or some supervisor how they process meaning as readers and writers. This can be a thought-engaging activity for the student, and depending on the viewer, may serve a particular assessment need well. (Some principals and supervisors, of course, may be more interested in looking at the working portfolio and be able to recognize its more ample display of process.)

In Chapter 6 and other places in this book, we have discussed having a student pull a show portfolio from his or her collection at the end of a school year to use in introducing himself or herself to next year's teacher. Other show portfolios might be selected for a display or assessment that will involve numerous portfolios—where the focus provided by the show portfolio would be very important to the viewer.

MISCELLANEOUS CONCERNS

36. Could there be such a thing as a single portfolio kept by a whole class or a group of students?

Teachers who have asked questions similar to this one are already exploring some of the interesting possibilities of portfolios—provided that the group project grows out of the opportunities for the students to keep individual portfolios. Group portfolio projects are highly appropriate for projects that involve team efforts.

For example, students who are producing a class newspaper, magazine, play, or program of some type can construct a portfolio that will demonstrate the kind of processes—including cooperation and interactions with language—that led to the final product. When such a group portfolio is collected, an unusual amount of focus on the audience that will look at it is involved. It can, for example, be prepared for other classes—with other teachers and of other years—as a kind of descriptive set of directions. The portfolio may be intended for administrators who will be deciding if the experience the portfolio details is worth school-time investment; it might be constructed to be on display for parents; or it may be intended for a variety of these and other audiences, including members of the media.

Doing such a portfolio also gives your students a genuine opportunity to weigh the value of their experience and to interpret it in terms of their individual development as language users. In addition, the cooperation needed to construct the portfolio creates just that much more esprit de corps.

37. I am considering working with my students to create a show portfolio that will move with them across the grades. It will give teachers a view of a student's longer-term language development. Does that sound like a worthwhile idea?

It is a very worthwhile concept. It builds on the notion of having students pull show portfolios from their working portfolios at the end of the year to introduce themselves to next year's teacher.

It should indeed give teachers who have a particular student in their classes across the years an idea of how the student is developing as a reader, writer, and thinker, including an indication of how interests and attitudes have developed. (That is a good reason to leave surveys of such things in the accruing portfolio.) The longer the portfolio has been developed, of course, the more revealing it can be. It can indicate over time, for example, how quickly or slowly a student's language abilities have been developing.

More important, however, don't overlook the value the portfolio will have to the student, who has more vested interest than anyone in his or her long-term development. The accruing show portfolio should be returned to the student near the end of the year so she or he can add selected materials from the current year to it before it moves on to the next teacher.

38. Can portfolios cover all subject areas?

Yes! Many teachers use portfolios focused on other kinds of development. And the language-focused portfolio discussed in this book can and should contain things and ideas that arise from numerous subjects. The more you encourage your students to react to what they read in social studies, science, mathematics, and other subjects, the more likely this is. The categorization of these disciplines is purely a practical decision that educators made years ago; the separation has little application beyond school. So you should encourage the inclusion of reactions to reading and writing done in any subject area.

PORTFOLIO AND
PERFORMANCE ASSESSMENT

Appendix B
Sources Cited and Other Relevant Reading

The sources cited, mainly in Chapters 1 and 6, are, of course, recommended as informative reading about portfolio assessment, performance assessment, and alternative assessment of language use and development in general. Yet they and the additional useful sources annotated in the four subsections that follow the sources cited are but examples of the vast and quickly growing base of descriptions, testimonies, analyses, considerations, and debate about these methodologies. The reader is encouraged to use now readily available and easily used databases such as that maintained by the Educational Resources Information Centers (ERIC) to identify and consider all the sources now available.

SOURCES CITED IN THIS TEXT

Afflerbach, Peter (ed.) (1990). *Issues in statewide reading assessment.* Washington, D.C.: Clearinghouse on Tests, Measurement, and Evaluation.

This paper presents six chapters that describe how statewide reading assessment is currently being performed and how the data are being used.

Aronson, Edith, and Farr, Roger. (1988). Issues in assessment. *Journal of Reading, 32* (2), pp. 174–177.

Discusses issues in reading assessment, including the concern that tests cannot measure the reading process. Concludes that tests will never be more than useful indicators; calls for more research and examination of existing and new types of reading comprehension tests.

Arter, Judith A. (1990). *Using portfolios in instruction and assessment.* Portland, OR: Northwest Regional Educational Lab.

Discusses the advantages of portfolios for both instruction and assessment.

Arter, Judith A. et al. (1995). *Portfolios for assessment and instruction.* ERIC Digest. Greensboro, NC: Clearinghouse on Counseling and Student Services.

Recounts the advantages of using portfolios in instruction and in assessment, with emphasis on the rationale for the methodology in assessment.

Austin, Terri. (1994). *Changing the view: Student-led parent conferences.* Portsmouth, NH: Heinemann.

Describes how turning the parent-teacher conference over to the student provides the impetus for the student to be self-reflective and to analyze his or her own work more thoroughly. Details on how to make such conferences successful structure the book.

Beck, Michael D. (April 1991). "Authentic assessment" for large-scale accountability purposes: Balancing the rhetoric. Paper presented at the Annual Meeting of the American Educational Research Association. Chicago.

Presents an argument challengng the viability and reliability of both portfolio and performance assessment in meeting the needs of audiences interested in educational accountability. (Can be obtained by writing BETA, Inc., 35 Guion St., Pleasantville, NY 10570.)

Benoit, Joyce, and Yang, Hua. (Spring 1996). A redefinition of portfolio assessment based on purpose: Findings and implications from a large-scale program. *Journal of Research and Development in Education, 29* (3), pp. 181–191.

Describes the developmental process of the Dallas Independent School District Chapter 1 portfolio assessment and compares the portfolio results to those of the standardized measures available within the district. Concludes that there are two different types of portfolios based on the purpose intended—those for instructional improvement and those prepared for accountability purposes.

Birrell, James R., and Ross, Sandra Kee. (Summer 1996). Standardized testing and portfolio assessment: Rethinking the debate. *Reading Research and Instruction, 35* (4), pp. 285–298.

Argues that portfolio assessment can be complementary to standardized testing, but that teachers have much to learn about using both methods effectively.

Black, Susan. (February 1993). Portfolio assessment. *Executive Educator, 15* (1), pp. 28–31.

Notes that reliability of teacher evaluation of portfolios is not high and thus it is important that teachers participating in a portfolio assessment program set acceptable standards, decide on content, and consider various reactions and potential problems.

Bond, Lloyd. (Winter 1995). Unintended consequences of performance assessment: Issues of bias and fairness. *Educational Measurement: Issues and Practice, 14* (4), pp. 21–24.

Uses the Vermont portfolio assessment program to discuss the difficulty of scoring performance assessments and other consequences of concern.

Bush, George. (October 1992). A revolution to achieve excellence in education. *Phi Delta Kappan, 74* (2), pp. 130, 132–133.

Then-President George Bush calls for national examinations among his education priorities and goals.

Callahan, Susan. (March 1996). Using portfolios for accountability: The ethic of care collides with the need for judgment. Paper presented at the 47th Annual Meeting of the Conference on College Composition and Communication, Milwaukee.

This case study of nine teachers in a Kentucky school details the problems and challenges they face in implementing court-ordered portfolio assessment in that state.

Case, Susan H. (October 1994). Will mandating portfolios undermine their value? *Educational Leadership, 52* (2), pp. 46–47.

Mandating portfolios on a systemwide or statewide basis may destroy their greatest assets: allowing students to reflect on their learning and feel a sense of hope and control. This article contends that once standards are defined by an outside authority, teacher-student collaboration is minimized and the importance of students' own goals and learning assessment diminishes.

Catterall, James S. (1990). *A reform cooled-out: Competency test required for high school graduation.* Los Angeles: Center for Research on Evaluation, Standards, and Student Testing.

Among 20 states that have instituted standardized testing to get a high school diploma since the mid-1970s, the four reported on here represent the two with highest and the two with lowest reported graduation rates. Found that students and their parents were not very aware of the requirement.

Cizek, Gregory J. (May 1991). Innovation or enervation? Performance assessment in perspective. *Phi Delta Kappan, 72* (9), pp. 695–699.

Questions whether performance assessment is a way of achieving educational goals.

Clinton, William. (Spring 1996). President urges standards that count. Excerpts from President Clinton's address to the National Education Summit. *American Educator, 20* (1), pp. 8–12.

Asserts that tougher standards and better assessments are necessary for educa-tional improvement and that once the standards have been defined, educators must hold students accountable for their achievement. In defining standards, the President argues, high accountability must be based on the premise that all children are capable of learning.

Cloer, Thomas, Jr. (1994). National standards movement: Inspiration or norm. In *Reading: Putting the pieces together,* Yearbook of the American Reading Forum, Vol. 14, Bernard L. Hayes and Kay Camperell (eds.)

This initial chapter in the yearbook focuses on the potential impact and advisability of national standards on the development of reading.

Coleman, Viralene J. (March 1978). Competency-based tests: What are the alternatives? Paper presented at the 29th Annual Meeting of the Conference on College Composition and Communication, Denver, CO. (ERIC document ED1623139)

Presents 13 alternatives to using competency based tests that it argues should be considered when diagnosing student competency in writing and that since English is too complex a subject to be measured by a single test, teachers can get a more accurate and fairer evaluation of student writing skills by using many kinds of evaluation methods.

Courtney, Brother Leonard (ed.) (1965). *The use of theoretical models in reading. Highlights of the 1965 Pre-Convention Institutes.* Newark, DE: International Reading Association.

Among the uses of theory in reading are applications to considerations related to assessment.

Dutcher, Peggy (1990). *Authentic reading assessment.* ERIC Digest. Washington, D.C.: Clearinghouse on Tests, Measurement, and Evaluation.

Authentic reading assessment is examined, focusing on its implementation within the Michigan Essential Skills Reading Test (MESRT). This indicated that reading is not a particular skill but an interaction among reader, text, and the context of the reading situation.

Farr, Roger. (September–October 1987). New trends in reading assessment: Better tests, better uses. *Curriculum Review, 27* (1), pp. 21–23.

This discussion of assessing students' reading abilities focuses on the need for developing better tests and better interpretation of test scores. Criterion-referenced tests versus norm-referenced tests are described, highlighting the Degrees of Reading Power and Metropolitan Achievement Tests: Reading, and the need for assessing the reading process is discussed.

Farr, Roger. (1991). *Portfolios: Assessment in language arts.* ERIC Digest. Bloomington, IN: Clearinghouse on Reading, English, and Communication.

This is a short summary of the rationale for using portfolio assessments, stressing how they can serve multiple purposes, address language arts goals, and serve as *authentic* assessments.

Farr, Roger, and Carey, Robert. (1986). *Reading: What can be measured?* Newark, DE: International Reading Association.

This comprehensive and critical analysis of methods and issues in reading assessment includes chapters on validity and reliability, the role of reading measurement in educational accountability, and issues and trends.

Farr, Roger; Carey, Robert; and Tone, Bruce. (1986). Research into the reading process Implications for assessment. In *Reading comprehension: From research to practice,* Judith Orasanu (ed.) Hillsdale, NJ: Lawrence Erlbaum.

This chapter reviews the effect of research and theory on reading assessment.

Farr, Roger, and Fay, Leo. (1982). Reading trends data in the U.S.: A mandate for caveats and caution. In *A Rise and Fall of National Test Scores,* Gilbert R. Austin and Herbert Garber (eds.) New York: Academic Press, pp. 83–137.

This chapter is an exhaustive consideration of the various types of performance assessment available from different states up until the early 1980s and what they seem to suggest about reading performance. It notes that the data are surprisingly limited and do not support sweeping conclusions.

Farr, Roger, and Olshavsky, Jill Edwards. (1980). Is minimum competency testing the appropriate solution to the SAT decline? *Phi Delta Kappan, 61,* pp. 528–530.

This article discusses the development of criterion-referenced tests nationwide as accountability measures.

Farr, Roger, and Roser, Nancy. (1974). Reading assessment: A look at problems and issues. *Journal of Reading, 17* (8), pp. 592–599.

Urges educators in reading to get on with the task of improving assessment programs and evaluation procedures

Farr, Roger, and Tone, Bruce. (1994). *Theory meets practice in language arts assessment.* ERIC Digest. Bloomington, IN: Clearinghouse on Reading, English, and Communication.

Reviews the applications of reading and language-development theory to the consideration of how best to assess development of language abilities.

Finn, Chester. (November 1992). National tests: Yes or no? The case for testing. *PTA Today, 18* (2), pp. 30–32.

This is a strong call for accountability from an outspoken national educational administrator.

Fontana, Jean. (October 1995). Portfolio assessment: Its beginnings in Vermont and Kentucky. *NASSP Bulletin, 79* (573), pp. 25–30.

In 1988, when a Maine test failed to measure educational accountability in Vermont, portfolios were adopted as a bottom-up response to the perceived need for reform. In 1990, Kentucky's Educational Reform Act mandated assessment by performance-based tasks, including portfolios. Both states feature scoring criteria (rubrics) based on four performance levels and sample portfolios.

Fremer, John. (June 1991). Changing large-scale testing programs: Learning from the experience of others. Paper presented at the Conference on Assessment of the Education Commission of the States. Breckenridge, CO.

Notes how the SAT moved increasingly toward critical reading based on longer reading passages.

Gearhart, Maryl, and Herman, Joan L. (1995). Portfolio assessment: Whose work is it? Issues in the use of classroom assignments for accountability. Los Angeles: Center for the Study of Evaluation and National Center for Research on Evaluation, Standards, and Student Testing.

This positive review of the use of portfolios in large-scale assessment is based on an examination of the Vermont program and a California study. It discusses the need for student input in what is assessed.

Gentile, Claudia A., et al. (1995). *Windows into the classroom: NAEP's 1992 writing portfolio study.* Princeton, NJ: Educational Testing Service.

This report of the 1992 National Assessment of Educational Progress Writing Portfolio Study of 3,000 students' writing gives an interesting and descriptive look at both the type of writing that students do and at the strengths and weaknesses: While most students demonstrated process, informative types of writing were not well developed.

Goldberg, Gail Lynn, and Kapinus, Barbara. (1993). Problematic responses to reading performance assessment tasks: Sources and implications. *Applied Measurement in Education, 6* (4), pp. 281–305.

This is an analytic examination of the tasks and scoring on a performance assessment battery by 123 elementary teachers.

Grady, Emily. (1992). *The portfolio approach to assessment.* Fastback series 341. Bloomington, IN: Phi Delta Kappa.

This booklet describes ways that portfolios can be used to assess what students know and can do.

Guskey, Thomas R. (March 1994). What you assess may not be what you get. *Educational Leadership, 51* (6), pp. 51–54.

In examining the Kentucky Education Reform Act, this article suggests that substantial time, resources, and teacher training are needed to effectively implement authentic assessment.

Hambleton, Ronald K. (Winter 1994). The rise and fall of criterion-referenced measurement? *Educational Measurement: Issues and Practice, 13* (4), pp. 21–26.

Depicts how accountability concerns led to the proliferation of criterion-referenced tests used in large-scale testing and examines how the type of testing may fall short of expectations placed on it.

Hamp-Lyons, Liz, and Condon, William. (1993). Questioning assumptions about portfolio-based assessment. *College Composition and Communication, 44* (2), pp. 176–190.

This author's perspective is oriented toward ESL students and throws light on our broader expectations about portfolio assessment.

Harnack, Andrew, et al. (December 1994). The impact of Kentucky's educational reform act on writing throughout the Commonwealth. *Composition Chronicle: Newsletter for Writing Teachers,* 7 (8), pp. 4–7.

This report on a survey of teachers found them skeptical about the changes. The new assessment system in Kentucky is clearly described.

Hayes, Bernard L., and Camperell, Kay (eds.) (1994). *Reading: Putting the pieces together.* Yearbook of the American Reading Forum, Vol. 14. Logan, UT: Utah State University.

Among the broad range of issues related to the teaching of reading are several of significance to assessment.

Henk, William A. (1993). New directions in reading assessment. *Reading and Writing Quarterly: Overcoming Learning Difficulties,* 9 (1), pp. 103–120.

Among the developments in reading evaluation discussed are the interest in the role of prior knowledge, strategic reading, process measurements, use of authentic texts, and the influence of habits and attitudes.

Herman, Joan L., and Winters, Lynn. (1994). Portfolio research: A slim collection. *Educational Leadership,* 52 (2), pp. 48–55.

The challenge in using portfolios for large-scale assessment lies in ensuring technical concerns such as equity, interrater agreement, and the validity and meaning of the scores.

Horowitz, Rosalind. (November–December 1995). A 75-year legacy on assessment: reflections from an interview with Ralph W. Tyler. *Journal of Educational Research,* 89 (2), pp. 68–75.

This article presents an interview with Professor Ralph W. Tyler, pioneer in the field of education and assessment, that lends some historical perspective to the current alternative assessment movement. After highlighting Tyler's contributions, the article provides caveats on assessment.

Huffman, Priscilla D. (January–February 1966). "Look what I did!": Why portfolio-based assessment works. *Early Childhood News,* 8 (1), pp. 20–23.

Describes a three-way planning and conferencing method involving teacher, student, and parents that incorporates the use of student portfolios.

Irwin-DeVitis, Linda. (Spring 1996). Teachers' voices: Literacy portfolio in the classroom and beyond. *Reading Research and Instruction,* 35 (3), pp. 223–236.

Examines three teachers' beliefs and attitudes as their school district moved toward mandated and standardized literacy portfolio assessment. Notes they value informal classroom portfolio assessment, but have concerns that the most valuable and authentic aspects of portfolio assessment will be lost.

Johnston, Peter. (1986). Assessing process and the process of assessment in the language arts. In *The dynamics of language learning: Research in the language arts,* James Squire (ed.) Urbana, IL: National Council of Teachers of English.

Discusses the influence of theory on a process perspective on language development and what that requires in assessing it.

Kannapel, Patricia J., et al. (1996). I don't give a hoot if somebody is going to pay me $3600: Local school district reactions to Kentucky's high stakes accountability program. Charleston, WV: Appalacia Educational Lab.

While few of the teachers studied in four Kentucky school districts believed in the state's new accountability program, this work produced evidence that the measures were beginning to drive the reform effort to some extent.

Kasse, Stacy. (November–December 1994). Student/parent conferences: A new generation. *Teaching PreK–8,* 25 (3), pp. 78–79.

An approach to parent-teacher conferences that involves fifth-graders as equal partners with their parents and teacher results in extensive exchange between all involved.

Khattri, Nidhi, et al. (1995). *Assessment of student performance.* Vol. I: *Findings and Conclusions.* Studies of Education Reform. Washington, D.C.: Pelavin Research Institute.

A three-year case study at 16 sites used extensive and varied methodologies to describe the status of assessment reform in United States education systems and offer recommendations for policy and future research.

Kinder, Dennis Ray. (Spring 1979). "On further examination of the SAT report. *Contemporary Education,* 50 (3), pp. 172–175.

Further discussion of declining SAT scores is presented.

Langer, Judith A., et al. (1995). Reading assessment redesigned: Authentic texts and innovative instruments in NAEP's 1992 survey. Princeton, NJ: Educational Testing Service.

Discusses how the NAEP's large-scale reading assessment is evolving in response to changing perceptions of reading development and assessment procedures. Included in the report is an overview of the theoretical framework underlying the assessment, a description of and presentation of reading materials used in the assessment, a discussion of students' performance on constructed-response questions, and a presentation of example questions. Major results of the 1992 assessment are reported.

Linn, Robert L. (1994). *Assessment-based reform: Challenges to educational measurement.* Princeton, NJ: Educational Testing Service.

Discusses how the role of assessment in educational reform has led to "waves" of testing emphases, such as the recent emphasis on performance. Proposes standards for assessment itself.

MacGinitie, Walter H. (ed.) (1973). *Assessment problems in reading.* Newark, DE: International Reading Association.

These papers treat a wide range of problems in assessment.

Maiorana, Victor P. (1992). *Critical thinking across the curriculum: Building the analytical classroom.* Bloomington, IN: ERIC Clearinghouse on Reading and Communication Skills.

Based on the idea that certain critical skills mark the thoughtful person, inform the workplace, and provide for lifelong learning, this book provides classroom teachers with the ability to teach various subjects to students in a manner that simultaneously develops students' critical thinking, reading, writing, listening, and speaking skills.

Manzo, Anthony, V. and Manzo, Ula C. (1995). *Teaching children to be literate: A reflective approach.* Orlando: Harcourt Brace.

This book on current focuses in literacy education is based on three assumptions: teachers must participate in examining and defining their philosophy and goals, and in selecting the teaching methods that will guide their efforts; teachers need to build familiarity with the research literature of the field; and teachers must be prepared to work in a variety of possible settings.

McCandless, Sam A. (1975). The SAT score decline and its implications for college admissions: A review of SAT score trends and the contexts in which they have occurred. Paper presented at the Western Regional Meeting of the College Entrance Examination Board. San Francisco.

A variety of explanations for the decline of Scholastic Aptitude Test (SAT) scores over the past several years are examined.

McRobbie, Joan (1992). *Using portfolios to assess student performance.* Knowledge Brief No. 9. San Francisco: Far West Lab for Educational Research and Development.

This issue describes what educators around the country are finding out as they use portfolios, indicating that while portfolio assessment is somewhat demanding, it is well worth the trouble.

Meisels, Samuel J. (1995). *Performance assessment in early childhood education: The work sampling system.* ERIC Digest. Urbana, IL: Clearinghouse on Elementary and Early Childhood Education.

Bills Work Sampling system as a performance assessment flexible enough to reflect individual academic achievement and designed to evaluate elements of learning not captured by standardized tests. Thus it is appropriate in early childhood education.

Miller, Wilma H. (1995). Alternative assessment techniques for reading & writing. Des Moines: Simon and Schuster.

This book provides a multitude of informal assessment strategies and devices, such as "kid-watching," retellings, journals, informal reading inventories, writing surveys, portfolios, and think-alouds. The book presents more than 200 reproducible assessment devices.

Millman, Jason. (Winter 1994). Criterion-referenced testing 30 years later: Promise broken, promise kept. *Educational Measurement: Issues and Practive, 13* (4), pp. 19–20, 39.

Argues that criterion-referenced measurement needs "higher item density" (more items per amount of domain) if it is to fulfill its promise.

Moss, Pamela, et al. (Fall 1992). Portfolios, accountability, and an interpretive approach to validity. *Educational Measurement: Issues and Practice, 11* (3), pp. 12–21.

Provides answers to questions related to the reporting of portfolio assessment results to audiences interested in in school accountability.

Murphy, Sharon. (March–April 1995). Revisioning reading assessment: Remembering to learn from the legacy of reading test. *ClearingHouse, 68* (4), pp. 235–239.

Suggests that both portfolio and performance-based assessment can be implemented in ways that retain vestiges of standardized testing. Compares aspects of standardized testing to aspects of portfolio and performance-based evaluation. Discusses responsibility to those assessed.

Myers, Joel, and Lytle, Susan. (October 1986). Assessment of the learning process. *Exceptional Children, 53* (2), pp. 138–144.

This discussion of how the learning process is assessed suggests the close relationships between learning, thinking, and language.

NAEP study casts doubt on national portfolio assessments. (April 17, 1992). *Education Daily, 25* (74), pp. 1–2.

This news item gives very mixed signals about the potential success of large-scale portfolio assessments.

O'Neil, John. (May 1992). Putting performance assessment to the test. *Educational Leadership, 49* (8), pp. 14–19.

Officials in Vermont, California, Kentucky, Maryland, and other states are betting that performance assessments may prove as powerful a classroom influence as paper-and-pencil testing used to be.

On further examination: Report of the Advisory Panel on the Scholastic Aptitude Test Score Decline (1977). Princeton, NJ: College Entrance Examination Board.

This thoughtful report, often referred to as "The Wirtz Report," gave careful consideration to potential influences on the SAT score decline, but went largely ignored by both media, decision makers, and the public.

On further examination of *On further examination.* Quick reference. (1977). Washington, D.C.: National Education Association.

A critical analysis of the Wirtz Panel's report.

Parker, Elaine F. (March 1995). Speaking of portfolios: Contrasting images. Paper presented at the 46th Annual Meeting of the Conference on College Composition and Communication, Washington, DC. (ERIC document ED390047)

A discussion of the appropriateness of the many metaphors used to describe portfolio assessment and its potentials.

Paulson, F. Leon, and Paulson, Pearl R. (1994). Student-led portfolio conferences. ERIC document ED377241.

Pulls together effective ideas for student/teacher/parent conferences built around portfolio collections.

Pearson, P. David. (1993). Standards for the English Language arts: A policy perspective. *Journal of Reading Behavior, 25* (4), pp. 457–475.

Examines the drive to develop a national set of standards for the English Language Arts curriculum. Addresses the issues of what standards are, what the current standards terrain looks like, what sort of standards could be set, and what the dangers are in the process. Offers suggestions for educators to begin the process of developing useful standards.

Popham, W. James. (Spring 1993). Educational testing in America: What's right, what's wrong? A criterion-referenced perspective. *Educational Measurement: Issues and Practice, 12* (1), pp. 11–14.

Current successes and failures in U.S. educational measurement are reviewed, focusing on criterion-referenced testing. Pluses and minuses are listed for the following: (1) the move toward authentic assessment; (2) the dominance of criterion-referenced assessment; and (3) item response theory applications.

Powell, Janet L. (1989). *How well do tests measure real reading?* ERIC Digest. Bloomington, IN: Clearinghouse on Reading and Communication Skills.

Discusses issues related to reading and reading assessment related to thinking and metacognition.

The primary program: Report from the Task Force on Improving Kentucky Schools. (1995). Lexington, KY: Prichard Committee for Academic Excellence.

A task force that examined Kentucky's primary program using multiple methodologies found marked improvement in student performance in the basics (reading, writing, and mathematics).

Ravitch, Diane (ed.) (1995). Debating the future of American education: Do we need national standards and assessments? Washington, D.C.: Brookings Institution.

A highly thought-provoking discussion of the possible outcomes of establishing national educational standards and assessments.

Reed, Lorrie C. (November 1993). Achieving the aims and purposes of schooling through authentic assessments. *Middle School Journal, 25* (2), pp. 11–13.

Examines what is measured by current standardized, criterion-referenced, and performance testing instruments and details the components of a comprehensive assessment system that includes testing and alternative, authentic measures as the basis for judgments about student progress.

Resnick, Lauren B., and Resnick, Daniel P. (October 1989). Tests as standards of achievement in schools. Paper presented at the Invitational Conference of the Educational testing Service, NY. (ERIC document ED 335 421)

The question of whether tests can be both curriculum neutral and effective means of monitoring and motivating educational practice is discussed.

Results from the NAEP 1994 reading assessment—at a glance (1996). Washington, D.C.: National Center for Education Statistics.

The 1994 National Assessment of Educational Progress Reading Assessment was administered to a national sample of students in grades 4, 8, and 12. National reading proficiency results were reported for students at each grade and within various subgroups of the population. State-level results were reported for individual states or jurisdictions that chose to participate in the 1994 Trial State Assessment. Major findings are reported in this concise report.

Rief, Linda. (March 1990). Finding the value in evaluation: Self-assessment in a middle school classroom. *Educational Leadership, 47* (6), pp. 24–29.

This testimonial to the effectiveness of portfolios cites several personalized examples and recommends immersing students in reading, writing, speaking, and listening activities; giving them sufficient time to develop projects they choose; and offering a lot of positive reinforcement. *This entire issue is themed and includes several valuable articles on portfolios.*

Robinson, Richard D., et al. (1996). *Issues and trends in literacy education.* Des Moines: Allyn and Bacon.

Among reprints of parts of key works on literacy are several chapters on assess-ment, including "Launching a revolution in standards and assessments" by Diane Ravitch.

Salinger, Terry. (December–January 1996). IRA, standards, and educational reform. *The Reading Teacher, 49* (4), pp. 290–298.

Summarizes the development of English language arts standards and discusses the role standards might play in achieving educational reform both in the classroom and within larger educational units.

Santa, Carol M. (April 1995). Assessment: Students lead their own parent conferences. *Teaching PreK-8, 25* (7), pp. 92–94.

Describes the use of student-led conferences in place of traditional teacher-parent conference. Notes that conferences reflect curricular change to reading and writing workshops and thematic studies, belief that students should take responsibility for their own literacy behaviors, and use of portfolio assessment.

Shane, Harold. (1977). The academic score decline: Are facts the enemy of truth? *Phi Delta Kappan, 59* (2), pp. 83–86, 145–146.

Presents an interview with W. Willard Wirtz, chairman of the College Entrance Examination Board panel, investigating the decline in Scholastic Aptitude Test scores.

Smith, Carl B. (ed.) (1991). *Alternative assessment of performance in the language arts: Proceedings.* Bloomington, IN: The ERIC Clearinghouse on Reading and Communication Skills and Phi Delta Kappa.

These papers, developed for a national symposium cohosted by Phi Delta Kappa and ERIC/PCS in August 1990, and the transcriptions of oral presentations and group sessions present extensive, varied, and confrontational perspectives on educational assessment in general and on alternative assessments that are informal or controlled.

Standards for the English language arts: Professional summary. (1996). International Reading Association, Newark, DE.

This summary reviews the rationale for defining English language arts for K–12 students and the perspective on language learning that informs it. After presenting 2 of the 12 standards and discussing them briefly, the summary provides a vignette to illustrate how the standards might be manifested in a classroom setting.

State student assessment programs. Midwestern region. (1993). Oak Brook, IL: North Central Regional Educational Lab.

Detailed information about student assessment programs of states participating in the North Central Regional Educational Laboratory is presented, describing design, purposes, and future plans.

Stewart, Susan C., et al. (Spring 1995). The revolution in assessment within and across educational settings. *Preventing School Failure, 39* (3), pp. 20–24.

The purpose and evolution of educational assessment are considered. Alternatives to standardized assessment include performance assessment, authentic assessment, and portfolio assessment. Issues concerning outcomes of the assessment revolution include appropriate standards, associated changes in curricula and grading, and questions regarding standards for students at risk.

Stiggins, Richard. (1987). NCME Instructional Module on Design and development of performance assessments. *Education Measurement: Issues and Practice, 6* (3), pp. 33–42.

This instructional module presents and illustrates rules for designing performance assessments in a step-by-step strategy through: (1) reason for the assessment; (2) type of performance evaluated; (3) exercises to elicit performance; and (4) systematic rating procedures. Guidelines for maximizing reliability, validity, and economy are presented.

"This Is My Best": The report of Vermont's writing assessment program, pilot year 1990–91. (1992). Montpelier: Vermont State Department of Education.

The early report on the Vermont portfolio program was unclear about its potential to be successful.

Tierney, Robert J., et al. (1991). *Portfolio assessment in the reading-writing curriculum.* Norwood, MA: Christopher-Gordon.

This book covers all aspects of portfolio assessment to both rationalize and inform its implementation in the classroom. It relies on research and actual implementations. It includes many practical examples and an extensive annotated bibliography.

Valencia, Sheila. (1990). A portfolio approach to classroom reading assessment: The whys, whats, and hows. *The Reading Teacher, 43* (4), pp. 38–40.

This short article argues that theory, research, and instructional experiences recommend a portfolio approach to reading assessment.

Wang, Chen Shih, and Ackerman, Terry. (April 1994). An examination of response dependency when there is more than one correct answer. Paper presented at the Annual Meeting of the American Educational Research Association. New Orleans.

This study reports on the interdependence of items on the Illinois Goal Assessment Program (IGAP) and includes a description of this atypical test on which there are multiple correct answers to items.

Wiggins, Grant. (April 1989). Teaching to the (authentic) test. *Educational Leadership, 46* (7), pp. 41–47.

A leading authority recommends portfolios as one form of authentic assessment, offering a descriptive example.

Wirtz, Willard, and Lapointe, Archie. (1982). Measuring the quality of education: A report on assessing educational progress. New York: Spencer Foundation.

This study assesses the National Assessment of Educational Progress and considers the anomaly of the gap between its reputed quality among experts and relatively slight public notice and influence.

Wirtz, Willard. (1978). What shall we do about declining test scores? Current issues in higher education. Washington, D.C.: American Association for Higher Education.

Discusses issues relating to score declines and the emerging trend toward competency testing in terms of egalitarianism and elitism and pluralism.

Wolf, Dennie Palmer, et al. (May 1992). Good measure: Assessment as a tool for educational reform. *Educational Leadership, 49* (8), pp. 8–13.

This article argues that portfolios are essential as tools of educational reform that will lead to individual and internal accountability in schools.

RELATED BACKGROUND AND OTHER SOURCES ABOUT ALTERNATIVE ASSESSMENT

Bouffler, Chrystine (ed.) (June 1993). *Literacy evaluation: Issues & practicalities.* Newtown NSW, Australia: Primary English Teaching Association.

This set of essays by Australian teachers underlines the importance of assessment and depicts numerous types and approaches in use by teachers in that country. Several help explain the role of more informal assessment and that which is compatible with whole language instruction in the broader assessment picture. Many of the chapters include practical advice and actual tools that teachers can use.

Brandt, Ron. (May 1992). On performance assessment: A conversation with Grant Wiggins. *Educational Leadership, 49* (8), pp. 35–37.

Wiggins expresses concerns about assessment reforms failing because high stakes will be attached to them too soon and judgments will be unreliable. He urges giving attention to task validity, score reliability, portfolio sampling, and solving problems related to generalizability.

Brooks, Jacqueline Grennon, and Brooks, Martin. (1993). *In search of understanding: The case for constructivist classrooms.* Alexandria, VA: Association for Supervision and Curriculum Development.

This pedagogy promotes teaching through the presentation of relevant problems and valuing student point of view and suppositions.

Burz, Helen L., and Marshall, Kit. (1997*). Performance-based curriculum for language arts: From knowing to showing.* Thousand Oaks, CA: Corwin Press.

This guide to performance-based curriculum is based on National Council of Teachers of English and the International Reading Association standards. It recommends making children themselves accountable for showing what they are learning and calls for performance that can be both observed and measured as a kind of accountability demonstration.

Butler, A., and Turbill, J. (1984). *Towards a reading-writing classroom.* Portsmouth, NH: Heinemann.

This source describes ways that the process approach to writing can be applied to the teaching of reading. Research on the integration of reading and writing is also discussed.

Calkins, L. M. (1983). *Lessons from a child.* Portsmouth, NH: Heinemann.

Observations in a classroom convince the author that reading and writing are inseparable activities.

Chapman, Carmen. (1990). Authentic writing assessment. ERIC Digest. Washington, D.C.: Clearinghouse on Tests, Measurement, and Evaluation.

This review considers some important ways of assessing student writing authentically, with some emphasis on the Illinois Writing Program for examples.

Coley, Richard J. (ed.) (August 1990). Testing. *ETS Policy Notes, 2* (3).

Two of three articles include one that discusses the role of testing in educational reform and one that describes some of the work done in Connecticut in the area of student performance assessment and in two other innovative assessment programs.

DiYanni, R. (1985). *Connections: Writing, reading, and thinking.* Portsmouth, NH: Heinemann.

This book presents questions and exercises that teach-ers can use to promote the integration of reading, writing, and thinking.

Floden, Robert E., et al. (September 1995). Capacity building in systemic reform. *Phi Delta Kappan, 77* (1), pp. 19–21.

Data from interviews with teachers in California, Michigan, and Vermont suggests a framework for shaping reform policies on strategies for enhancing teacher capacity.

Gardner, Howard. (1991). *The unschooled mind: How children think and how schools should teach.* New York: Basic Books, HarperCollins.

An expert on understanding the development of the human mind makes an eloquent plea for education reformation that will help students move beyond rote learning to achieve genuine understanding. Gardner makes use of what is known about human development and cognitive science, turning it into well-grounded advice that is both practical and very readable.

Goldstein, Arnold A., and Carr, Peggy G. (April 1996). Can students benefit from process writing? *NAEPfacts, 1* (3).

Discusses the classroom frequency and effectiveness of process-oriented activities based on 1992 National Assessment of Educational Progress data. Findings suggest that use of prewriting activities is associated with the highest average proficiency scores.

Guskey, Thomas R. (ed.) (1996). *Communicating Student Learning.* ASCD Yearbook. Alexandria, VA: Association for Supervision and Curriculum Development.

Thirteen chapters treating the effective reporting of assessment results and student performance to a variety of audiences with a range of interests in accountability and instructional accountability. A thought-provoking and highly useful source.

Hansen, Joe B. (1992). A purpose driven assessment program. Paper presented at the annual meeting of the American Educational Research Association, 1992.

This describes the assessment program of the Colorado Springs (Colorado) Public Schools. It includes norm-referenced, criterion-referenced, and performance-based assessment, which includes "direct writing" and portfolio assessment.

Harp, Bill (ed.) (1991). *Assessment and evaluation in whole language programs.* Norwood, MA: Christopher-Gordon.

Twelve chapters describe and discuss assessment and evaluation compatible with the whole language approach to language instruction, ranging from miscue analysis to holistic strategies. Applications to bilingual, multicultural, and special education students are discussed, as are other practical concerns such as record keeping and reporting assessment results.

Henry, George H. (1974). *Teaching reading as concept development.* Newark, DE: International Reading Association.

This book presents an approach that relies completely on the synthesis of several different texts into each of several subsets, which are laddered into a general concept, such as *nature*. That concept, for example, would approach nature as beautiful and grand, then destructive, then vulnerable to man's mismanagement. Understanding Henry's approach can be highly useful to those planning language performance assessment.

Irwin, Judith W., and Doyle, Mary Anne (eds.) (1992). *Reading/writing connections.* Newark, DE: International Reading Association.

This collection of analyses of the reading-writing connection is historic and research-based, yet practical in its perspectives. It covers various types of student writing based on reading and focuses on language processes. It is an invaluable source for teachers who would ground their performance assessment in compatible instruction and a sound understanding of the theory and research that recommends it.

Jaggar, A., Carrara, D., and Weiss, S. (March 1986). Research currents: The influence of reading on children's narrative writing and vice versa. *Language Arts, 63* (3), pp. 292–300.

The interaction of meaning construction while reading and while writing is examined.

Johns, Jerry L. (compiler) (1993). *Informal reading inventories.* DeKalb, IL: Communitech International Incorporated.

Numerous sources are abstracted and indexed.

Johnson, Peter. (1987). Teachers as evaluation experts. *The Reading Teacher, 40* (8), pp. 744–748.

Since the bulk of educational decision making takes place in the classroom, Johnson argues, assessment must serve teachers in the creation of optimally effective instruction.

Marzano, Robert, and Kendall, John S. (1996). The fall and rise of standards-based education. Issues in brief. Aurora, CO: Mid-Continent Regional Educational Lab.

A guidebook on the history of standards-based educational reform with considerations of its implications.

McTighe, Jay, and Ferrara, Steven. (1994). *Assessing learning in the classroom. A report from professional standards and practice.* Washington, D.C.: National Education Association.

The common principles underlying all types of classroom assessment are explored with attention to how they inform instruction and improve learning, how many sources of information they tap, and how valid, reliable, and fair those are.

Morrow, Lesley Mandel, and Smith, Jeffrey K. (1990). *Assessment for instruction in early literacy.* Englewood Cliffs, NJ: Prentice-Hall.

These papers prepared for the Rutgers Symposium on Education interpret and synthesize current theory, research, and practical information by offering five perspectives on assessment of the concept *emergent literacy:* historical, developmental, psychometric, sociolinguistic, and pedagogic. Chapters review formal measures, argue for informal approaches, insist on adherence to measurement principles, call for a new discourse on assessment of early literacy, and describe and discuss alternative strategies for assessing it.

Pikulski, J. J. (1989). The assessment of reading: A time for change? *The Reading Teacher, 43* (1), pp. 80–81.

This article argues that the assessment of reading must shift from being test-centered to being teacher- and pupil-centered and that it must reflect dynamic, constructionist, process-oriented instructional goals.

Reading framework for the National Assessment of Educational Progress: 1992–1998. (1997). NAEP Reading Consensus Project. Washington, D.C.: National Assessment Governing Board.

Presents the framework for the 1992, 1994, and 1998 NAEP reading assessment, which is "more consistent with contemporary knowledge about reading and more relevant to the needs of education decision-makers than earlier assessments have been." Discusses how both the framework and the assessments were developed with a goal for constructing, extending, and examining meaning. Special studies, including one on portfolios, are addressed in this booklet as well.

Robbins, Sarah, et al. (Spring 1995). Negotiating authority in portfolio classrooms: Teachers' use of assessment theory to critique practice. *Action in Teacher Education, 17* (1), pp. 40–51.

Presents a model for theoretical consideration of classroom practices by teachers themselves. This case study of two teachers' use of portfolios depicts examples of an interpretive process of theory informing practice, and reflection on practice then reshaping theory.

Roderick, Jessie A. (ed.) (1991). *Context-responsive approaches to assess children's language.* Urbana, IL: National Conference on Research in English.

This book's chapters cover numerous focuses on alternative assessment and evaluation in language education. It includes rationales for its use in both instruction and reporting to accountability-focused audiences and describes methodologies that provide a dynamic view of student and school performance.

Ross, Pat O'Connell. (Fall 1991). Advocacy for gifted programs in the new educational climate. *Gifted Child Quarterly, 35* (4), pp. 173–176.

Among initiatives that are recommended in the education of the gifted student are performance-based assessment and portfolios.

Ruddell, Martha Rapp. (1993). *Teaching Content Reading and Writing.* Boston: Allyn and Bacon.

This broadly scoped, textlike account of the many aspects of teaching reading and writing has an idea-centered, content-focused emphasis that can help ensure authentic language experiences for students. Although this 419-page book discusses portfolios only briefly, everything in it is highly compatible with portfolio assessment. It is very readable and offers many specific classroom examples.

Sensenbaugh, Roger. (1991). Developing strategies for reading, writing, and critical thinking: The intermediate grades. *Reading Research and Instruction, 31* (1), pp. 77–80.

This ERIC/RCS column selects and annotates 10 excellent sources for the teacher.

Smith, Carl B. (1996). Integrating the language arts. ERIC Digest. Bloomington, IN: Clearinghouse on Reading, English, and Communication.

Notes that research advocating the integration of the language arts has not had great impact on classroom instruction and reviews it to recommend that impact.
Stanton, Jana. (1987). *Dialogue journals.* ERIC Digest. Urbana, IL: ERIC/RCS.

A description of a dialogue journal illustrates an explanation of their usefulness for involving even reluctant students in the use of language. ERIC document ED 284276.

Stiggins, Richard J., and Conklin, Nancy Faires. (1992). *In teachers' hands: Investigating the practices of classroom assessment.* Albany, NY: State University of New York Press.

This look at the ways that teachers assess and at what teachers learn from them offers an array of instructional and professional perspectives that are supported by extensive reports of the research that revealed them.

Valencia, Sheila W. (ed.) (1994). *Authentic reading assessment: Practices and possibilities.* Newark, DE: International Reading Association.

Nine case studies describe new authentic approaches to assessing reading.

Walters, Joseph. (1992). Application in multiple intelligences: Research in alternative assessment. In *Focus on evaluation and measurement.* Proceedings of the National Research Symposium on Limited English Proficient Student Issues, 1991.

These reports discuss how the view of *multiple intelligences* forces the rethinking of the assessment of learning, and point out several implications for teaching bilingual and multicultural students.

Wetzel, Keith, and Best, Anita (eds.) (1992). *Computers and the writing process. Teacher's guide to organizing and evaluating student writing.* Eugene, OR: International Society for Technology in Education.

Written by educators who believe that writing and word-processing strategies and skills are best taught as students do real writing for a variety of readers.

Wharton-McDonald, Ruth, et al. (1997). *Outstanding literacy instruction in first grade: Teacher practices and*

student achievement. Reading Research Report No. 81. College Park, MD: National Reading Research Center.

Nine outstanding teachers were observed and interviewed to determine outstanding approaches and methodologies for developing literacy. Among the distinguished instruction reported are encouragement of student self-regulation and throrough integration of reading and writing activities.

Worthen, Blaine R., Borg, Walter R., and White, Karl R. (1993). *Measurement and evaluation in the schools.* New York: Longman.

This comprehensive examination of educational measurement covers all traditional concerns—creating and selecting assessment for the classroom and designing school- and districtwide assessment programs.

OTHER SOURCES ABOUT PORTFOLIO ASSESSMENT

Arter, Emily. (Fall 1992). *The portfolio approach to assessment.* Fastback Series. Bloomington, IN: Phi Delta Kappa.

This booklet describes ways that portfolios can be used to assess what students know and can do.

Arter, Judith A., and Spandel, Vicki. (1992). NCME instructional module: Using portfolios in instruction and assessment. *Educational Measurement: Issues and Practice, 11* (1), pp. 36–44.

This training module rationalizes portfolio assessment and helps teachers design it. It applies practical answers to special questions and considerations, and it gives sequenced steps for developing a sound portfolio approach.

Au, Kathryn H. (1993). *Literacy instruction in multicultural settings.* Fort Worth: Harcourt Brace Jovanovich.

In discussing the full range of developing the language abilities of students from diverse backgrounds, this book argues that portfolios are an appropriate and effective way to assess progress because they invite the consideration of work reflecting goals influenced by circumstances outside the classroom.

Au, Kathryn. (October 1996). When parents serve as writing critics. *Teaching PreK–8, 27* (2), pp. 61–62.

Describes a strategy that involves parents in reviewing folders of students' work that results in parents acknowledging progress.

Ballard, Leslie. (February 1992). Portfolios and self-assessment. *English Journal, 81* (2), pp. 46–48.

A teacher finds portfolios successful in getting students to recognize their own strengths and weaknesses as writers.

Bushweller, Kevin. (July 1995). The high-tech portfolio. *Executive Educator, 17* (1), pp. 19–22.

Describes a project in Vermont that had students keep electronic portfolios with some focus on the technical problems that resulted.

Calfee, Robert C., and Perfumo, Robert C. (April 1993). Student portfolios: Opportunities for a revolution in assessment. *Journal of Reading, 36* (7), pp. 532–537.

A survey reports rapid growth in the use of portfolios and raises concerns about their effective use.

Calfee, Robert C., and Perfumo, Pamela (eds.) (1996). *Writing portfolios in the classroom: Policy and practice, promise and peril: Evaluating writing through portfolios.* Final Report. Berkeley: National Center for the Study of Writing and Literacy.

This book presents an extensive collection of essays by researchers, practitioners, and policy makers who study the impact of classroom portfolios in the assessment of writing achievement by elementary and middle-grade students.

Cole, Donna J., et al. (1995). *Portfolios across the curriculum and beyond.* Thousand Oaks, CA: Corwin Press.

A guidebook that defines portfolios as a systematic and organized collection of evidence used by the teacher and student to monitor growth of the student's knowledge, skills, and attitudes. Accountability uses are also discussed.

Cook, Jimmy.(January 1995). A call to action. *Teaching PreK-8, 25* (4), pp. 30–31.

Describes development of a process-oriented writing curriculum that provides continuity through the use of portfolios passed on to the students' next teacher.

The Crest Line (Newsletter of the National Center for Research on Evaluation, Standards, & Student Testing). (Fall 1992). Special portfolio issue.

Several articles on portfolios include comments from the center's directors, Eva Baker and Robert Linn, on "portfolios and accountability"; a description of a videotape on portfolios at the elementary level produced by the center; an article by Ron Dietel about a study of the time demands of portfolio programs, using those in Vermont and Michigan as examples. The article suggests, however, that they are worth the burden.

Deming, Mary P., and Valeri-Gold, Maria. (Fall 1994). Portfolio evaluation: Exploring the theoretical base. *Research and Teaching in Developmental Education, 11* (1), pp. 21–29.

Explores the growing body of theory supporting the use of portfolios in student evaluations, including a review of the method's theoretical underpinnings and an account of additional supporting evidence.

Despain, LaRene, and Hilgers, Thomas L. (Fall–Winter 1992). Readers' responses to the rating of non-uniform portfolios: Are there limits on portfolios' utility? *WPA: Writing Program Administration, 16* (1–2), pp. 24–37.

This article discusses the problems of grading or rating nonuniform portfolios.

Farr, Roger et al. (1997). *Portfolio assessment teacher's guide, Grades K-8.* Orlando, FL: Harcourt Brace.

This guide proposes portfolio assessment that is quite similar to that proposed in this book but is considerably shorter (42 pages, including blackline masters). The authors of this book are grateful to the publisher for the permission to expand the material considerably.

Farr, Roger. (1990). Setting directions for language arts portfolios. *Educational Leadership 48* (3), p. 103.

While identifying the strengths of portfolio assessment for informal assessment, this article recommends careful consideration before assuming that they replace standardized tests.

Feuer, Michael J., and Fulton, Kathleen. (February 1993). The many faces of performance assessment, *Phi Delta Kappan, 74* (6), p. 478.

Performance assessment is defined as seven common forms that include both analysis of student writing in general and portfolios.

Fogarty, Robin (ed.) (1996). *Student portfolios: A collection of articles.* Palatine, IL: IRI/Skylight Training and Publishing.

A collection of discussions about a variety of philosophical, organizational, and implementational questions surrounding portfolio assessment.

Frazier, Darlene M., and Paulson, F. Leon. (May 1992). How portfolios motivate reluctant writers. *Educational Leadership, 49* (8), pp. 62–65.

An Oregon teacher's project to create a classroom portfolio for an education class led to volunteer contributions from her students and to the students keeping their own individual portfolios.

Gambrell, L. B. (1985). Dialogue journals: Reading-writing interaction. *The Reading Teacher, 38* (6), pp. 512–515.

Guidelines for the use of dialogue journals and for teacher participation are given.

Gentile, Claudia. (April 1992). *Exploring new methods for collecting students' schoolbased writing.* NAEP's 1990 Portfolio Study. Washington, D.C.: Prepared by Educational Testing Service for the National Assessment of Educational Progress 1990 Writing Assessment for National Center of Education Statistics, Office of Educational Research and Improvement, U.S. Department of Education. (Available from the U.S. Government Printing Office, Superintendent of Documents, Mail Stop: SSOP, Washington, D.C. 20402-9328.)

This is a report on an extensive study that analyzed 4,000 student portfolios collected at grades 4 and 8. It was conducted in conjunction with National Assessment of Educational Progress and evaluated the writing in the collections. It was evaluated in terms of its *narrative, informative,* and *persuasive* qualities. This inductive study is an important landmark in research that can help describe what portfolio assessment can show educators and how well it may serve the interests of audiences interested in school accountability.

Gill, Kent (ed.) (1993). *Process and portfolios in writing instruction.* Classroom Practices in Teaching English, Vol. 26. Urbana, IL: National Council of Teachers of English.

This volume has 16 chapters on teaching and evaluating student writing with an emphasis on process and is loaded with good ideas that tie portfolio assessment to effective writing instruction.

Grace, Cathy. (1992). The portfolio and its use: Developmentally appropriate assessment of young children. *ERIC Digest*. Urbana, IL: Clearinghouse on Elementary and Early Childhood Education.

This describes portfolios for lowest grades and notes that it is extra important for the children and parents to be involved with the teacher in the assessment. Includes numerous references.

Graves, Donald H. (November 1989). Research currents: When children respond to fiction. *Language Arts, 66* (7), pp. 776–783.

This review of research stresses the possibility of involving students in fiction that they read by having them write about the story characters.

Hansen, Jane. (April 1992). Literacy portfolios emerge. *The Reading Teacher, 45* (8), pp. 604–607.

A professor, a teacher, and an elementary class begin to examine themselves as readers and writers, an exercise that evolves into portfolio assessment.

Hansen, Jane. (May 1992). Literacy portfolios: Helping students know themselves. *Educational Leadership, 49* (8), pp. 66–68.

Keeping portfolios leads students in a New Hampshire classroom to designing activities that help them reach their own goals to grow as readers, writers, and thinkers.

Hayes, Betty, and Kretschmann, Daren-Johnson (compilers) (1993). *Portfolio assessment: An annotated bibliography of selected resources*. Madison, WI: Wisconsin State Board of Vocational, Technical, and Adult Education.

Lists and summarizes 33 sources on portfolio assessment.

Herbert, Elizabeth A. (May 1992). Portfolios invite reflection from students and staff. *Educational Leadership, 49* (8), pp. 58–61.

This article describes an alternative assessment program that became more meaningful through the use of learning experience forms and "portfolio evenings," in which children presented their portfolios to their parents.

Herter, Roberta J. (January 1991). Writing portfolios: Alternatives to testing. *English Journal, 80* (1), pp. 90–91.

This article tells how assessing the development of eleventh-grade students' writing skills using portfolios promoted self-reflection and a sense of self-responsibility for the improvement of their writing.

Hiatt, Evelyn L. (Fall 1991). An update on the Javits Project: Identifying and serving disadvantaged gifted youth. In *Identifying and serving diverse populations*, Evelyn Levsky Hiatt and Jeanette Covington (eds.) A themed issue of *Update on Gifted Education, 1*(3).

The project stresses creative and thinking-related criteria for evaluating student progress with portfolios. There is, as well, a guide, *Texas Student Portfolio,* that spells out these worthwhile criteria. Contact: Division of Gifted/

Talented Education, Texas Education Agency, 1701 North Congress Avenue, Austin, TX 78701-1494.

Howard, Kathryn. (Spring 1990). Making the writing portfolio real. *The Quarterly of the National Writing Project and the Center for the Study of Writing and Literacy, 12* (2), pp. 4–7, 27.

Jervis, Kathe (1996) *Eyes on the child: Three portfolio stories*. The Series on School Reform. New York: Teachers College Press.

Three extensively detailed stories of teachers developing authentic new portfolio-assessment strategies in schools involved in reform and restructuring. Issues that arise in different situations and the resulting portfolios themselves are described.

This describes how eighth-graders who were developing portfolios went through five phases that could be useful indicators of the language-development progress of students.

Johns, Jerry L., and Leirsburg, Peggy Van. (Fall 1992). How professionals view portfolio assessment. *Reading Research and Instruction, 32* (1), pp. 1–10.

In comparing current results of an ongoing study to previous studies, it was found that educators' familiarity with portfolios is increasing and that fewer practical problems in using them are being reported. Still, users express concerns with planning, managing, and "organizing" them.

Johnson, Bil. (1996). *Performance assessment handbook: Portfolios & Socratic seminars*. Vol. 1. Princeton, NJ: Eye on Education.

A guide to portfolios assessments with indications of the future of portfolio assessment.

Johnson, Paul B., Sr. (September 1996). Sharing portfolios with parents. *Principal, 76* (1), pp. 44–45.

A very sensible and appealing example of a "portfolio-sharing night" works to improve public relations and communication with parents while promoting self-evaluation and goal-setting in the students.

Jongsma, Kathleen Stumpf. (1989). Portfolio assessment (questions and answers). *The Reading Teacher, 43* (3), pp. 264–265.

Three educators offer their suggestions for using portfolios to evaluate reading and writing.

Kemp, Donald; Cooper, Winfield; and Davies, Jon. (January–February 1991). The role of administration in portfolio assessment. *California Curriculum News Report, 16* (3), pp. 3–4.

These guidelines are intended to help administrators consider, implement, and support portfolio assessment.

Koretz, Daniel. (1992). *The Vermont portfolio assessment program: Interim report on implementation and impact, 1991–92 school year*. Project 3.2: Collaborative Development of Statewide Systems. Los Angeles: Rand Corp.

This is the interim report of the first year of a state assessment program at grades 4 and 8 that focuses on math and writing portfolios made up of students' best pieces. It reports on surveys and interviews with teachers, portfolio raters, and principals. Teachers report positive effects on instruction and learning.

Krest, Margie. (February 1990). Adapting the portfolio to meet student needs. *English Journal, 79* (2), pp. 29–34.

A teacher with several years of experience using portfolios describes how they can be used successfully to motivate and evaluate student writing. She tells how portfolios can be graded with a score for the amount of revision and risk-taking and a score based on one to three products. A few papers are required, but need not be graded; otherwise the student takes full responsibility for his or her writing.

Lankes, Anna Maria D. (1995). *Electronic portfolios: A new idea in assessment.* ERIC Digest. Syracuse, NY: Clearinghouse on Information and Technology.

Reviews the application of computerized composition and storage as an alternative to portfolio collections in folders.

Manning, Maryann, and Manning, Gary. (September 1996). Teaching reading and writing. Keeping writing portfolios. *Teaching PreK–8, 27* (1), pp. 132, 134.

Describes the method as one that encourages students to take responsibility for their learning and includes six usable forms for such an approach.

Martin, Bill. (September 1992). Literature and teaching: Getting our knowledge into our bones. *English Journal. 81*(5), pp. 56–60.

Stressing process in both learning and teaching, a teacher includes portfolios as one means of helping students experience literature.

McRobbie, Joan. (1992). Using portfolios to assess student performance. *Knowledge Brief,* No. 9, Far West Laboratory for Educational Research and Development.

This nine-page issue describes what educators around the country are finding out as they use portfolios, indicating that while portfolio assessment is somewhat demanding, it is well worth the trouble.

Miller, Michael A. (June 1992). The ins and outs of portfolios. *Communique, 20* (6), pp. 3–.

This perspective in a publication of the National Association of School Psychologists describes portfolio assessment as a viable multidimensional evaluation.

Moersch, Christopher, and Fisher, Louis M. III. (October 1995). Electronic portfolios—some pivotal questions. *Learning and Leading with Technology, 23* (2), pp. 10–14.

Discusses some technical and nontechnical aspects of using electronic portfolios in the classroom.

Murphy, Sandra, and Smith, Mary Ann. (1990). Talking about portfolios. *The Quarterly of the National Writing Project and the Center for the Study of Writing and Literacy, 12* (2), pp. 1–3, 24–27.

Discusses questions that should be answered before beginning a portfolio project and describes the way that three schools answered them; suggests how teachers can make decisions using portfolios.

Paris, Scott G., and Ayres, Linda R. (1994). *Becoming reflective students and teachers with portfolios and authentic assessement.* Psychology in the Classroom: A series on Applied Educational Psychology. Washington, D.C.: American Psychological Association.

This guide for teachers is aimed at creating reflective students and teachers by providing specific descriptive examples of classrooms, teachers, and students involved in this approach.

Paulson, F. Leon; Paulson, Pearl R.; and Meyer, Carol A. (February 1991). What makes a portfolio a portfolio? *Educational Leadership, 48* (5), pp. 60–63.

This article presents guidelines for using portfolios in developing self-directed learning and a way of getting students to value their own work. It defines the closeness of portfolio assessment and instruction as an "intersection."

Pierce, Lorraine Valdez, and O'Malley, J. Michael. (Spring 1992). *Performance and portfolio assessment for language minority students.* Program Guide Series. Washington, D.C.: National Clearinghouse for Bilingual Education.

This offers directions for assessing the oral proficiency, reading, writing and language-arts portfolios of minority students, with rubrics that are recommended and that use a 0–5 scale.

Portfolios illuminate the path for dynamic, interactive readers. (May 1990). (Secondary Perspectives). *Journal of Reading, 33* (8), pp. 644–647.

This discusses how portfolios can be used to evaluate strengths and development in reading.

Portfolios resources bibliography: Innovative assessment (Fall 1994; 1993; 1991). Portland, OR: Northwest Regional Educational Lab.

A critical and annotated bibliography of 216 sources (1994), 182 sources (1993), and 94 sources (1991) on portfolios with descriptors and index along with information on how to acquire the sources.

Raju, Nambury. (1991). *Integrated literature and language arts portfolio program.* Chicago: Riverside.

These tests use intact selections of authentic literature and an open-ended testing format. The system, which has the student synthesize and respond to prompts, is performance-based assessment designed to match new language arts objectives in the classroom, and it focuses on speaking and listening as well as on reading and writing.

Ronda Woodruff: Fourth-grade teacher in Beaverton, profile. (May 1, 1990). *Portfolio Assessment Newsletter, 1* (2). Published by the Northwest Evaluation Association, 1–2.

A teacher joins her students in keeping and analyzing personal writing portfolios. This issue also has an annotated bibliography on portfolios and numerous opportunities to exchange information with those using portfolios.

Schmitt, Maribeth Cassidy. (March 1990). A questionnaire to measure children's awareness of strategic reading processes. *The Reading Teacher, 43* (6), pp. 444–461.

This article offers a highly structured approach to assessing and promoting the metacognitive reading behavior highly compatible with self-assessment using portfolios.

Sloan, Megan. (April 1996). Assessment at work. I love this piece because . . . *Instructor, 105* (7), pp. 30–31.

Describes ways to use portfolios to help students evaluate their own progress and think more reflectively habitually.

Smith, Robert L., and Birdyshaw, Deanna (eds.) (1992). *Perspectives on assessment,* Vol. I. Grand Rapids: Michigan Reading Association.

This collection of essays considers all types of educational assessment, with some emphasis on the Michigan Educational Assessment Program, before turning to classroom assessment and six chapters with much practical advice on informal assessments. A third section offers three chapters on portfolios.

Solomon, Gwen. (February 1991). Electronic portfolios. *Electronic Learning, 10* (5), p. 10.

This brief article describes how high school students kept their language arts portfolios as computer files.

Stecher, Brian M., and Hamilton, Eric G. (1994). Portfolio assessment in Vermont, 1992–93: The teachers' perspective on implementation and impact. Paper presented at the Annual Meeting of the National Council on Measurement in Education, 1994.

Mixed results are reported on the state's portfolio assessment of mathematics and writing at grades 4 and 8. Teacher concerns and concerns about reliability are detailed.

Stewart, Roger A., et al. (March 1993). Portfolios: Agents of change (Have you read?) *The Reading Teacher, 46* (6), pp. 522–524.

This review of three textbooks on portfolios in the reading and writing classrooms published in 1991 and 1992 recommends portfolios, but with some caveats.

Sunstein, Bonnie S. (1992). The personal portfolio: Redefining literacy, rethinking assessment, reexamining evaluation. *Writing Noteoook: Creative Word Processing in the Classroom, 9* (4), pp. 36–39.

This advocacy of portfolios for students and teachers alike stresses the importance of self-evaluation.

Tierney, Robert. (September 1992). Portfolios: Windows on learning. Setting a new agenda for assessment. *Learning, 21* (2), pp. 61–64.

Describes and promotes portfolios as dynamic asssessment that promote thinking and independence while providing a multidimensional view of development.

Valencia, Sheila, et al. (1990). *Assessing reading and writing: Building a more complete picture for middle school assessment.* Technical Report No. 500. Center for the Study of Reading, University of Illinois. Cambridge, MA: Bolt, Beranek and Newman.

This report builds a strong case for a portfolio approach to assessment of reading and writing during the middle school years, stressing how the approach can be continuous, multidimensional, collaborative, knowledge-based, and authentic. Portfolio assessment is described in some detail in five "scenarios." Appendices include: A Schema for Scoring Retellings (The Retelling Profile), A Holistic Scoring Scale, An Analytic Scoring Scale, A Writing Analysis Checklist, and A Self-Evaluation Questionnaire.

Valencia, Shelia W., and Calfee, Robert. (1991). The development and use of literacy portfolios for students, classes, and teachers. *Applied Measurement in Education, 4* (4), pp. 333–345.

This sensible article explores uses of portfolios—including a whole-class portfolio. It considers portfolio assessment a valuable complement to externally mandated tests, but notes that there are technical issues that must be addressed and that portfolios must be closely linked to instruction.

Vavrus, Linda. (August 1990). Put portfolios to the test. *Instructor, 100* (1), pp. 48–53.

This article treats the implementation of classroom portfolios as five major decisions: what it will look like, what will go in it, how and when contents are selected, how the portfolio is evaluated, and how and why portfolios can be passed on to other teachers.

Wolf, Dennie Palmer. (1989). Portfolio assessment: Sampling student work. *Educational Leadership, 46* (7), pp. 35–39.

Administrators, teachers, and researchers used the portfolios of artists, musicians, and writers to model those for students that were offered as an assessment substitute to audiences who have depended on standardized testing.

Yancey, Kathleen Blake (ed.) (1992). *Portfolios in the writing classroom: An introduction.* Urbana, IL: National Council of Teachers of English.

Ten essays present the advantages of using portfolios by sharing stories of teachers who have used them in varying situations.

ADDITIONAL SOURCES ON LARGE-SCALE APPLICATIONS OF PORTFOLIO ASSESSMENT

Howell, Kenneth W., et al. (Fall 1993). Bias in authentic assessment. *Diagnostique, 19* (1), pp. 387–400.

A survey of teachers involved in Arizona's program of authentic assessment of student writing reveals serious concerns about several aspects, including "fairness"—particularly to minority students.

Meyer, Caroll; Schuman, Steven; and Angello, Nancy. (September 1990). *Aggregating portfolio data,* rev. ed. Lake Oswego, OR: Northwest Evaluation Association.

Answers numerous questions about the viability of aggregating analyses of portfolios to report and meet the needs of audiences that have depended on standardized tests and about the potential impact of those uses on the usefulness of the portfolio in the classroom.

Mills, Richard P. (1996). Statewide portfolio assessment: The Vermont experience. In *Performance-based student assessment: Challenges and possibilities,* Joan Boykoff Baron and Dennie Palmer Wolf (eds.) Ninety-fifth Yearbook of the National Society for the Study of Education. Chicago: The University of Chicago Press.

A descriptive report on the Vermont portfolio program—its rationale, contents, and some results.

An initial report on the use of portfolios for statewide assessment in Vermont.

New Mexico Portfolio Writing Assessment 1991–92: Administration Manual. (1992). Santa Fe: New Mexico State Department of Education.

This is the manual for the procedures for the first year of portfolio assessment in the state of New Mexico with guidelines for each teacher to follow in grades 4 and 6 (and optionally grade 8). Requirements for the portfolios include responses to three prompts and "best pieces."

Northwest Policy. (August/September 1991). Northwest Regional Educational Laboratory. (Entire issue)

This issue of the laboratory's newsletter is dedicated to issues in assessment, particularly as it informs educational decision makers and other audiences interested in accountability.

Simmons, Jay. (March 1990). Adapting portfolios for large-scale use. *Educational Leadership,* 47 (6), p. 28.

Reports research indicating that portfolios can be used to produce the information that accountability audiences need.

ADDITIONAL SOURCES ON PERFORMANCE ASSESSMENT

Arter, Judy. (1993). Designing scoring rubrics for performance assessments: The heart of the matter. Paper presented at the Annual Meeting of the American Educational Research Association. Portland, OR: Northwest Regional Educational Lab.

Argues that carefully prepared rubrics can help performance assessment fulfill its potential to serve as an effective instructional tool.

Ferrett, Robert T. (October 1991). Reading & writing. *Thrust for Educational Leadership,* pp. 38–41.

The director of research and evaluation for the Riverside Unified School District in Riverside, California,

describes the use of integrated language performance assessment as a part of the district's pupil testing program, which used a published series.

Linn, Robert L.; Baker, Eva L.; and Dunbar, Stephen. (November 1991). Complex, performance-based assessment: Expectations and validation criteria. *Educational Research,* 20 (8), pp. 15–21.

Rather than doubting the viability of alternative performance assessments, this article argues, we should be developing assessment criteria that are sensitive to the expectations for such new assessments. It has an excellent list of 51 relevant references.

Lutrario, Chris. English INCA (Integrated National Curriculum Assessment) Teacher's Guide. (1991). London: Harcourt Brace Jovanovich Limited.

Nine of the prompt/writing activity combinations developed for the *Integrated Assessment System: Language Arts Performance Assessment* by The Psychological Corporation (1990) are presented in a single-volume guide to administering them and interpreting results in England.

Macon, James M.; Bewell, Diane; and Vogt, MaryEllen. (1991). *Responses to literature.* Newark, DE: International Reading Association.

A rationale for having students write in response to reading, this booklet—which is intended to be used with workshops—presents a set of prewriting activity charts, story maps, story frames, summary forms, and other guides to help students organize their thinking.

Mitchell, Ruth, and Stempel, Amy. (1991). *Six case studies of performance assessment.* Report on *Testing in American Schools: Asking the right questions.* Washington, D.C.: U.S. Congress Office of Technology Assessment.

This detailed description of the different performance assessment programs at six U.S. schools emphasizes that the purpose for the assessment must be clear and that the variety of types of performance assessment creates psychometric problems.

Roeber, Edward D., et al. (1990). *Performance assessment: A national perspective.* Policy Briefs Numbers 10 and 11. Elmhurst, IL: North Central Regional Educational Lab.

Views performance assessment as an exercise in which students demonstrate specific skills and competencies as opposed to selecting one of several predetermined answers to an exercise; various perspectives related to test construction and applications are discussed.

Russavage, Patricia McGrath. (1992). Building credibility for portfolio assessment. In *Literacy: Issues and practices.* 1992 Yearbook of the State of Maryland International Reading Association Council, Vol. 9.

This reports on the Maryland School Performance Assessment Program as implemented at the Lettie Marshall Dent Elementary School. It tells how the program is anchored in authenticity, is continuous, is a sampling of multidimensional responses, and is a promoter of active, collaborative reflection.

Werner, P. H. (February 1992). Integrated assessment system. *Journal of Reading,* 35 (5), pp. 416–418.

This is a descriptive review of the *Integrated Assessment System* published by The Psychological Corporation and the source of numerous samples in this book.

PORTFOLIO AND PERFORMANCE ASSESSMENT

Appendix C
Getting Some Help: Tools You Can Use!

Blackline Masters/Models of
    Records
    Forms
    Note Sheets
    Letters to Parents
    Announcements

for use by
Students and Teachers Assessing With Portfolios

Forms
Records
Reaction Sheets

for Kindergarteners and First-Graders to Use

Name _____

Teacher _____

Reading and Writing Log

Date	Title and Writer	R/W	How I liked it
			☺ ☺ ☹
			☺ ☺ ☹
			☺ ☺ ☹
			☺ ☺ ☹

Teacher's Notes:

Telling About My Portfolio

Name _____

(Teacher note: Have the children organize the materials into different piles. Suggest that they draw a picture about the reading and writing in each pile. They may want to draw a picture about one of the things in the pile if they cannot think of a picture that represents the entire part.)

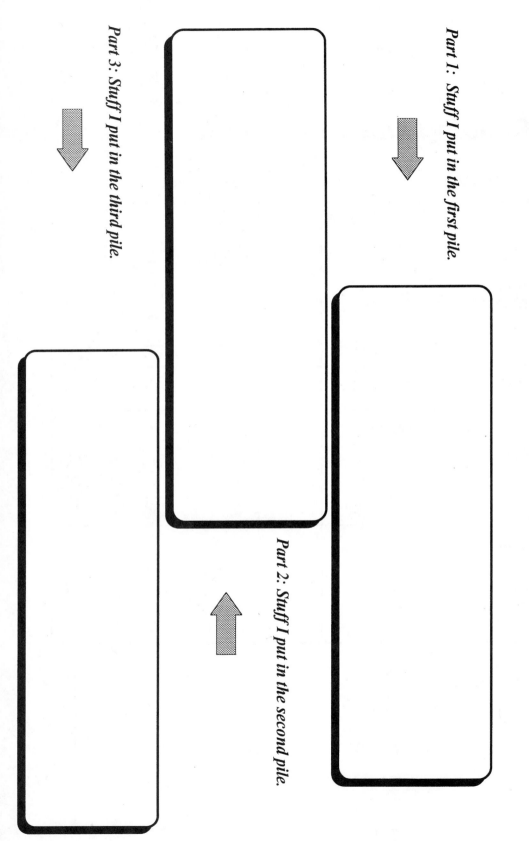

Part 1: *Stuff I put in the first pile.*

Part 2: *Stuff I put in the second pile.*

Part 3: *Stuff I put in the third pile.*

Attitudes and Interests (Reading and Writing)

Name _____ Date _____

1. How do you feel when someone reads a story to you?

2. How do you feel when you read a story?

3. I like to read . . .

magazines	letters	books	newspapers

4. I like to read about . . .

science	travel	animals
adventure	make-believe	real people

5. These are other things I like to read about (draw your own) . . .

6. Do you like to read at home?

7. Do you think you are a good reader?

8. Do you like to write?

9. Do you like to write at home?

10. Do you think you are a good writer?

11. These are the things I like to write about (draw your own).

Thinking About My Reading

Name _____ Date _____

---

1. I picture in my mind what I am
   reading about.
   😊 😐 ☹️

2. I think about what is going to
   happen next in a story.
   😊 😐 ☹️

3. When someone reads to me, I
   feel like this.
   😊 😐 ☹️

4. When I read to myself, I feel
   like this.
   😊 😐 ☹️

5. My favorite kinds of books are _____

_____

6. When I come to a word I don't know, I _____

_____

7. When I finish reading a story, I sometimes _____

_____

This is a picture of my favorite story.

Thinking About My Writing

Name _____ Date _____

This is what I will look for in my writing.

I found what I was looking for.   ☺ ☺ ☹

1. This is how my writing makes me feel.   ☺ ☺ ☹

2. This is how my writing makes other people feel.   ☺ ☺ ☹

3. I picture in my head what I am writing about.   ☺ ☺ ☹

4. When I write, I think about the person who will read my writing.   ☺ ☺ ☹

5. I read over my writing to make it better.   ☺ ☺ ☹

6. I like to write things I have a drawn a circle around.

   stories   notes   reports   plays   poems   journals   comics

Name _____   Date _____

Story Title _____

Ask the students to draw a picture of what they liked best in a story that you read together. Encourage them to write about what is happening in the picture. If they want to look back at the story to check on words, encourage them to do so.

Aha!

Something that I thought was very exciting in something I read (or something I read with the teacher).

Name of the story _____

Date _____

My Partner's Ideas About My Portfolio

My name _____

My partner's name _____

This is a picture of the things my partner
liked best in my portoflio.

This is a picture of the things my partner thinks
I should write more about.

Name _____

Teacher _____

About My Portfolio

Write or draw about . . .

What I most like to read and write about.

```
┌─────────────────────────────────────┐
│                                       │
│                                       │
│                                       │
│                                       │
│                                       │
└─────────────────────────────────────┘
```

The things I write and read about the most.

```
┌─────────────────────────────────────┐
│                                       │
│                                       │
│                                       │
│                                       │
│                                       │
└─────────────────────────────────────┘
```

The things I want to read and write about more.

```
┌─────────────────────────────────────┐
│                                       │
│                                       │
│                                       │
│                                       │
│                                       │
└─────────────────────────────────────┘
```

Forms
Records
Reaction Sheets

for Other Students to Use

Reading and Writing Log

Name _____

Super	☆ ☆ ☆ ☆
Good	☆ ☆ ☆
Fair	☆ ☆
Poor	☆

School _____

Date	Title and Writer	R/W	Comments: . Why I read/wrote it . Why I like/dislike it . Other comments	Rating

Teacher's Notes:

Organizing My Portfolio

Name _____ Date _____

What's in my portfolio:

Topics I like to read about:	*Topics I like to write about:*
1.	1.
2.	2.
3.	3.
4.	4.

Favorite books and stories I read:	*Favorite things I wrote:*
1.	1.
2.	2.
3.	3.
4.	4.

Kinds of books and stories I want to read next:	*Things I want to write about next:*
1.	1.
2.	2.
3.	3.
4.	4.

Name _____ Date _____

My Portfolio
Table of Contents

How do you want to organize your portfolio? What kinds of things go together? You could sort the things in the portfolio into piles and then you could think about a title for each chapter. Don't forget to include the books and stories you have read as well as the things you have written.

Chapter One Title: _____

Things I included in this chapter: _____

_____

_____

_____

_____

_____

Why I included these things in this chapter: _____

_____

_____

_____

_____

Chapter Two Title: _____

Things I included in this chapter: _____

_____

_____

_____

_____

_____

Why I included these things in this chapter: _____

_____

_____

_____

_____

Chapter Three Title: _____

Things I included in this chapter: _____

_____

_____

_____

_____

_____

Why I included these things in this chapter: _____

_____

_____

_____

_____

Summary–Reading/Writing Interests

Student _____   Date _____

Topics	Writing	Reading	Genre	Writing	Reading
Adventure	☐	☐	*Short Stories*	☐	☐
Mystery	☐	☐	*Novels*	☐	☐
Sports	☐	☐	*Poetry*	☐	☐
Nonfiction	☐	☐	*Biography*	☐	☐
Humor	☐	☐	*Nonfiction articles*	☐	☐
Romance	☐	☐	*Newspaper articles*	☐	☐
Historical	☐	☐	*Plays*	☐	☐
Science fiction	☐	☐	_____	☐	☐
_____	☐	☐	_____	☐	☐
_____	☐	☐	_____	☐	☐

Teacher comments:

_____

Thinking About My Reading

Name _____   Date _____

Teacher _____   Grade _____

✓ The topics I like to read about most are: _____

_____

✓ The kinds of things I like to read most are: _____

_____

✓ I use my imagination when I am reading by: _____

_____

✓ I guess what is going to happen next when I read by: _____

_____

✓ I like to read books and stories that: _____

_____

✓ I don't enjoy reading books and stories that: _____

_____

✓ I (do, do not) talk with my friends about things I read because: _____

_____

✓ I think I would be a better reader if: _____

_____

✓ I get the the ideas about what I want to read from: _____

_____

Thinking About My Writing

Name _____ Date _____

Teacher _____ Grade _____

✓ When I write, I like to include these kinds of things in my writing: _____

_____

✓ I like these things about my writing: _____

_____

✓ I can improve my writing by: _____

_____

✓ I (do, do not) like my writing when: _____

_____

✓ I get most of my ideas for my writing from: _____

_____

✓ I think that other people (like, dislike) my writing because: _____

_____

✓ I'd like to write more about: _____

_____

✓ I think that one of the best things I have written is: _____

_____

✓ One of the things that I think is my worst writing is: _____

_____

Thinking About My Writing

Select something you have written (it could be something you liked writing or something you didn't like writing) and tell about what you did when you wrote.

Name _____

What is the writing piece you are going to tell about? _____

_____

Tell what you did as you were getting ready to write. Did you make notes, draw a picture of your story, jot down ideas, or just think about what you wanted to write? Did you think about other stories or articles that were like the one you wanted to write? Did you talk with anyone about your ideas?

_____
_____
_____
_____
_____

Tell what you did as you were writing. Did you change your mind very often? Did you stop to look up information? Did you talk with anyone about what you were writing?

_____
_____
_____
_____
_____
_____
_____

Tell what you did after your first draft. Did you reread what you had written? Did you think about confusing parts? Did you think about your audience? Did you have anyone else read what you had written and get their ideas?

Tell what you did when you went over your paper the last time. Did you check for spelling errors and correct punctuation? Did you ask a friend or the teacher to help with the editing? Did you look up any words in the dictionary?

Now that you have had a chance to think about one piece of writing, what do you think that you did or didn't do that was the most help to you? What do you think you could do to make your writing even better?

Thinking About My Reading and Writing

Name _____ Date _____

Write your thoughts about how you have grown as a reader and writer. What do you like most about your reading and writing? What would you tell a friend about your best reading and writing?

A Summary of My Work

NAME: _____ **DATE:** _____

What is getting better about my work?	What do I need to work on?
What will I read next?	**What will I write next?**

An Update on My Reading and Writing

(Based on the analysis of my portfolio)

Name_____ Date _____

1. **My goals in reading have been to:**_____

_____

_____

_____.

2. **My goals in writing have been to:**_____

_____

_____

_____.

3. **I think I have succeeded in:** _____

_____

_____

_____.

4. **I still need to:**_____

_____

_____

_____.

5. **Some new goals in reading are to:**_____

_____

_____

_____.

6. **Some new goals in writing are to:**_____

_____

_____

_____.

Ways to Reach My Reading and Writing Goals

Name_____ Date _____

My goal is to...	*So I need to...*

Teacher's comments:

About This Piece of Writing

Name_____ Date _____

Name of piece I wrote: _____

_____

Why I wrote it: _____

_____.

I wrote it for these people to read: _____

_____.

I got the idea for this piece from/by _____

_____

_____.

This is the ___first ___second ___third draft of this piece.

The hardest thing about writing this was _____

_____

_____.

Things I could do to make this a better piece of writing: _____

_____

_____

_____.

I had _____ read it, and this is what s/he thinks:

_____

_____

_____

_____

_____

_____

My Partner's Suggestions for Making My Writing Better

What my partner said about my writing

My name _____

Title of my writing _____

My writing partner's name_____

The best ideas in the writing: _____

_____

What my partner thought about when s/he read my story: _____

_____

An idea my partner had to make my ideas more interesting: _____

_____

Who my partner said would like reading my story: _____

_____

My partner said my story was most like this book/story that he or she had read

before: _____

More comments from my writing partner: _____

_____

_____

_____

_____

ONE OF MY BEST PIECES OF WORK

because

_____

_____

_____

_____

Parent's Comments:

My Classmates' Comments:

_____

_____

_____

_____

My comments about this:

_____

_____

_____

_____

_____

When you read and write, REMEMBER!

1. What do I want to know or say?

5. Do I picture what is happening?

2. What do I already know?

6. Do the ideas make sense to me?

3. Do I think about the ideas before I start to read and write?

7. Do I make changes if things don't make sense?

4. Do I think about what is coming next?

8. Do I get help when I need it?

Welcome to my portfolio!

My name is _____.

I am in Grade _____ at _____school.

My teacher's name is _____.

Date of this note:_____ I began my portfolio _____.

- **How my portfolio is organized:**

  _____

  _____

  _____

- **What my portfolio shows about me:**

  _____

  _____

  _____

- **What my portfolio shows about my reading:**

  _____

  _____

  _____

- **What my portfolio shows about my writing:**

  _____

  _____

  _____

- **Be sure to watch for these things:**

  _____

  _____

Telling About a Story

Name _____ Date _____

Name of the story _____

_____

Written by _____

_____

Who (Main Character): _____

Story Problem: _____

_____

_____

1st Major Event: _____

_____

_____

2nd Major Event: _____

_____

_____

3rd Major Event: _____

_____

_____

4th Major Event: _____

_____

Solution: _____

_____

Reporter's Fact Sheet

*Reporter:*_____

*Story:*_____

What happened?

What else happened?

How did it happen?

Who was involved?

Who else was involved?

When did it happen?

Where did it happen?

Why did it happen?

Notes for Adding a Story Ending

Name:_____

The story we read was:_____

When the story ended:

This had just happened:

This character....	Was doing this:

This is what I will have happen next:

Notes for Adding a New Beginning to a Story

Name:_____

The story we read was:_____

When the story begins:

This is happening:

This character....	Is doing this:

I will have this happen before that:

A Table for Making Comparisons

Name:_____

I am comparing/contrasting in order to :

I'm comparing/ contrasting by looking at these:	I am comparing/contrasting this: A. _____ It is like/different from B:	To this: B. _____ It is like/different from A:
1.		
2.		
3.		
4.		

Forms
Records
Reaction Sheets
Notes
Letters

for the Teacher to Use

Name _____   Date _____

Conference Notes

Purpose	What do I know?	Predict before?	Predict during?	Picture?	Make sense?	Make changes?	Get help?

Teacher's Notes:

Student's Notes:

Portfolio: Initial Conference Notes

This check is to provide you with a place to record your observations after an initial portfolio conference. Use the back of this page for topics or concerns not included on this sheet. (*This form is designed for use with beginning readers and writers.*)

Student's Name _____   **Date** _____

1. Reading Experience

_____ **HIGH** (Seems to know many stories, has been read to extensively, engages in make-believe reading)

_____ **MODERATE** (Knows some stories, has been read to some, limited attempts to read on his/her own)

_____ **LOW** (Seems to be aware of few stories, does not discuss times s/he has been read to)

Comments:

_____

_____

_____

_____

_____

2. Background Knowledge

_____ **HIGH** (Familiar with many topics and readily discusses his/her ideas, has visited widely and talks about personal experiences)

_____ **MODERATE** (Discusses some ideas and experiences, seems reluctant to talk about his/her own views, experiences)

_____ **LOW** (Does not discuss everyday experiences, seems unwilling to discuss ideas or experiences)

Comments:

_____

_____

_____

_____

_____

3. Reading/Writing Awareness

_____ **GOOD** (General understanding of purposes for reading and writing)

_____ **FAIR** (Some understanding of purposes for reading and writing)

_____ **POOR** (Very Limited understanding of purposes for reading and writing)

Correctly Identifies:

_____ letters

_____ names of letters

_____ words

_____ sentences

Knows how to:

_____ handle a book to read

_____ follow print as story is read

_____ turn pages

_____ write name

_____ write numbers/letters

Getting Started (Primary Level)

Name _____ Date _____

Teacher note: These questions can be used as part of an initial portfolio conference with a student. Space is provided for you to write the student's responses.

Reading

Do you like to have someone read to you? Who? _____

_____

Does anyone read to you at home? What do they read with you? _____

_____

What kinds of stories do you like best? Funny? Make believe? Scary? Do you have any favorite story characters? Tell me about them? _____

_____

Do you know someone who is a good reader? What makes him or her a good reader? _____

_____

Writing

Do you like to draw pictures about stories? _____

_____

Do you like to write or "or make pretend write" about your pictures? _____

_____

Do you know someone who is a good writer? What makes him or her a good writer? _____

_____

What would you like to write about? _____

Students' Interests as Determined from Portfolio Conferences for Forming Reading/Writing Interest Groups

Teacher's Name _____

Students' Names	Animals	Sports	History	Mysteries	Science Fiction	Romance	Adventure	Biographies	Collecting	Comments

Reading and Writing Inventory

Student:_____

Teacher:_____ **Date:** _____

A. To get a sense of the student's attitude about reading and writing, ask:

1. Are you a good reader? Why or why not?
2. Are you a good writer? Why or why not?
3. What are the most important kinds of things that you read? Why?
4. What are the most important kinds of things that you write? Why?
5. Do you like to read? Why or why not?
6. Do you like to write? Why or why not?
7. Do you read or write at home? What?

Reading and Writing Inventory   **Page 2**

Student: _____ Date: _____

B. To learn about the student's interests, ask:

8. Tell me about your favorite book.

9. Tell me about something you wrote that you like a lot.

10. What are your favorite two things to do?

11. Do you have any hobbies? What other things do you enjoy doing regularly?

12. What are your favorite TV shows? Why?

13. Name two persons that you admire the most. Why do you admire them?

14. Who is the most interesting person you know well? Why do you find him or her interesting?

Reading and Writing Inventory   **Page 3**

Student: _____ Date: _____

C. To get a sense of the student's command of reading and writing strategies, ask:

15. How do you decide what to read?

16. How do you decide what to write?

17. What do you do to start writing something?

18. If you are looking for a book to read, what do you look for?

19. Do you like to guess what is going to happen when you are reading a story?

20. Do you see pictures in your mind when you read? How does that work?

21. What happens if things aren't going well when you are reading and writing? What do you do?

22. What do you do when you don't know what a word means or the word to use when you are writing?

How We're Doing

Name of Student _____

Teacher's Name _____

Date of this report _____

STRENGTHS	Teacher's Comments:	Student's Comments:

SHOULD WORK ON	Teacher's Comments:	Student's Comments:

Portfolio Evaluation

Student _____

For the portfolio collected between _____ and _____

Reading

Amount of Reading and Writing	Extensive	Moderate	Limited

Comments _____

Attitudes and Interests	Positive	Neutral	Negative

Comments _____

Progress as a Reader and Writer	Impressive	Noticeable	Too Limited

Comments _____

Writing

Amount of Reading and Writing	Extensive	Moderate	Limited

Attitudes and Interests	Positive	Neutral	Negative

Progress as a Reader and Writer	Impressive	Noticeable	Too Limited

Summary Statement

| Statement Number _____ | Period: from _____ to _____ |

Student:_____ Teacher:_____

Amount of Work Produced	Progress Shown
Attitudes and Interests	**Evidence of Self-Asssessment**

Review of Portfolio Reading Materials

Student's Name _____
Teacher's Name _____
Date _____ **Grade** _____ **School** _____

1 = Limited 2 = Below expectation 3 = Average 4 = Above expectation 5 = Outstanding

Assessment	1	2	3	4	5	Teacher Comments
Amount of reading						
Reads a variety of topics						
Reads a variety of genres (i.e., stories, poems, magazine articles)						
Reads during free time						
Reads outside of school						
Attitudes toward reading						
Talks about favorite books and stories						
Completes reading self-assessments						
Reacts to what has been read						
Reading interests						
Makes use of reading ideas in writing						
Shares book/story interests with others						
Is developing reading interests						
Reading ability						
Relates reading to background						
Shows an appreciation for new ideas						
Shows confidence as a reader						

Summary Assessment

Assessment	For This Review			Since Last Review		
	Outstanding	Average	Limited	Improving	About Same	Not as Good
Amount of reading						
Attitudes toward reading						
Reading growth						

Review of Portfolio Writing Materials

Student's Name _____

Teacher's Name _____

Date _____   **Grade** _____   **School** _____

1 = Limited 2 = Below expectation 3 = Average 4 = Above expectation 5 = Outstanding

Assessment	1	2	3	4	5	Teacher Comments
Amount of reading						
Writes on a variety of topics						
Writes in a variety of genres (i.e., stories, poems, magazine articles)						
Revises ideas						
Shows awareness of audience						
Organization of writing						
Sticks to topic						
Shows good planning						
Sentence/Vocabulary						
Uses varied and appropriate word choice						
Uses a variety of sentence types						
Mechanics						
Spells correctly						
Correct/appropriate usage						
Punctuates appropriately						
Good sentence construction						

Summary Assessment

Assessment	For This Review			Since Last Review		
	Outstanding	Average	Limited	Improving	About Same	Not as Good
Amount of writing						
Attitudes toward writing						
Quality of Writing						

Teacher's Checklist
of the Writing Process
(Kindergarten and First Grade)

Teacher _____   **Date** _____

Grade _____

<u>Marking Key</u>
+ Regularly
0 Sometimes
- Never

Children's Names

Planning

Jots down notes and ideas											
Uses prewriting discussions to plan and think about writing											
Develops a plan before writing											

Revising

Focuses on an audience											
Makes changes in meaning to better achieve his/her writing purpose											
Edits work for mechanical errors and to enhance communication											

Self-evaluating

Asks others to review writing											
Uses reactions of others in revising											
Revises enthusiastically											
Takes pride in final product											

Comments _____

_____

_____

Teacher's Checklist
of the Writing Process

Teacher _____ Date _____

Grade _____

Children's Names

Marking Key
+ Regularly
0 Sometimes
- Never

Uses pictures and words to tell stories												
Writes from left to right												
Shows knowledge of words by grouping letters in words												
Sounds out letters while writing words (i.e., seems to know that letters represent sounds—phonemic awareness)												
Sentences have a reasonable syntactic structure												
Shows awareness of punctuation: capitalization. end marks. commas. quotation marks.												
Likes to talk about the stories he or she is writing or drawing												

Comments: _____

Teacher's Checklist
of the Reading Process

Teacher _____ **Date** _____

Grade _____

Children's Names

Marking Key
+ Regularly
0 Sometimes
- Never

Using Effective Strategies

Reads for personal purposes and focuses on a purpose for reading											
Uses background knowledge and experiences to expand meaning											
Predicts events and happenings in a story											
Summarizes while reading											
Uses context clues as meaning clues											
Rereads to make changes if things don't make sense											
Gets help from the teacher or from other resources											
Seems to understand conversations											
Is able to use notes and diagrams as comprehension aids											

Comments _____

_____

_____

Teacher's Observation Checklist
of the Speaking/Listening Process

Teacher _____   *Date* _____

Grade _____

Children's Names

<u>Marking Key</u>
+ Regularly
0 Sometimes
- Never

Speaking

Volunteers for speaking activities										
Comments contribute to conversations										
Expresses ideas clearly and logically										
Seems to use background information appropriately										
Responds logically to comments made by others										
Takes turns in discussions										

Listening

Pays attention to conversations										
Seems to understand conversations										
Follows directions appropriately										
Able to ignore distractions										

Comments: _____

_____

_____

A Checklist of Student Reading and Writing <u>Processing</u>

Student_____ **Teacher** _____

Processing Strategies	Time Period 1 Date: _____	Time Period 2 Date: _____	Time Period 3 Date: _____	Time Period 4 Date:_____
Identifies purposes for reading and writing				
Relates reading and writing to his/her background and experience				
Thinks about what s/he will read or write before beginning				
Predicts/thinks about what is coming next while reading and writing				
Pictures/visualizes the meaning s/he is making				
Challenges meaning to see if it makes sense				
Adjusts meaning as s/he reads and writes				
Seeks help/ information when s/he needs it				

Reading/Writing Strategies Checklist (Teacher's Notes)

Student _____   Date _____

Teacher _____   Grade _____

Strategy	Comments	Strategy	Comments
1. What do I want to know or say? (*Does the student focus on purposes for reading and writing?*)		**5. Do I picture what is happening?** (*Does the student visualize story events in both reading and writing?*)	
2. What do I already know? (*Does the student use background knowledge from previous reading and other experiences to make sense in his or her reading and writing?*)		**6. Do the ideas make sense to me?** (*Does the student reflect about the ideas in an attempt to develop a coherent understanding?*)	
3. Do I think about the ideas before I read and write? (*Does the student discuss the genre and the types of things that one expects to find in a particular kind of reading, and the kinds of things that are included in a particular kind of writing?*)		**7. Do I make changes if the things don't make sense?** (*Does the student go back in his reading to check out why things don't make sense? Is there evidence of revision in writing?*)	
4. Do I think about what is coming next? (*Does the student talk about predictions in reading and writing?*)		**8. Do I get help when I need it?** (*Does the student know how to use resources such as the dictionary? Does s/he collaborate with other students?*)	

Teacher's Comments:

Date:_____

Teacher's Comments:

Date:_____

Teacher's Comments:

Date:_____

Teacher's Comments:

Date:_____

Upperville Elementary School

Portfolio Notes

This Month:
*How are
we doing?*

February 1998/ Volume I, No. 1

First Student-Teacher Conferences Are Completed

Mrs. McMilburn and each of the 29 students in her second-grade class have completed their first round of conferences. The students met one at a time with their teacher for up to a half an hour each.

Students had spent over six weeks picking things they have written and keeping records about what they have read and written.

Before they met with Mrs. McMilburn, each student had finished two things:

➤ The student had organized all the different things in the collection and had made a Table of Contents. Actually, most of the students had already done this, and checked or reorganized things.

➤ The student had looked at all the things in the portfolio and had looked hard at it to decide what was good, what was getting better, and what needed to improve more.

Mrs. McMilburn had looked at these things, too. She and each student discussed all this and they made *Conference Notes* together.

When they were finished, each student had decided on some goals for the next grading period. These included things to read and things to write. They also included ways to make their writing stronger and more interesting.

Why We Keep All the Old Versions of Stories and Essays That We Do Over

by Billy Stillserman

"What do you do when you re-write a story?" Mr. Dondelburg, our Assistant Principal asked me.

I wasn't sure what to say at first. I mean, I know all the stuff that I do. It's lots of stuff. So I just went through the portfolio and found that story, "My Fine & Fussy-Frog." I redid that thing at least four times, and I saved three of them, I was sure.

"Look," I said, pointing to some words that I had circled on the third one I wrote about the frog. "I fixed some words that I didn't spell right." I pointed to the same words in the last draft to show that they were OK there.

"Oh, I see, you do your spelling over when you rewrite."

"Well, yeah," I said. "I do that." This wasn't going the way I wanted it to go. "I do some other stuff, too, you know."

"Sure," Mr. Dondelburg said, "I see a question mark that was missing in this draft." He pointed at a period after a question in the one I wrote before the last one. Then he found the question mark in the final copy of the story. I shook my head.

"You would make a good editor for our newsletter," I said. He seemed happy enough for a little bit. Then he said, "But why did you save this older one? This really messy one. Why do you want something like it in your portfolio?

"Well...." I'm still not happy at the way this was going. "I try to fix all the spelling and stuff, but I do other stuff, too. And that's what I worry about most. So sometimes I still miss a word or a question mark or something like that."

"What other stuff?" Mr. Dondelburg said.

I pointed at that draft with the words circled. "Well, see," I said. "I moved all this stuff up near the front. It was describing the way the frog looked. You know the yellow marks on his back and stuff. It was too late to be doing that. It got in the way of the ending. So I moved it up."

He was looking at the first two copies of the story carefully now. "Wow," he said. "You really turned this into a great story!"

Dear Parent,

This year in your child's class, each student will collect drawings they make, writing they do, and other materials that interest them. These will be kept in *portfolios* that the students help make and decorate themselves. These portfolios will be an important part of the reading and writing instruction your child experiences this year. They will be used both to teach and as one way to assess each student's development as a reader and writer.

Many of the student products that your child puts into the portfolio will be done in response to stories we have read as a group and to stories you have read to or with your child at home. Some will be original stories explained with words written on or beside the pictures.

Some students may add materials to their portfolios that make them think of things they would like to draw and write. These may include something that is in a color your child likes or a picture of a favorite animal or activity. *Hopefully, some of these things will be drawn, written, and found at home—not as homework, but because your child is enjoying language. Many may be about stories that the student has read or had read to him or her at home.*

Another important part of the student portfolios will be some records. One of these is a log which will show all of the things that your child has read at school, remembers reading at home, and has drawn and "captioned" at school and home. These include a student reaction that indicates how he or she likes each thing entered. There will be some other notes about items in the portfolio—drawn and written by your child or written by me. There will also be some notes that your child and I will make at regular conferences we have to discuss the contents of his or her portfolio. We will be talking about them regularly, of course—as often as several times a day; but these conferences will be special times to set new goals for reading and writing.

You, too, will have opportunities to write comments that can go into the portfolio. One thing you may notice about this *working portfolio* is that it is a full and "busy" collection that promotes self-analysis—not some tidy showpiece for us to see. The student needs to think hard to organize all the things in it. That is the *major purpose* of portfolios: *to develop readers and writers eager to get better and better.*

During this year there will be several opportunities for you to examine the portfolios, for you to ask questions about their contents and about this approach to instruction and assessment, and for us to talk about your child's development as a reader, writer, and thinker. Meanwhile, if you have any questions, please feel free to contact me whenever you can do so.

There are numerous other ways for you to become involved. You can continue reading to your child and encouraging him or her to draw and write at home. It is very important to include stories read and heard and drawn outside the classroom in the portfolio. These can be added to the log and can be brought to school and added to the portfolio, if the student wishes. *Also, continue to praise strengths and improvements in language use that you notice.*

Sincerely,

Dear Parent,

This year in your child's class, each student will collect pieces of writing and other materials in a *portfolio*. Many of the papers that the students will keep in their portfolios are ones they have written after reading something that was of particular interest to them. For example, the student may add something to a favorite story, may write something about its characters and the way they behave, or may analyze the reasons that certain things happen. They will also write about nonfiction. For example, they may suggest solutions to problems that are presented in several non-fictional articles, charts, and the like.

The students will also be collecting other things in their portfolios, such as poetry and other creative things they write. Some may keep journals. They can add favorite clippings from old magazines and other sources as ideas for other things to be written. *Hopefully, some of these pieces of writing and other materials will be created or found at home—not as homework, but because reading, writing, and thinking about things are fun and satisfying!*

Another important part of the student portfolios will be some records. For example, there will be a log of the things your child reads and writes, both at school and at home. It will include comments by your child about the things read and papers written. There will also be longer notes in the portfolio that tell about writing particular pieces in it and that analyze his or her progress as a reader and writer. There will be notes from other people who look at the portfolio, too. I will write a few, and classmates may look at it and write notes. Your child and I will make important notes at conferences we will have about the portfolio. We will be talking about the contents of the portfolio regularly, of course, as they accumulate. We may be doing that every day; but the conferences will be special times to set new goals for reading and writing.

You, too, will have opportunities to write comments that can go into the portfolio. One thing you may notice about this *working portfolio* is that it is a full and "busy" collection that promotes self-analysis—not some tidy showpiece prepared for you and me. That is the *major purpose* of portfolios: *to develop self-assessors*: people concerned about becoming better readers and writers.

During this year there will be several opportunities for you to examine the portfolios, for you to ask questions about their contents and about this approach to instruction and assessment, and for us to talk about your child's development as a reader, writer, and thinker. Meanwhile, if you have any questions, please feel free to contact me whenever you can do so.

There are numerous other ways for you to become involved. You can continue encouraging your child to read and write at home. It is very important to include things read and written outside the classroom in the portfolio. Things that are read at home can be added to the log, and things written there can be brought to school and added to the portfolio, if the student wishes. *Also, continue to praise strengths and improvements in language use that you notice.*

Sincerely,

Dear Parent,

As you are probably aware, we are using portfolios for language instruction and assessment of reading and writing progress in your child's classroom this year. Our portfolios are *working collections* of things that each student has written and of other materials. Much of the writing is in response to things read and thus reveals development in reading comprehension. The collections also include numerous records and self-analyses of the materials in them.

The students and I realize that portfolio assessment may be new to some of you, and that even if you are familiar with it, you may have questions about it. Therefore, we have prepared a ***Portfolio Workshop*** to 1) explain how portfolios work and help the students learn and develop, 2) give you a chance to ask any questions that you have, and 3) give you an opportunity to examine your son's or daughter's portfolio collection and to discuss it with your child and with me.

The workshop will last approximately an hour and allow time for those of you who wish to stay to examine and discuss your child's collection. It will cover the following:

- · What most authorities think portfolios should and can accomplish
- · What goes into portfolios and how it is selected
- · What is done with the materials once they are in the portfolios
- · What the students feel they get from keeping portfolios
- · What the teacher feels is learned from the portfolios
- · How portfolios fit into the whole assessment picture—what they tell which audiences
- · Answers from students and teachers to your questions

The ***Portfolio Workshop*** will be held:

- · on
- · from
- · in
- · at

Both the students and I would be very pleased if you are able and interested in attending. If you have any questions about the workshop, please feel free to contact me.

Sincerely,

Dear Parent,

Earlier this year, I wrote you about the portfolio that your child is keeping in our class this year. It contains many examples of his or her writing, much of it in response to reading; and it also includes records and analyses of its contents. The intention in keeping the portfolios is to develop self-assessors who are keenly aware of and interested in their development as readers and writers.

I believe that the portfolio has played an important role in the language development of your child. Many parents have been to the classroom to look over the portfolio's contents and to discuss its contents and the teaching and assessment approach with me; and I am eager to discuss these matters with you again at your convenience.

We are now sending you a collection of materials that have accumulated in the past weeks and that have been carefully analyzed by both your child and me. As I explained earlier this year, these collections are *working portfolios*, not showpieces. That means they contain many types of materials, some of them early drafts of pieces that were rewritten. They are not intended to be merely a collection of your child's best work but a demonstration of how he or she processes language and thought.

The collection has now become so bulky that it is too cumbersome for its student owner to manipulate while analyzing it. Since many of those materials have served their purpose to promote self-analysis, the collection has been culled. Out of the collection, your son or daughter has kept some key records and analyses, some pieces of writing that are slated to be revised, and some ideas for future writing. These have formed the core of a new collection that will be analyzed in the immediate future.

The remainder of the materials are being sent home for you to examine and for you and your son or daughter to save. I encourage you to look them over carefully and to share your reactions with your child. It is a fine idea to examine them at one point with the young writer, who may have some valuable insights you might otherwise overlook. It is important that you offer positive comments as you can and engage in conversations about the things read.

Hopefully, you will learn a great deal about your child's use of language. If you note particular problems or shortcomings in the collection, be assured that we are addressing them in the classroom. Your child has probably made note of needs to emphasize certain reading and writing behaviors in the analyses that accompany these papers, so they can be discussed in terms of working to turn them into strengths. I will be eager to discuss any such matters with you when you can contact me.

Also, experience has shown that papers of this sort are valued as life records more and more as time goes by. Thus I encourage you to save them for your child if at all possible.

Thanks for your support and assistance with this portfolio assessment initiative.

Sincerely,

CREDITS

Chapter 3 Page 82: "Good Models" from *The Gooch Machine: Poems for Children to Perform*. Copyright © 1997 by Brod Bagert. Published by Wordsong/Boyds Mills Press. Reprinted by permission.

Chapter 6 Pages 208–209: "A Teacher Uses Portfolios to Get Parents Involved." Used with permission of Traci G. Jones.

Chapter 7 Page 241: Prewriting Activity "Reporter's Fact Sheet: Kate Shelley and the Midnight Express." From *HBJ Treasury of Literature*, 1993 Edition, Unit Integrated Performance Assessment, Teacher's Edition, Grade Five by Roger Farr, copyright © 1993 by Harcourt Brace and Company, reprinted by permission of the publisher.

Page 241: Prewriting activity "Who was doing what?". From *HBJ Treasury of Literature*, 1993 Edition, Unit Integrated Performance Assessment, Teacher's Edition, Grade Three by Roger Farr, copyright © 1993 by Harcourt Brace and Company, reprinted by permission of the publisher.

Page 242: Prewriting activity "A Comparison/Contrast Chart: Growing Up in The Old West." From *HBJ Treasury of Literature*, 1993 Edition, Unit Integrated Performance Assessment, Teacher's Edition, Grade Eight by Roger Farr, copyright © 1993 by Harcourt Brace and Company, reprinted by permission of the publisher.

Chapter 7/Chapter 8 Page 255: General Scoring Rubric (Expanded and Abbreviated Versions). From *HBJ Treasury of Literature*, 1993 Edition, Unit Integrated Performance Assessment, Teacher's Edition, Grade Five by Roger Farr, copyright © 1993 by Harcourt Brace and Company, reprinted by permission of the publisher.

Pages 245, 267, 269: Pre-writing Activities, itemized explanations of "Accomplishment of Task," "Writing," and "Reading," the full rubric for "Accomplishment of Task," the task and an example of a paper that scored a 3 out of 4 for the "Water Problem Essay." From the *Indiana Performance Assessment '92*, The Center for Reading and Language Studies at Indiana University, September 1993. Sponsored by The Department of Workforce Development; Commission on Vocational and Technical Education, Employment, and Training Services; The Indiana Vocational Technical College; The Lilly Endowment; and the Indiana Commission for Higher Education.

Chapter 8 Page 260: General Scoring Rubric. From the *Integrated Assessment System: Language Arts Performance Assessment*. Copyright © 1990 by Harcourt Brace and Company. Reproduced by permission. All rights reserved. "Integrated Assessment System" and "IAS" are registered trademarks of The Psychological Corporation.

Page 262: Scoring Rubric for Rhetorical Effectiveness in Story from *Integrated Performance Assessment, 1997*, copyright © 1997 by Harcourt Brace and Company, reprinted by permission of the publisher.

Pages 268–69: Description of the task for Grade Four prompt/writing activity combination entitled "What's Up Amelia" followed by the complete annotation and response for a paper scored as 4. From the *Integrated Assessment System: Language Arts Performance Assessment*. Copyright © 1990 by Harcourt Brace and Company. Reproduced by permission. All rights reserved. "Integrated Assessment System" and "IAS" are registered trademarks of The Psychological Corporation.

Pages 269–70: Prompt and Writing Task for Grade One accompanying "You Look Funny" by Joy Kim, including annotation and complete scored page. From *HBJ Treasury of Literature*, 1993 Edition, Unit Integrated Performance Assessment, Teacher's Edition, Grade One by Roger Farr, copyright © 1993 by Harcourt Brace and Company, reprinted by permission of the publisher.